A-TRAIN

Memoirs of a Tuskegee Airman

Lieutenant Colonel Charles W. Dryden

United States Air Force (Retired)

With a Foreword by
Lieutenant General Benjamin O. Davis, Jr.
United States Air Force (Retired)

The University of Alabama Press
Tuscaloosa and London

First Paperback Printing 2002

Typeface: Sabon

∞

The paper on which this book is printed
meets the minimum requirements
of American National Standard
for Information Science–Permanence of Paper
for Printed Library Materials,
ANSI Z39.48-1984.

Library of Congress Cataloging-in-Publication Data

Dryden, Charles W. (Charles Walter)
    A-train : memoirs of a Tuskegee Airman / Charles W. Dryden;
with a foreword by Benjamin O. Davis, Jr.
      p. cm.
    Includes bibliographical references and index.
    ISBN 0-8173-0856-3 (alk. paper)
    ISBN 0-8173-1266-8 (pbk: alk. paper)
   1. Dryden, Charles W. (Charles Walter) 2. World War,
1939–1945—Aerial operations, American. 3. World War,
1939–1945—Participation, Afro-American. 4. World War,
1939–1945—Personal narratives, American. 5. Afro-American
air pilots—Biography. 6. United States. Army Air Forces—
Biography. 7. Tuskegee Army Air Field (Ala.) I. Title.
D790.D78 1997
940.54'4973—dc20   96-24118

British Library Cataloguing-in-Publication Data available

A-TRAIN

>> >>

P-40 *A-Train II* with Lieutenant Charles W. Dryden seated and Lieutenant Colonel Benjamin O. Davis, Jr., on the wing. (Acrylic on canvas, by Ric Druet, 1996, commissioned by Willis Brown. Used by Permission.)

To
Beloved Wife
and
to the memory of
BROTHER ROB AND SISTER VIE
Revered Parents

Contents

Part II: After Desegregation

Foreword

A-Train: Memoirs of a Tuskegee Airman by Charles W. Dryden, Sr., Lieutenant Colonel, USAF (Retired), is an autobiography of a prominent and very active member of the group of several hundred Black airmen who were trained to fly in the skies over Alabama in the early 1940s, who fought the air war in Europe during World War II, and who simultaneously lived through the tempestuous life that the United States has imposed upon its Black citizens throughout all of our lives.

Dryden depended heavily upon frequent telephone conversations with some seventy of his wartime and postwar friends to check and cross-check most of the "recollections" he reports in his book. I can attest to this fact because I was an active participant in his process of discussion and verification of details of some of the historical material he presents. And, of course, as commanding officer of the 99th Fighter Squadron and, later, the 332nd Fighter and 477th Composite Groups, I shared many of the experiences he describes.

Chuck's book has two major logical divisions, the first prior to desegregation of the United States military, and the second after desegregation. It is an honest rendition of his life experience throughout the time period covered by his book. It could well have been titled: "The TRUTH as I Saw It." Chuck's book contains a wealth of interesting detail that should appeal to all Tuskegee Airmen. It would also be an educational read for anyone who is slightly acquainted with the existence of the Tuskegee Airmen but who does not fully understand the details of the World War II experience of Blacks—overseas—and desires to know more. This book consists of material that can provide the reader with the background for comprehension of the ongoing struggle with racism in the United States.

Chuck Dryden is a sincere, honest, friendly person who has fought the good fight throughout his long life and now, through the medium of his autobiography, desires to share its important details with all Americans but particularly with Americans of goodwill, who need all the information they can muster to arm them for the antiracism fight that will continue for the remainder of our lives and those of our descendants.

Benjamin O. Davis, Jr.
Lieutenant General
United States Air Force (Retired)

Prologue

Due to the rigid pattern of racial segregation that pre-
vailed in the United States during World War II, just
short of one thousand, i.e. 992, Black military aviators
were trained at an isolated training complex near the
town of Tuskegee, Alabama, and at Tuskegee Institute.
Four hundred and fifty Black fighter pilots under the
command of Colonel Benjamin O. Davis, Jr., fought in
the aerial war over North Africa, Sicily and Europe
flying, in succession, P-40, P-39, P-47 and P-51 type aircraft. These gallant men flew 15,553 sorties and completed 1,578 missions with the 12th Air Force and the
15th Air Force. Colonel Davis later became the U.S. Air
Force's first Black general and rose to the rank of Lieutenant General.

They were called the "Schwartze Vogelmenshen"
(Black Birdmen) by the Germans who both feared and
respected them. White American bomber crews rever-
ently referred to them as "The Black Redtail Angels"
because of the identifying red paint on their tail assemblies and because of their reputation for not losing
bombers to enemy fighters as they provided fighter escort to bombing missions over strategic targets in
Europe.

The 99th Fighter Squadron, which had already distinguished itself over North Africa, Sicily and Anzio, joined three other Black squadrons: the 100th, 301st and 302nd. These four squadrons, designated as the 332nd Fighter Group, comprised the largest fighter unit in the 15th Air Force. From Italian bases they also destroyed enemy rail traffic, coast-watching surveillance stations and hundreds of vehicles on air-to-ground strafing missions. Sixty-six of these pilots were killed in aerial combat while another thirty-two were either forced down or shot down and captured to become prisoners of war.

These Black Airmen came home with 150 Distinguished Flying Crosses, Legions of Merit and the Red Star of Yugoslavia.

Other Black pilots, navigators, bombardiers and crewmen were trained for medium bombardment duty and were joined by 332nd combat returnees and formed into the 477th Composite Fighter-Bomber Group (flying B-25s and P-47s). This group never entered combat because of the surrender of Germany and Japan in 1945. Significantly, the 477th's demands for parity and recognition as competent military professionals combined with the magnificent war record of the 99th and the 332nd led to a review of the U.S. War Department's racial policies.

For every Black pilot there were ten other civilian or military Black men and women on ground support duty. Many of these men and women remained in the military service during the post–World War II era and spearheaded the integration of the armed forces in the U.S. Air Force in 1949. That the "Tuskegee Experiment" achieved success rather than the expected failure is further recorded by the elevation of three of these pioneers to flag rank: the late General Daniel "Chappie" James, our nation's first Black Four-Star General; Lieutenant General Benjamin O. Davis, Jr., USAF, Retired; and Major General Lucius Theus, USAF, Retired.

Three Tuskegee Airmen share the distinction of having flown combat missions in World War II, the Korean War and the war in Viet Nam: Colonels Hannibal Cox and Charles McGee, and Lieutenant Colonel Charles Cooper, all USAF, Retired. Three other Tuskegee Airmen flew combat in Viet Nam in other type aircraft and all retired as Lieutenant Colonels: John "Mr. Death" Whitehead; William Holloman and George Hardy. (Excerpt from "The Tuskegee Airmen, A Brief History," an official fact sheet published by Tuskegee Airmen, Inc.)

That brief essay is just the tip of the iceberg. By digging below the surface one finds more interesting history about the Tuskegee Airmen—history that can be found in books by or about the Tuskegee Airmen. Most such histories, whether biographical, autobiographical, or just descriptive of events, are didactic in form and content. They are good materials for use as textbooks and references. By contrast, my autobiography is written in the form of a historical drama.

A drama with a story line about the "Tuskegee Experiment" in which the ability of "Negroes" to fly airplanes as pilots and to keep them flying as mechanics, armorers, radiomen, and the like was doubted, and tested.

A drama describing a continuing plot to dump the "experiment" in a dustbin of history.

A drama in which the villain of the piece was Jim Crow.

A drama in which the villain appeared often, and oftentimes unexpectedly, in the form of various "ugly Americans."

This historical drama of mine is replete with anecdotes. In most instances the anecdotes are narrated by the use of dialogue. Admittedly, due to the passage of decades since the anecdotes occurred, the dialogue is not verbatim but is, in most cases, a reasonable facsimile of things said more than a half century ago.

Moreover, by literary license the sometimes salty language of warriors, such as the Tuskegee Airmen were, has been softened to suit the tastes of all readers, especially young innocents who, it is my hope, will read these memoirs. As a senior-citizen author I feel obligated to protect our junior citizens from soldierly profanity.

It needs be said that as the exploits of the Tuskegee Airmen become more widely known and acknowledged we may begin to appear larger than life. Not so. We had our share of goofs and gaffes. And goof-offs. In narrating some incidents I have protected the person(s) involved from embarrassment by using nicknames, other names, or no names.

I must also declare that I do not claim that *A-Train* . . . is THE complete history of the Tuskegee Airmen. Obviously, no one person can tell the entire story of the Tuskegee Airmen because there are as many stories to tell as there were actors in the melodrama, each actor having a unique perspective of numerous events.

The saga of the Tuskegee Airmen had a cast of thousands, literally. There were heroes: the men who flew aloft and the men on the ground who kept them flying. And there were heroines: some in uniform as nurses, some in uniform as WAACs; others in mufti—the mothers, wives, sweethearts, sisters, daughters who supported their heroes "over there" and back home with V-mail, "care packages," and prayers. Heroines who, like their men in uniform, encountered the mean spirit and ways of Jim Crow even as they supported the war effort on the home front.

Finally, like any melodrama worthy of the label, the saga of the Tuskegee Airmen had a musical score of sorts. The score was made up of "our" songs and tunes: ballads that distilled the pain of being apart from our beloveds, like, "I'm making believe" (that you're in my arms), sung by the Ink Spots, and tunes that kept alive memories of home and happier times, peace times, jazz tunes like "Take the A-Train" played by Duke Ellington's orchestra that I liked so much I named my World War II combat airplane, "A-Train."

Such is the stuff of my memoirs, from infancy until military retirement.

Charles W. "Chuck" Dryden
Atlanta, Georgia

Acknowledgments

Because this is an autobiography, I feel compelled to salute not only those persons who urged and encouraged the writing of the book but also those who nurtured and impacted the life about which it has been written. The length of the honor roll of each group humbles me as I realize how blessed I have been with so many fine friends and kinfolk.

For starters, of course, my parents: Charles Levy Tucker Dryden ("Brother Rob") who never owned a house or a car but who boasted, proudly, "I invested in my children," and Violet Adina Dryden ("Sister Vie") whose gentle patience tempered Dad's firm discipline. Their abiding faith in God and dedication to educating their three children set me in motion, and my debt to them is incalculable. Likewise my brother Denis Alvin and sister Pauline because of whose presence I learned early on, as big brother, the need to be unselfish and to share and love kinfolk. Kinfolk like my beloved, flower-named aunts who nicknamed their Sister Vie and who helped her raise me: Lilly, Daisy, Myrtle, Hyacinth, and Iris.

During thirty-two years of a failed first marriage there were, as in most marriages, good things and bad. Grateful I am to my former wife, Irma Cameron "Pete" Dryden, for at least four good things: our three sons, Charles, Jr. ("Thumper"), Keith, and Eric, and the fourth, her mother, Charlie Pearl Cameron ("Mother Pearl"), my first beloved mother-in-law.

Now, praise the Lord, there is Marymal, my wife of twenty years at this writing, who has brought into my life the love of flowers, gourmet foods, and fine arts as well as my love for her, her mother Florence (my second beloved mother-in-law), and Marymal's four children—George, Tony, Kenny, and Cornelia—and the pursuit of happiness with all of them.

For my spiritual growth several ministers did as much by the example of their lives as by their preachments, for which I must express my gratitude: the Reverends Edler Garnet Hawkins, pastor at Saint Augustine Presbyterian Church, Bronx, New York, and later the first African American to be appointed Moderator (top official) of the United Presbyterian Church in the USA; Joseph Roberts, pastor at Elmwood Presbyterian Church, East Orange, New Jersey, and later senior pastor at Ebenezer Baptist Church, Atlanta, Georgia, where Dr. Martin Luther King, Jr., was once the pastor; Joseph Lowery, pastor of Central United Methodist Church in Atlanta and president of the Southern Christian Leadership Conference (SCLC); Cornelius Henderson and Walter Kimbrough, former senior pastors at Ben Hill United Methodist Church, Atlanta. All of these ministers of the gospel provided spiritual balance for the demands of my professional life as a military officer, a warrior.

Other persons who affected my career as an aviator number in the hundreds, too numerous to mention here, but at least these demand public acknowledgment for the impact that they exerted on my life: Bill Pyhota, CPT flight instructor; Milton Crenshaw and Charles A. "Chief" Anderson, civilian flight instructors at Tuskegee; Lieutenant General Benjamin O. Davis, Jr., my squadron commander and, later, group commander; Brigadier General Noel F. Parrish, commander of Tuskegee Army Air Field; Sidney Brooks and Clarence Jamison, aviation cadet classmates and squadron mates in the 99th along with Herbert E. Carter and Spann Watson, and especially James B. Knighten, who saved my life in the skies over Sicily.

The other group of steadfast friends, those who added their voices to Marymal's urging me, encouraging me, indeed goading me to write these memoirs, comprises a number of people whose help in getting the job done has been immeasurable, some because of the sense of urgency that they imparted and facilities they made available to me, others because of the information they provided. First and foremost among the "facilitators" is my mentor and motivator, Maceo Dailey, Ph.D., scholar and professor of history and herstory at Spelman College who encouraged me to write my story utilizing the computer in his office on campus. To ensure that I was diligent in getting the job done he offered me a ride to the college daily until it was completed, which put me in debt to his wife and sons as they squeezed into the family car to make room for me. For their gracious gift of daily rides "to work," and for Dr. Dailey's teaching me the fundamentals of "WordPerfect" on the computer, I am most grateful.

Sometimes my instructions to the computer were less than perfect and it would balk. That was when the two "whiz kids" of the Social Sciences Computer Lab at Spelman came to my rescue and got the computer to behave; I thank Mrs. Iris Aikens-Singleton and Ms. Jennifer Means for their expertise in taming the computer gremlins, Ms. Laurette Quaye of the History Department for her help with some clerical problems, and Spelman College for being the launching pad for *A-Train*.

For the contents of the book I have resorted to two main sources of information. In nine books written by or about Tuskegee Airmen I was able to find a wealth of information that was either old hat to me, helping me accurately recollect dates, places, and persons involved in events I had lived through but about which, a half century later, my memory was either flawed or totally failed, or information that was brand new to me. Those books are listed in the bibliography.

Because this work covers my memoirs, I have relied on my memory as the main source of information. However, cognizant that memory fades with time I have leaned heavily upon fellow Tuskegee Airmen for corroboration. Early on I became convinced that because of their personal experiences they are like the griots who made it possible for Alex Haley to write *Roots*. Accordingly I have kept hot the telephone lines of almost seventy of my buddies and many kinfolk with phone calls to corroborate one thing or another that I seemed to remember. Most times the callee said, "Yeah,

Chuck!" as he or she concurred in my recollection. Once or twice, however, I was told, "No, Chuck, it wasn't like that!" and I had to abandon a long-cherished, but dubious, "memory."

So, for their part in helping me recall accurately various bits and pieces of my story, I salute and thank: Charles A. "Chief" Anderson, Lee Archer, Ernest S. Banks, Howard Baugh, Omar Blair, Roscoe Brown, Charles Bussey, William A. Campbell, Herbert E. Carter, Huey Charlton, Rodney Coleman, Toy Conley, Oleta Crain, Benjamin O. Davis, Jr., Alvin Downing, Edward Drummond, Irma Cameron Dryden, Jean Esquerre, Kenneth Frank, Willie Fuller, George Haley, James H. Harvey, Milton Henry, Harold A. Hillery, William Holloman, Willis Hubert, James Hurd, Fred E. Hutchins, Clarence Clifford Jamison, Alexander Jefferson, Clovis Jones, Elmer Jones, Elmore Kennedy, James Bernard Knighten, Gerald Lalor, Nancy Leftenant-Colon, Roy LeGrone, Hiram Little, Lewis Lynch, Charles E. McGee, Richard Macon, William Melton, Thomas Money, Oliver Morse, James Nabbie, Fitzroy Newsum, Ira O'Neal, Alan M. Osur, Walter Palmer, Henry Perry, George Prather, Bernard S. Proctor, Louis R. Purnell, James Reed, Wiley Selden, Clarence Shivers, John Silvera, Gordon Southhall, Harry Stewart, John Suggs, William Thompson, Mildred Twigg, George Watson, Sr., Spann Watson, Shelly Westbrook, James T. Wiley, Arthur Williams, Charles I. Williams, Ray Williams, Robert Williams, Leroy Willis, Jr., O. B. Young.

Five years after completion, the manuscript finally passed muster thanks to editing suggestions by Ms. Beverly Green, Ms. Dee Robinson, and two anonymous reviewer-critics for The University of Alabama Press, and thanks to the copy-editing of Mrs. Beverly Denbow.

For the quantity of material contained in my memoirs, and the accuracy of it, I am much indebted to all the above. As for the quality, insofar as it may be flawed, the fault is entirely mine.

Part I

Before Desegregation

1 Dismissed!

» July 1944

"The accused will rise and face the court."

"Does the accused have anything to say before sentence is pronounced?"

"No, Sir."

"Having found First Lieutenant Charles Walter Dryden, Serial Number AO 789 119, guilty as charged of one count of violating the 96th Article of War, this general court-martial sentences Lieutenant Dryden to be dismissed from the United States Army Air Corps."

2 Why?

» July 1944

Dismissed from the United States Army Air Corps!

Dismissed from . . .

Dismissed . . . Dismissed . . . DISMISSED!!!

The words rang in my ears. Rattled around my skull. Ricocheted through my brain: from the cell that interprets language, telling me, "Dismissal means dishonorable discharge, loss of citizenship"; to the cell that controls body temperature—it went haywire as I broke into a cold sweat in that hot, humid courtroom; to the cell that controls self-control—I began trembling uncontrollably. The truth is I "tweaked" harder than I had ever "tweaked" before and thought: "Thank God for a tight sphincter to control my bowels."

Then came the questions. Questions I asked myself: "Why me?" "How come this has happened to me?" "Why have I been tried and convicted and sentenced by general court-martial?"

Everyone who knows me knows that I have been gung ho about flying all my life. That I am proud to wear the silver wings of a U.S. Army Air Corps pilot and the silver bars of a first lieutenant. That I am grateful to God for having survived combat. So: Why? Why? Why?

No need to ask, really. I knew the answers: I was court-martialed because I had led a flight of four P-39 "Airacobras" on a low-altitude pass across Walterboro Army Air Base on a Saturday in May 1944. How low? The fact is the control tower deck was seventy-five feet above the ground. When asked on the witness stand how

4

Extra!

Court-Martialed

CAPT. CHARLES W. DRYDEN, of Bronx, N.Y., former 99th Fighter Squadron pilot, who has faced court-martial and been acquitted since his return to this country after six months overseas. The decision of the court exonerating him is up for review. He was charged with low flying.

Published in the *Baltimore Afro American,* July 29, 1944, this picture should have been captioned: 1st Lt. Charles W. Dryden . . . was acquitted of flying low over the town of Walterboro, South Carolina, on Sunday but convicted for "buzzing" the air base the day before.

high the planes appeared to be as they flew across the base, the control tower operator on duty at the time said: "I looked down at them as they passed the tower!"

In short, we were "buzzing."

At that time buzzing was severely frowned upon by military brass because a rash of incidents had occurred recently involving crashed airplanes, injured or dead military pilots and civilians, and destroyed property. Just shortly before my transgression a particularly gruesome incident involved a military pilot who buzzed a pair of fishermen in an open boat on a lake in Florida. He flew so low that his propeller decapitated one of the men in the boat. That did it! The War Department put out the word that any future buzzing would be punished by dismissal from the service.

Did I know this? Yes, I had read it in an Army Air Corps flying safety bulletin.

Then why buzz? Why defy the rules? Why risk the loss of my flying career? ("A fate worse than death," I thought. "After all, flying is my whole life!")

The questions flashed through my mind and, as many persons facing death have testified, my whole life passed in review, as if to provide answers.

3   The Fledgling

"Air'pwane! Air'pwane!"

That is how, lisping, a typical two-year-old, tearing paper into bits and throwing them into the air, tried to tell the world that: "I want to, I was born to, I MUST fly!"

That is what "Sister Vie" used to tell me about my early yearning for the sky. To me she was "Mom," the gentlest, most devout, loving mother anywhere, ever. Christened Violet Adina Buckley, her middle name should have been Patience. I remember Mom teaching me to count by tens, even before I began first grade, by using bundles of match sticks, ten to a bundle. And spelling words using phonetics—the "at" family: bat, cat, hat and so on—long before anyone ever thought about Sesame Street. And grammar. The "King's English" way of proper speaking, although I must admit that answering, "It is I" when asked, "Who is it?" never did sound right to me. She needed patience, a lot of it, to get me started on the road to education.

Together, she and Dad emphasized four things in my rearing: love and serve God, obey your parents, be loyal to your family, and get a good education.

Dad was . . . Dad. Not Pop. Not a "take-me-out-to-the-ballgame" sort of father and yet not a rigid disciplinarian. Make no mistake, he was firm in demanding no-nonsense obedience, and I made sure to make as few mistakes as possible to avoid encounters between his razor strop and my hind parts. But I felt his love for me from his tender lullabies as he rocked his firstborn infant to sleep. We never went to baseball or football games because he did not know those games. He knew cricket because he was a Jamaican: A trip or two to see a cricket match at Van Courtlandt Park in the Bronx was about as close as I ever got to sharing fun with my father at a spectator sporting event.

He could swim like a fish and delighted the family with weekend picnics to Long Island beaches (Coney Island, Rockaway Beach, Riis Park Beach) and Interstate Park on the New Jersey side of the Hudson. Half the fun was going and coming home on the Long Island Railroad trains to the beaches and the Dyckman Street ferry across the Hudson River to Interstate Park. The other half was wading in the surf and riding the amusements at Coney Island: For me no roller coaster was too fast, no ferris wheel too high, no merry-go-round too dizzying. Aboard them I was "flying"; I was close to my fantasy heaven.

Charles Levy Tucker Dryden, "Dad" to me, was my first hero. A sergeant in the Jamaican Expeditionary Force during World War I, he was deployed to Europe by way of Egypt. His unit came under heavy fire in Belgium and he caught a hunk of shrapnel in his chest. It came within a quarter inch of ending these memoirs before they could even begin.

Before his military stint he was a teacher at Mico College (for men) in Kingston. Violet was a teacher at next-door Wolmers College (for women). They met and fell in love but had to postpone marriage plans until Dad's return from the war. Keeping the faith until the Armistice, Mom moved to New York City to await her beloved "Robin." Nine months, two weeks, five days later, on September 16, 1920, I saw the light of day, blessed from the start with two nurturing, loving, in-love parents.

To Mom's five sisters, Dad was "Brother Rob," and that became his nickname, used by all adult kinfolk. They were my aunts, all named for flowers: Lilly, Daisy, Myrtle, Hyacinth, and Iris. Affectionately, they called my mother "Sister Vie." So to all our kinfolk my parents were "Brother Rob and Sister Vie"—compatible, unflappable, devout cherubim and seraphim.

My aunts Lilly, Daisy, and Myrtle helped rear me, more than they will ever know. Older by a few years, their bearing, presence, manners, and behavior taught me what to expect of proper ladies when I began dating. Hyacinth and Iris, one year older and younger than I, respectively, were more like sisters to me, though when we were young they taunted me by insisting that I address them as "Aunt." Of course, in later years whenever introductions to young suitors were required, they declined the title, threatening painful consequences if I dared say, "May I introduce you to my Aunt ——."

My good fortune, of being born into a tranquil home and supportive family, increased six years later when my brother Denis Alvin was born and when, after another five years, along came my sister Pauline. Thus my world was complete in a family with both parents present plus a brother and a sister, because of whom I learned how to share, unselfishly. And many kinfolk close by who helped teach me respect for elders, knowledge of my Jamaican roots and folklore, and loyalty to family. And last but certainly not least, they taught me about the universal authority shared by all adults—kinfolk, teachers, preachers, policemen, yea even total strangers—that all children must behave and display good manners at all times, in all places, especially away from home. To disgrace one's family by misbehavior was to court disaster—like a good, this-hurts-me-more-than-it-hurts-you spanking.

In his quiet but forceful way my Dad used to say: "Son, you have two sets of ears. One set on your headsides, the other set on your backside. And if I can't get you to hear through your ears up top, I know you will hear through your bottom."

Education was the order of the day, day after day, school term after school term. Summer vacations included reading at least one book of our choice and attending some craft activity at a local school or playground. And year round there was time for a hobby.

My hobby was building model airplanes. Solid models: The Boeing P-12B and Curtis P-6E were my favorites, complete with U.S. Army Air Corps insignia on the wings, fuselage, and tail. Rubber band–powered flying models whose parts were painstakingly laid out on wax paper covering the blueprints of the model, fastened on top of a card table with straight pins; the ribs and spars and stringers held in place by more pins until airplane acetate glue, squirted carefully on adjacent parts, hardened and bonded them together. Then came the tough task of covering the fuselage, wings, and tail surfaces with thin tissue paper that was made taut by being sprinkled lightly with warm water. Growing up, my pride and joy were my model airplanes suspended from strings strung across the ceiling of my room from wall to wall to wall. Everyone on the block knew about the crazy Black kid who wanted to fly.

Spare time, after homework and home chores, was spent reading anything and everything about flying, especially a pulp magazine, *G-8 and His Battle Aces*. Each month I could hardly wait to read the latest feats of "derring-do" by "G-8," the fictional Yank World War I pilot, and his squadron of "battle aces" flying Spad VIIs as they shot down the hated Boche in Albatrosses, Fokkers, and Pfalzes above the trenches in France. Every child has a fantasy world. Mine was flying as a bird, higher than the highest mountain, farther than the ends of the earth, faster than a shooting star.

Apart from, and higher in priority than my hobby, was book learning in school. Whenever an adult visited, the first thing said to kids was, "How's school?" Kinfolk or strangers, it was almost always the same greeting. Not "Hello!" or "How are you?" but "How are you doing in school?" So, at an early stage I got the message that book learning could earn points, and rewards, from adults. Ignoring the benefits of education earned penalties. My Aunt Myrtle drove the latter point home painfully when I was in first grade. One day when she visited our home she gave me a quarter to buy a composition book for school. Quickly forgetting why she had given me the money, I ran around the corner to the candy store and bought the shiny cap pistol I had seen in the window. A couple days later she visited again and said, "Charlie, let me see the composition book you bought."

I thought: "Uh, oh! Now I remember why she gave me the money."

I said: "I forgot what you told me to buy, Aunt Myrtle, but I got this cap pistol that I always wanted. Isn't it a beauty? It shoots a roll of caps and . . . and . . . ouch!"

"Young man," she said, grabbing me by the ear, "this will help you remember next time you are told to do something for your schoolwork. Now you show me where the store is and we will return the cap pistol and get the book you should have gotten in the first place!"

I got the point. Education was high on the list of priorities when I was growing up. With that kind of prompting at home to excel, my teachers had no trouble with me. The truth is I really enjoyed school. It was a case of the appetite growing with the eating. Hard work with studies brought good grades, good grades brought rewards, rewards encouraged hard work, and so on.

By the time my formal education began in kindergarten at P.S. 169, in the Washington Heights section of upper Manhattan, I was ready. I could spell. I was proud that I could spell. And I got into trouble because I could spell: One day I spelled a four-letter word I had heard for the first time in my life and didn't know that it was a "bad" word. Wrote it on a piece of paper that had my name on it. As luck would have it the slip of paper fell out of my pocket. My teacher found it. Shocked by my profane prose, she said to me, sternly, "Charles, I want to see you after school!"

"Yes, Ma'am," I quavered, wondering why.

After all the other children had left to go home she confronted me with my paper. My punishment was a mouthwashing with some harsh brown laundry soap. I don't remember that teacher's name but I will never forget the incident.

Another "unforgettable" experience at P.S. 169 happened during a recess play period. Standing in a circle and rotating our hands in circles in front of our tummies, as if winding yarn, we sang with the teacher leading the chorus:

> Wind, wind nigger baby
> Wind, wind nigger baby
> Pull and pull
> And one, two, three.

I sang as loudly and as lustily as any of the other kids. In all my five years, until then, I had never heard "the" word, the hated word, the hateful word. It was never used in our household.

At supper that night Mom asked, "Son, what did you do at school today?"

"We learned a new song."

"Oh? Would you sing it for us?"

"Sure, Mom." And I sang the ditty.

Dead silence, for just a moment, Mom and Dad looking at me with strange expressions on their faces. Anger? Disbelief? Shock? I saw all of these but most of all, ANGER! Breathing hard, speaking in a tone I had never heard before, Dad said: "Son, I am not angry with you, but don't you ever sing that song again. *Nigger* is a bad word and we never use it. We will talk to your teacher about it, so don't you worry, Son, y'hear?"

"Yeah, Dad."

Someone talked to someone at school. Either Mom or Dad. Perhaps both. In any case we never sang that song again. That was my initiation into the world of hate and hurt based upon skin color.

When the time came for me to begin first grade we had moved from 164th Street between Edgecombe and Amsterdam Avenues in Washington Heights to 152nd Street and Saint Nicholas Avenue on Sugar Hill. P.S. 46 between Amsterdam and Saint Nicholas Avenues on 156th Street became my school home for the next six years.

Although I cannot recall all of my teachers, I do remember fondly three who worked hard to fill my head with knowledge and ambition. Like many a schoolboy, once upon a time I had a crush on a teacher. The object of my affections presided over sixth grade at P.S. 46: Mary Elizabeth Sullivan, I shall never forget. She was so kind and patient. And beautiful. I was inspired to study hard and excel—to please her.

Graduation from elementary school was both good and bad for me. Good because I was promoted from P.S. 46 to attend Edward Walmsby Stitt Junior High School, J.H.S. 164, at Edgecombe Avenue and 164th Street. Bad because I was leaving my beloved Miss Sullivan. Later at home, alone in my room, I sobbed my heart out for my lost love.

Among my teachers at Stitt was a lady who taught me to love the correct use of language "by the rules." In me Miss Laura Balfour had a pupil with ears attuned to the proper use of English. From twelve years of hearing my Jamaican parents speak "King's En-

FIRST LEADERSHIP ROLE. Elected president of the
senior class by his classmates at Stitt Junior High School,
fourteen-year-old Charles Dryden sits front and center in this
1934 picture with Principal Thomas Halligan and peerless
algebra teacher, Agnes L. Mackin, in the third row.

glish" I had learned the what and how of good English. In her
grammar class Miss Balfour taught me the why.

In my last year at Stitt my classmates elected me class president,
my first leadership opportunity. More important, we were taught
algebra by Miss Agnes L. Mackin, the best of all my teachers. Miss
Mackin made algebra crystal clear to the entire class and taught us
to love math. Lucky for me, because in order for my dream of flying
to come true I needed the curriculum of a science high school with
high standards and good credentials. Peter Stuyvesant High School
on the lower east side of Manhattan was the place to go. Stuyvesant
had tough entrance requirements, but I got in.

Four years later I got out with a diploma and acceptance in the
freshman class at City College of New York (CCNY). During the
four years at Stuyvesant I had made some new friends, two of

whom later shared military service with me at Tuskegee Army Air Field (TAAF)—Willie Batten and Leroy Gillead. Several other boyhood friends from high school days also showed up at TAAF during World War II, including Vinnie Campbell, Kenneth Frank, Conrad Johnson, Humphrey Patton, and Mike Smothers. Two others crossed my path in other places at later times: Horace McCoy in Oran, Algeria, during World War II, and Bryce Anthony in Japan during the Korean War. More about them in later chapters.

Matriculation at CCNY was a compromise and a blessing—and a near disaster—for me:

A compromise, because I really wanted to be either a military or an airline pilot. However, because neither the U.S. Army Air Corps nor any airlines was open to African American pilots, I would have settled for an aeronautical engineering degree at New York University. Unfortunately, my family could not afford the tuition at NYU. My next option was tuition-free CCNY, where I enrolled in the School of Mechanical Engineering (CCNY did not offer the aeronautical engineering degree).

A blessing, because just getting into CCNY was just that. The entrance requirement at that highly rated college was an 82 percent average on high school regents exams. I made it by the skin of my teeth.

A near-disaster, because my academic record at CCNY was just that. As one professor said to me as he saw me agonizing over a problem on one of his Physics 6 tests: "Mr. Dryden, why don't you change your major? You'll never make it as an engineer!" And Professor Zinn was right. Engineering was not my cup of tea.

However, a good thing happened at City College in 1940 during my third year there. A Civilian Pilot Training Program (CPTP) was started. I signed up for it and was accepted for the training. Successful completion of the ground school and forty hours of flying would earn a private pilot license. Hallelujah! That was my blessing!

Ground school classes were at the uptown campus of City College, and the flight training was at Roosevelt Field near Mineola, on Long Island, New York. That meant leaving home in the Bronx at 5:00 A.M., riding the subway to Pennsylvania Station, then the

Long Island Railroad to Mineola and a bus to Roosevelt Field. A long trip? Sure, but what of it? All I cared about was learning to fly. Besides, Roosevelt Field was where Charles "Lindy" Lindbergh took off on his historic nonstop flight to Paris in 1927. I felt it might launch my flying career also.

Matthews and Rappaport (Roy and Max) were the CPTP contractors with Uncle Sam at Roosevelt Field. They operated a small fleet of about three J-3 Piper Cubs. A secretary/operations clerk, Ethel Verbeek, kept all the flight records up to date and kept the morale of us trainees upbeat by cheerful friendliness. A half dozen or so trainees started the program in June 1940, including: Floyd Borneman, the "all-American boy" who knew a lot about flying; easygoing Orest Maurice Garin, of French descent; Bobby Maxwell, African American, smart mechanical engineering student, and cousin of Johnny Hodges, the peerless alto saxophonist with Duke Ellington's orchestra; Savchuck, the son of Russian immigrants; Shaaf, the Jewish comedian of the class who always had a joke handy to lighten our mood whenever any of us worried about how we were doing in the program; and Dryden, the kid from the Bronx whose Jamaican parents wanted him to finish college more than anything else but were willing to go along with his reaching for his dream. I was delirious with joy when Dad signed his approval for me to enroll in the CPT Program.

Three flight instructors stand out in mind. Frank O'Brien was my friend and Bobby Maxwell's instructor. Bobby was the first to solo and Frank was obviously proud of him. So was I. Bobby greased his first landing—he wouldn't have cracked eggs on the ground! Frank grinned from ear to ear. We almost lost Frank later during the program when he slipped on a patch of mud as he was cranking the propeller to start the engine on one of the Cubs. He stumbled toward the prop and one of the blades cut him across the abdomen. Rushed to a nearby hospital, Frank was patched up and was flying again in a few weeks.

Bill Pyhota was my instructor. Tall and broad shouldered, he filled the front seat in the small cabin of the Piper Cub. Because of his size I had trouble seeing the ground straight ahead on landing approaches from my very first airplane ride in June 1940. In fact, I had to develop a technique of judging height above the ground, during landing approaches, by focusing my peripheral vision on the ground as seen through the left and right side windows of the cabin. Although our training planes were based at Roosevelt Field, which had paved runways and taxiways, hangars, a control tower, fences, and objects that help in judging height above the ground, we flew during the day from a grassy field that had been a potato patch. Height perception was trickier at the potato patch than at the airport where landing, at the end of the day, was much easier for me.

About a week of daily flights trying to teach me how to take off and land the Piper Cub prompted Bill Pyhota to give up his front seat and say to me, one afternoon at the potato patch, "OK, Mr. Dryden, take it around the traffic pattern and bring it back here."

I couldn't believe my ears. I felt I was ready to solo, but . . . I began trembling from a slight case of nerves. I was a bit jittery because this was the day I had dreamed of all my life. From "Air'pwane! Air'pwane!" in my pram, to *G-8 and His Battle Aces,* to model airplanes, the trail had led to here, and now! As I taxied to the edge of the field and turned into the wind for takeoff it dawned on me: "I can see straight ahead! Bill's broad shoulders are not there blocking my view!" I exulted. "Yeah, but he ain't here to land this plane either, Dummy," my inner voice responded. "Well, I can't quit now," I thought. "All the guys saw Bill get out of the plane and they know I'm about to solo. So I've got to do it. There's no turning back."

Kinda like that time at the 135th Street YMCA pool when I was about ten years old. I got in line on the diving board with a bunch of other kids, jumped off when it came my turn—and almost drowned. I didn't know how to swim! Talk about peer pressure!

"Well," I told myself, "this is different because, first of all, I know how to fly. And besides, I have made at least twenty takeoffs and landings. Just remember what Bill has said over and over again: 'Dryden, fly the airplane. Don't let the airplane fly you!' "

So. Here we go, Piper Cub, just you and me. Throttle forward all the way, smoothly, swiftly. Light pressure on the rudder pedals, left or right as necessary to track straight ahead until the tail skid lifts

off the ground as airspeed increases and suddenly, SUDDENLY—
I'M FLYING! After twenty years of dreaming about it, I'm doing
it . . . I am actually FLYING! Shouting it at the top of my lungs,
laughing like a loon—ecstatic!

But wait—something's wrong. Something is loose up there in the
front seat. It looks like a black round stick moving from side to
side. What can it be? Why would Bill get out of the airplane and
leave some piece of equipment flopping around like that? It looks
something like the control stick back here.—Of course! That's it!
That THING is the control stick in the front seat. It's just that I've
never seen it before because Bill Pyhota has always been in the front
seat, until now.

OK. Now that we've solved that mystery, let's get this flying machine back on the ground. Turn left onto downwind leg at 800 feet,
fly straight and level to the road with the big red barn that Bill used
to set his base leg when he was showing me how. Now turn left 90
degrees onto the base leg and throttle back, holding airspeed at 60
mph and descending straight ahead on base leg until almost abreast
of the lane in which you plan to land. Turn left into final approach,
gun the engine briefly to clear it and, as the plane is at about treetop
height, begin easing back on the stick, close the throttle, and—
pray! Then, bump, bump, kiss, kiss we were on the ground, Piper
Cub and me.

I had soloed!

That was just the beginning for a fledgling. With the traditional
ritual (of having my shirttail cut off by the other guys) behind me,
as well as a sleepless night of excitement, on a "high," I settled
into the groove of training flights: dual instruction flights with Bill
Pyhota demonstrating power-on and power-off stalls, pylon 8s,
overhead landing approaches, spot landings, and forced landings;
solo flights to practice all the above.

One sunny afternoon, flying solo in a cloudless sky, I got into
trouble while practicing power-off stalls. It all started normally
enough: At 5,000 feet in the practice area, turn 90 degrees left then
90 degrees right, scanning the sky above and the space below to
"clear" the area for the presence of other planes; fly straight and
level lined up with a road on the ground and pull back on the stick

smoothly and steadily to raise the nose steeply above the horizon while simultaneously closing the throttle.

Oh boy, Piper Cub is hanging on its prop. Then—WHAM! The Cub's nose has flipped forward and downward violently, throwing me up and off the seat and backward. My feet can't reach the rudder pedals; I can barely reach the top of the stick. Piper Cub is shuddering, wind whistling/roaring past its struts as we dive toward the ground. My pulse is racing and I'm suddenly in a cold sweat. This is not like anything Bill ever demonstrated!

What do I do now? Pray hard. Act fast. Remember Bill's words: "Fly the airplane. Don't let the airplane fly you!"

So. Pull back on the stick firmly, raising the nose to the horizon. Throttle forward about halfway. Settle down squarely in the seat. Head toward the field and land. Tell the instructor what happened and ask, "What was that?"

"A whipstall," said Bill.

"Sometimes called a tail slide," Charlie Gregson chimed in. (He later became my instructor to get me ready to take the CAA [Civil Aeronautics Authority] flight exam for the private pilot license.)

By whatever name it was called I knew I would be careful not to raise the nose too steeply in future stalls and risk tearing the wings off the plane. "That's what could have happened," Charlie said.

By the time of the CAA flight test, some weeks later, and with forty hours of flying time in my logbook, I had learned enough to pass with flying colors. I became the proud possessor of a private pilot license.

That was something. REALLY something! But it wasn't enough. It was only the beginning. I wanted to fly bigger airplanes, faster than the 65-horsepower Piper Cub.

I envied the U.S. Navy ensign who landed his Grumman F4F Wildcat at Roosevelt Field one day during our Primary CPT Program, taxied up to the ramp, and hopped out. As a few of us student pilots walked around the stubby, dark blue–painted navy fighter plane, the pilot invited us to climb up on the wing to look into the cockpit. I gulped as I looked at the myriad gauges, dials, switches, and lights on the instrument panel and consoles on the

WACO PILOT. The Waco UPF-7 was a great airplane for aerobatics in the Advanced CPT Program at CCNY in the fall of 1940.

sides of the cockpit. Although somewhat overwhelmed, I thought to myself, "If he can do it, I can too."

Another time, I envied the second lieutenant, U.S. Army Air Corps, who visited the Matthews and Rappaport hangar one day. He was assigned to the pursuit squadron stationed at Mitchel Field, next door to Roosevelt Field. I was fascinated by his tales about flying the Curtis P-40 "Tomahawk" with which his squadron was equipped. Because of many crashes, the P-40 was nicknamed the "Flying Coffin." Still, more than ever, I wanted to be a military pilot flying a sleek, fast, all-metal pursuit plane.

My next chance at reaching my goal came with being selected for the Advanced CPT course. Matthews and Rappaport had a contract to conduct the advanced course using a Waco UPF-7 biplane with two open cockpits and 250-horsepower engine. And their plane had a U.S. Army Air Corps paint-job: yellow wings with a white star in a blue circle located near the tips on the top of the top wing and on the underside of the bottom wing; alternate red and white horizontal stripes on the rudder; sky blue fuselage. Very glamorous looking!

My advanced course instructor was, again, Bill Pyhota. And I had great fun as he taught me acrobatics: chandelles, loops, Immelman turns, split-"S's," Cuban 8s, lazy 8s, snap rolls, slow rolls, vertical reverses, falling leaves, spin recovery. Precision flying techniques were learned in performing 360-degree and 720-degree overhead landing approaches to power-off "spot" landings.

Toward the end of the forty-hour flying program I had to plan and fly a solo cross-country navigation flight with landings at two strange fields and final landing at Roosevelt Field. The final *"pièce de résistance"* was a dual night flight with Bill Pyhota in the Matthews and Rappaport Stinson Reliant, a deluxe, closed-cabin, high-wing monoplane.

With Bill at the controls we took off from Roosevelt Field at dusk on a cold, clear, moonless night in February 1941. As we climbed, turning toward New York City, I gasped at the awesome sight of thousands of lights on buildings in lower Manhattan and Brooklyn, ships in the harbor, cars in the streets, and stars twinkling above. It all looked to me like a bucketful of diamonds spilled on black velvet, and the lights strung on the suspension cables of the George Washington Bridge across the Hudson in the distance looked like a giant necklace, completing the illusion.

I had mixed feelings about that flight because it was my first flight at night (fantastic!) and my last CPT flight (saddening). I knew it would be the last time I would fly with this peerless young pilot-instructor with the half smile and a twinkle in his eyes whenever a student pilot did something really right. Eighty hours of flying under his tutelage had earned him my respect and admiration.

I hope that life has dealt him fair skies and tail winds through the years, for it was Bill Pyhota who first unfurled the wings of this fledgling.

4   Off to Tuskegee

>>   August 1941

By the end of the Advanced CPT course in February 1941 I was broke. Round-trip subway fare plus Long Island Railroad fare plus bus fare almost daily for eight months had eaten up all the savings my folks had earmarked for my carfare to City College. Tuition was free but books and student fees would add up to a tidy sum for my junior and senior years. So when the Primary CPT course ended in late August, I had to make a choice: either resume classes at City or accept the offer to go through the Advanced CPT Program.

Choice? No choice, that! Can the sun choose not to rise in the morning? Can the lowly caterpillar choose not to molt and become a butterfly, free to fly the air? No. No more than I could choose to return to plodding, miserably, toward total disaster in some mechanical engineering class at City College. Besides, with a CAA private pilot license in my wallet along with a letter offering me a slot in the Advanced CPT Program, I regarded the offer as one I could not refuse.

My buddy, Bobby Maxwell, turned down an offer to do the advanced course and chose instead to finish his studies for a mechanical engineering degree. I knew I would miss his friendly, easygoing manner and the companionship of the only other Black in the Matthews and Rappaport CPT school. Not only was Bobby a fine pilot but he was a brilliant mechanical engineering student as well. In later years his choice proved to be obviously correct as he graduated with flying colors. And when we met again at a social affair, for the first time in a dozen years, he was successful, wealthy, and still one of the most likable men I've been privileged to call "friend."

For me, as the saying goes, "the appetite grew with the eating." I had tasted flying and was hungry for more. "Hungry" is an understatement—"greedy" describes my appetite better because, even as I began flying a bigger, faster airplane in the advanced course and learning acrobatics, I wanted more. I wanted the P-40. I wanted the silver wings and gold bars of a U.S. Army Air Corps pilot!

To get them one had to complete air corps training as an aviation cadet. The first step, of course, was to apply at a recruiting station. So I tried to apply at the army recruiting office at 39 Whitehall Street in lower Manhattan, not far from city hall. I just knew that my brand new private pilot license would earn me a quick enlistment as an aviation cadet.

"Crazy nigger!" To tell the truth, I didn't hear the sergeant say it, but the look on his face when I asked for an application told me what he must have been thinking. What he said was: "The United States Army is not training any Colored pilots, so I can't give you an application."

Stunned, angry, near mad from frustration, I fought to control tears of rage. Was this to be the end of my dream? This was the second time White America had rejected me!

The first time had occurred two years earlier during my sophomore year at City College. Under the tutelage of my Drafting 101 professor, Mario Carbone, I had turned out some pretty good drafting plates. Seeing a help wanted ad for a junior draftsman in the *Bronx Home News*, I wrote requesting an interview and included several samples of my work. Next day a telegram came with an urgent invitation for an immediate interview. "Thrilled" doesn't describe my feelings. "Feverishly excited" is closer to the mark. In any case, I slept very little that night but daydreamed of landing a real job.

Bright and early the next morning I dressed in my one Sunday-go-to-meeting suit and reported to the company's office with portfolio containing several other examples of my work and, of course, THE TELEGRAM—my ticket to the future.

"Waddayawant!" she sneered at me.

I thought: "What a surly receptionist!"

I said: "I'm here for an interview. I received this telegram from your company yesterday."

Eyeing me suspiciously, she grunted, "Wait here," and disappeared through a door marked "Manager." Moments later a short, dumpy, bald man emerged with "Miss Surly" in tow. I heard him say some nice words, pleasant words. Words like: "Your work is very good. I would like to hire you."

("Good!" I rejoiced.)

"But," he continued, "you see, boy, if we hire you we would surely have trouble with our other employees. I'm sorry."

Oof! I felt as though I had been kicked in the stomach. Speechless. Breathless. Stunned. I left in a daze. I had just had my first knockdown by Jim Crow and it made me sick at heart.

A month later came Round Two, with the recruiting sergeant— another knockdown.

Yet another month later it was October 1940. Tucked way back in the back pages of the *Bronx Home News* one Saturday was an article that I happened to see. Just a few lines announcing that the U.S. Congress had passed a bill enabling the War Department to accept applications for aviation cadet training from "Negroes."

H-A-L-L-E-L-U-J-A-H! Thank you, Jesus!

Of course the recruiting office was closed on Saturday. That was the longest weekend of my life, but finally it was Monday and I "opened" the recruiting office at 39 Whitehall Street. I was already there when the same sergeant arrived just before 8:00 A.M. He didn't seem overjoyed at seeing me but, wordlessly, after piddling around for about a half hour, he shoved the application form to me across his desk and handed me a pen to fill it out. About an hour later, after having labored over it, I handed it to him. Scanning it, he snapped, "You have a pilot's license?"

"Yeah," I replied. "Got it last month."

"Oh yeah? How?"

"CPT Program."

"CPT? What's that?"

I thought: "To be a sergeant he sure is dumb."

I said: "Civilian Pilot Training Program."

Next question: "How old are you?"

"Twenty, last month on the sixteenth."

"Well," he said triumphantly, "you can't enlist. You have to have your parent's permission if you're not twenty-one." And he threw the application back across the desk to me.

"And you have to get it back here in forty-eight hours."

Twenty-two hours later, on Tuesday, I was right back at the recruiting office with the application signed on the proper line by my Dad in his beautiful handwriting. Holding the form gingerly, as though it was too hot to handle, Sergeant What's-his-name grunted: "You'll hear from us. Don't call us; we'll contact you when we're ready. That's all!"

I couldn't help wondering if that was, indeed, all. Wondered if I would ever hear from 39 Whitehall Street.

As luck (i.e., providence) would have it, I did. Six months later in early April a letter, THE LETTER, arrived at 800 Home Street, Bronx, New York, saying, in effect: Report to the recruiting office for a physical examination and, upon passing same, an interview by a board of U.S. Army officers.

"Oh, hot damn!" I exulted. But I worried: I'll never pass the physical. At only 150 pounds, soaking wet, they'll never let me fly big planes.

Well, at some point of my young life I had heard that "nothing beats a trial but a failure." So, what the hell! Let's go try anyway!

So I did. And I passed the physical! There were nine of us, all Blacks—obviously this was a special occasion—taking the exam that day. Only two of us passed the physical. The other guy, Lloyd Singletary, was from Connecticut. We were happy to have passed the exam but sad about the other guys' failure. One, Jimmy Plinton, whom I met that day for the first time, was flunked for a temporary condition that was later corrected; he took the physical again, passed it, later became an instructor pilot, and after the war was the first African American to be a vice president of Eastern Airlines.

With the physical exam completed just before noon, and the fluid in the eye test causing me to have slight double vision, I was told to go to lunch and return at one o'clock for an interview by a board of officers.

Crossing the wide avenue to the hot dog stand on the other side of the street was unnerving, especially with the double vision blurring oncoming cars and trucks. But with God's help I made it across. While wolfing down what looked like two hot dogs (although I had ordered only one), I was thinking how blessed I was to have been born to strong, healthy parents who had fed me the proper foods, insisted on my getting an education, and were, themselves, models of decent God-fearing people. Mother: gentle, patient, gracious. Dad: stern but reasonable—and multitalented. He could fix anything.

I remembered the time when I was about ten years old and my dreams of flying almost came crashing down. I had almost lost the index finger on my left hand trying to slice a hard loaf of stale bread with one of Dad's razor-sharp carving knives. The blade slipped off the top surface of the stonelike bread; slid down the side, and sliced my finger to the bone at the middle knuckle. Blood spurted, then gushed. Pain seared and I hollered, "Help!"

Mom came into the kitchen from somewhere in the apartment, saw my predicament, made a tight bandage with a dish towel, and told me to squeeze the base of the finger. Saying, "Be brave, Sonny, I'll go get your father," she rushed out of our first-floor apartment to the lobby of the building to summon Dad. He was on duty as elevator operator at the time but came to me at once. First he unwrapped Mom's dish-towel bandage. Then he held my finger in the cold tap water to wash away the gushing blood, painted the wound edges with iodine (I howled), and with a tourniquet of sterile gauze stanched the flow from a gusher to a slow ooze.

He then half-ran, half-walked me to a nearby emergency clinic. Lucky for me it was only two blocks away because I could hardly keep up with his long strides. The doctor dressed the wound and told me to keep the bandage dry and return a week later.

I did. He removed the bandage and the scab that had formed. Of course the wound began to bleed, whereupon he painted it with iodine. I yelped. He put on a fresh bandage and said, "Come back again next week."

On about the fourth or fifth such visit the doctor told me to tell my parents that the finger was not responding to treatment and would have to be amputated. But they would have to give their permission. I went home and told them.

"Never!" my father roared. He was a God-fearing man. I had never heard him swear or curse, but I think he must have muttered some Jamaican bad word followed by: "They will not cut off your finger—I will not allow it! You are not going back to that butcher shop. From now on I will take care it." And he did.

He took off the bandage, washed the wound in cold water, dusted it with talcum powder, and put on a fresh bandage. One week later he removed the bandage. No blood flowed or even oozed. My finger was saved. Saved, too, were my dreams of flying for Uncle Sam—with one finger missing I could not have passed the physical exam for aviation cadet training!

So. After lunch came the interview.

Seated stiffly, nervously, and alone about six feet in front of a long table behind which my three inquisitors sat with their brass buttons and assorted ribbons, I felt like a prisoner in the dock. The first questions were easy: What is your full name? Where were you born? When? Where did you attend grade school? Junior high? High school? College?

Answering easily, smoothly, I thought: "This is a breeze." And I relaxed.

"Your parents, where were they born?"

Uh, oh, I thought. Mom and Dad had never applied for American citizenship, although they had often expressed their intention to do so. Like many other immigrants, they had kept putting it off. However, I myself am a natural-born American, so, "Not to worry, press on regardless!" I reassured myself with that typical Jamaican expression I had learned from my kinfolk. With these thoughts in mind I settled down, calm, cool, and collected as I answered: "My mother and father were born in Jamaica, British West Indies. They are applying for American citizenship this month."

Almost immediately, with the next question, I became shaken

up, lost my cool, and felt that my dream of flying had been cashed in. The question was: "Have you ever been arrested?"

"Oh [expletive deleted]!" I thought. I was afraid they might ask that question. Two years earlier I had used a slug instead of a five-cent coin to go through the subway turnstile on my way to classes at City College. Using slugs was a common practice among high school and college students, who got away with it most times. That morning, however, a plainclothes detective was watching the early morning rush hour crowd going through the turnstiles. He spotted my slug as it showed up in the large illuminated magnifying glass window on the side of the turnstile, walked over to me, and, grasping my shoulder in a firm grip, said: "You're under arrest!"

Omigod! My world came crashing down. My knees knocked. I trembled all the way to Bronx County Courthouse where I was booked, fingerprinted, and then locked in the "tank," a holding cell for miscreants awaiting a hearing in municipal court at 10:00 A.M., two hours later. Two hours to call myself every variety of "stupid," "dumb," "immature" in the dictionary and to wonder, miserably, "What will my parents think of me?" I, who they thought was a good boy who never gave them any trouble in all my eighteen years.

Well, resigned to my grim fate as a fingerprinted felon, I decided to cross that bridge when I got to it. My immediate problem was the judge and what penalty he would impose for my transgression.

Finally, it was ten o'clock. Herded into the courtroom with the rest of the dregs from the tank—drifters, vagrants, and drunks— I slumped onto a hard bench, awaiting my fate. Barely heard my name when the clerk called it and directed me to stand at a podium directly in front of the high desk where the judge was seated. So help me God, I cannot remember if I was asked to swear on a Bible to tell the truth. I was in a fog. I heard: "What is your name?"

"Charles Walter Dryden, Your Honor."

"How old are you?"

"Eighteen, Sir."

"Your occupation?"

"Student."

"Where?"

"CCNY, Sir."

"What?" he exploded. "Do you mean to tell me that you are a college student and you were dumb enough to use a slug to ride the subway?"

"Y-Y-Yes, Sir, Your Honor," I quavered.

"Now I've heard it all," he said, shaking his head in disbelief. Then he launched into a scathing but mercifully brief lecture about honesty, integrity, and obedience of the law, punctuated by a $50.00 fine, and ended saying: "I am suspending sentence. Now get out of my courtroom and don't let me see you in here again, ever! And remember, you now have an arrest record."

The courtroom clock showed 10:47 A.M. I had missed my calculus and Spanish classes but could still make it to CCNY's uptown campus in time for my afternoon classes. Good! Even better news than that—my parents would not know what had happened.

"Mr. Dryden, let me ask you again: Have you ever been arrested?"

Jerked back to the present by the repeated question, I thought. Fast! My options? Lie, say "No" and risk being exposed as a liar, eventually. Say "Yes" and kill my dream with the truth about my arrest three years ago. Parents' and teachers' impact on me through the years of molding my character saved me. I chose the truth and, barely audibly, said: "Yes, Sir."

"Oh?" With raised eyebrows, the major who was leading the questioning said, "Tell us about it."

As I was telling my sorry tale I watched the faces of the three officers, trying to maintain eye contact and hoping, desperately, for some sign of sympathy. Perhaps just the flicker of a smile, however slight and fleeting. Nothing! All three sat stone faced, staring (glaring?) at me. While I was speaking the major kept glancing at a folder that lay open on the table. When I had finished, I thought: "I am finished now, for sure." Then the major shocked me. He said: "Mr. Dryden, that is an interesting story, mostly because it is a true story. Of course, the air corps doesn't want any thugs or criminals. However, we certainly don't want any pantywaists either. Most of all, we don't want any liars. Now we know that this is a true story because we already knew all about your arrest record. It's all right here in this file. We just wanted to see if you would tell the truth. Well, you did, and so you have passed everything today with flying colors. Congratulations! You will hear from the War Department in about ninety days."

"Thank you, Sirs!" I croaked through a dry throat.

Thank you, Jesus! I exulted, inwardly. Talk about happy! But for the ninety-day wait I would have been delirious.

Somehow I managed to endure the wait for travel orders with the help of my family, neighborhood friends, my pastor, the Reverend Dr. Edler G. Hawkins, and the wonderful, caring, nurturing folks at Saint Augustine Presbyterian Church in the Bronx. And my girl friend, Jackie.

Jackie was just about the prettiest girl I had ever seen. And, too, she had both style and class. We had met several months before, while I was learning to fly in the CPT Program. A senior at Hunter College, she was popular with her girl friends at the all-girl school and much admired and pursued by guys in our neighborhood and our college crowd. Her cute figure on a petite brown frame was topped by a cameo face crowned with bangs covering her forehead. I loved bangs. I loved Jackie. Dancing together, slow drag style, to Duke Ellington's "All Too Soon" at a party given during the Christmas holidays by Norma, a friend of hers, Jackie whispered to me, "*Je t'aime.*" And I flew, without wings. Soared clear out of this world! She and her family—parents, grandparents, two brothers, and two sisters—became some of my greatest, most encouraging supporters.

With so many wonderful people urging me onward and upward I felt I was already on top of the world and that only the sky was my limit. On my job as an elevator operator at the Lotos Club on 57th Street, just a few doors east of Carnegie Hall, I fantasized that every ascent was a takeoff in an airplane and every descent was a landing: At every stop I concentrated on making sure that the floor of the lift was absolutely flush with the floor of the landing itself. I felt it was necessary to get in the habit of doing everything with utmost precision.

The Lotos was a private, lily-White male club that counted many prominent men in its exclusive membership. My six months of employment there enabled me to observe the social elitism of such clubs — bastions of White American males, breeding grounds of Jim Crow. I shall never forget the night of June 18, 1941, when heavyweight champion Joe Louis fought Billy Conn in the Polo Grounds, home of the New York Giants baseball team. Conn's strategy was to hit and run and try to evade the Brown Bomber's knockout punches and win on points. Conn bobbed and weaved, tempting fate for thirteen rounds.

The Lotos bar lounge was jammed with members and guests gathered to hear the blow-by-blow radio broadcast and cheer for Conn. At the end of each round various members came to the elevator for a quick trip to their rooms and to bait me.

"How do you like the fight, boy?" gloated one.

"Looks like Louis can't beat Conn, eh, Charles?" needled another.

"How much will you lose when Conn is the new champion?" taunted still another.

I kept my silence. Agonized for Joe. Prayed for Joe. And was answered! Finally catching up with Conn in the thirteenth round, Joe put Billy's lights out, later coining the now-famous phrase, "You can run but you can't hide!" Joe Louis never knew how he turned around the mood at the Lotos Club that night. The elevator became icy as the members tried to cope with the egg on their faces, as I needled them with:

"Great fight, right?" and

"Louis sure whipped his butt, didn't he?" and

"I bet you lost a bundle on Conn, eh?"

No answers. Just stony silence. For once Jim Crow was speechless. That experience gave me a preview of a similar type of elitism laced with bigotry that I found in officers clubs later in my career.

But let me not get ahead of my story.

The War Department finally came through with Special Orders Number 197, dated August 19, 1941, issued by United States Army, Headquarters, New York Recruiting District, 39 Whitehall Street, New York. In part, the order stated: Aviation Cadet Charles W. Dryden, 12032421, having enlisted this date for assignment to Air Corps Flying School, Tuskegee, Alabama, will proceed from New York, New York, to Tuskegee, Alabama.

That was it! I was in the army now! A great-fun going away party by Jackie and her family the day before my departure was unforgettable. The next day, on the noon Pennsylvania Railroad train to Washington, D.C., my journey south began. The "Pennsy" racketed along at a good clip, arriving at the D.C. terminal in plenty of time for me to make my connection with the Southern Railroad to Atlanta.

My orders included a U.S. Government TR (transportation request) for an upper berth. However, the conductor told me I would have to stay in the "Colored" coach until the Pullman cars were made up. That would be about ten o'clock, four hours later.

So I settled down in a seat behind a grandmotherly lady who was traveling with two young children, a boy about eight and a girl about six. Cute kids.

"Where're you going, Son?" the old lady asked.

"To Tuskegee, Ma'am," I replied.

"Ever been south before?"

"No, Ma'am."

"Going to college, eh? Tuskegee's a good school. Famous, too. Booker T. Washington was a great man."

"Yes, Ma'am. But I'm not going to college at Tuskegee Institute. I am going to the army flying school there."

"Oh!" she said, excitedly. "I read about the 99th Pursuit Squadron just last week in the *Pittsburgh Courier.* So you're going to be a pilot. Now you be careful, y'hear? And don't forget to pray, always, Son, and you'll be alright. And I will pray for you, too."

"No, Ma'am, I won't forget. And thank you for your prayers."

There was more to thank her for about an hour after the train left Washington and the sandwich and drinks vendor came through the "Colored" coach. "Grandma" invited me to share some of the fried chicken and corn bread she had in a large picnic basket.

"You don't have to mess with that mess," she said. "The bread is probably stale and they don't taste too good anyway. That's why when Colored folks travel down here we bring our own food. Here, Son, have some of this."

"Thank you, Ma'am, but I have government orders that pay for my meals during the trip. And I don't want to eat up what you have for yourself and the children."

"Fiddlysticks!" she snorted. "I always bring extra for young people like you who may not have much eating money on the way home or back to school and would prefer home-cooked vittles, anyway. Don't you?"

"Yes, Ma'am."

By now my mouth was drooling and I protested no more. As I bit into the proffered drumstick, I was glad she had insisted.

"Delicious!" I mumbled between bites while she smiled the smile of an appreciated cook. Her kindliness made me feel at home and helped me forget how uncomfortable the Colored coach was with its windows open to admit "fresh" air into the sweat-box car. "Fresh" the air was not. Located just behind the baggage car, which was next behind the steam locomotive, the Colored coach caught a constant flow of cinders from the coal-burning engine. A film of cinders soon covered everything: clothing, baggage, seats. Even lungs. Once when I sneezed into my handkerchief I was appalled to see a residue of soot staining it.

At about seven o'clock that evening the porter came through the coach checking tickets. Looking at my ticket, he saw the notation about government-authorized meals.

"Don't you want to have dinner in the dining car, Son?" he asked.

"Yes, I sure do."

"Well, you wait here 'til I see the conductor."

About ten minutes later the conductor came into the car with the porter in tow. Frowning, he asked me: "You the one wants to eat in the dining car?"

"That's right," I replied.

"Follow me," he growled.

About ten coaches and Pullman cars later we arrived at the last car on the train, the dining car. At the front of the car, just inside the door, were two tables, one on each side of the aisle. Both had a heavy, green cloth curtain on a ceiling track that could be closed to hide from view anyone seated at the table. A kitchen helper took my order; the two waiters were busy serving the diners at the tables in the rest of the dining car . . . all White folks.

After "Grandma's" delicious chicken and corn bread, I had little appetite, or space, for a full meal. The truth is I went to the dining car only to see for myself "the curtain" about which I had heard from some sleeping-car porters who lived in our neighborhood. I saw the curtain and got the message: You're in the South now; stay in your place; facilities for Colored people are separate but equal.

Separate? Assuredly! I thought.

Equal? Obviously not! I observed.

I ordered a ham and cheese sandwich on whole wheat toast, some cookies, two pints of milk, and a Coca-Cola for my new friends and took it all back through the ten railway cars to the Colored coach. Their smiles of greeting warmed my heart.

I was seeing the faces of southern hospitality: spontaneous friendliness on the Black face, instant hostility on the White.

At about ten o'clock the porter came into the car again. Beckoning me to follow him, he said, "Son, the Pullman car is ready. You can get into your upper berth now."

I said good-bye to "Grandma." The cute kids were already asleep, sprawled across the bench.

The Pullman car had been transformed into a narrow aisle with green curtains covering upper and lower berths on both sides. When we reached my upper berth, my porter friend showed me the ladder to climb up into the berth and handed my satchel up to me, with the suggestion that I use the lavatory right away while he stood outside the door, and "Hurry up, before someone else comes to use it!"

Nobody did. I climbed back up into my berth and slept fitfully, awakening each time the locomotive started off with a jerk, or two, or three after several stops during the night. Just before dawn, George the porter (I learned later that all porters were called George) awakened me.

"Come now, Son, while everyone is still asleep so you can wash up."

"Thank you, Sir," I said. I couldn't call him George any more than I could have called him boy. He was an elderly man and I had been reared to respect my elders. Besides, his calling me "Son" and helping me to use the train facilities, while avoiding any unpleasantness, earned my gratitude.

After dressing and collecting my gear I went back to the coach. "Grandma" and the cute kids were not there. They had gotten off at one of the many stops during the night. I felt a sense of loss. I had grown to love that old lady and her "grands."

At about 8:00 A.M. the train reached Atlanta, where I was to change trains. I went up the stairs into the terminal to use the "Colored Men's" rest room and to get directions to the track where the Central of Georgia Railroad train was waiting to leave for Montgomery, Alabama, and drop me off at Tuskegee along the way.

Back down the stairs to the train platform. Walk to the Colored coach just behind the baggage car, and climb aboard, hauling my suitcase. There were only two young men in the car, lounging across seats on opposite sides of the aisle. As I settled into a seat in the row next to theirs they greeted me.

"Hey, man, I'm Sid Brooks from Cleveland," said the stocky, broad-shouldered one. "Where you from?"

"And I'm Clarence Jamison, also from Cleveland," the smaller-built but wiry guy chimed in. "We just got into Atlanta on the L&N Railroad."

"I'm Charlie Dryden from the Big Apple. I caught the Pennsylvania Railroad to D.C. yesterday at noon and then the Southern to Atlanta last night."

"Where you heading, Charlie?"

"To Tuskegee. The aviation cadet program."

"Hey! How 'bout that! We're headed there, too. Looks like we're all going to be in the same class," Brooks said.

And so we were.

About four hours after the train left Atlanta, four hours of getting acquainted, we heard the porter's shouted announcement:

"C-H-E-H-A-W! C-H-E-H-A-W! I'm talking 'bout C-H-E-H-A-W!"

The train slowed jerkily to a stop. We looked out the window for a terminal. We saw a shack with a sign: CHEHAW.

"Why are we stopping here?" one of us asked the porter.

" 'Cause this is where you get off to go to Tuskegee."

So we got off. Good Lord, it was hot! August in Alabama was wicked.

Small as it was, the railroad station nevertheless had its separate but "equal" waiting rooms for Colored and White travelers. Outside, on the dirt road side of the shack, we found a station wagon from Tuskegee Institute waiting to take us to the campus. Fifteen hot, dusty minutes later we reached our destination. We had finally arrived. Tuskegee, "the pride of the swiftly growing South."

Now, immediately, began our eight months of training as aviation cadets.

5   Aviation Cadets

» August 1941–April 1942

"All right, 'Dummies,' let's get with the program! Get the lead outta your butt. Get your bags out of the bus and line up right here in front of the cadet barracks. Move it!" he barked.

"He" was a bullet-headed man about my height, about twenty pounds heavier, light complexion, dressed in starched khaki long-sleeve shirt tucked into pants with knife-edge creases held up by an olive drab web belt fastened by a gleaming brass buckle. Spit-shined brown shoes, overseas cap set with the front crease just above the eyelashes, and tan necktie, with the ends tucked in between the second and third buttons from the top, completed his uniform.

"My name is Aviation Cadet George Spencer Roberts of class 42-C. My friends call me 'Spanky.' To you I am 'Mister Roberts.' To me you are 'Dummies.' Now, what are your names? Sound off, Dummies!"

That was our introduction to the cadet corps. No "Hello, glad to meet you." No "Welcome aboard!"

Dripping with sweat from the heat and the double-breasted wool suit I had on, all I wanted was a shower and a change into light-weight clothes. But that was not to be until after Mr. Roberts had proved to me that I knew nothing about how to make a bed. At home I had been making my bed almost every day of my life since age six but had never had to make it so taut that a quarter dropped

36

from a foot above the army blanket would rebound about half that height.

Finally, about three hours later, after having had clothing items issued to us, we were allowed to shower and look around the cadet barracks. Located adjacent to a quadrangle near the north end of the campus, and flanked by men's dormitories, Sage and Phelps Halls, the building was known on campus as "the bathhouse." It had once housed an indoor swimming pool. Now, with the pool area covered over by a floor, the building housed the aviation cadets of the "Tuskegee Experiment." On the floor about twenty double-decked bunks had been set up, aligned in two rows. In place at both ends of each double-decker were footlockers, one each for the occupants of the top and the lower bunks.

Just inside the entrance was a small office that served as an administrative office of sorts. At the far end of the large open area a wall separated the living/sleeping area from an open shower room in which were a dozen showers, with drain boards, on one side of the lavatory area and a half dozen commodes on the other. On the bunkroom side of the wall about a dozen face basins with mirrors were installed.

The first class of cadets had already been in the program exactly one month. Thirteen African American young men had begun their primary flight training on July 19, 1941. A historic date to be remembered! Scheduled to complete their training in March 1942, they were designated class 42-C. They were upperclassmen to class 42-D, my class.

Twelve of the thirteen members of 42-C were cadets, all of whom were college graduates or had at least two years of college; many had private pilot licenses earned in the CPT Program; one had military experience in the U.S. Army field artillery.

The thirteenth, and most prominent, man on the roster of 42-C was Benjamin O. Davis, Jr., Captain, U.S. Army Infantry, the son of Brigadier General Benjamin O. Davis, Sr. The elder Davis (who had come up the ranks from buck private) was the first African American to wear the stars of a general officer in the nation's history. Captain Davis, Jr., had graduated from the United States Mili-

A platoon of aviation cadets march in formation with a guidon bearer out in front. Although the identity of this large class is unknown, it must have been at TAFS several months after Dryden's cadet class (42-D), which began with eleven and graduated only three.

tary Academy at West Point, New York, in the class of 1936, surviving and succeeding through four years of "silent treatment" by his classmates and without a roommate. He went through flight training as an officer and did not live in the bathhouse barracks with us cadets. However, his impact on our cadet corps was immediately apparent.

My 42-D classmates and I felt the impact at once. It was obvious that Captain Davis had taught his aviation cadet classmates a great deal about military bearing and procedures—and about how to be upperclassmen: that is, how to deal with, how to guide, how to discipline "Dummies" like my ten classmates and me.

By midafternoon all of my classmates had reported in, thus completing the roster of class 42-D, including: Robert L. Boyd, Washington, D.C.; Sidney P. Brooks, Cleveland, Ohio; Earl Brown, Tallahassee, Florida; Earl Bundara, Baltimore, Maryland; Charles W. Dryden, New York, New York; Clarence C. Jamison, Cleveland, Ohio; "Red" Joyner, Plant City, Florida; "Sneezy" Lewis (hometown unknown); John McClure, Chicago, Illinois; James Moore (hometown unknown); James Smith, Cincinnati, Ohio.

Suited up in our spanking new GI uniforms, we were getting acquainted with each other, stowing our gear in our footlockers and wall lockers when we heard:

"Fall out, Dummies, on the double!"

Outside on the patch of lawn in front of the bathhouse we began learning how to form up in ranks—open ranks, close ranks; how to do facing movements—left face, right face, about face; how to move as a coordinated group without tripping over ourselves, without bumping into others, all upon commands by upperclassmen:

"Forward, 'harch!" "To the rear 'harch!" "Column left, 'harch!" "P'toon, halt!"

A few such movements stirred up the gnats in the lawn. They found new homes in the eyes, ears, nose, and, if you were foolhardy enough to open your mouth, in your throat, too. It seemed to me that all the gnats in Alabama lived in that lawn.

Adding to our misery was the fact that we were in the army now and had to stand at attention, which meant we could not swat at the critters. All we could do was try to blow a stream of air at the pesky insects by twisting our mouths this way and that.

About a half hour of close-order drill seemed like a half day and helped to work up an appetite. I didn't need any help for that as I had had nothing since a sandwich on the train from Atlanta several hours before. So when the cadet captain of 42-C, Marion A. B. Carter, maneuvered the formation, comprising all the cadets of 42-C and 42-D, along the campus street to the mess hall, I was more than ready. His command to "double-time, 'harch!" was most welcome as it meant we would get to chow faster. I was starved!

Next, seated on the edge of our chairs in the dining hall we Dummies learned how to eat a "square meal." Our mess hall was in Tompkins Hall, the student and faculty dining room on the Tuskegee Institute campus. Built by students, as were many of the campus buildings, Tompkins Hall was completed in 1910. Its imposing facade, highlighted by its columns, dome, and clock tower, was calculated to impress. I was much impressed, both by its majestic appearance and by the knowledge that it was built by students, an example of founder Booker T. Washington's emphasis on manual arts and skills.

Just down the street from Tompkins Hall was the laboratory of the world-renowned Dr. George Washington Carver. I was more than impressed; I was thrilled and felt truly privileged to be a part of it all. I couldn't wait for dinner to end so I could double-time, in formation, back to the cadet barracks and write letters to the folks back home about all I had experienced since boarding the train at Penn Station thirty hours before. It had been a long day.

The next day and the rest of the week were full of activities having nothing to do with flying. From reveille at 5:00 A.M. until taps at 10:00 P.M. we were occupied with PT (physical training—calisthenics), close-order drill, manual of arms with rifles, inspections of self and barracks. And Dodo verses.

We were issued a pocket-size booklet with Dodo verses we had to memorize quickly, the sooner the better to avoid penalty tours imposed by upperclassmen. Most Dodo verses were inanities. For example, when asked by an upperclassman, "Mister, how is the cow?" the cadet's top-of-the-voice, verbatim response must be: "Sir, she walks, she talks, she is full of chalk. The lacteal fluid extracted from the female of the bovine species is highly prolific to the nth degree, Sir!"

Or, when asked, "Dummy, what time is it?"

Respond: "Sir, I am deeply embarrassed and greatly humiliated but due to circumstances over which I have no control, the inner workings and mechanisms of my poor chronometer are in such a state of discord with the great sidereal movement by which time is so commonly reckoned that I cannot, with any degree of accuracy, state the correct time. However without fear of being too far off, I will state that it is exactly —— minutes, —— seconds, and —— tick tocks past the hour, Sir!"

Other Dodo verses were sage axioms, like:

> There are old pilots
> And there are bold pilots
> But there are no old, bold pilots!

For manual of arms training our instructor was Sergeant Henry Beasley, an instructor of the Army ROTC unit at Tuskegee Institute. He was the epitome of patience as he taught us:

> Right shoulder arms!
> Present arms!
> Order arms!
> Stack arms!
> Et cetera, et cetera, et cetera.

His barked commands were so clear we wondered how he could project his voice so well. We found out soon enough in barracks bag drill, a fiendish but effective exercise in which, with barracks bag (laundry bag) over his head, each cadet had to practice barking phrases in a loud, deep bass voice, rather than a high-pitched voice, by using the tightened muscles of his diaphragm to project his voice. Phrases like:

> Yes, Sir!
> No, Sir!
> No excuse, Sir!

The latter was the most important phrase to be learned. No matter what the circumstances, regardless of the reason or reasons for failure to perform some task or comply with some order, the cadet's only acceptable response was: "No excuse, Sir!"

I learned about the "No excuse, Sir!" rule as early as the second day when 42-D went through physical exams.

In addition to the usual tests of blood pressure, body temperature, chest sounds and X rays, muscle reflexes, hearing acuity, eye charts, and so on that are part of typical physical exams, we were also introduced to a gadget I had never seen before: the depth perception test apparatus. On a long narrow table two wooden pegs, about six inches tall, were mounted, one fixed to the table, the other mounted on a slide in a channel so that it could be moved back and forth past the fixed peg when pulled by a rope. Seated at one end of the table, about ten feet from the stationary peg, the cadet must pull the rope until the pegs appear to be lined up next to each other.

Sailing through all phases of the physical, including the depth perception test, I felt confident. Until the shots. Not the kind you hear—the kind you feel! Immunizations for about four maladies. Although I cannot remember all the shots—one was tetanus, which I remember because it burned like a hot poker—I shall never forget my reaction.

I passed out.

Moments later, I guessed, I came to, stretched out on the floor, my head cradled on the arm of the pretty nurse who had shot me. She smiled, asking, "Are you OK, Cadet?"

"Yeah, I think so."

Looking up at the ring of faces around me, my classmates, I also saw the flight surgeon. Scowling, he asked me: "What happened, Dryden?"

"I don't know, Sir. Guess I just got nervous when I saw all those needles."

"That's no excuse, Mister. And if it happens again I'm going to wash you out of the program. You understand?"

"Yes, Sir!"

Thank heaven, it never did happen again. But that was not the end of the incident. My new so-called friends, my classmates, nicknamed me "Diapers."

"Diapers," indeed! "Dummy" was bad enough. Now I had another put-down to live with. "Well," I thought, "if that's a part of what I have to go through to win my wings, so be it!"

Although there was no flying during our first four weeks, there were many memorable events.

Meeting Dr. George Washington Carver was such an event. His laboratory was located between our bathhouse barracks and the chapel. After attending chapel service on Sunday morning some of us cadets visited the laboratory and talked with genius in the form of a gentle, brown-skinned man with a high-pitched voice and a friendly, almost shy, manner.

Unforgettable!

Unforgettable also were the Negro spirituals I heard sung by the Tuskegee Institute choir. Some I had learned listening to the "Wings Over Jordan" radio programs on Sunday afternoons when I was growing up in New York, for instance: "Swing Low Sweet Chariot" and "Oh Mary, Don't You Weep, Don't You Moan." Others were new to me.

"Lift every voice and sing" were the first words of James Weldon Johnson's "Negro National Anthem." By ending his third and last stanza with the words

> Shadowed beneath thy hand
> May we forever stand
> True to our God
> True to our native land

the composer caused me to thrill with emotion every time I heard or sang the anthem. Powerful prose!

Another spiritual new to me was "Steal Away." The opening words, "Steal away, steal away, steal away to Jesus," seem innocent enough. But I learned that during the years of slavery whenever an escape to freedom was planned the slaves passed the word by singing "Steal away." And "Ole Massa" was none the wiser. Clever conspirators!

I learned this fact and much more folklore from my classmates who had been raised in the South. They knew much more about the history of our people than those of us from above the Mason-Dixon line. I had a lot to learn, and not only about flying.

Of course our upperclassmen had begun flying training one month earlier, long enough for a couple of them to have been washed out already. As 42-D began flight training, our upperclassmen were already scheduled to fly in the mornings and attend ground school classes on campus, so our schedule was just the reverse.

Mornings found 42-D marching to ground school classes to learn about theory of flight, aircraft engines, meteorology, funda-

PRIMARY PHASE FLIGHT INSTRUCTORS. This December 1942 group photo presents some of the most skillful pilots in the annals of aviation. They are, in the top row, left to right: Bob Terry, John Young III, Charles W. Stevens, Charlie Foxx, Roscoe Draper, Sherman Rose, James A. Hill, Adolph Moret, Ernest Henderson, Matthew Plummer, Linkwood Williams, Daniel "Chappie" James, Lewis Jackson, Milton Crenshaw, and in the front row: Perry Young, Charles Flowers, Claude Platt, Charles Alfred "Chief" Anderson, C. R. Harris, Wendell Lipscomb, J. E. "Muscles" Wright.

mentals of navigation, and army regulations. Except for the latter I had studied all of these subjects in CPT so I enjoyed ground school and had an easy time of it. Clarence "Jamie" Jamison was also a CPT graduate and between us we were able to help tutor some of our classmates whenever they were stumped by some subject.

Our afternoons were out of this world! Flying began for 42-D after the month of preflight training. All eleven of us had made it through preflight. So far, so good. Now the fun began in the primary phase. After that would come basic training, followed by advanced training, each requiring almost three months and involving a different type of aircraft to be mastered.

In primary we were introduced to the Stearman PT-17 "Kaydet," an open-cockpit, two-seater biplane that resembled the Waco UPF-7 that I had learned to fly in the advanced phase of the Civilian Pilot Training Program. So at first I felt confident that primary would be a "piece of cake." That confidence evaporated after only a couple of flights with my instructor.

Milton Crenshaw, one of the three primary phase flight instructors, all of whom were Negroes, was a tall, slim, brown-skinned man of quiet mien, serious expression: a no-nonsense pilot who insisted on precision in everything, from the preflight inspection of the aircraft to the filling out of the Form 1, aircraft log, at the end of a flight. It did not take him long to detect my overconfidence.

Aloft one day Mr. Crenshaw, in the front cockpit with me in the rear, told me to fly straight and level. "Piece of cake," I thought, and kept it just so—straight and level. Then he said, "Turn left 90 degrees, then right 180 degrees."

Midway through these maneuvers he reached back with both hands and pinned my feet to the rudder pedals. Meanwhile my flight helmet was almost blown off my head as he bellowed through the gosport, "Mr. Dryden, if you don't start using the rudder in turns, I'm going to wash you out!"

Back on the ground he continued the humbling of a cocky cadet by lecturing: "Mr. Dryden, I know that you have a private pilot license and that you've been through the CPT advanced course. So you should know how to fly already. But let me tell you something, Mister. You're here to learn how to fly the army way, with precision, by army standards, and you'd better learn to do things by the book. Understand?"

"Yes, Sir!"

The next few flights were a challenge. We were flying from Moton Field, a large, open-meadow grass strip located about ten miles from the Tuskegee Institute campus. It reminded me of the pea patch in Long Island where I had first soloed in a Piper Cub. And that presented me with a challenge: to be among the first of 42-D to solo the Stearman. To do so I would have to meet Mr. Crenshaw's standards. So I concentrated on using the rudder in turns. And it worked!

After about a week of takeoffs and landings, I soloed. I wasn't the first in my class to do so, but neither was I one of the 42-D unfortunates who never soloed, one of those who were washed out.

That night, after soloing, I was doused with beer: Hudepohl beer in a green bottle, which was appropriate, for green beer, though unaged, could still make you feel no pain after two or three bottles.

Flying during the rest of primary was a mixture of dual flights with Crenshaw to learn the army way of doing precision landings and acrobatics in the Stearman and solo flights to practice what I had been taught.

All went well: stalls (power-on and power-off), spins, chandelles, vertical reverses (cartwheels), loops, split-"S's," lazy 8s, Immelmans, falling leaves, slow rolls. But not snap rolls! For some reason, for the life of me, I couldn't do a snap roll with a precise ending with wings level on the horizon and no flopping around. Fortunately for me, Crenshaw didn't give up on me. He turned me over to Charlie Foxx, nicknamed "Mr. Acrobatics." As tall as Crenshaw and about the same complexion, Foxx was "a pilot's pilot." He took me aloft one day. At about 5,000 feet, he said, "OK, Mr. Dryden, hold it straight and level, line up with that road down there, and give me a snap roll to the right."

So I did. That is to say, I tried. His comment told me I failed.

"No, no, Mister! It started out OK but your ending was sloppy with your wings flopping up and down across the horizon. It must have a crisp ending, like this—watch the controls as I show you how to do it right."

Taking over the controls Mr. Foxx demonstrated a crisp snap roll as I watched the movements of the control stick, rudder pedals, and throttle. He made it look so easy! Then he said. "Now, you do one."

I did. Several very crisp "snaps." With the Foxx technique they were easy. More than that, they were fun!

Some weeks later, near the end of primary, I had another maneuver to master: pylon 8s, a basic maneuver I had learned both in CPT and in army primary flying but not well enough to satisfy Mr. Crenshaw. So he turned me over to the "Chief."

Charles Alfred Anderson, the chief instructor in the primary phase at Tuskegee Army Flying School, was the grandfather of

Black aviation. He had taught himself to fly in 1926 when he bought an airplane, a Velie Monocoupe, but could find no one to teach him. So he practiced taxiing the airplane for about six weeks until he got his nerve up and took off—and taught himself to fly. And he kept on learning—about night flying, instrument flying in bad weather—eventually earning his commercial and transport pilot licenses, the first African American to do so.

Chief took me up late one afternoon just before dusk and, just as Charlie Foxx had taught me how to do snap rolls, Chief made pylon 8s look easy. And he taught me how. That helped me over the last hurdle in primary. Along with Sid Brooks, Jamie Jamison, and "Smitty" Smith, I passed the flight test. We were promoted to the basic phase. We four were all that remained of the original eleven cadets of 42-D. The other seven had been washed out for various reasons: medical, ground school failure, flying performance.

By now it was Thanksgiving and we four were given a ten-day leave of absence to begin on December 1. Off I went to New York. The Big Apple. My hometown where, just a year before, a recruiting sergeant had told me, "The United States Army is not training any Colored pilots." I could hardly wait to "just happen to drop by" and gloat while watching his face when I walked in in my aviation cadet uniform.

First, though, I wanted to visit my family at home in the Bronx, my girl friend, Jackie, and her family just two blocks away, and my kinfolk and Sugar Hill buddies in Manhattan. Next, I longed to attend worship service at Saint Augustine Presbyterian Church where my Dad was an elder, my Mom a deacon. The congregation was like an extended family and the pastor, the Reverend Dr. Edler Garnet Hawkins, was without question the most Christian clergyman I had ever known. And, finally, I looked forward to visiting Matthews and Rappaport, the flying school operators at Roosevelt Field out on Long Island to thank them for their excellent Civilian Pilot Training Program in which I learned to fly before becoming an aviation cadet.

That was a lot to accomplish in a ten-day leave of absence, especially when two days had to be spent traveling by rail. Luckily, happily, I was able to do it all, with a couple "Welcome home,

Charlie!" parties to boot—all, that is, except the visit to the recruiting sergeant. I had planned to save that task for my last day
before returning to duty. But then something happened when I still
had three days of leave left. Something unexpected.

On December 7.

That Sunday morning, at Saint Augustine Presbyterian Church
with my family, I was greeted and congratulated by my pastor and
my church family. After church, Jackie and I visited her younger
brother, who was recovering from an illness in a local hospital.

So far it had been a lovely day for me in spite of the gray overcast
sky that hugged the skyline from dawn. The vibes of love and affection from those whom I loved most in all the world had engulfed
me all day. Riding home from the hospital on a bus with Jackie
beside me, I thought, "God is in His heaven and all is right with the
world." Sometime in my past I had come across that phrase and it
seemed to fit my mood perfectly. Until . . .

Until one lady passenger shattered my euphoria.

"Soldier," she said, "do you know we're at war?"

Startled, I responded to her question with one of mine.

"What did you say?"

"We're at war. Japanese bombers attacked Pearl Harbor in Hawaii and sank many ships. Haven't you heard the news?"

Her comments triggered murmurs and discussions among the
other passengers. Most, like me, expressed disbelief, comparing
this announcement to Orson Welles's "War of the Worlds" broadcast three years before. When we arrived at Jackie's home, however,
her parents, brother, and sisters were all listening intently to radio
news reports. So I was wrong in disbelieving the lady on the bus.

"Charlie, will you have to go back to Tuskegee right away?"
Jackie's father asked.

"Don't know, Sir. I don't think so. You see, I still have five months
to go before my flight training is finished, so I really can't see why
I would have to rush back before my leave ends. I'm not due back
until Wednesday, the tenth."

Wrong again!

When I returned to my home an hour or so later, my Dad handed
me a telegram. He and Mom wore worried expressions on their

faces as I ripped open the envelope and read the message addressed to Aviation Cadet Charles W. Dryden:

REPORT TO BASE NLT 9 DEC 41 STOP
(SIGNED) MAJOR T. SMITH, COMMANDANT

No doubt about that!

So, when the Pennsylvania Railroad train to Washington headed south at noon the next day, I was on it. Arrived at the cadet barracks at about noon on the ninth. Mission accomplished.

As my three classmates returned from leave we all wondered why we had to return so quickly. We soon learned the reason why. It was because, with our primary flying over, we were to begin the basic phase immediately.

A couple of days later we were ordered to pack our footlockers and prepare to move to the main base, Tuskegee Army Air Field (TAAF), about eleven miles from the campus. It was still under construction but, no matter! We were going to live on a real, honest-to-goodness army air base. Our upperclassmen had already moved to TAAF and were eagerly awaiting the arrival of their Dummies—us!

With some feelings of nostalgia, 42-D left the Tuskegee Institute campus, thinking, "Good-bye bathhouse, hello Tent City!" Cadet barracks at TAAF were still abuilding so we were billeted in a four-man pyramidal tent.

Built on a square wooden platform, the tent had wooden walls and a door up to about five feet above the floor. From each corner a two-by-four beam angled toward the apex about ten feet above the floor. A wood stove sat in a sandbox on the floor in the center and the metal flue went straight up through a hole in the apex of the four angled beams. A canvas tarpaulin over the beams formed the roof. To protect the tarpaulin from sparks drifting up and out of the flue, there was a semispherical wire mesh spark arrester atop the flue. The spark arrester had to be removed frequently and wire brushed vigorously to remove soot from the soft pine wood that tended to clog the wire mesh.

Our upperclassmen were already housed in such tents. Their spark arresters clogged several times daily, requiring someone to shinny up the roof and wire brush the spark arrester. That is why they were so glad to see their Dummies arrive. Our welcome to basic was the command: "Alright, Dummies, fall out and climb up on the roof and clean off the spark arresters, on the double!"

We lived in Tent City for about a month. The streets in our area, and all over the base, were rivers of mud with deep ruts cut into the ooze by earth-mover "Turn-a-Pulls" rolling on six-feet-tall tires, caterpillar tread bulldozers, six-by-six GI trucks and jeeps. Tent City was located on a slope rising gently, gradually above the flight line, on a site where the various permanent buildings were taking shape: base headquarters, base hospital, base theater, officers quarters, NCOs' and enlisted men's barracks, and aviation cadet barracks. We could hardly wait for the cadet barracks and paved streets to be completed.

Meanwhile life in Tent City, with the occasional cold rains of January in Alabama, was an added detraction from our peace of mind. Temperatures outside the tent sometimes dropped into the twenties. Oftentimes inside the tent it seemed colder than that until a fire was started in the wood stove. The four of us in 42-D's tent took turns starting the fire in the morning. While the "fireman" of the day struggled to start the fire, the others, shivering under blankets, egged him on or snoozed until the time to get up for reveille (5:00 A.M.).

Whenever it was Smitty's turn to light the fire, he delighted in shaking me roughly and hissing in my ear: "Diapers! Oh, Diapers! Time to get up and pee. Time to get up and pee!"

I could have gladly killed him. Or at least whup him. But he was bigger than I. Six feet, over 200 pounds, all bone and muscle toned by football at Central State College, versus my five feet nine inches, under 150 pounds, barely more than skin and bones. Besides, he was cadet captain of our class. So, I would get up cussing and fussing, dress, fall out from the tent, and fall into ranks with the rest of the cadets for reveille formation to start the day. Before the dawn's early light.

In basic we got into a new type of airplane: BT-13, the "Vultee Vibrator." A low-wing monoplane with the power of 450 horses up front—more than double that of the 220-horsepower engine in the primary trainer, the PT-17, we had just mastered—and capable of 185 mph as compared to the 120-mph Stearman. Also, with its sliding canopy we would not shiver in an open cockpit any more, nor would we have to cope with a top wing obscuring planes above us. Inside the cockpit were more instruments to be mastered than in the Stearman. And there were new controls and equipment to cope with: wing flaps, trim tabs, fuel mixture, variable pitch propellor. And radios for air-to-ground communication as well as intercom between instructor in the back seat, student in the front. And heat, which made the flying less uncomfortable than it had been in the open-cockpit Stearman but which was not hot enough to eliminate the need to wear bulky, fleece-lined, leather winter flying jackets, pants, and boots. The boots were so bulky and heavy that I had no more trouble using the rudder pedals in turns as my primary instructor had admonished me in the Stearman. Quite the contrary, I had to overcome a tendency to overcontrol the rudder in the BT-13.

Flying the "Vultee Vibrator" BT-13 was fun once the new controls were mastered. Acrobatics especially were easier than in the Stearman because of the more powerful engine. The only problem was in inverted flight: Fly upside down for more than about five seconds and the engine might quit!

My instructor in basic was Captain Robert Lowenberg, a big (six feet four inches), rawboned, humorless man. I don't remember ever seeing him smile. Perhaps that was because he was also commandant of cadets. Or perhaps he had come to regret having volunteered for assignment to TAAF. We had heard that all of our instructors in basic and advanced phases, all White officers, had volunteered to train Negro pilots.

Whatever the reason, Bob, as we called him behind his back, never gave me the impression that he was pleased with my flying. He was satisfied, apparently, because he didn't wash me out, but he never seemed pleased. My former flight instructors, Bill Pyhota in the CPT Program and Milton Crenshaw in primary, had smiled now and then at my performance, bolstering my confidence. But not Bob. So I sweated out basic, fearing the "washing machine" the entire ten weeks.

The first thing we had to learn to do prior to a flight in the BT-13 was no different than in the Stearman or, indeed, any airplane: an outside walk-around visual check of the propellor, engine, fuselage, wings, ailerons, tail surfaces (rudder and elevators), landing gear, and tires.

Inside the cockpit was something new, a printed checklist we had to memorize: CIGFTPR, meaning

C - Controls unlocked and moving freely
I - Instrument readings OK
G - Gas tanks full and selector on main tank
F - Flaps set for takeoff
T - Trim tabs set for takeoff
P - Propellor set for takeoff
R - Run up (check) engine for proper power output.

Once aloft our repertoire was similar to that of the primary phase: takeoffs and landings, forced (emergency) landings, acrobatics. One added activity became my favorite: formation flying. I loved it with a passion. Taking off singly and joining close up on a leader's wing by swiftly judging the necessary curve of pursuit got my adrenalin flowing. Sliding smoothly, safely, from one position in the formation to another with only inches of clearance between props and wings turned up my pulse with excited pleasure. In other words, I got my kicks in formation.

Ground school in basic introduced us to some new subjects not seen in primary. Morse code was one new subject. We had to learn the dits and dahs of the Morse code alphabet and be able to send and receive twenty-five words per minute in order to pass the subject and avoid the "washing machine." What a relief the day that the Morse code instructor, Sergeant Ronald Fielleteau, who had just put me through a speed test, said: "Cadet Dryden, you have passed it."

Another new subject was the Link trainer, a flight simulator in which we began learning to fly the radio beam for radio navigation and for takeoffs and landings in bad weather. Sergeant Bob Wilson, the Link trainer instructor, also taught us all about the "A" quadrant, the "N" quadrant, the cone of silence, orientation methods, and instrument landing procedures.

Other subjects we had first met in primary, such as aerodynamics and theory of flight, power plants and propellors, meteorology. In basic phase navigation we learned that True Virgins Make Dull Companions. That was not a social commentary but merely a phrase to help us remember the correct sequence in converting from true course, from point A to point B as measured on a map, to magnetic course taking into account the earth's magnetic effect along the route, to compass course allowing for deviations from the norm of the aircraft compass caused by metal objects in the cockpit. Thus:

True Course	True
+ or − Variation	Virgins
= Magnetic Course	Make
+ or − Deviation	Dull
= Compass Course	Companions

Cross-country navigation flights gave us a chance to apply such knowledge and other things we learned about dead reckoning and radio navigation. Sometimes navigation flights were made with the instructor on board, others solo. It was on such a flight, near the end of basic, that we lost Smitty to the "washing machine."

The four of us, Brooks, Jamison, Smith, and I, each in a BT-13, were scheduled for a four-leg cross-country flight from TAAF to three other towns and a return to TAAF. Smitty was to lead the formation to checkpoint number one, followed by each of the rest of us leading on one of the other three legs. Captain Lowenberg went along in my back seat; I wasn't happy about that. However, we took off, in string, into a beautiful, cloudless afternoon sky and formed up crossing directly over the base before heading on course. Having settled into number four position in the formation, I throttled to normal cruise setting, checked my compass reading, and noted to my horror that Smitty was leading us on the return leg! Quickly checking my map strapped to my knee pad, I knew for sure that he was on the wrong leg.

"Oh Lord, let him discover his mistake and pick up the correct heading before it's too late," I prayed. I knew that a mistake like that could "wash" a cadet. Class 42-D was already down to only four of the original eleven who had begun basic six months before, and we had become tightly knit buddies after having endured so much together in that half year.

Unfortunately for Smitty it was too late. Over the intercom Captain Lowenberg growled, "I've got it, Dryden!" as he grabbed the control stick in the rear seat, rammed the throttle full forward, and pulled ahead into the lead position, swooping around in front of Smitty's ship and barking over the radio: "Cadet Smith, return to base and land immediately! And the rest of you land also."

Poor Smitty! Back on the ground he got a royal chewing out while Sid, Jamie, and I had to stand at attention and witness his embarrassment. I felt very uncomfortable throughout the harangue as Cadet Captain Smith, a proud young man with good leadership qualities, was humbled in front of his classmates. We hoped that the chewing out was the end of it, but no such luck. Smitty was washed out a day or so later, the last of 42-D to be dropped from the cadet corps.

That left only three of us, coincidentally the same three young men who had left Atlanta together, six months earlier, on the train bound for Chehaw: Brooks and Jamison from Cleveland, Dryden from New York.

By now, mid-February, the third class, 42-E, had arrived at TAAF. They had been our Dummies in primary, ten of them, and afforded us the experience of being upperclassmen while we were all living in the bathhouse cadet barracks. The apparent reason for this upper-to-lower classmen status was to authorize the uppers to harass the lowers and make their life miserable, ostensibly to test their mettle and their ability to "take it." As an upperclassman, however, I saw this difference in rank more as a relationship offering me opportunities to learn something about leadership rather than a status weapon for hazing.

In any case, by the time 42-E finished primary and transferred to TAAF, only half of the original ten were still in the cadet corps. Our upperclassmen, 42-C, with only three weeks to go before graduation, had been whittled down to five. Thus there were just thirteen cadets who left the mud and misery of Tent City to take up residence in the spanking new cadet barracks completed in February: indoor showers and latrines, central heat in brightly lit rooms, two cadets to a room. Sheer luxury after the rigors of Tent City! Aviation cadet training became "a piece of cake" with such amenities. Icing on the cake were the locations of the cadet mess next door to the barracks, the post theater a half block away, and the PX (post exchange) directly across the street.

For many GIs and civilian employees on the base, the PX was a mecca where one could buy various personal items, socialize with friends, learn the latest "spratmo" about happenings on the base and in town, and enjoy the latest sounds on the juke box. For me the juke box sounds brought memories of home and created nostalgia for years to come: from Duke Ellington's "Take the A-Train," to Glenn Miller's "String of Pearls" and "Moonlight Cocktails," to the Ink Spots' "If I Didn't Care," Louis Jordan's "I'm Gonna Move," Lil Green's "Since I Fell for You" and "In the Dark," Tommy Dorsey's "Sunny Side of the Street," and Benny Goodman's anything and everything!

Such music, wafting through the night air from the PX across the street to the cadet barracks, soothed us after each long day of flying, ground school, calisthenics, inspections, and marching on rutted, muddy streets and dodging earth-moving vehicles. After dinner in the cadet mess hall we had about three hours for studying, writing letters to the folks back home, and relaxation, sometimes going to the base theater to see the latest movie, before taps sounded.

One evening after supper in the cadet mess I ambled over to the theater to see *Springtime in the Rockies* featuring the Harry James band. I loved jazz and had been looking forward to enjoying the music. A few minutes after the house lights dimmed and I had settled down to enjoy the movie, I heard an announcement over the public address system: "Cadet Dryden, report to the cadet lounge. You have a visitor."

"Dammit," I thought. "Who the hell can it be, visiting me just when I don't want to be bothered?"

I left the theater grumbling to myself and walked the half block to the cadet barracks, hoping to dispose of the intruder quickly and return to the movie. As I entered the cadet lounge I felt sheepish and overjoyed. There, seated in one of the lounge chairs, was my pastor from Saint Augustine Presbyterian Church in the Bronx, the Reverend Edler G. Hawkins! He rose to greet me with a bear hug.

"Hi, Revvie!" I exulted. "I'm so glad to see you. How come you're here?"

"Well, Charles, I have some church business to take care of in this part of the country and I decided to check up on one of my flock to see how you're doing and to bring you greetings from the folks at Saint Augustine's."

I forgot all about the movie. For the next three hours, until taps, we talked, reminisced, guessed the outcome of the war. Before he left we prayed together and he gave me a pocket edition of the New Testament in a zipper-bound book, a treasure to be cherished.

About two weeks after moving into the cadet barracks, 42-D completed basic flight training and entered the home stretch in the advanced phase.

The North American AT-6 "Texan" was our new trainer. It had more power: 600 horses up front. Inside the cockpit were some features similar to the BT-13: controls for flaps, trim tabs, variable pitch propellor. Other features were different, new—for instance, a gunsight, trigger on the control stick, and controls to raise and lower the landing gear, which meant we had to learn at least one more checklist for landings. The GUMP checklist:

> G - Gas selector on the fullest tank, fuel pumps on
> U - Undercarriage (landing gear) down and locked
> M - Mixture (fuel) control on full (or auto) rich
> P - Propellor(s) pitch control set for landing (low pitch,
>   high RPM).

Three advanced phase instructors took charge of our flight training, one-on-one: Sid Brooks was assigned to Captain Robert "Mama" Long, Jamie Jamison to Captain Robert "Rapid Robert" Rowland, and I drew Captain Clay "Buckwheat" Albright.

Checkout in the AT-6 began on the first day of advanced: takeoffs and landings on the only runway that had been completed so far.

BASIC AND ADVANCED PHASE FLIGHT INSTRUCTORS. When this picture was taken in early 1943, Col. Noel F. Parrish (front row, fourth from the left) was base commander of Tuskegee Army Air Field (TAAF). Posed with him are the flight instructors of the basic and advanced phases of the aviation cadet training program: front row, left to right: Lt. William H. George, Lt. Rudebaugh, Capt. Clay Albright, Col. Parrish, Maj. Robert R. Rowland, Capt. Robert Long, (last two officers' names are unknown); back row, left to right: Lt. Charles H. DeBow, Lt. Mac Ross, Capt. Robert Dunham, Maj. Don McPherson, Capt. Robert Lowenberg, Capt. Gabriel Hawkins, Capt. Robert L. Boyd, Lt. Lemuel R. Custis. Lieutenants Custis, DeBow, and Ross were graduates of the first class (42-C). All the others are White officers, most of whom volunteered for the assignment at TAAF.

In basic we had become accustomed to making crosswind landings on the one runway whenever the wind was not blowing directly in line with the runway, so that was not a problem. In fact there were few problems in flying the AT-6 early on. Acrobatics and formation flying were much easier and more fun in the higher powered airplane. I especially enjoyed formation takeoffs and landings, which we practiced on Shorter Field, an auxiliary grass strip midway between TAAF and Montgomery.

Night flying was another skill for us to learn in advanced. TAAF did not yet have the necessary facilities for night flying, so we were driven the fifty miles to Maxwell Air Base just west of Montgomery. We didn't get back to our cadet barracks until around midnight, shivering from the cold night air in our fresh-air taxi, an open-sided command car.

My only night flight before then was my last flight in the CPT Program one year before when the night lights of New York City dazzled me. Montgomery's lights were not nearly as numerous or as brilliant, but flying the AT-6 at night was more thrilling. Especially the night I soloed. After that milestone we had to make a night cross-country navigation flight to show our ability to use radio beams as navigation aids as well as light lines.

Light lines were visible aids for night flying. Between cities throughout the United States were light beacons spaced about twenty miles apart. Each beacon flashed a Morse code letter in a red light, continuously, in a prescribed sequence, which we remembered by memorizing this phrase:

W - When
U - Undertaking
V - Very
H - Hard
R - Routes
K - Keep
D - Direction
B - By
G - Good
M - Methods.

The next beacon started the phrase over again with W, and so on. The geographic location of each beacon was shown on aeronautical charts whereby the pilot could fix his position, provided visibility was good.

After completing my night cross country, I felt I had only one more hurdle: gunnery!

This last hurdle almost became my Waterloo. Two types of gunnery had to be learned: ground and aerial. Against targets on the ground I was a terror. Tore them up. On the other hand, hitting the banner towed behind an airplane was quite another ball game for me. I almost struck out, barely scoring enough points during our week at the Eglin Field, Florida, gunnery range to meet the Army

Air Corps requirements for graduation. But I did, and 42-D returned to TAAF with all requirements for graduation completed. With about two weeks to go before graduation day, during which all we had to do was pass final ground school tests and flight checks, we were home free! Or so we thought.

We had been senior cadets in the barracks since March 7 when 42-C graduated as the first five Negroes in the nation's history to be commissioned as flying officers. Historic heroes, they were: Captain Benjamin O. Davis, Jr., Washington, D.C.; and Second Lieutenants Lemuel Rodney Custis, Hartford, Connecticut; Charles Henry DeBow, Indianapolis, Indiana; George Spencer Roberts, Fairmount, West Virginia; and Mac Ross, Dayton, Ohio.

With their graduation the declared intention of the War Department to commission Negro flying officers became credible. Because of the high washout rate since the beginning of the "Tuskegee Experiment" eight months earlier, many observers had begun thinking that we had been let into flying training only to be programmed to fail. So, as I sat in the post theater with the rest of the cadet corps watching wings being pinned on our upperclassmen, I thought: "They have made it all the way through and so will we. We're next!"

When the brand new officers moved out of the cadet barracks that afternoon, 42-D became top dogs of the corps. By then the corps numbered about thirty-one, including three in 42-D, five in 42-E, fifteen in 42-F, and eight in 42-G.

At the top of the heap we felt secure enough to invite Master Sergeant Fred Archer to our quarters to brief us on how the .30-caliber machine guns on the AT-6 were synchronized with the engine to prevent shooting off the propellor. Our motive was good: We wanted to know just in case our final ground school exam had a question about synchronization. But our method was bad: The cadet barracks were off limits to all personnel except cadets, tac (tactical) officers, and authorized enlisted men. Although Sergeant Archer had accompanied us and flight instructor Captain Albright to gunnery at Eglin Field to service our guns, he was not authorized to enter our barracks at TAAF.

As luck would have it, the commandant of cadets happened to

walk through the building on a spot inspection. Barking us to " 'ten hut!" he ordered Archer to leave and announced: "You misters have disobeyed a standing order about unauthorized visitors in this building. Do you understand?"

"Yes, Sir!" we chorused.

"Did one of the tac officers authorize the sergeant to come in here?"

"No, Sir!"

"Then why did you disobey orders?"

"No excuse, Sir."

"Well, you've got to be penalized. I will decide how and notify each of you before taps. At ease!"

Designed to release us from the rigid posture we had assumed when Captain Lowenberg first entered our room hollering " 'ten hut!" his last order did everything but put us at ease. As he strode out of our room, I thought, "Omigod! He now has the grounds to wash the rest of 42-D out of the program. After all we have been through, how could we have been so stupid?"

Anguished about what our penalty would be, I had no stomach for dinner, waiting for the axe to fall. We had seen one of the first class washed out within the last week before his graduation. So we feared the worst.

Just before lights out Sergeant Dickie Lee, a hip cat from Washington, D.C., who was a clerk in the commandant's office, came to our room and announced: "Bob says you misters are to report to the supply room first thing, before reveille, and pick up fatigues. You gotta have them on for inspection at the reveille formation."

"Why the fatigues?" Brooks asked.

"Lawdy, Miss Claudy, le's have a pahty, invite ev'bahdy!" Dickie Lee clowned.

"Come on, Sergeant, cut the comedy!" Jamie exclaimed.

"Yeah, why the fatigues?" I echoed.

Dickie Lee dropped the bomb. "It ain't funny, y'all. Right after reveille you're supposed to report to the cadet mess and go on KP."

"What?" we exploded in unison.

"That's right, Gentlemen. See you in supply at 4:30 in the A.M. G'night, Sirs."

"G'night, Sarge."

After Lee left we discussed our fate.

"Well," Brooks said, "KP is better than being washed out."

"Yeah," Jamie agreed. "It's mo' better. In fact, it's much mo' better."

Jamison, a graduate of the University of Chicago, of course knew proper grammar but he also knew how to lighten the mood and get us to chuckling whenever things got heavy. So we were relieved by the punishment although we knew the rest of the cadets, all underclassmen to us, would razz us unmercifully.

Their fun at our expense began at breakfast. We reminded them that in two weeks we would be officers and would return to inspect the barracks. Then, woe to them! It didn't matter—they razzed us anyway.

The word about the senior cadet class being on KP spread around the base like wildfire and reached town as well. We still had some ground school classes to attend, and as we marched from place to place during the days we heard words of encouragement from all quarters.

Saluting the director of training, Lieutenant Colonel Noel F. Parrish, one day as we passed him on the street, we heard him say: "Cadets, I know about your punishment and I want you to know I'm pulling for you. I want you to stick it out. Don't give up."

Others who went out of their way to urge us on were Ground School Commandant Captain Roy Morse, Base Hospital Chief Nurse Captain Della Raney, and Cadet Mess Dietician Mrs. Lillian Drew. NCOs and enlisted men we passed on the streets greeted us with: "Hi, Lootenants! Don't give up. We're pulling for you!" And they saluted us although we were not yet officers. Our former upperclassmen, now officers, joined the chorus of supporters, as did our advanced flight instructors, Captains Albright, Long, and Rowland. With all these people urging us on, KP was tolerable.

One morning, after about three days on KP, Sergeant Lee brought us good news. Captain Lowenberg had issued orders for us to put on our regular cadet uniforms then ride a staff car he had arranged to drive us to a military uniforms tailor in Montgomery to be fitted for officer uniforms. That was an exciting experience in itself, but the seeming assurance that we were going to graduate was heady stuff. Every night thereafter, until graduation, polishing the bill of my garrison cap and burnishing the eagle insignia on the front of the cap was my favorite way of relaxing at the end of an exhausting day in the kitchen of the cadet mess hall.

One last incident could have wiped out 42-D completely. One hot, steamy afternoon about two days before graduation day the three of us were in the cadet mess doing various KP chores: peeling potatoes, scrubbing pots, sweeping the floor. In walked the commandant through the front door, and he barked in a loud voice, "Drew!"

That did it. Our cups (of anger and frustration) "ranneth over." As one man we stood up, walked from the kitchen toward him just as the cadet mess hall dietician came out of her office next to the dining area. Mrs. Lillian Drew was a petite, brown-skinned lady clad in an immaculate, starched, white smock. She had the demeanor of a gracious, competent professional. And she deserved respect!

Sid Brooks, taking the role of spokesman, said icily: "Captain Lowenberg, the lady's name is Mrs. Drew. We hope you will show her respect in the future and address her properly." Or words to that effect.

The commandant turned beet red, said nothing, turned on his heels, and stomped out. We heard nothing further about the confrontation. Indeed we heard nothing further about plans for our graduation ceremony. We had known the scheduled date, April 29, from the beginning of the advanced phase. Based upon that information, Brooks and Jamison had invited some family members from Cleveland, and all three of us had friends at Tuskegee Institute whom we wanted to invite to our graduation ceremony.

As late as the eve of graduation we had not been told anything about the next day's events. Captain Morse, commandant of the ground school, sent a message to us that the ceremony was scheduled for 10:00 A.M. We notified our guests from out of town and our friends in town.

Next morning, after reveille, we reported to the kitchen as usual because we had not received any orders relieving us from KP. Finally, at about 8:00 A.M., Sergeant Dickie Lee came to the cadet mess hall with a startling message.

"Captain Lowenberg wants you cadets to report to the post theater dressed in class-A cadet uniform for graduation ceremony at 9:00 A.M."

"Dammit!" I fumed. Why did Bob do this to us? It would be impossible for our invited guests to arrive here on time with such short notice about the one-hour-earlier time. Mrs. Drew heard about the change and walked the half block from the cadet mess hall to the post theater. And so it was that she was the only witness present as aviation cadet class 42-D, the second group to graduate from Tuskegee Army Flying School—and probably the smallest graduating class in the history of the U.S. Army Air Corps—received their silver wings and gold bars: Second Lieutenants Sidney Paul Brooks, Charles Walter Dryden, and Clarence Clifford Jamison.

As my wings were being pinned on my cadet tunic by Colonel Parrish, I exulted inwardly: "I've made it! I've made it! I HAVE MADE IT!" My heart was racing so fast I feared I might pass out from excitement, for now, at last, it was over. All the hurdles that could have killed my dream were now, themselves, washed out. The medical exams, physical stamina tests, ground school quizzes, Morse code qualification, Link trainer proficiency, flight checks, evaluations by tactical officers and upperclassmen were now, and forever, just history. Hallelujah!

Leaving the post theater after handshakes from the officers on the platform, Colonel Parrish, Captain Davis, and Captain Morse (Captain Lowenberg declined to proffer a handshake), I was approached by a rather short, stocky NCO grinning broadly from ear to ear as he popped to rigid attention with a snappy salute.

"Congratulations, Lieutenant Dryden!" he said. "I'm Corporal Nick Quinones and I would like to be your orderly, Sir."

"Thanks, Corporal," I grinned back, returning his salute and reaching for a dollar to reward him for being the first person to salute me as a brand new lieutenant. "Call me at the BOQ after I have moved in there and we'll talk about the orderly job then."

"Thank you, Sir. And, again, congratulations, Lieutenant! Everyone on the base is proud of you pilots!"

During our last lunch in the cadet mess hall we said good-bye to

GRADUATION DAY FOR 42-D. Possibly the smallest
graduating class in the history of the U.S. Army Air Corps,
aviation cadet class 42-D at TAFS received their silver wings
and gold bars on April 29, 1942. Pictured next to an AT-6 advanced
trainer on the flight line, 2nd Lts. Clarence C. Jamison, Charles W.
Dryden, and Sidney P. Brooks (left to right) are congratulated
by ground school commandant Capt. Roy F. Morse.

the cadets, wishing them good luck and encouraging them to press
on to their own graduation. And we thanked Mrs. Drew for having
been so supportive.

Next we turned in our GI equipment to the cadet supply office
and received copies of our orders for ten days' leave of absence.
We were told that for the next twenty-four hours our status was
in limbo—we were neither cadets nor officers—and that we must
wait that long before donning our officer uniforms.

Our invited guests, upon arriving for a 10:00 A.M. ceremony,
were miffed by the commandant's double cross. However, everyone
was so elated over the successful completion of the training by a
second group of cadets that anger evaporated as we all left the base
and rode to the Tuskegee campus area. By midafternoon, at the
home of a friend of Jamie Jamison, I had changed into my pink

Second Lieutenant Charles Walter Dryden,
United States Army Air Corps—
A dream come true!

trousers and green blouse with silver wings pinned above the left pocket and a gold bar on each shoulder, garrison cap with the highly polished bill and gleaming eagle set rakishly on my head. It seemed that the afternoon hours dragged on until the six o'clock train to Atlanta left the Chehaw whistle-stop station to begin my journey back home to New York. Finally, when the train chuffed its way out of the station, I began to relax, anticipating with pleasure a triumphant homecoming. All the way north, as the train wheels clickety-clacked over the rails, a phrase drummed in my head: "I am one of eight. I am one of eight. I am one of eight." I was indescribably thrilled to be one of the only eight African Americans qualified and authorized to wear the silver wings of a United States Army Air Corps pilot!

By the time the train reached Pennsylvania Station at about noon the next day, I could scarcely bear my own conceit. Then, in the vast terminal teeming with troops of all sorts—army, navy, marines, Coast Guard—all in their distinctive uniforms, as well as policemen, and porters wearing their red caps, I was accosted by a small, frail, elderly White lady who said to me in an imperious, grande-dame voice: "Here, boy, carry my bag!"

Drawing myself up to my full five feet ten inches and thrusting my chest forward, I replied with all the hauteur I could muster: "Madame, I am an officer of the United States Army air forces. You need a porter. They are everywhere around here in the terminal. You can tell them by their red caps. In fact, here's just such a gentleman passing by. I am sure he will be able to help you. Good day, Madame!"

I felt annoyance. A bit of anger. But also I felt as though I had been brought back to earth. I had been made to realize that no matter what I might achieve in life I must never allow myself to "get too big for my britches." I must always remember that clothes don't make the man.

After that humbling encounter I found my way to the IRT (Interborough Rapid Transit) subway, rode it to the Bronx, caught a taxi from the Prospect Avenue station to my folks' 800 Home Street home. Knocked on the door. Stepped back. It opened. Then, BEDLAM!

"Welcome home, Charlie!"

That is how ten days of leave began. Days of parties, visitors to our home coming to see a local boy who had had a dream that came true, visits with kinfolk at their homes and with family friends and neighborhood buddies, many of whom were already in uniform and others who were expecting a call to arms momentarily. So many invitations to dinners, parties, and speaking engagements that I couldn't make them all. Happy days!

This time home I did get to "just happen to be in the neighborhood" and visit the army recruiting office at 39 Whitehall Street in Manhattan, a mission I couldn't accomplish five months earlier when Pearl Harbor Day cut short my leave. However, again I missed seeing the recruiting sergeant who had seemed so reluctant to give me an application for aviation cadet training in the first instance. He was no longer there. Gone off to war, I supposed.

A day or so later, when my leave ended, I was gone too. Gone from the Big Apple, back to duty. Back to Tuskegee Army Air Field to begin the next chapter of my life as a changed creature: earthbound before now; henceforth and forever able to fly, with the new, hard-earned wings. Like an eagle.

Back to the nest.

6   Nest of Black Eagles

»   April 1942–April 1943

Arriving at Chehaw at about noon the day after leaving Penn Station, I was really anxious to get started with my new life. During the overnight train ride I had plenty of time to ponder a raft of questions about what the new life would be like. Questions about my new duties: What would they be? How many? I had heard that new "Second Looies" are always loaded down with every imaginable extra duty, every undesirable task that higher ranking officers avoid. Would I be able to handle them?

About my new responsibilities: Would I have staff or command responsibilities? Deal mainly with men, money, or matériel? Would I be in charge of some activity? So many slots had to be filled at the almost-brand-new Tuskegee Army Air Field. Or would I be an assistant to some other officer in charge?

What about new relationships? With other officers—of higher rank? Of equal rank—especially our former upperclassmen? With cadets? With NCOs and enlisted men? With an orderly?

The most burning questions, of course, were: Where on the post will I be assigned? What will be my outfit?

The answer to those questions was awaiting me at post headquarters when I signed in, reporting for duty. The post adjutant handed me a large brown envelope containing several papers. Riffling rapidly through the stack I found the most important of all— my assignment orders:

Special Orders No. 68, dated 5 May, 1942,
issued by HEADQUARTERS,
TUSKEGEE ARMY FLYING SCHOOL,
Tuskegee, Alabama

7. The following named Officers having reported this
station per par.
1, S.O. #64, this Headquarters, dated 29 April 1942, are
assigned to the 99th Pursuit Squadron, effective this date:
2nd Lieutenant Sidney P. Brooks (0–789118) A.C.
2nd Lieutenant Charles W. Dryden (0–789119) A.C.
2nd Lieutenant Clarence C. Jamison (0–789120) A.C.

"Good! All three of us are in the 99th. That's great!" I thought.
My next thought was, "Where will I be billeted?"

Another document in the envelope was a post clearance form. It
directed me to visit several offices on the post and check in. First
was the billeting office where I was assigned a room in the BOQ
(bachelor officers quarters).

My room was on the second floor of the two-story wooden barracks. At the far end of the hall, it was the inner room of a two-
room suite, not at all plush as the term *suite* might imply. My room,
was at a corner of the building, so I had two windows giving me
cross ventilation. However, because the only door to the suite was
in the other room, I had to go through my roommate's room to get
to mine.

Fortunately my roommate was an amiable man, a veteran of over
twenty years of army service: Major Fleetwood McCoy, an attorney by profession, TJA (trial judge advocate) by military assignment. He didn't appear until late in the afternoon. He came into
his room, heard me stirring around in my room, stowing my gear
and settling in, and knocked at the connecting door.

"Hi, Roomie!" he greeted me brightly. "I'm Major McCoy. Fleetwood McCoy, from Chicago."

"Pleased to meet you, Sir. I'm Lieutenant Charles Dryden from
New York City. I just returned from ten days' leave there. Signed in
at post headquarters a couple of hours ago, Sir."

"Have you gotten your assignment yet?"

"Yes, Sir. The 99th."

"Fine, Roomie. I'm glad to have one of you young shavetail pilots as a roommate. Maybe we can go on a flight sometime."

"Sure thing, Major."

And so a new friendship was born. Major McCoy became my mentor as well as my roommate. At dinner at the officers mess that evening I admitted to him that the prospect of being an officer was somewhat overwhelming to me and that the need I felt to know everything about everything in a number of sources and references was mind boggling: "Everything" meaning army regulations, the *Manual for Courts-Martial,* the officers guide, aircraft tech orders, et cetera, et cetera, et cetera.

The major tried to put me at ease with the advice to just "Be yourself, keep your eyes and ears open, and, when you don't know something, ask somebody who does."

Good advice, I thought, as I remembered how, when I was an aviation cadet in primary, I had met an army veteran at Moton Field one afternoon while waiting my turn to fly. A six-striper, master sergeant, White, graying and grizzled, with a beer belly and fore-arms like tree trunks, he looked all the world like Wallace Beery, the film star of the 1920s and 1930s. I had asked him about army life and military traditions. His words were wisdom distilled from over twenty years in uniform. He taught me about the proper rela-tionship between officers and enlisted men: "First of all," he said, "you must earn the respect of your men. Look out for them, they'll take care of you by doing a good job of whatever they're doing. Go to bat for them and they'll bust their butts for you."

"What do you mean, 'go to bat for them,' Sarge? If I make it all the way through and get my commission, how do I do that?"

"Very simple. You look out for them. Make sure they have the best chow available. And the best equipment and supplies the army has for them to do their jobs. Show interest in what they're doing and tell 'em you appreciate it. Spend some time on the flight line while the mechanics, armorers, radiomen are working. Ask ques-tions. Not only will you learn things you should know but they'll get a chance to show what they know. Be sure to say you appreciate a chance to learn from them. After all, they are the ones who will keep you flying.

"And don't forget the cooks, the medics, the GIs in the motor pool, in the mail room, and for goshsakes don't forget the finance clerks 'cause if they don't keep your pay records straight you'll be outta luck on payday.

"Whenever one of your men does a good job, congratulate him in front of the other troops. On the other hand, when a man screws up, if he deserves to be chewed out, chew him out. Just be sure to do so in private, never in public, unless he has been insubordinate or disrespectful when other troops are around.

"Stand up for your men. Back them up if something goes wrong when they are following your orders. In other words, don't pass the buck if you're at fault when higher headquarters raises hell about something. But don't hesitate to jack 'em up to get them on the ball, if necessary."

"What about when your outfit does a good job, what do you do?"

"Give them some time off when you can. Three-day pass, overnight pass, whatever, whenever things slack up a bit. Your topkick should be able to help you keep track of who's doing good and who's goofing off."

"How about socializing with the troops?"

"Never!" he roared. "Don't gamble with your men. If you win their money some will feel that you took advantage of your rank. If they win yours you will have a problem if you ever have to discipline them at some later time—whatever punishment you give out will look like revenge. So, whatever you do, don't gamble with your men. Or drink with them unless it's a squadron picnic or party or something like that. In any event, don't ever, ever let them see you drunk!

"These are all common sense rules, Cadet, and if you follow them when you become an officer, you'll get along just fine in this man's army," said Master Sergeant "Wallace Beery."

So now, a half year later, I was an officer. Still "wet behind the ears" trying to get used to the world of second lieutenants. A different world, to be sure, than anything I had known before. True enough my primary assignment was to the 99th Pursuit Squadron where my main activity was to be flying. However, in order for my former 42-D classmates and me to gain some on-the-job training as officers, each of us was given a TDY (temporary duty) assignment to one of the ground support units on the post.

I was assigned to the 367th Service Squadron on TDY as adjutant. The commanding officer, First Lieutenant Nat Freeman, had more than ten years of military service under his belt when he was assigned to Tuskegee Army Air Field.

Slightly taller and stockier than I, he was about the same complexion. Mild mannered, friendly, and wise in the army way of doing things, he was just what a brand new officer needed in a CO to learn about the world of "Second Looies."

In the squadron orderly room he started me reading army regulations and gave me some basic tasks to perform like monitoring the daily morning report and inspecting our NCOs' and enlisted men's barracks. One day he handed me the keys to "Betsy," his pride and joy, a 1939 Buick sedan, parked outside the orderly room.

"Do me a favor, will you, Lieutenant? Take Betsy up to post headquarters and deliver this envelope to the post adjutant. It has a classified document that requires an officer as courier."

"Yes, Sir, I'll deliver it, but I won't need the keys, thank you. I'll walk the three blocks to headquarters. I need the exercise."

"But not in that blazing, noonday sun, Lieutenant. Go on, take the car," he insisted.

"Can't do that, Sir."

"Why not?" he asked, with a bit of an edge in his voice. He was getting annoyed.

"I can't drive, Sir."

"You WHAT? You mean to tell me that you can fly airplanes but you can't drive?"

"That's right, Sir."

"That's hard to believe, Dryden. Tell me something: Are you doing anything this evening?"

"No, Sir."

"Well then, come by my room in the BOQ and we'll start teaching you to drive. I can't have an officer in my outfit who can't drive."

That evening, after dinner at the officers mess, I had my very first driving lesson. At nearly twenty-two years of age.

The next evening my second driving lesson was cancelled because it started raining hard before Lieutenant Freeman and I could get out to the car. So he said: "Let's just talk about how you're doing. In the squadron you're doing OK; I'm glad to have you in the 367th, even though only on TDY. But how's it going otherwise? Got any problems?"

"Not really, Sir, but I am puzzled by some of the customs I've read about in the officers guide and others I've heard some of the guys discuss at the O Club."

"For instance?"

"For instance, officers never carry an umbrella, never carry packages, never push baby carriages."

"Oh, those are just military traditions of the officers' code of conduct," he said. And we talked on about the significance of what was taking place at Tuskegee Army Air Field: the inescapable fact that everyone, officers and enlisted men, pilots and ground crewmen, were being watched constantly and that we dare not fail. We dare not disgrace ourselves, our families, our race by our actions. The rain continued and seemed to get heavier as we talked. Around eight o'clock the phone in the hall jangled a couple of times. A moment later there was a knock at the door.

"Telephone for you, Lieutenant Freeman."

Excusing himself, he went down the hall to the phone, returning after a few minutes.

"Lieutenant," he said to me, "I have a job for you. I've just been informed that we have about thirty men arriving at Chehaw in about an hour. I want you to meet them there, take charge, and bring them back to the post in a couple of six-by-six trucks that the motor pool dispatcher is sending to the station. You go on down to Chehaw in Betsy."

"Are you serious, Sir? You know I have had only one driving lesson."

"That's alright, Dryden. You can do it. I know you can."

And I did. How, I don't really know. By guess and by God, I guess. In any case it was my first chance to put to work some of the advice that the kindly master sergeant, who reminded me of film star Wallace Beery, had given me that day back in primary.

First of all I had to drive Betsy to Chehaw through a downpour over muddy, narrow, unlighted country roads, praying all the way. Arriving at the station about twenty minutes after leaving the BOQ, I found two six-by-sixes already there, awaiting the train's arrival. The drivers were sitting in the Colored waiting room.

"Good evening, Lieutenant," one greeted me as they both rose to stand at attention when I entered.

"At ease, men. You're here to take some troops to the post, is that right?" I asked.

"Yes, Sir."

"Where are they coming from, do you know?"

"No, Sir. The motor pool dispatcher just told us to be here to meet a train at 2100 and take about twenty men and their duffel bags to a barracks in the 367th Service Squadron area."

"Well, if the train is on time they'll be here in about fifteen minutes. So we'll just have to wait."

"Yes, Sir."

The train pulled in to the station at about 2105. A group of Black soldiers dismounted from the coach behind the baggage car and hustled through the storm into the waiting room, hauling their duffel bags on their shoulders. When they were all inside I greeted them.

"Good evening, men. I am Lieutenant Dryden. Welcome to Tuskegee. Who's in charge?"

"I am, Sir," a buck sergeant spoke up.

"Where are you all coming from?" I asked.

"We left Fort Dix yesterday, Sir."

"Uh, Uh, Uh! I know you must be beat from that long train ride. So let's get you men out to the base and into your barracks and get some hot chow. There are two trucks here to take you there. I'll meet you in the 367th squadron area."

"OK, Lieutenant," the sergeant replied. Then turning to his men he barked: "Alright, load 'em up. Make sure you got all your gear. Le's go, on the double!"

When they were all aboard the trucks I spoke to the drivers.

"I'll meet you at the 367th orderly room when you get there."

"OK, Lieutenant."

As the drivers were cranking up to drive off I made a dash through the downpour to get to Betsy and get on the road before they did. I wanted to make sure that they were behind me just in case I ran into a ditch or had some other mishap and needed to be rescued. Upon arriving at the base I drove to the squadron orderly room to check on the readiness of the barracks. The CQ told me that one of our squadron barracks was ready and waiting for its new occupants but no cots or bedding were available in our supply room because no advance notice had been given about the arrival of these troops. He also told me that the CO wanted me to call him as soon as I arrived. I dialed the BOQ number and heard: "BOQ, Lieutenant Freeman speaking."

"Hi, Lieutenant," I replied. "This is Dryden. I made it OK. Betsy performed like a champ. We've got twenty-eight new troops from Fort Dix. The train arrived about a half hour ago and the trucks are on their way here now. CQ tells me there are no cots or bedding in our new, empty barracks. Should I call the OD to see if we can get base supply to issue what we need?"

"I've already tried that. Had no luck at all. Everything is locked up tighter than a drum—Sunday night, y'know. Same thing with the mess halls. This isn't the first time that higher headquarters has kept us in the dark about incoming troops and we have had to improvise. So do what you can to get the men settled, Dryden, and keep me posted."

"Yes, Sir."

About ten minutes later the trucks arrived in the squadron area, throwing up geysers of water as they braked to a stop in front of the barracks. The men piled out over the tailgates, jumping into puddles of water, and dashed up the half dozen stairs of the stoop and into the building. They were pretty well soaked as they dropped their duffel bags and dripped little pools of water where they stood peeling off their waterlogged raincoats. I heard one of them "signifying": "Damn, man, I don't see no cots in this place. Are we gonna have to put up cots before we can hit the sack? Man, I'm too beat to wrestle no cots!"

After their long train ride they had been looking forward to just falling out onto a cot and calling some hogs. I sensed that they were new recruits, knew that they were wet and miserable, and figured that they were hungry to boot. So this was my first test of dealing with troops in a difficult situation. What to do?

I remembered some words of wisdom from my NCO mentor during the primary phase of cadet training, the master sergeant who had told me, "Never ask your men to do something that you are not willing to do yourself." So I knew what I had to do. I told the sergeant in charge to call the men to attention.

"Atten'-hut!" he barked. They all popped to attention.

"At ease, men!" I said. "I am Lieutenant Charles Dryden of the 99th Fighter Squadron and on TDY with the 367th as adjutant. The CO didn't get word about your arrival until a couple hours ago. He ordered me to meet you while he tried to get bedding and chow for you all. But it's late Sunday night and everything is closed.

"So. We are going to bunk on the floor tonight. At least we are out of the rain. And I'm going to go out and see what I can scrounge in the BOQ: candy bars, crackers, potato chips. Go ahead, pick yourself a spot, dry out as best you can, and I'll be back with some grub."

I left and drove past the post exchange on the way to the BOQ. The PX was just closing but I was able to buy a couple dozen Baby Ruths and some potato chips. On to the BOQ where I reported to Lieutenant Freeman what the situation was and took a blanket from my bed. Then back to the 367th barracks.

There I found the newcomers spread out in the big open room of the barracks, each man having staked out a space for himself in which he had set his duffel bag as a pillow. They had pulled out some dry clothes and were changing into them after having peeled off their soaked uniforms, which were spread out to dry. One near the door saw me as I entered and hollered: " 'Ten-hut!"

"As you were!" I countered, as the men scrambled to their feet.

"Sit down and relax for a few minutes while I give you a rundown on the situation here." They all sat while I remained standing.

"First of all, men, I haven't had much luck rounding up bedding and hot chow for you. The mess halls and supply rooms are all closed since it is pretty late and this is Sunday night. Now, the base would have been ready for you if advance notice of your arrival had been sent to the base, but it was not. I spoke to the CO, First Lieutenant Nathaniel Freeman, while I was out scrounging and he said that he tried to get what we need but with no luck, and so he promised to straighten things out first thing in the morning when everything opens up. Meanwhile we will have to make do with what we have.

"What we have is a couple dozen candy bars and some snacks I bought at the PX just as it was closing and some things I begged and borrowed from some of my buddies in the BOQ. It's a bit more than two fish and five loaves but at least we don't have to try to feed five thousand with it, thank the Lord!"

Chuckles rippled through the group of men and I felt that the edge of their anger at our being unready to receive them was beginning to soften somewhat. I continued: "Another thing to be thankful for is that since we don't have any cots you won't have to wrestle with them to put them together." That drew laughter and joshing remarks aimed at the man who had grumbled about having to assemble cots.

"So, Gentlemen, since it's getting late and I know you guys are bushed, let's divide up these snacks so that everyone gets something to eat. Hold your questions—I know you must have a lot of them—until morning, and get some shuteye. Although the building is brand new the commodes and showers, complete with hot water, are working. So make yourselves as comfortable as you can. I see an empty spot over there by the stairwell and I'm claiming it. Let's have lights out in fifteen minutes. See you in the morning!"

The looks on their faces as I went over to my chosen spot on the floor, took off my blouse, loosened my tie, lay down on the blanket and pillow I had brought from my BOQ room, and covered myself with my raincoat assured me of the wisdom of my "Wallace

Beery"–NCO mentor who had told me, "Never ask your men to do something that you are not willing to do yourself."

As I rolled over and fell asleep I felt that I had passed my first real test in "the world of the Second Looies."

The next morning, at 0500, the CQ came over to the barracks from the orderly room and awakened me as I had asked him to do the night before. I dressed quickly, quietly, and asked him to rouse the sleeping men with lights on at 0600. Though still dark outside, the rain had stopped. I drove Betsy to the BOQ and went to Lieutenant Freeman's quarters to return his car keys to him and gave him a report of how the new troops had spent the night. His "Well done, Lieutenant," convinced me that I had, indeed, passed my first test as an officer responsible for troops. Later that afternoon I had proof positive when I heard a knock on the door of my BOQ room. When I opened it, there stood Corporal Nick Quinones, who had been the first to salute me as a brand new second lieutenant and had asked me if he could be my orderly.

"Hello, Corporal Quinones! Come in, come on in."

"Thank you, Lieutenant," he said, entering. "I remember that on your graduation day from cadet training you invited me to visit you after you moved into the officers quarters to see if you would take me on as your orderly. Do you remember that, Sir?"

"I sure do, Corporal."

"Well, Sir, the spratmo all around the base today is about how you bunked on the floor of the barracks with some new 'croots from Fort Dix and everyone is saying you're the kind of officer they'd like to have in charge of them. Me too. So, how about it, Sir, can I be your orderly?"

I was flattered by his words. And pleased. And grateful to "Wallace Beery" for his wise advice. And I determined right then that whatever knowledge I might gain in years to come, I would pass it on to some younger novice in need of guidance. So I said:

"Yes, Corporal Quinones, you've got the job."

A big grin split his face from ear to ear. "Thanks a million, Lieutenant! Now please tell me what you want me to do."

"Keep my shoes polished, my brass insignia on my belts and caps and uniforms gleaming, the bill of my garrison cap shined. Keep my room tidy. And that's about it. I'm going to give you a key to the room and notify the billeting officer that you are authorized to enter the building and my room on a regular basis. And because you have to come through my roommate, Major McCoy's, room to get to mine, I will clear the arrangement with him. He does not have an orderly right now and he may want to hire you too.

"Just remember one thing, and I'm sure I really don't have to overemphasize this: Honesty is a must in this job. Especially since Major McCoy is the trial judge advocate on the base and you certainly don't want to have any things missing in our quarters and wind up in a court-martial. Do you understand?"

"Yes, Sir, I do. And you don't have to worry, Lieutenant. I'll take good care of yours and the major's quarters."

"OK. Now let's talk about pay. How about $10.00 per week?"

"That's great, Lieutenant!"

"OK. Then it's a deal. I will speak with Major McCoy to see if he will agree to your having access to our quarters and let you know tomorrow."

Quinones saluted, I returned the salute, we shook hands, and he left. So now my accoutrements as an officer, in the tradition borrowed from the British military, were complete—I had a "batman." And for only $10.00 per week!

I could afford it because, after all, my monthly income had tripled upon graduation from the $75.00 of an aviation cadet to the $150.00 base pay of a second lieutenant plus the $75.00 flying pay (50 percent of base pay), for a total of $225.00 per month.

To earn the flying pay I had to perform the other new role besides that of a new second lieutenant—the role of a fighter pilot. Both roles developed concurrently: Usually my mornings were spent on the flight line where I flew various types of airplanes as a member of the 99th Fighter Squadron; afternoons were usually spent "up on the hill" in the 367th Service Squadron area.

My first flight as an officer was a scant three days after I returned to TAAF from graduation leave. On May 11 I flew an hour and ten minutes in a BT-13 in the morning. Later that afternoon I had two and a half hours in a round-robin cross-country flight to Atlanta in an AT-6. What great fun! From that day on I knew that what I wanted more than anything in all the world was a longtime career in the Army Air Corps.

My flying during the next few days was in the training planes I had flown as a cadet. Then, one week to the day after my debut as a 99th pilot, came my moment of truth—I was scheduled to check out the notorious "flying coffin," the P-40 "Tomahawk"! I had been studying the tech orders all week about its various systems: fuel, electrical, hydraulic, landing gear, radios. I had talked with the graduates of 42-C who had already checked it out and had some flying time in it. And I had watched their takeoffs and landings as my buddies, Brooks and Jamison, and I sat outside squadron ops while our former upperclassmen were flying.

So now it was my turn—my turn to show that the hours of sitting in the cockpit getting acquainted with the myriad dials, gauges, indicators, levers, switches, and controls had not been wasted, that the blindfold cockpit check was not just an exercise but that I could make all of the cockpit gadgets work in flight and master this monster that breathed hot, hot air within its innards.

Walking out to my assigned airplane I mentally pushed aside the caterpillars that were thrashing around in my gut and tried to concentrate on what I had learned about normal procedures—how to start the Allison engine without starting a fire, takeoff power, how to raise the gear, the stall speeds with various configurations of the landing gear, wing flaps, cowl flaps, et cetera, et cetera, et cetera. By the time I reached my "coffin" the caterpillars had metamorphosed into full-fledged butterflies in my churning gut.

When I had completed the outside walk-around check of the plane sitting on the ramp in the blazing, over-ninety-degrees-temperature sunshine, I was dripping with sweat. As was the case every time one of us went out to fly the P-40, scores of flight line people were watching, urging the novice on to conquer "the beast."

So. There was no turning back now. I remembered how I had had the same thought the day of my very first solo flight in the CPT Program almost two years before. But there was a helluva lot of difference between the 65-horsepower, 70-mph Piper Cub and the 1300-horsepower, 240-mph P-40! With such thoughts racing through my mind, I climbed up on the wing, into the cockpit, and fastened my seat belt and shoulder straps. The crew chief helped me get fastened in and assured me that the tanks had been topped off and that his plane had checked out perfectly during the morning preflight check. I thanked him and said, "I'm ready."

He jumped off the wing and stood by the fire extinguisher.

I pulled on my gloves, goggles down over my eyes, and hollered "Clear!" as I began the starting procedure.

After a few "Chuff! Chuff! Chuff's" the engine roared into life. Indicator needles on various gauges began moving, some lights lit up, and the airplane itself began throbbing slightly. It was alive! The monster was alive and ready to do battle with the hapless, puny human who dared to try to ride it. Funny, the kind of thoughts that cross one's mind when under stress. From somewhere in the deep recesses of my mind came the limerick:

> There once was a lady from Niger
> Who smiled as she rode on a tiger.
> They returned from the ride
> With the lady inside,
> And the smile? On the face of the tiger!

The baleful orange-colored eye of the coolant temperature warning light jerked me back to the here and now. It meant that I had just a few minutes to get airborne and get some cooler air flowing over the engine before it would be overheated and seize up. So I signaled the crew chief to pull the chocks from in front of the wheels, and I started to taxi out to the active runway.

Because of the big nose tilted at about a 30-degree angle to the horizon in front of the cockpit, the pilot had to "S" the aircraft while taxiing in order to see where he was going. And because of the weight of the plane it took a lot of brute strength to move the rudder pedals using the attached brakes alternately to "S" from side to side of the taxiway. By the time I reached the end of the runway my legs were trembling from the exertion of taxiing. And the cockpit had become a veritable sauna from the heat of the engine swirling into the open canopy. And worst of all, the needle of the coolant temperature gauge was up against the peg.

Suddenly, inexplicably, my near-panic evaporated. All signs in the cockpit told me: "Get moving! Take off! Now!" And my brain reminded me that our former upperclassmen had already flown the P-40. That's all I needed as I thought: "If they can do it, so can I."

Lining up with the runway I looked at the tower, saw the green light, heard, "P-40 on the runway, you're clear to take off."

I "gave it the needle" (full throttle), fought the torque of the 1,300 horses straining to pull the plane around to the left by applying hard, I mean HARD, right rudder, held the stick slightly aft of neutral, and FLEW IT OFF THE GROUND! Instantly the coolant temp began to drop to normal and the warning light went out as I climbed cautiously straight ahead to 1,000 feet then turned left, then right to leave the traffic pattern, and proceeded to the practice area, about ten miles away from the base.

During the next forty minutes the butterflies in my gut flew away as the Tomahawk and I got acquainted. At first I was intimidated by its brute strength as I tried some basic flight maneuvers. Pulling the nose up, to climb steeply by moving the control stick aft of neutral, but forgetting to roll the trim tab slightly for nose-up attitude, and having to strain to bring the nose up, I finally thought, "Use the trim tab, Dummy!" and Tomahawk responded beautifully. From then on, using the trim tab with changes of flight attitudes, I found that finger-tip pressure on the control stick was all I needed. Aileron and rudder trim tabs also helped relieve the brute strength needed to make this beast respond to my demands.

Some words of my instructor in the CPT Program, Bill Pyhota, came to mind. He had drummed into my psyche: "You fly the airplane—don't let the airplane fly you!"

So, OK, Tomahawk, let's see how you act in turns—gentle and steep, descents—gliding and diving, stalls—power-off and power-on, spins—left and right. Do you act differently in these various maneuvers when you are "clean," with everything retracted, than when you are "dirty" with "garbage"—landing gear, wing flaps, cowl flaps—hanging out? Do you shudder to warn me when you're about to whipstall or whip into a spin when I have pulled your nose too high and manhandled your 1,300 horses up front? Or do you just take charge and live up to your alias, the "flying coffin"?

Thirty minutes of trying various maneuvers convinced me that Tomahawk was really a pussycat, not a tiger. That is, if you stroked it right—at least up in the air, at altitude. The final question was still to come, however, when my scheduled forty-five minutes was running out: "Tomahawk, how do you act on landing? I've heard you would rather ground loop than taxi in to the ramp any day. Is that true?"

I soon found out. With confidence gained from having put the beast through its paces aloft, I descended from the 10,000-feet level to the 800-feet traffic pattern and called the tower for clearance to land. Then I turned onto downwind leg and throttled back to traffic pattern airspeed, about 120 mph. The nose got heavy so I used the trim tab; I lowered the landing gear by first putting the gear handle in the down position, then with the pinkie of the right hand held the landing gear electrical switch on the control stick closed until the landing gear indicator light glowed green. The landing gear warning horn stopped sounding and I felt a thud as the wheels locked into place. Now "dirty," with the gear hanging down, the nose got heavy again—so I used the trim tab to reduce the strain of pulling back on the stick. Now I turned into the base leg and then into the final approach lined up with runway, "crabbing" the aircraft with the nose turned slightly into a mild crosswind to compensate for drift. All the while Tomahawk was losing altitude in a gentle descent to the runway with the 1,300 horses up front merely idling. To keep them from quitting altogether the throttle was advanced partially and briefly to "gun" the engine. Now we were over the end of the runway at about treetop height and my moment of truth was at hand. I eased the stick back to bring the nose up to three-point landing attitude and held it there, left hand ready on the throttle in case Tomahawk shuddered on the edge of a stall before the ground came up to meet the wheels. Then bump, bump, as the main wheels touched down.

"Hallelujah!" I shouted into my oxygen mask. "I've made it!"

Not quite. Tomahawk wasn't finished teaching me a lesson yet. The beast wanted to fly some more and bounced back into the air. I added a little power with the throttle, held the stick about neutral and the rudder pedals even, then closed the throttle again and Tomahawk came back to earth, this time to stay. Good! So I get credit, or discredit, for two landings. "Not bad," I thought.

But the beast still wasn't through with me. Just as I was congratulating myself for having conquered it, I noticed that its big nose was beginning to move on the horizon from right to left and Tomahawk was not lined with the centerline of the runway.

"Uh, oh! Ground loop," I knew. "Gotta act fast!"

I applied hard, I mean HARD, right rudder to straighten it out and just a quick jab of the throttle to regain direction down the runway, then played the rudder pedals to keep it straight until it had slowed almost to a stop. Turned into the taxiway, "S"-ing to the ramp, opened the canopy, and greeted the crew chief with a grin to match his as he chocked the wheels, climbed up on the wing, and I shut off the engine.

"How'd it go, Lieutenant?"

"Great, Sarge! The P-40 is great and your airplane runs like a sewing machine—smoooooth! Everything worked OK and I really enjoyed the ride. I don't have any gigs to write up on the Form 1, and I want you to know I appreciate the chance to fly your plane on my checkout. Thanks!"

"Oh, you're welcome, Lieutenant. Any time. Thank you for making a soft landing in my baby."

"You mean two landings, don't you?" We both laughed at that.

The backslapping, handshakes, and congratulations from my classmates and other pilots in operations when I walked in were like winning a special trophy. I remembered the fighter pilot from Roosevelt Field who had put the fear of the "flying coffin" into us CPT students several months before, and I thought: "Today I put that fear to rest. I FLEW that airplane. Bill Pyhota would be proud of me!"

Four days later I got my second chance to fly the Tomahawk. This time I tried some acrobatics (chandelles, loops, slow rolls, split-"S's," Immelmans) and shot a few landings. The more I flew it the more I liked it—the appetite grew with the eating. And not only when flying the P-40. Many days I was scheduled to fly one of the trainers, which suited me just fine. There was no such thing as too much flying for me, and by the end of May my total for the month was nearly fifty hours.

One especially pleasant "fun" thing was "rat racing" on Sundays. Once the flow of pilots began coming out of the pipeline, many people on the base were anxious to go up for a ride with them: the mechanics, armorers, radiomen, parachute riggers, clerks from the flight line, and nurses, MPs, cooks, clerks, and nonflying officers from up on "the hill." All week long we pilots would be asked by various persons: "Can I get a ride with you next Sunday?"

About midmorning on Sunday a dozen of us would each check out an AT-6 "Texan" trainer and get our passenger suited up with a parachute and radio headset and strapped into the rear cockpit. Then we would take off in string, one after the other, and form up into one huge echelon formation. Upon reaching 5,000 feet the leader peeled off, followed in turn by all the rest. Then the "rat race" began with the leader doing every acrobatic maneuver in the book and each pilot following the leader through rolls, loops, Immelmans, split-"S's"—everything! Needless to say some of the backseat passengers didn't fare too well being wrung out like that. And by the time the formation landed, about an hour after takeoff, some passengers had to get a bucket and clean up their breakfast that they had upchucked in the rear cockpit. The next week brought another batch of eager beavers who wanted to experience the thrill of flying.

As the weeks passed from May into June, aviation cadet classes 42-E and 42-F graduated with their wings, and there were more pilots to fly the "orientation" flights for personnel on the base. The main purpose of the flights, of course, was to increase the flying proficiency of the pilots, but the very important bonus was the motivation of various ground support persons to do their level best to see to it that the "Tuskegee Experiment" was a success. Everyone at TAAF was proud of the pilots, "our boys," and for our part we pilots were grateful to everyone who was making it possible for us to disprove the myth that Negroes could not fly or keep airplanes flying.

One of my "home boys" from the old Sugar Hill neighborhood in New York was among the mechanics keeping us flying at TAAF.

Sergeant Kenneth Frank was in the 890th Maintenance Squadron. One day he looked me up on the flight line and asked, "How about a flight sometime?"

"Sure, Ken. How about tomorrow night? I'm scheduled to fly in a T-6 at 1900. Can you make it?"

"That's great, Lieutenant."

"Charlie to you, Kenny. I haven't changed. See you at base ops at 1800 tomorrow."

The next afternoon a monstrous thunderstorm swept over the base, cleansing the air with its torrents of rain. By 1800 when Kenny and I met at base operations, the thunderhead had spent its fury and had retreated about twenty miles off in the direction of Atlanta. Its anvil top looked to be way up above 40,000 feet; its billowing, bulging contours, seeming to spread over forty miles, were changing color from stark white to bronze bathed in the golden glow of the setting sun as dusk set in. A magnificent sight! I wanted to get airborne without delay to see it close up. Donning our parachutes quickly and climbing aboard, we got off the ground in short order.

I headed toward the cumulonimbus cloud, climbing up to about 8,000 feet, and flew around its edges, up and down and around its contours, just skimming the edges but not penetrating the cloud. I had been taught well the way to fly through a thunderhead: "Don't!"

After about a half hour the sun set below the horizon and I asked Kenny over the intercom, "Are you game for some acrobatics?"

"Sure!" he replied.

Then I did every acrobatic I had ever learned: loops, slow rolls, snap rolls, split-"S's," Immelmans, cartwheels, chandelles. Through it all Kenny grinned and hollered: "More! More!"

Finally our hour and a half was up, all too soon. We were having such a good time: two old friends who had dreamed of flying ever since they could remember. After landing, Kenny thanked me for the ride. "It was my pleasure," I replied, as I thought of the many pleasant hours I had spent at his home just "hanging out" with him and the rest of the guys on Saint Nicholas Place.

A number of the guys from the old Sugar Hill neighborhood

were also at TAAF, making me feel at home: Mike Smothers who, along with Kenny and me, had been a member of the "7 Boys and a Girl" social club that hosted one of the most prestigious teenagers' affairs on Sugar Hill; Humphrey Patton, an aviation cadet; and Bert Braithwaite, who played a mean tenor sax in the Imperial Wings of Rhythm, TAAF's top-flight jazz band. A couple of my former schoolmates at Stuyvesant High School—Willie Batten, an aircraft mechanic, and Leroy Gillead, who later was commissioned as a navigator—were reminders of home. Having all of these friends from the past helped me cope with grief when tragedy struck TAAF.

On June 8, TAAF went into mourning over the first loss of life in an airplane crash. Two cadets in the advanced phase were flying an AT-6 on a routine training mission when they attempted to fly under a bridge across the Tallapoosa River west of the base. Somehow they didn't make it. The plane crashed and broke in half between the front and rear cockpits. Cadet Richard "Red" Dawson, in the front seat, was killed instantly. Cadet Walter I. Lawson was found sitting on the bank of the river, dazed and bruised, but alive. Miraculously, surprisingly alive! Not surprisingly he became nicknamed "Ghost" Lawson.

Checkouts in the P-40 continued as each class graduated from aviation cadet training, and the 99th's roster of assigned pilots increased with each passing month. With the exception of the commanding officer, operations and assistant operations officers, and engineering officer, all pilots were assigned to either A-, B-, or C-Flights, each of which had eight pilots. The full complement of twenty-eight pilots was not assigned until the end of August. As each cadet class graduated, almost all the new pilots were assigned to the 99th. Exceptions were Lieutenants Charles DeBow and Mac Ross of the first class, 42-C, and George Knox of the third class, 42-E, who were assigned to the 332nd Fighter Group as the nucleus of that unit.

A graduate of the fourth class, 42-F, Lieutenant Faythe McGuiness, was a 99th original, but he was killed in a crash during a routine training mission in a P-40. The tragedy of his untimely death engulfed the entire population of the base and the campus community in grief because of the particular pathos of the tragedy.

ORIGINAL PILOTS OF THE 99TH PURSUIT SQUADRON: (left to right, front row): Herbert E. Carter, Amory, Miss.; Lee Rayford, Washington, D.C.; George S. Roberts, Fairmount, W.Va.; Benjamin O. Davis, Jr., Washington, D.C.; Lemuel R. Custis, Hartford, Conn.; Clarence C. Jamison, Cleveland, Ohio; Charles B. Hall, Brazil, Ind.; (middle row): Walter I. Lawson, Newtown, Va.; Spann Watson, Hackensack, N.J.; Allen G. Lane, Demopolis, Ala.; Paul G. Mitchell, Washington, D.C.; Leon C. Roberts, Pritchard, Ala.; John W. Rogers, Chicago, Ill.; Louis R. Purnell, Snow Hill, Md.; James T. Wiley, Pittsburgh, Pa.; Graham Smith, Ahoskie, N.C.; (back row): Willie Ashley, Sumter, S.C.; Charles W. Dryden, New York, N.Y.; Irwin B. Lawrence, Cleveland, Ohio; William A. Campbell, Tuskegee, Ala.; Willie H. Fuller, Tarboro, N.C.; Richard C. Davis, Fort Valley, Ga.; Sidney P. Brooks, Cleveland, Ohio; Sherman W. White, Montgomery, Ala.; George R. Bolling, Phoebus, Va. Missing from the photo are Sam M. Bruce, Seattle, Wash.; Herbert V. A. Clark, Pine Bluff, Ark.; James B. Knighten, Tulsa, Okla.; James L. McCullin, Saint Louis, Mo. (Photo taken in March 1943 at Tuskegee Army Air Field; birthplaces also noted)

He was going to be married the next day to a beautiful girl from the local Tuskegee Institute campus community. Everyone knew about the storybook romance: He was handsome, dashing, and he "wore a pair of silver wings," which was the title of a popular ballad of the time; she was cute, pert, pretty, and they were very much in love. Theirs was a scenario fit for Hollywood. But it was not to be. When Faythe crashed, the euphoria of the folks on base, and for miles around, crashed too. He was the first victim of the "flying coffin" at TAAF.

The roster of 99th pilots, when the squadron first had its full complement of twenty-eight pilots, included commanding officer: Lieutenant Colonel Benjamin O. Davis, Jr., operations officer: Captain George S. Roberts, assistant operations officer: Lieutenant Erwin B. Lawrence, engineering officer: Lieutenant Herbert E. Carter; A-Flight: Captain Lemuel R. Custis, flight leader, and Lieutenants Herbert V. A. Clark, Willie H. Fuller, Allen G. Lane, Paul G. Mitchell, Louis R. Purnell, Graham Smith, James T. Wiley; B-Flight: Lieutenant Clarence C. Jamison, flight leader, and Lieutenants Willie Ashley, Sidney P. Brooks, Charles W. Dryden, Lee Rayford, Leon C. Roberts, John W. Rogers, Spann Watson; C-Flight: Lieutenant Charles B. Hall, flight leader, and Lieutenants George R. Bolling, William A. Campbell, Richard C. Davis, Earl E. King, James B. Knighten, Walter I. Lawson, Sherman W. White.

Every one of these pilots was a competent aviator, a distinct individual on his own merits. Some were strictly by-the-book individuals, others were innovators, "hot rocks" who could make the Tomahawk "talk" and cry "Uncle!" All soon became team members as we flew together in our assigned flights almost daily. With the tutelage of a visiting team of technicians, we learned a British system of intercepting invading enemy aircraft by responding to vectoring directions from a ground control center—a forerunner of radar-controlled interception.

We practiced defensive patrol techniques and dogfighting tactics, which, in one practice session, almost wiped out half of B-Flight when Flight Leader Jamison and his wingman, Brooks, challenged Deputy Flight Leader Dryden and his wingman, Ashley, to a dogfight. After taking off and joining up into our four-ship formation, we flew to the practice area and split up into two elements. With our wingmen flying in tight formation, Jamie and I turned toward each other when we were about five miles apart to "get it on!"

Flying toward each other at top speed, "balls to the wall," about 240 mph, the two pairs of airplanes had a rate of closure of almost 500 mph, allowing little more than a half minute to swerve from a head-on collision. But we were daredevils, and each was determined not to "chicken out." So we pressed the attack, straight ahead, neither one swerving, each expecting the other to change course. Then quickly, soon—too soon—the half minute was gone, the five miles were gone, and the four planes were about to smash into each other. All I remember seeing was the two planes rushing toward me as I threw my left arm up in front of my face, pushed the control stick down sharply, and sobbed, "Oh God!"

Somehow, by the grace of God, we missed each other. None of the four planes struck any part of any of the others. A miracle! Over the radio, on squadron frequency, I heard Jamie: "B-Flight, join up, return to base!" His voice sounded shaky. I felt shaken. To the bone. We were back on the ground a scant twenty minutes after taking off. The ops officer asked why we were back so soon. It would have sounded imbecilic to say, "because we had to change our underwear," so we said nothing.

The squadron's daily flying activities included cross-country navigation missions to various bases, usually in the South: Meridian, Mississippi; Birmingham, Alabama; Tallahassee, Florida. Such flights were always just one-day trips—never RON (remain overnight). For us to remain overnight would have required us to occupy billets in the BOQ, and on all such bases Jim Crow was very much in command, regardless of what the base commander's name might be. It was bad enough when we landed in daytime and taxied in to the ramp to park our planes. Many a flight line mechanic blanched several shades paler than normal when we unsnapped our oxygen masks and jumped off the wings of our fighter planes to walk into base operations. And in the flight line snack bars we were amused, at first, as the attendants were amazed to see us clad in flying gear. Of course our amusement changed to anger as quickly as their amazement turned to hostility when we demanded to be served. Often we flew back to base starving rather than submit to Jim Crow.

One consolation on such flights to other bases was the smiles and the thumb-to-index-finger OK signal flashed at us by the Negro workers in the cafeteria kitchens and by ditch diggers and truck drivers wherever we passed by. Returning the greeting I felt a bond impossible to describe. It was almost as though we were declaring, long before I ever heard the words of the civil rights movement spiritual, "We shall overcome!" They were proud of us and we were fiercely determined to make them proud of us. So, when we took off we joined up into the tightest, prettiest formation ever seen, anywhere, as we roared across their base on our way back to TAAF.

By the summer of 1942 the word had gotten around about a squadron of Negroes flying fighter airplanes at Tuskegee, and we began to have visitors. Wing Commander Donaldson, an RAF officer who had seen combat against the Luftwaffe in the Battle of Britain, flew in to TAAF in his P-40 with its triple-band markings painted on the fuselage aft of the cockpit. With his typical walrus mustache and clipped British accent, he was impressive.

Another visitor was RAF Squadron Leader McLachlan who flew his P-36, a radial engine–powered forerunner of the P-40, with a prosthetic attachment on his left arm. The forearm was missing, the result of a wound in the Battle of Britain.

Yet another visitor was an airplane, flown in to TAAF by a pilot whose name was not known to us pilots of the 99th and, anyway, was unimportant to us. What was important to us was the name of the plane: P-39 "Airacobra"! Of course we had all seen pictures of Bell Aircraft Company's unorthodox tricycle-landing-gear fighter with a cannon in the nose spinner and the in-line engine mounted behind the pilot's cockpit and doors that opened like the doors on a car. But none of us had ever seen one in the flesh. More exciting than just seeing one was the prospect of flying it.

When it landed we heard spratmo that one of the pilots at TAAF was going to be given a chance to check it out. Of course all of us wearing wings thought, "Let me at it; I can fly that machine!" As it turned out, none of us got to do any more than stand on the wing and peer into the cockpit and drool at the thought of flying the P-39. The lucky guy was a cadet in the advanced phase, Ed Gleed. We did not know why he was selected but we did see that he was a good pilot, because after a hasty briefing about the 39's systems and SOPs (standing operating procedures) he took off, flew some basic maneuvers upstairs, and brought it back in a good landing to the cheers of hundreds of base personnel who had heard about the flight and had rushed to the flight line to see it. Although I envied Gleed for having had the chance to fly the Airacobra, I was truly proud of the way he had handled it. It was a fact of our life at TAAF that every time one of us scored a victory of some sort, all of us were victors. On balance, receiving that kind of credit was only fair because the converse was also a fact of our life: Whenever one of us made a mistake, all of us were labeled inept.

Our life at TAAF was made pleasant and memorable by other visitors, the likes of heavyweight champion of the world, in the uniform of the U.S. Army, Joe Louis; our favorite pinup Lena Horne; and blues singer Lil Green moaning "Since I Fell for You" and "In the Dark, In the Dark." They and many other entertainers came to TAAF with USO shows to boost the morale of all the troops. In the summer of 1942 I had a visitor who made my life ecstatic: Jackie! She had written me to ask if she and her mother could stay at the guest house on Tuskegee's campus for about a week while visiting me and touring the base and the famous campus. My answer? "Come on! Come quickly!"

I made arrangements for them to stay at Dorothy Hall on campus and called them to inform them and to ask their train arrival information. On the day of their arrival I was scheduled for a flight that would prevent my meeting them at Chehaw. So I asked my buddy, Knighten, to meet them and escort them to the BOQ lounge. He agreed. Meanwhile, I took off early enough before my assigned practice patrol mission to intercept their train from Atlanta to Chehaw, about halfway between West Point and La Grange, Georgia. It was easy to spot as it was the only train smoking on that line that day.

Flying parallel to the rail line about a half mile to one side at about 500 feet, I rocked my wings several times in greeting and

Lena Horne, our pinup girl, visited the troops at Tuskegee
Army Air Field and, later, Godman Field, Kentucky. Morale
was lifted by her songs and by her very presence.

then repeated the greeting on the other side of the train to make
sure that they saw my special "welcome" gesture. It was partially
in vain, I later learned from Jackie's Mom, who saw the plane.
Jackie didn't—she was in the ladies' room at the time.

No matter. I was delighted to see them when I landed and rushed
up to the BOQ. After introducing them to some of my buddies, all
of whom scoffed at my saying, "Meet my girl friend, Jackie, and
her mother, Gwendolyn," by signifying: "Naw, that pretty fox
can't be your girl friend! How can a homely cat like you ever win a
cute kitten like her?"

If the truth were known, I never knew the answer to that either.
But Jackie had said she loved me and I never dared ask why. I just
was thankful for my blessings.

The next week was idyllic, showing off my two lovely guests as
I showed them around the base at the officers club, flight line, post
exchange, and at the theater and on the Tuskegee campus at the
chapel, in the dining room, and at the Propellor Club near the

campus where dancing and socializing were the very best the community had to offer. All too soon the week ended and Gwendolyn had to return to New York to look after the rest of her family. Jackie did not have to return to classes at Hunter College until mid-September, so she asked her mother to let her stay another week. Gwendolyn said to me: "Charlie, I'm going to leave my daughter in your care. I know you will take care of her."

That evening Jackie and I took her mother to the Chehaw station where she boarded the train to Atlanta on her first leg of the trip back to New York. The second week of Jackie's visit was like an instant replay of the first week, only more so. But again, all too soon, it too was ended and it was time for her to leave. Sorrowfully we went to Chehaw for her to board the train to Atlanta. When it arrived I couldn't leave her so I bought a ticket and rode to Atlanta, too. But then I had to face facts—either say g'bye and return to TAAF or go AWOL. In truth, I was crazy about Jackie, but I wasn't a complete fool, so I said, "Good-bye, my love!" She got on the train going north to New York; I boarded the southbound train to Tuskegee—and I never saw her again! Why? I was not really sure why. I did receive a "Dear Charlie" letter around the end of the year from which I concluded that absence makes the heart grow fonder—for somebody else. Whatever. In any case the memory of Jackie lingered on through the years, especially on Pearl Harbor days because we had shared that moment in history together.

The summer of 1942 ended. Flying continued. Just about every day I was up flying some kind of airplane, honing my skills, averaging thirty hours of flying time per month. From the last week in August my time was flown almost exclusively in the P-40. And I had begun to really love flying it.

In autumn, leaves began to turn color and the air changed from searing hot to cool and crisp. On November 10 my gold bars turned to silver and my title changed from second lieutenant to first lieutenant. To me life at TAAF was mighty sweet.

There were so many things to be enjoyed, and savored, on that new base that was still abuilding. On that 1,600-acre tract set about six and half miles northwest of the Tuskegee Institute campus, brand new buildings were being completed in rapid succession. New facilities, services, and amenities appeared almost miraculously. Militarily there was never a dull moment at TAAF. When my cadet class, 42-D, had first reported to the base, just before Christmas 1941, the base commander was a pleasant fellow, Major James A. Ellison, who had assumed command in October 1941. Three months later Colonel Frederick Von Kimble, a rather dour, somewhat humorless officer, took command in January 1942. He lasted the year until Colonel Noel F. Parrish became base commander in December.

Colonel Parrish had been at TAAF from its very beginning, first as a flight instructor, then as director of flying training, and finally as the man in charge at the top. All along the way to the top he had been a friendly, enthusiastic supporter of the "Tuskegee Experiment," sensitive to the needs, aspirations, and obstacles faced by all of us at all levels—officers, enlisted men, aircrews, and ground support personnel. He used his position as best he could to make sure that we succeeded in spite of the Jim Crow policies of the army air forces and racist practices in the surrounding communities. Because of his staunch support of his Negro troops on the base, his critics rancorously, and raucously, labeled him "nigger lover." For the same reason we humorously, and affectionately, referred to him as "the great White father." By his actions he truly earned our respect.

Life at TAAF was also made pleasant by the attention that the "experiment" was getting from "our" public and "our" press. Except for an occasional article here and there, for example in *Life* magazine, the general media ignored us. However the "Black Dispatch" lionized us. Almost every issue of the weekly newspapers featured articles about the men of TAAF and their experiences. Every graduating class of cadets was spotlighted, and hometown "soul" newspapers applauded their hometown heroes when they won their wings. Promotions of our enlisted men were publicized, such as when, on April 1, 1942, Jim Reed, top aircraft mechanic on the flight line, and Sidney Johnson, in base headquarters up on "the hill," became the first noncommissioned officers at TAAF to be promoted to the top NCO rank—master sergeant. With all those six stripes on their sleeves I referred to them, with all due respect for their know-how and position at the top of the enlisted ranks, as "zebras."

Articles, complete with glamorous pictures of us in flying gear, that appeared in "our" newspapers—the *Afro American, Amsterdam News, Chicago Defender, Cleveland Call and Post, Norfolk Journal and Guide, Pittsburgh Courier*—brought us fan mail: lots of it for handsome brutes like Lee Rayford of Washington, D.C., and George Knox from Indianapolis, a few letters for even plain runts like me. There were requests for autographed pictures and pairs of silver wings for use as charms; and there were propositions of all kinds, including proposals of marriage with pictures of the smitten lady enclosed. Although hardly any of the guys replied to their fan mail, it was a great boost to the ego.

The daily routine of life on the base began at dawn with the sound of airplane engines coughing to life on the flight line, each one adding its roar to the chorus of all the others as the crew chiefs preflighted their "babies." Every mechanic was proud of his machine and worked his damnedest to keep his "baby" from becoming a crippled "hangar queen" unable to fly for some mechanical flaw or other. Then came the boom of the cannon and the strident trumpet sounding reveille as the officer of the day, and his detail of military policemen (MPs), officially started TAAF's day by raising Old Glory to the top of the flagpole in front of base headquarters.

Then, all day long in various parts of the base, one heard the measured cadence of marching troops going from place to place. The cadets added fighting chants as they marched to and from the flight line and ground school:

> Contact! Joystick back! Nose up in the blue
> Gallant men of the 99th, brave and tried and true,
> For we are heroes of the night,
> To hell with the Axis might!
> Fight! Fight! Fight! Fight! Fighting 99th!

Overhead, almost constantly all day long, various types of planes were flying and attracting attention with their maneuvers, especially whenever a tight formation roared into the traffic pattern and peeled off to land. That was always a thrilling sight!

Officially the day ended with the lowering of the flag at base headquarters and the trumpet sounding "retreat" as the new officer of the day led the detail of MPs. Heard all over the base, the sounds of "retreat" brought all ground activity to a halt. Vehicles stopped moving and the occupants got out and stood at attention facing toward headquarters. Likewise, pedestrians and marching troops stood still at attention until the last bugle note faded away. Retreat took place promptly at 1700 hours.

Then, for the most part, TAAF quieted down for the night as the mess halls began feeding the supper meal. The flight line often continued to hum with activity when night flying was scheduled and, occasionally, when a transient aircraft landed to refuel. About an hour before dusk the base lit up with its myriad lights of many colors, and when the sun finally set TAAF was like a gleaming kaleidoscope of colors: green rotating beacon, red hazard-warning lights on tall radio towers and the control tower, amber lights marking the sides of the runways, blue lights showing the pilots where to taxi, and white lights everywhere.

Taken altogether, the sights and sounds of the air base were pleasant and memorable, making me feel privileged to be part of this Army Air Corps experience at TAAF—the sort of experience that was "old hat" to White Americans who took it for granted but that was altogether new to African Americans who relished and appreciated the chance to experience life on an air base, at last, after having been excluded by U.S. Army policy from the very beginning of the Army Air Corps.

Once the decision to build an air base for the training of Negro pilots and support personnel was made and TAAF was built, equipped, and staffed, the War Department still was not sure how to use their new "secret weapon." Consequently the 99th pilots kept building up flying time in their P-40s, sharpening their combat flying skills, and awaiting a call to go overseas. The "Black Dispatch" newspapers clamored, "Why can't our boys be sent overseas to fight for our country like all other Americans?"

Finally, on September 15, 1942, the 99th was placed on alert for deployment overseas. We expected movement orders momentarily. However, the squadron did not leave TAAF until six months later.

Meanwhile, we began to prepare seriously for such a move. Squadron Adjutant Captain Hayden Johnson coordinated the activities of various sections of the organization to acquire the necessary equipment for overseas duty. Interestingly enough his brother, Captain Maurice "Pie Train" Johnson, was also a member of the 99th as our flight surgeon.

As time marched on we pilots kept flying and our ground crews kept our planes flying with a high rate of availability. The one thing that put a crimp in their near-perfect record was when a plane was AOCP (aircraft out of commission, awaiting parts). At times AOCP was the bane of the flight line crews and really put them to the test just before the Christmas holiday season when the squadron received movement orders—not for the entire outfit to move overseas but for the pilots, mechanics, armorers, and some mess hall cooks and orderly room clerks to go TDY to Dale Mabry Field near Tallahassee, Florida, for gunnery practice.

We flew our planes down to Dale Mabry a couple of days before Christmas and began flying aerial and ground gunnery missions immediately. Because it was the main gunnery-practice base for many fighter squadrons in the Southeast, Dale Mabry was an extremely busy base with large gaggles of airplanes of various types flying roundabout the traffic pattern during daylight hours. One day, upon returning to the base from a ground gunnery mission leading a four-ship flight of P-40s, I called the tower for landing clearance and was told, "P-40 flight, you are number twenty-two to land!" As I put my flight into a stepdown echelon to the right and orbited the base waiting for the twenty-one planes ahead of me to land, I glanced over my right shoulder to see how my other flight mates were doing and I saw four "Jugs," P-47s with their big barrel-like fuselages, tucked in right echelon behind my number four man! Their leader was told by the tower, "You are number twenty-six to land!"

On Christmas Eve, having flown three gunnery missions, we all figured that we would have a day off on Christmas Day. Some of the guys knew the daughter of the president of Florida A&M College who invited us to a party at her home. Her family and friends were most cordial, entertaining the pilots of the much heralded 99th, and we relaxed and enjoyed their hospitality. We returned to our billets late and, some of us, "looped" (inebriated) because we had figured that we would not have to fly on Christmas. We figured wrong!

Early Christmas morning Ops Officer Spanky Roberts came through the barracks with bad news: "Awright, you guys, off and on!" he blasted us awake. "Off your butt and on your feet. We've got a TWX ordering the 99th to fly gunnery today."

We thought he was kidding and I, for one, rolled over trying to ignore what I thought was a poorly timed April Fool joke. He wasn't joking. He read the TWX (teletype message) from Brigadier General Adlai H. Gilkeson. Talk about the grinch stealing Christmas! Some of us were going to be at risk because of much libation at the Christmas Eve party. It was difficult enough landing on the camouflage-painted runways at Dale Mabry when stone sober. How were we going to make out with our depth perception clouded by demon rum? In fact, one of the guys did misjudge the runway and ran off the end of it into a coal pile. He walked away without a scratch and the rest of us refrained from teasing him about his misadventure mainly because each of us knew that "there, but for the grace of God, go I."

A day or so after New Year's Eve we returned to TAAF and resumed routine flying but with a new sense of urgency. We expected to be told to "pack up and git!" almost any day. No such orders appeared, but we did hear some sad news on January 5 when a gentle genius, a giant among men, passed on: Dr. George Washington Carver. I thanked God for having had the privilege of meeting him.

By that time TAAF had been equipped to support night flying. And by then I had logged more than 150 hours in the P-40 and felt at home in it. However, my first P-40 night flight was a bit of a shocker when I saw bright red exhaust flames shooting out of the exhaust stacks on both sides of the long nose of the beast. Of course the exhaust flames were nothing new to the beast—it had been breathing flames every time I had ridden it before. I just hadn't been able to see the flames in daylight. At night the flames lit up the area in front of the cockpit so brightly that the pilot could have a problem judging his height above the runway on landing. After a few flights we got used to it.

We had much more trouble getting used to the effects of a night flight on January 30, 1943. That night our squadron mate, Richard C. Davis, was killed in the crash of his P-40. "Big Dave" from Fort Valley, Georgia, had graduated from cadet training in 42-G, the fifth class to do so. We were just barely getting used to missing his dry, homespun humor when, less than two months later, on March 24, we lost Earl "Wamba" King, from Birmingham, Alabama, who also was a 42-G graduate. King's plane crashed into Lake Martin about twenty miles north of the base while on a daytime routine training mission. When I heard about this second fatal crash in such a short time, I couldn't help thinking that the "flying coffin" reputation of the P-40 was not to be taken lightly, ever!

Two new members of the 99th were assigned to replace the late Lieutenants Davis and King. Both were notable athletes: Sam M. Bruce had been a CIAA (Central Intercollegiate Athletic Association) wrestling champion and James L. McCullen handled a basketball as though he had been born with one in his hand. They were classmates/graduates of cadet class 42-H and they both fitted into the vacant slots in Charlie "Seabuster" Hall's C-Flight with hardly a ripple.

Time was running out on the 99th. The time of the glory days in the nest of Black eagles had only about a week to run after King's death. We had received orders to deploy overseas and we felt that we were as ready as we would ever be. During a visit to TAAF in mid-February the secretary of war, Henry Stimson, had declared that in his opinion the 99th was "outstanding by any standards."

During the final week of March, each of us was busy winding up his affairs at the base and on campus. As the twenty-one months from the entry of the first class into aviation cadet training until the entry of the first Negro flying squadron into war was coming to an end, the mood in the Tuskegee community began to change. What had been a joyous, pride-provoking adventure—in which a group of Americans of color proved that, in spite of all odds and obstacles, they could fly and maintain airplanes in tip-top condition to fly to meet the highest standards—now became a nightmare: the specter of war was now a grim reality.

Nevertheless, morale was high. Farewell parties were hosted by campus families and at the officers and NCO clubs on base. Finally, D-Day (departure day) arrived. All day long the 99th's squadron area was a scurry of activity, packing boxes of personnel records, army regulations, documents of all kinds vital to the proper running of the unit, and crates of various sizes and shapes containing supplies and equipment of all sorts. Also in the BOQ area the single guys, like myself, were packing up our personal belongings, emptying our rooms, and getting ready to clear out of them that night. We were scheduled to board a train at the railhead down near the flight line just before midnight. The married officers who lived off base, in town, like my classmates, Brooks and Jamison, brought their personal stuff to the squadron supply room to be packed into crates for shipment overseas.

The officers club hosted a final farewell party for the squadron's officers, beginning with supper. Dress code for the party was class A, so I got sharp in my pinks and greens and walked over to the club. Despite the prospect of leaving our "home" of the past year and a half and going "over there," almost everyone was in a party mood. Almost everyone was trying to ignore the sadness of farewell, chatting, joking, dancing—except for Lieutenant Allen Lane, the broken-legged bridegroom: He had gotten married just a day or so before and had somehow broken his leg, which was in a hip-to-thigh cast. Poor Allen, he took a merciless ribbing from the guys.

As I was standing, chatting with a group of folks, one of our ground (that is, nonflying) officers, Lieutenant Jimmy Freeman from New York, approached me with one of the army nurses from our base hospital in tow. She was petite and cute with a figure that her uniform could not completely conceal.

"I think you two New Yorkers should know each other," Jimmy said by way of introduction. "Lieutenant Dryden, I'd like you to meet Lieutenant Cameron. Charlie meet Pete—she just got in today from the city and I had a tough time convincing her to come to the club tonight. Now that she's here, perhaps you can convince her it was worthwhile."

"I'll sure try, Jim. Thanks for introducing us," I said as he moved away. Turning to her, I said, "Hi, Lieutenant, did I hear Jim right? Did you just arrive from New York today?"

"That's right, just a few hours ago."

Nice voice, melodious, I thought: Let's hear more.

"How long have you been in the Army Nurse Corps?" I asked.

"Only three days, since Monday when I was sworn in."

"Whereabouts in New York are you from, Pete? Did I get your name right? Pete—is that right? The music and all were so loud I couldn't really hear what Jim said."

"That's right, it's Pete, as in 'Peter loved the Lord.' Actually, I'm not from New York now, although I was born there. My home is now in Belleville, New Jersey, and I met Jim Freeman when I was in nurses training at Harlem Hospital, at one of our dances."

In the background I heard the sounds of one of my favorite jazz numbers, Jimmy Lunceford's "For Dancers Only."

"Care to dance?" I asked.

"I dunno, I'm kind of tired from that long train ride from New York. As a matter of fact there were three of us Harlem Hospital nurses who came down together and arrived this afternoon. We were so tired that all we wanted to do was retire early, and we were getting ready to do that when our chief nurse, Captain Della Raney, told us that the 99th is leaving tonight and that the whole base is turning out to see them off."

"And she ordered you to come to the club?"

"No, not quite, but she said we would regret it if we missed the party. So here we are: Mary Rickards is over there by the window and Alice Dunkley is seated by the piano."

"And here you are beside me, and we're missing out on that good Lindy-hopping music. How about it, Pete, care to dance?" I asked again.

"Sure, Charlie."

We danced an off-time Lindy hop that was oh-so-smooth. Pete

was light on her feet, like a feather. A perfect dance partner. After my breakup with Jackie I had not become involved with anyone. I had not had a girl friend since then, and as Pete and I did a number on Jimmy Lunceford's number, I thought to myself: WhyOhWhy did she wait until today to come to Tuskegee? And then I blurted it out loud: "Why haven't you been here before now? In fact, where have you been all my life?" Before she could answer, I said: "Look, Pete, the squadron is shipping out in a couple of hours and when we get the word to report to the squadron the party will be over. I don't have anyone to say good-bye to me." (Seeing the other guys with wives or sweethearts wishing them farewell, I was beginning to feel sorry for myself.) "So would you spend the rest of the evening here at the party with me?"

Looking me straight in the eyes, she shocked me! She said, almost in a whisper, "I think I could spend the rest of my life with you."

Whoa! Heady stuff! But I liked the sound of it and I was beginning to fall, hard!

The next number on the jukebox was a slow ballad, popular at the time: "Sweet Slumber," by Buddy Johnson—one of her favorites, she said, as we clung together, slow dragging to the music. Dance after dance we had eyes only for each other until time ran out on us. Over the PA system we heard an announcement: "Attention! Attention! All officers of the 99th Fighter Squadron are to report to the squadron orderly room by 2100. Repeat, 2100."

"That's it, Pete. Gotta go now. I'll write you the first chance I get. Will you answer?"

"I will. I will. You know I will." Her eyes brimmed. Mine too, as I thought how sad and unfair it seemed that we had not met before now. After last-minute good-byes to families and friends at the club, we had only about ten minutes before 2100, so several of us double-timed over to the 99th area. There we saw a small fleet of trucks lined up outside the orderly room. As we arrived there we heard Captain Rod Custis's barked command: "Officers platoon, fall in!"

Forming in the three parallel ranks to which we had become accustomed during inspections, parades, and ceremonies, each man found his usual position and stood at parade rest until all were in ranks. Although all of us were still clad in our class-A uniforms, many of us were hanging loose, sort of unmilitary in posture, which was understandable because, after all, we were about to go off to war, some might never return and, most of all, we had just come from a farewell party with an open bar.

No matter. We were officers and had to act the part. So. Captain Custis called out: " 'Ten-hut! Dress r-i-g-h-t, dress!"

We all popped to attention, raised our left arms horizontal to the ground, snapped our heads to look to the right as we shuffled to our right until our right shoulders touched the upraised fingertips of the men to our right. That is, all of us but one. That one was Lieutenant Sherman White. Sherman sort of wobbled his way from his spot in the rear rank through the other two ranks to the front of the formation, stuck his hand out to shake the captain's hand, and greeted him with a silly grin and words that became a sort of squadron slogan: "Carry on, Hoss!"

That brought gales of laughter and relieved some of the tension that had gripped us all day.

After calling the roll Captain Custis reported to the CO, Lieutenant Colonel Davis: "Officers platoon all present and accounted for, Sir!" In turn our NCOs reported to the CO the same information about their platoons. Every man of the squadron was present and accounted for—no one was AWOL. The fighting 99th was ready to leave home and go to war!

We loaded aboard the trucks for the ride to the railhead, only a short fifteen minutes away. Once there we jumped off, each man taking his own bedroll, stuffed with his clothing and toilet articles, to make sure that he would have it handy during the train ride to . . . most of us did not know where. The CO had kept our orders from higher headquarters a dark secret to avoid any slip of the lip that might give aid and comfort to our Axis enemies.

About five minutes after we arrived at the railhead one of my buddies said to me, "Hey, Dryden, there's a cute nurse looking for you over there where those cars are parked."

I covered the hundred yards or so in a flash, and there she was leaning against Chaplain Douglas Robinson's car. He and his wife had taken pity on her at the club when they heard her bemoaning her sudden loss of a newfound romance and wondering when she would ever see him again. Like hundreds of others they drove to the railhead for last good-bye hugs and kisses of their young, young men going to war. And they brought her with them.

We fell into each other's arms and sighed promises: "I'll wait for you." "I'll pray for you." "I'll write to you."

And we exchanged tokens to seal our promises. She took a class ring from her finger and gave it to me, saying: "Take this with you. Promise you will bring it back. That way I'll know for sure you will return to me."

"I promise, Pete. Here, take my scarf." It was the only thing I had handy to give her because I had changed into field gear and my wings, pinned to my blouse, were packed deep into my bedroll. "It will keep you warm and remind you of me whenever nights turn cold like tonight here in 'Skegee."

We clung to each against the cold fresh breeze, waiting for the train that would separate us. All around the railhead others waited too. Base Commander Colonel Parrish, moving among the clusters of people, saying his good-byes and wishing us Godspeed, was heard complimenting Colonel Davis on the decorum and discipline of the officers and enlisted men of the 99th.

Finally, off in the distance the sound of the train whistle split the cold night air and the ground began to rumble as the locomotive rounded the bend coming from the direction of Montgomery. It ground to a halt with a shower of sparks and clouds of steam. Now there was just enough time for one last kiss, one last "Good-bye!" before climbing aboard. In less than a half hour we were all on board.

" 'Board! All aboard!" the conductor chanted. We started moving and, although it was a moonless night, I could see the TAAF kaleidoscope of colored lights slide out of view as we left behind loved ones, memories, and the familiar scenes of the "Nest of Black Eagles."

So. Finally, twenty-six months after being authorized by the War Department on January 16, 1941, the 99th Fighter Squadron, manned entirely by Americans of color, African Americans, was on its way to defend the nation against foreign enemies. The fighting 99th was going to war!

The date was April 2, 1943.

7 Fighting 99th: Over There!

» April 1943–September 1943

Sleep came easily that night. We had had a full day from reveille to midnight, packing, partying, departing. Once the train moved off from TAAF we were assigned to specific coaches where we flopped down, one man to each seat, and surrendered to Morpheus as the train thundered into the night heading toward a POE (port of embarkation) somewhere on the coast. Which coast? Most of us did not have a clue—only the CO and, perhaps, his immediate staff knew. The rest of us, we hoi polloi, did not know and I for one did not care as I fell asleep with bittersweet memories of a nurse just met, perhaps for the last as well as the first time.

I awakened to someone walking through the coach hollering: "Chow time! Chow time! Chow in the dining car in fifteen minutes!"

After breakfast, in the officers coach, spratmo was running wild as everyone tried to guess where we were headed. Attempts to pry any information out of Adjutant Johnson or Ops Officer Roberts were fruitless. And Intelligence Officer Cornelius Vincent, when asked, "Where are we headed?" responded only with his stock advice about how to get along in the army: "You've gotta be shrewd, like G-2!"

So we tried to be shrewd and figure out the answer by noting the names of train stations that we were passing. As the morning wore on it became evident we were heading north through the Carolinas (Alabama and Georgia were left behind while we slept) and Virginia. We crossed the Mason-Dixon shortly after noon and continued north through so-called God's country, reaching the west bank of New York's broad Hudson River just before dusk. Staying on the New Jersey side, the train chugged its way along the rails hugging the foot of the Palisades, finally screeching to a halt at its destination: Camp Shanks, New York.

All day long the talk in all the coaches had been about where we were going, on the train and after that: England? North Africa? the Pacific? Now, at least we knew the first answer. As we visited other coaches and chatted with our NCOs and enlisted men, we began to feel the stirrings of comradeship and, if there is such a word, "teamship." In all the months while the squadron was being staffed and trained we had been identified by outsiders in the way we were designated, "the 99th." But now, with no outsiders, that is, no "nonmembers" near, I felt a strong sense of being a part of a special group. I felt an unusually strong bond, a linkage with each and every man of the squadron. And I sensed that others had similar feelings. I sensed it because of so many things said by so many different men during that long train ride from TAAF to Camp Shanks.

I sensed that the 99th was ready in all respects save one—none of its pilots had any experience in aerial combat. It was quite unusual—almost unheard of—for a fighter squadron to begin flying combat missions without having at least a few seasoned combat veterans in its ranks.

But, not to worry. In all other respects it was ready. Thanks to the almost twenty-four months of training that its ground crew officers and enlisted men had absorbed in classrooms and on the job and the average eighteen months of flying training that its twenty-eight pilots had received, the 99th was ready for combat.

In addition to the twenty-eight pilots, the squadron was staffed with eleven nonflying officers, all with vital roles as members of the combat team nicknamed "the Fighting 99th." They were: George Currie, ordnance officer; James O. Freeman, ordnance officer; Hayden Johnson, adjutant; James L. Johnson, engineering officer; Maurice Johnson, flight surgeon; Henry Letcher, transportation officer; George Petross, personnel officer; Bernard Proctor, mess officer; Dudley Stevenson, communications officer; William

Thompson, armament officer; Cornelius Vincent, intelligence officer; Benote Wimp, supply officer. (Hayden Johnson and Maurice Johnson were captains; the others were lieutenants.) James L. Johnson was transferred to another unit shortly after arrival at overseas base; Lieutenant Herbert Carter replaced him as engineering officer.

In addition to the above officers, the 99th Fighter Squadron had two ground officers of AAF Service Detachment Number 99 attached to it to provide field maintenance for its aircraft and vehicles. They were: Captain Elmer Jones, commanding officer, and Lieutenant Thomas Malone, administrative officer.

As for noncommissioned officers and enlisted men, there were 292 listed on Special Orders Number 85, Headquarters, Tuskegee Army Flying School, dated April 1, 1943, including 35 assigned to the AAF Service Detachment Number 99. They were among the best trained in the army air force as witness the fact that 75 percent of them were qualified for OCS (Officer Candidate School) and that most of them had technical training at Chanute Air Field and other specialist training schools. Most important, perhaps, was the fact that they had more than two years of experience in their particular skills on the job. Some of the key NCOs were: First Sergeant Percy Gary, squadron first sergeant; Technical Sergeant Fred Archer, armorer NCO; Technical Sergeant Clovis Bordeaux, communications NCO; Master Sergeant Alexander Crawford, flight line chief; Master Sergeant Ellsworth Dansby, flight line chief; Staff Sergeant Wendel Le Fleure, operations chief clerk; Technical Sergeant Donald Quander, instrument NCO; Staff Sergeant William Warner, parachute-rigger NCO.

Considering all of the expertise of our ground support officers, NCOs, and enlisted men, we were ready for combat. Except for the lack of any seasoned combat veterans, our pilots were ready, too. Quiet as it was kept, we were almost overtrained, near jaded, and bored by the long delay in being ordered into combat to put our skills to the test. For example, most of our pilots had more than 300 hours in their Form 5 (flight log) including the 200+ hours of aviation cadet flying time and, in the P-40, flying time from checkout flights, formation flying, navigation trips, aerial and ground gunnery, acrobatics, instrument flying, and night flying. After my last flight at TAAF, my Form 5 showed a total of 538 hours, including 207 hours in the P-40; add to that the 90 hours flown in the CPT Program, I had 628 hours of experience as a pilot. I personally felt ready.

So. Why the delay in ordering the squadron overseas? The problem was an old one, older than the Republic itself. Its name? Jim Crow!

Jim Crow delayed—almost killed off—the "Tuskegee Experiment" before it was born. The fact is that the top brass of the War Department did not want Negroes in the U.S. Army Air Corps. At the very top of the corps, the commanding general, Henry "Hap" Arnold, expressed the view that it would take too long to train pilots and ground crews to be of any use in the war. And when the decision was reached to form the 99th, he recommended that the unit be deployed to a remote location such as Antigua or Saint Lucia in the Caribbean.

With such an attitude at the very top one wonders how the "Tuskegee Experiment" ever got started at all! The problem of how to get the air corps to accept and train Negroes as pilots, mechanics, armorers, and radio technicians could be stated in two words: racial prejudice, with all its aspects, shades, and dimensions. The solution came through the efforts of several persons.

One was the wife of the president of the United States of America. During a visit to Tuskegee Institute to check on a polio treatment facility at the hospital on behalf of her polio-stricken husband, Eleanor Roosevelt discovered that the airplanes she saw flying around the area were piloted by Negroes. Curious, she inquired and was introduced to "Chief" Charles Alfred Anderson, the "granddaddy of Black aviation" who had taught himself to fly in 1926 when no White instructor would teach him. After a pleasant flight with "Chief," against the advice of her Secret Service entourage, she returned to Washington and urged the president to remove the barriers against Negroes in the Army Air Corps.

Another was Yancey Williams, who filed a suit to compel the army to accept his application for flight training. Yet another was Spann Watson, who had also filed suit as a backup to Williams's suit. Interestingly enough, the announcement that the U.S. Army was beginning to accept applications from Negroes was made on January 16, 1941, the day that Yancey Williams's suit was filed in the Superior Court of Washington, D.C. Both Williams and Watson got into the aviation cadet program and won their wings and commissions as second lieutenants in the U.S. Army Air Corps.

Judge William Hastie, civilian aide to the secretary of war, had been a gadfly goading the War Department to do the right thing about enlisting Negroes in the Army Air Corps through his efforts beginning in the late 1930s.

Some of this background information about the origins of the "Tuskegee Experiment" was common knowledge. Much of it was news to me, however, which I learned during the long train ride from TAAF. Now, at Camp Shanks, I knew much more. But like most of the guys I was still in the dark about where the 99th was bound next.

During the next twelve days we were issued equipment of all kinds needed for combat overseas: bedrolls, gas masks, .45 automatic pistols.

Winter clothing was issued to each man. Aha! So now we knew. We were going to England. "Good!" I thought. "I may get a chance to meet my Uncle Wilmot, my mother's brother who lives in a London suburb and whom I have never seen, except in a snapshot."

Each evening some of us were given liberty to visit relatives and friends or just to "do the town" — the Big Apple. Because it was my hometown, my classmates, Brooks and Jamison, went with me to meet my folks in the Bronx. After a bus ride across the George Washington Bridge we caught a taxi for the five-mile trip to my home. Along the way I pointed out points of interest:

"The George Washington Bridge that we just crossed was opened the same day my sister, Pauline, was born, October 25, 1931.

"There's Presbyterian Medical Center," and "Now we're passing Stitt Junior High where I attended," and "We are now going through 'Sugar Hill' where I grew up. . . . Now we're at the top of the viaduct, seventy-five feet above the ground. Over there on the left is the Polo Grounds, home of the New York Giants, and over there on the right is . . . is . . . my gosh! It's my Aunt Daisy, waiting at the trolley car stop! Driver," I said, "pull over to the curb!"

He did. Leaning out of the window I greeted her; we hadn't seen each other since I had gone away to Tuskegee nineteen months before.

"Hi, Aunt Daisy! Where are you going? Can we give you a lift?"

"Charlie! What are you doing here? I thought you were at Tuskegee."

"I was until last week. My squadron is heading overseas and my buddies and I are on liberty tonight. So we were heading to see the folks in the Bronx."

"Guess what?" she said. "That's where I'm going. I was just waiting for the trolley."

"Great! Come on with us, Aunt D."

As she was settling into the front seat I introduced Brooks and Jamison to her. We all surprised my parents, sister, and brother when we knocked at their door and spent a pleasant, although emotion-charged, farewell-we're-off-to-war/God-go-with-you visit. Mom's tears as she hugged me when we left almost did me in!

Back at Camp Shanks we kept gearing up to go. Our CO and about six members of his staff were going off somewhere every day, returning late in the evening. We rank-and-file people wondered what was going on. We soon found out. After supper on April 15 we were told to pack up our gear and load on buses outside our barracks. A short, one-hour trip to a dock brought us to our troop ship, the USS *Mariposa*. That's when we learned that Colonel Davis was the executive officer aboard ship and his staff held all the key positions aboard that ship during the voyage. I was extremely proud to be a member of the 99th! We had not yet proved our mettle in combat but this was an auspicious start. And soon the world would learn about our exploits overseas because we had with us a war correspondent assigned to accompany us wherever the war took us, namely Tom Young, Jr., of the *Norfolk Journal and Guide*.

Early next morning the good ship *Mariposa* eased out of New York harbor through fog. As it moved out onto the broad Atlantic and the fog lifted, I expected to see a flotilla of ships sailing east-

The Dryden family at home, at 800 Home Street, Bronx, New York, April 1943. Left to right: Pauline (12), Denis (17), Charles Levy Tucker ("Brother Rob") Dryden, Violet Adina ("Sister Vie") Dryden, and 2nd Lt. Charles W. Dryden on farewell visit before going overseas with the 99th Fighter Squadron.

ward in a huge convoy. I saw . . . nothing! There was no convoy. We were going to run the gauntlet of the Nazi sub–infested Atlantic alone. A chilling thought.

My billet was the middle bunk of a triple-decked bunk in a cabin shared with eleven other officers with just one commode and shower for that room. Somehow we survived the inconveniences of the voyage. Daily "abandon ship" drills were held, and we were required to wear our life vests at all times when moving about.

On the stern of the ship was a gun position that was test fired by a gun crew every day. Movies were shown topside every night. We were lucky to have a fair weather crossing, which enabled us to see the stars and try to figure out where we were headed—to no avail, however, because one night the Big Dipper was at the stern, the next night at the bow, the next at port, and the next on the starboard side. Wondering why we were wandering all over the Atlantic, we asked a crew member. He said: "We're trying to outrun a sub on our tail!"

We didn't know if he was spoofing us, but in any case we made port safely, after nine days at sea, when we docked at Casablanca, French Morocco. So much for our "shrewd" guess about England and my hopes of seeing my Uncle Will. Instead here we were in North Africa, in tropic temperature, clad in winter woolens and sweating profusely by the time we disembarked down the gangplank to load onto trucks to go to . . . wherever. But there were no trucks. Instead we marched about three miles under the broiling African sun, in full field gear, to our bivouac area on a hillside on the outskirts of Casablanca. As if that trek were not irksome enough, as we were marching along first on the hot, asphalt streets of Casablanca and then the dusty roads on the outskirts, we saw our broken-legged bridegroom, Lieutenant Lane, pass by riding on a jeep, his cast-encased leg resting on the fender, his face wreathed in a big smile as he needled us with: "OK, you Dummies, on the double!"

Good-natured threats to break his other leg filled the air turned blue with cusswords. He was probably saved from bodily harm by the fact that the next day was Easter Sunday, April 24.

Soaked with sweat we flopped on the ground in the shelter of a large pyramidal tent, most of us dropping off to sleep that late afternoon from sheer exhaustion. It had been a trying day with nothing but C-rations for chow. I, for one, had no interest in supper that night. After a full night's sleep I was refreshed when awakened for reveille and an inspection by the CO. We learned that "the Old Man" was ticked off by our unmilitary conduct the night before and that we would be expected to conduct ourselves in a military manner even though we were in the field. Spit and polish was still the order of the day.

On Easter Day, Colonel Davis and his staff were busy finalizing arrangements for movement to our first home in North Africa. The rest of us got acquainted with that part of our motherland, the sights, sounds, and smells of Casablanca.

Bands of Arab boys were moving about the hillside constantly, like shifting desert sands driven by the winds, the difference being that these clusters of boys were drawn from one place to another on the hillside by the groups of GIs bivouacked there. As they scuttled from group to group, the boys hawked their wares, which they carried inside their mattress-cover garments. A GI mattress cover with two holes cut into its closed end for leg holes, two holes near the top, one on each side, for arm holes, and the open end, with the drawstring tied loosely around the neck, was the standard garment for all of the Arab boys. All of them had their heads shaved except for a topknot of hair near one side of the head and tied with string at the base of the topknot, the ends of the hair hanging loose so that the topknot looked like a palm tree on the top of a dune.

Inside their closed-bottom garments they carried unbelievable merchandise. I saw different ones with a pair of GI shoes, oranges, carton of cigarettes, a roll of francs that would choke a horse, C-rations. One boy had a live chicken in his mattress coverall! They kept up a constant stream of chatter: "Hey, GI, you want shoes? You want cigarettes? I got sister, you want . . . ?"

They were between the ages of about seven to about fifteen. We were warned by some GIs who had been there a day or so before we arrived to beware of these accomplished young thieves and pimps. The boys made me think of Fagin's boy thieves in Dickens's *Oliver Twist*.

The strangest Easter I had ever experienced ended with orders to prepare to board a train into the interior the next day.

By midafternoon the squadron was loaded aboard a rickety train of ancient vintage. One coach hooked up behind the steam engine was followed by about a dozen cattle cars, the *quarante huite* ("forty and eight"), that hauled the doughboys around France during World War I. It was our home for the next twenty-four hours, which is how long it took for the train to cover the 150 miles to our destination: Oued N'Ja, French Morocco. Nothing more than a rural meadowland at the foot of the Atlas Mountains and about ten miles north of the French-Arab town of Meknes, Oued N'Ja had been bulldozed level to be used as an airfield and had a large race-track-like circle, a few hundred yards in diameter, cut out in the meadow grass, for use as a simulated dive-bombing target.

Very soon after disembarking, the squadron's pyramidal tents were erected for the housing of all personnel and for orderly room and flight line activities. Already standing was a wooden operations shack and a small one-story control tower. So we were ready to begin flying operations the day after we arrived. However, there were no airplanes on the field, and a week passed before the squadron got word that planes were available for our use.

We used that week to settle in and get acquainted with the surrounding terrain, the local people, and customs. First of all we were advised by our flight surgeon, Captain Maurice "Pie Train" Johnson, about health and hygiene precautions: Don't eat fresh fruit obtained locally because the farmers fertilize their crops with "night soil" (human excrement), which produces very big oranges and the like but also causes big gastric problems, like diarrhea; drink only water from the Lister bag, located in the mess hall area, that has been treated with halazone tablets to avoid various intestinal maladies; take quinine tablets daily to ward off malaria.

The latter gave me a problem. Quinine tablets caused me to suffer severe headaches and the substitute, atabrine, was not much better. The daily dose of either one put me out of action and caused me to miss marching with the squadron in a parade of Allied units in the city of Fez to celebrate the defeat of Nazi armies at Bizerte and Tunis on May 9 and their ouster from Africa. That's when I decided that the remedy was worse than the malady could ever be, and I stopped taking the medications. The result was no more headaches, so I was able to visit Fez anyway on another occasion.

Josephine Baker, the celebrated African American entertainer, resident of France, and darling of Europe's music halls and bistros, was performing in Fez at the sultan's palace. She invited the men of the 99th to a performance that was a showstopper, really something to write home about, which I did in my second letter to the folks back home. My first letter was written the day after we landed in Casablanca and, like everybody else in the squadron, I tried to be clever and tell my family in New York and Pete at TAAF that we had landed after nine days at sea and that I had a great time at "Rick's Place" that night. "Rick's," of course, was the nightclub in the film *Casablanca,* which was going the rounds of movie theaters at that time. I learned later that the ruse didn't work because the censors had deleted that reference from my letter, and although the folks at home learned from the news articles filed by our two

A Curtis P-40 and some of the ground crewmen who
kept them flying somewhere "over there" in 1943.

war correspondents that we were in North Africa, they never knew
exactly where.

The 99th remained at Oued N'Ja four weeks, from April 27 until
May 30. V-mail from the States began to catch up with us after
about a week. We had been given our APO (army post office) address before leaving Camp Shanks and had informed our families
and friends, who began writing right away. So the first mail call
brought a bonanza of letters for almost everyone. Besides letters
from my family in New York, my batch included a few from Pete at
TAAF. Her letters introduced me to the romantic poetry of Walter
Benton: It took only a few excerpts from "This Is My Beloved" to
seal her conquest of my heart, for her to become my beloved.

Our airplanes also became available after about a week at Oued
N'Ja. For a couple of reasons, all of us, pilots and ground crewmen
alike, were glad to get our hands on the spanking new P-40Ls that
were waiting for us at an Army Air Corps depot a few miles away.

First of all, a month had passed since the last time either pilots or mechanics had had anything to do with a P-40, and we were all anxious to get back into business. Second, we pilots were eager to get into the air and tangle with some pilots who had been on the *Mariposa* with us. There were seventy-five of them who had been flying P-39 "Airacobras" in the States. Now they were at a nearby grassy field similar to ours and had already received their combat airplanes: A-36s, fast forerunners of the P-51.

With their new planes our former shipmate/friends became our "enemies" as they delighted in using our airfield as a practice simulated dive-bombing target. Several times during our first week without airplanes the Invaders came screaming down toward us in simulated dive-bombing attacks, roaring across our compound and blowing down our tents with their propwash. We were itching for revenge—nothing malicious, of course, just good-natured, clean fun.

We ferried our planes from the depot to our field and promptly began getting acquainted with our assigned plane and ground crew. Staff Sergeant Cecil Curl and Corporal Fritz Mayers were my crew chief and armorer, respectively. Like me they were both from New York, so what could be more fitting than to give our high-speed "baby" the same name as the famous subway express in New York: A-Train. We agreed on the name but I suggested it not because of the subway train but because I loved the jazz number played by Duke Ellington's orchestra that was rocking the USA: "Take the A-Train." For whatever reason, the squadron painter emblazoned on both sides of the nose of my airplane a large "A-Train."

Just to have new planes rather than hand-me-down relics such as we had at TAAF was a motivator for us. But we also got our kicks from mock dogfighting with our A-36 neighbors next door and returning the favor of blown-down tents as we buzzed their airdrome.

With daily flights we retuned our skills in formation flying, sometimes by Flights A, B, or C, other times the entire squadron, and occasionally just a single ship. On one such flight Lieutenant Bud Clark had a malfunctioning landing gear system that failed

"A-Train II," Lt. Dryden, and crew chief, Sgt. Cecil Curl,
at Fardjouna, Tunis, June 1943.

to lower the gear completely. Coolly he circled the field to burn off the fuel then bellylanded with minimum damage to the plane. For his professional airmanship Bud was designated Yank of the Month by the popular Army Air Corps newspaper, *Yank*.

Another feat of airmanship was performed by Lieutenant Leon Roberts, who flew his plane back to base after the top of his rudder and vertical stabilizer were chopped off as he flew under an unseen cable while flying in formation. Reporting to his flight leader that he had felt a jolt and then noticed that his directional control seemed strange, he was told by one of the other members of the formation that part of his tail was missing. Although urged to bail out before losing control completely, he doggedly flew the plane several minutes to return to base. Such was the determination of the 99th pilots to succeed that they showed themselves to be among the best pilots anywhere in the theater of operations.

We still lacked a vital ingredient, however: combat-wise veterans among our leaders. The next best thing was to be tutored by combat veterans. Soon after we got our planes we were visited by one of the best fighter pilots in the business at that time: Colonel Philip Cochran, the real-life model for the Colonel "Flip Corkin" of the popular "Terry and the Pirates" cartoon. During the Allies' desert campaign against Field Marshal Erwin Rommel's Afrika Corps, Colonel Cochran had proved his dive-bombing skill by dropping a 500-pounder smack atop a Nazi high command headquarters. He had also developed dogfighting tactics in several skirmishes with Luftwaffe pilots. Along with two other P-40 combat veterans of the desert campaign, Major Ralph Keyes and Major Robert Fackler, he spent about a week with us at Oued N'Ja.

We learned much about our adversaries from that trio. For me the most important information was about how our P-40L "Kittyhawks" compared with Field Marshal Hermann Goering's fleet of fighters. Colonel Cochran told us that because both of the primary fighter planes being used by the Luftwaffe in the theater of operations, the ME-109 and the FW-190, could outrun, outclimb, and outdive the P-40, we were going to be among the most courageous pilots in the war. We would have to stay and fight simply because we were too slow to be able to run away!

"Don't worry about that, however," he told us, "because the P-40 can outturn every fighter the Germans have except one built by the Italians, the Macchi 202. But there are not many of those in the theater. So all you have to do when you get jumped by an ME-109 or a Focke Wulfe is to get into a tight turn, reef it in as tight as you can without stalling, and just wait him out. If he tries to stay with you in the turn you will eventually end up on his tail."

With such information, and many other tidbits of tactics and techniques of survival in aerial combat, I felt more than ever ready for my baptism of fire. The time for that initiation was approaching as the squadron received orders to move to a forward base on Cape Bon, south of Tunis. Our new airdrome was in a dried lake bed in a rural area with the Arab name Fardjouna, located near the small town of Menzel Temime, 40 miles due east of Tunis. The move was organized in two echelons: The ground echelon was to travel by motor vehicles in convoy on the spotty—sometimes good, other times terrible—roads of Morocco, Algeria, and Tunisia; the air echelon was flight planned to cover the 980-mile trip with refueling stops at Oran, on the Mediterranean coast, and at Blida, 20 miles south of Algiers where we would RON (remain overnight), then, next morning, take off to Fardjouna with a refueling stop at Telergma, 20 miles south of Constantine, Algeria. The air echelon was organized into two sections of fourteen airplanes each, with the CO, Colonel Davis, leading the first section followed about a half hour later by the second section led by operations officer, Captain Spanky Roberts.

All eight of us in B-Flight were in the second section. Midmorning of May 30 we shook the dust of Oued N'Ja and took off heading east on the first leg to our first stop, Oran, 313 statute miles, as the crow flies, over some low but rugged mountains. At normal cruise the ETE (estimated time en route) figured to be one and a half hours. Willie Ashley was my wingman.

About an hour after takeoff, Willie began having engine trouble and he couldn't keep up with the formation. He called: "Dryden, Ashley here. My coolant light is on. I'm overheating. Gotta put this thing down somewhere. Over."

"Roger, 'Beefly' [his nickname]," I answered. "Oujda is about thirty miles to the right of our course in a valley. You can make it from this altitude even if it quits. Just hold it at 10,000 until we're over the airport, if you can, then we'll spiral down to land. I'll lead you in. Over."

"Roger, Hoss!"

Although Jamison, our flight leader, was probably monitoring the transmissions, I made sure he was clued in on what was happening by calling him.

"Jamie, Dryden here. Going down with Ashley into Oujda airport to check on his engine. Rejoin you at Blida. Over."

"Roger, Dryden. See you there."

The rest of the squadron continued on as Ashley and I dropped out of formation and landed at Oujda. Our flight briefing had included information about the airport at Oujda, especially the fact that a U.S. Army Air Corps depot was located there with facilities to repair planes and engines. Even better than that was the fact that there were acres upon acres of brand new P-40s parked there in open storage.

After taxiing in to the ramp we located the aircraft maintenance officer, told him about Ashley's engine trouble, and requested repairs as soon as possible so that we could rejoin our outfit flying east to the war zone.

"Sorry, Lieutenant," he said to me. "We're backed up here at the depot trying to get all these new airplanes ready for combat so we can't take the time to repair your engine. But I can get you out of here today if you just go out there on the field, pick out a plane you like, come back in here and sign an MR [memorandum receipt] for it and go on your way, OK?"

"Sure thing, Major!" Ashley said.

I followed Willie out to the field as he climbed the wing of one of the many planes there and settled into the cockpit to get the feel of it—like trying on a new pair of shoes. A-Train's engine had been acting up a bit back at Oued N'Ja, so I decided to trade it in for a newer one inasmuch as it would only cost my signature on an MR.

We got our new planes gassed up and took them up for a test hop. Satisfied that everything was working OK on both planes, we retrieved our bedrolls from the small baggage compartment aft of the cockpits of our old planes. By then it was dusk, so we decided to RON in a transient BOQ and strike out for Blida in the morning.

We took off at first light, headed for Blida 300 miles further east, hoping to catch up with the rest of the squadron. After one and a half hours in the air we landed at Blida only to find that the squadron had already left on the next leg—that is, except three guys who were having a variety of problems with their airplanes and required maintenance. With Ashley and me there were now five of us trailing behind the outfit. My new plane purred like a kitten on the flight to Blida, but Ashley's new one acted up. The next day was spent trying to get all five planes ready to go. No such luck.

Our squadron SOP (standing operating procedure) required that we operate at least in pairs on all missions, and because I was the senior ranking officer of the group of stragglers I should have remained at Blida until all five airplanes were ready. However, I got antsy, anxious to rejoin the outfit, and I rationalized that because my airplane was OK, my duty was to rejoin the squadron as soon as possible. So early the next morning I took off to Telergma,

203 miles east of Blida, flying above more rugged terrain that included a 7,572-foot mountain peak just 8 miles to the north of a course that provided virtually no navigation aids such as rivers, roads, railroads, or towns. Fortunately my dead reckoning brought me to Telergma right on my estimated time of arrival (ETA). After refueling, off I went on the final leg to Fardjouna, 262 miles, one hour and fifteen minutes distant.

One hour after takeoff the city of Tunis and the Bay of Tunis came into view about 5 miles off to the left. Dead ahead I saw a large dry lake bed with P-40s parked in revetments clustered in groups around the perimeter.

"I've made it!" I crowed, as I stopped worrying about possibly running across the path of some Luftwaffe pilot looking for a target of opportunity. Although the Germans had been chased off the continent three weeks earlier, there were sporadic air raids against Allied forces. I would have been a choice victim for some kill-hungry Nazi because I had no ammo in my guns.

There were no paved runways on the vast lake bed but there appeared to be tracks beside some of the clusters of revetments. "Probably carved out by takeoffs and landings," I thought.

Figuring that there were a few different squadrons using the lake bed and not knowing which cluster of planes was the 99th's, I peeled off over one area, landed, and taxied up toward a ground crewman who was signaling me where to park. After I had shut down the engine he jumped up on the wing and I knew at once that I was in the wrong area. So did he, when I unsnapped my oxygen mask. Before I could ask my question, "Where is the 99th area?" he volunteered the answer with a thick drawl: "You must be lookin' for them there Cullud boys. They're over there, 'bout two miles from heah, Lootenant," pointing in the general direction of the coast.

Two miles was too far to taxi across the lake bed, so I took off and didn't bother to retract my wheels. By the time I reached 800 feet I was over the cluster of revetments the GI had pointed toward, and I landed again, this time for good, as I saw one of our squadron flight line mechanics signaling me where to park as I taxied in. Now I knew I was "home," among friends. I was elated over having navigated, solo, the 465 miles from Blida to Fardjouna, over rugged, virtually trackless mountain terrain, strange territory I had never seen before.

In the operations tent Spanky Roberts greeted me with: "Hi, Dryden. What kept you? How come you're solo? Where are the rest of the guys? And how come you're not in the A-Train? The plane you just got out of doesn't have your A-Train on the nose!"

Briefing him on what had happened since I had dropped out of formation to escort Willie Ashley to the Oujda airport two days before, I answered all his questions and guessed that the other four guys would arrive probably in a day or so. As we were talking a flight of eight of our P-40s thundered overhead and peeled off to land, returning from a dive-bombing mission on the island of Pantelleria. A few minutes later the pilots piled out of the flight line jeep and trooped into the ops tent for G-2's mission debriefing.

"Hey, JP," one of them ribbed me, "where've you been while we're fighting the war?" The rest chimed in, teasing, signifying that I was a mere "junior pilot," still wet behind the ears. After two days of combat they fancied themselves "veterans," and I had to admit they had faced shot and shell—and I had not. That changed the next day when Spanky scheduled me to fly a dive-bombing mission as wingman for Jamison, B-Flight leader.

Midafternoon, June 4, I saw shots fired at me in anger, with malice aforethought and with intent to kill! And certainly with provocation because, in a screaming dive, the way Colonel Cochran had taught us to do when we were just learning back at Oued N'Ja, I was attempting to place a 500-pound bomb on a German target on Pantelleria. Following my leader in the dive I saw red tracers streaking past my cockpit, hundreds of them, looking like a river of red sparkles that I saw out of the corners of my eyes and not directly because I was focused on the gunsight mounted atop the instrument panel. Concentrating on hitting the target, I didn't have time to get scared. It wasn't until I pulled up from the bomb run that the thought crossed my mind: "They were trying to kill me!" Only then did I tweak a bit.

Pantelleria was only forty-seven miles due east of our airstrip, out in the Mediterranean. At first all that open water was worrisome but I got used to it by the time of my first encounter with the Luftwaffe in the air. That encounter came a few days later, on June 9. I was leading a flight of six B-Flight members on a patrol just west of Pantelleria. Willie Ashley, Sid Brooks, Lee Rayford, Leon Roberts, Spann Watson, and I were at about 8,000 feet flying in the "company front," sometimes called "line abreast," formation that we had been taught by Colonel Cochran, Major Keyes, and Major Fackler back at Oued N'Ja.

In "company front" all the pilots fly their planes abreast, that is, on a line with the leader and looking toward the leader while maintaining proper position in the formation. When any member of the flight sights a bogey he calls the leader and reports the "clock" location of the bogey relative to our formation as well as the relative altitude, for example: "Trooper Leader, Trooper Three here. 'Bogies,' five o'clock high."

That is just about what I heard on our squadron frequency that afternoon. I responded with: "Trooper Three, Leader here. Watch 'em."

So far, Trooper Three's sightings were "bogies" (unknowns) and he was now responsible to alert the flight members if he later identified them as "bandits" (enemies). A couple minutes later my headset crackled:

"Trooper Leader, Trooper Three here. Several bandits, seven o'clock, diving."

"Trooper Three, call the break!" I said as I jerked my head around, straining my eyes to pick up the attacking bandits. The reflection of the bright sun on the Mediterranean blinded me to the dots that were rapidly closing in on our formation. I could not see the enemy but I heard a tense voice in my headset.

"Trooper Flight, Three here, break right, NOW!"

Instantly, without any hesitation, six P-40s wheeled around "on a dime" in a gut-wrenching, 180-degree tight turn to confront the enemy, the pilots flicking their gun switches and gun sights ON as they prepared for this first air battle with the enemy by any of the 99th pilots. Suddenly facing the thirty-six .50-caliber machine guns of our flight, the attacking planes scattered. So did we as we took off after them.

Up until that very moment I had harbored a fear deep within myself. It wasn't as much a fear of the enemy as it was the fear of which President Franklin Roosevelt spoke when he proclaimed that "the only thing we have to fear is fear itself." When I saw the swastikas on those ME-109s and felt the urge to "go get 'em" and a surge of adrenaline at the prospect of being the first Negro to shoot down an enemy airplane in aerial combat, I knew that I had conquered my fear of possibly turning yellow and turning tail at the first sign of the enemy.

As it turned out none of us scored a victory on that mission. Ashley damaged one of the enemy planes but wasn't able to follow the smoking plane to see if it crashed, and we did not have gun cameras at that stage of the war so he could not confirm a victory. After the break right into the attacking fighters I saw a formation of medium bombers several thousand feet above us and I climbed to engage them. No luck there as my P-40 couldn't climb fast enough to catch up to them and we were not equipped with oxygen for flights above 12,000 feet. Somewhere around 16,000 feet I passed out briefly. I came to a few seconds later with my plane in a shallow dive.

By now, about fifteen minutes after the initial "Break right!" call, the sky was clear of enemy fighters and our guys had begun to form up. I rallied them by rocking my wings and calling: "Trooper Flight, Trooper Leader here, rocking my wings. Join up. Let's return to base," as I started a wide turn to the west, heading home to Africa.

Twenty minutes later we landed, ending a historic flight. True enough we had no confirmed victories but, happily, no losses. As for me, I was relieved to know that although my nickname in the cadets may have been "Diapers," in combat it would never be "Chicken." That in itself was a personal victory.

In higher headquarters' reports about that first-encounter mission, we were criticized for having scattered, "panicky" in the face of the enemy. The truth of the matter is that each man was eagerly trying to be the first to down an enemy.

The bombing of Pantelleria continued around the clock for the next five days. In addition to our own dive-bombing missions there was a constant stream of medium and heavy bombers flying high above our airstrip on their way to dump their loads on the hapless island on which the Germans had built an airstrip and hangars with repair shops and stores of ammunition. By June 11 the defenders had had enough. Probably shell shocked by the incessant pounding, they literally waved the white flag. Thus Pantelleria became the first target ever to surrender to air power, exclusively, with no need for ground troops.

That campaign earned for each member of the squadron our first battle star on our Mediterranean-African-European Theater ribbon.

The next step in the war in the Mediterranean was Sicily. The Germans had retreated to the island off the toe of the Italian boot after being evicted from North Africa and had beefed up their defenses, airfields, and antiaircraft batteries all along the southern coast. That's where our next targets would be. Before the start of Operation Husky, the invasion of Sicily, however, we had a few days' breather, which allowed us time to get acquainted with our surroundings.

The squadron's ground echelon had arrived from Oued N'Ja covering the 1,000+ miles in a convoy of trucks and various motor vehicles over rough, mostly dirt roads. "Junior," our squadron mascot, was with them. "Junior" was an Arab boy, orphaned by the war, about eleven years old, who attached himself to the outfit back in Oued N'Ja, endearing himself to everyone by his good manners and his willingness to take on little tasks in the camp, like shining shoes or doing KP in the mess hall. He spoke little English at first but picked up GI jargon quickly. And he was honest. He was not like the Fagin-type hustlers we had seen on the hillside outside Casablanca when we first landed.

In Fardjouna we were "adopted" by another Arab boy, Tony, a young teenager who, like the young hustlers on the Casablanca hillside, would lie, steal, and provoke fights with "Junior." Tony was banished from our campsite *toute suite*.

I got a chance to try out my high school French during the breather following the fall of Pantelleria. The CO approved one-day passes to visit Tunis, about forty miles from our strip. Each day one of the flights was given the use of two five-passenger weapons carriers for twenty-four hours. When B-Flight's turn came, I drove one of the vehicles. I thought of Lieutenant Nathaniel Freeman, who had taught me to drive his "Betsy" back at TAAF, and was glad not to be embarrassed by not knowing how to drive.

The road into Tunis was sometimes good, in short stretches of asphalt, most times bad, in long stretches of dirt ruts carved out by tank treads during the ground battles that had led to the ouster of the Germans just weeks before. Approaching the outskirts of Tunis, downwind, a strong aroma of olive oil suggested that every house in the city was cooking lunch. The fragrance of French-Arab cuisine was mouth watering, so the five of us in my vehicle stopped in a small restaurant for a snack, using a combination of English and schoolboy French to place our orders.

Afterward we explored Tunis. Lieutenant Jimmy Freeman, one of our ground support officers, and I teamed up and we went looking for the USO, where he had heard that a friend of his was on the staff as a hostess. As we were walking at leisure through the narrow streets, looking in shop windows and at the wares of sidewalk vendors, we were accosted by an MP coming toward us.

"Soldiers!" he barked. "What are you doing with .45s on your hip and impersonating officers? I'm gonna run you in; you're under arrest!"

Jimmy Freeman was a bear of a man, over six feet tall and about 220 pounds of bone and pure, hard muscle. He had the strength of a weight lifter—he delighted in bench pressing guys who weighed more than he by just lifting them high over his head—and the skill of a boxer who had competed in the 1936 Olympics in the heavyweight division. Fearless and usually even-tempered, slow to anger, this time he virtually exploded with rage. Taking out his wallet he extracted his ID card, which identified him by name, rank, and serial number as an officer of the U.S. Army Air Corps. Then he demanded the MP's name and the name and location of his unit, saying sternly: "Soldier, don't you recognize rank when you see it? Don't you see these gold bars on my collar and the silver bars on this other officer's collar? We think your commanding officer needs to know how stupid and insubordinate you are. I'm going to report your insulting manner and recommend that you be relieved as a military policeman. Do you understand me?"

"Y-Y-Yes, Suh," the hapless MP drawled, stammering as his face turned beet red. I almost felt sorry for him because Jimmy's size would intimidate anyone. However, I was just as enraged by the MP's insulting manner. Jim and I found the MP's unit and filed a report with his CO, who didn't seem at all impressed by our complaint against one of his troops. I had the notion that no disciplinary action would ensue, but at least we had gotten the matter off our chests. I felt that we had met Jim Crow overseas and that the poison of bigotry had already been spread abroad by some GIs in the theater who displayed plantation attitudes even as they fought to defeat the "master race" Nazis and their notions of racial superiority.

In their headlong rush to escape advancing Allied armies, the Germans left a lot of equipment in the vicinity of our airstrip. Some of our men claimed ownership of abandoned vehicles: J. B. Knighten had found a German jeep; Gene Carter had a motorcycle. Here and there one could see the hulks of crashed airplanes, both Allied and German, that were great sources of souvenirs. The main problem with scrounging mementos from German equipment was the risk of being booby-trapped and suffering injury or death. The only souvenir I got up enough nerve to take was the clock from the instrument panel of a wrecked British Spitfire.

Booby traps could be found out in the fields around Fardjouna. The most common ones were the Italian-made "tomatoes," red hand grenades that were left behind by fleeing Nazis who had sown the surrounding area with a number of the lethal "fruit." The local Arab men avoided the danger of the "tomatoes" by riding their spindly legged donkeys while their wives walked ahead. One day an Arab woman came to our dispensary to ask our medics for help. Her hand had just been blown off by a booby trap. That's all I needed to convince me that the only souvenir I wanted to take home from the war was me, intact, uninjured.

During the short-lived lull in hostilities the 99th flew practice missions to keep our combat formation skills sharp. Between flights our two war correspondents were busy interviewing various men and writing human interest articles and filing them with their news offices back in the States. One day Tom Young of the *Norfolk Journal and Guide* singled me out and asked me, "Who is your favorite person in the entire outfit?"

I begged the question with the truth: "Tom, I have no favorite person. First of all there are the guys I fly with who help me get through our missions and return to base in one piece. Then there are my crew chief who keeps A-Train II running, my armorer who keeps my guns firing, the radioman keeps me in touch with others when danger threatens, the cooks feed me, supply guys clothe and equip me, medics keep me healthy, pay clerks pay me, and mail clerks bring me the V-mail from home that boosts my morale. So, you see, I've got a whole lot of 'favorites' in this outfit." He incorporated some of my comments in one of his articles.

The lull ended after about a week and we resumed daily missions with a new scenario. Target: Sicily, the next step in attacking the "soft underbelly" of Adolf Hitler's Third Reich. Sicily was more than twice the distance from our Fardjouna airstrip as Pantelleria: 120 miles over open water to our first target on the island, German strongholds near Castelvetrano. Our first mission as part of the fighter escort for a large formation of medium bombers attacking that area turned out to be my first taste of combat in dogfights with Luftwaffe pilots. The action was so vivid that even as this is being written a half century later, it is as though my baptism by fire in the sky above Sicily were in the present tense:

» »

"Trooper Blue Three, Trooper Blue Four here—break right!"

Flying number four slot on Bill Campbell's wing, I have yawed A-Train to the inside of a standard rate left turn at about half throttle, just enough thrust of my V-1650 Packard engine to hold position slightly below Bill's plane. We are a two-ship element that is a small part of a huge gaggle of about seventy-two fighters, mostly P-40s, escorting about an equal number of medium bombers: some B-25 "Mitchells," some A-20 "Bostons," but mostly B-26 "Marauders."

All, fighters and bombers alike, are based at various airstrips in North Africa, from Algiers to Tunis.

The targets for the bombers are a network of Luftwaffe airstrips around Castelvetrano near the southern coast, western tip of Sicily. From 8,000 feet I can see the airstrips clearly. The morning sky is cloudless. Visibility is clear as far as the eye can see. There is no haze to impair vision. And yet, for some reason the bombers have not dropped their loads of 500-pounders on their first run over the target area.

"What's wrong?" I wonder. "Can't they find their Initial Point [IP]?" Whatever the reason, the bombers are now doing a full circle to try again. That will take at least three minutes. Plenty of time for the Nazis to scramble their fighter-interceptors.

SOP (standing operating procedure) for Allied fighters escorting bombers calls for the fighters to fly a miles-wide circle around the target while the bombers are dropping their loads. This procedure was designed to avoid exposing the fighters to flak (antiaircraft artillery) unnecessarily. After the bombers have completed their mission, bombs are away, and they head for home, the fighters re-form above, on both sides and behind the formation of "Big Friends," to ward off attacks by enemy "bandits." Ideally this all happens before enemy interceptors can scramble.

Not this time. At least, not the last part. While our Big Friends have been trying to get set to wipe out their targets, all of the seventy-two or so Allied escort fighters have been flying in four-ship flights, following each other around in a wide circle about 1,000 feet above the bombers. Pretty soon we begin to see streaks of dust appearing on the five or six airstrips near Castelvetrano as enemy interceptors scramble. Watching them climb, out of range, to positions above us I tense, anticipating baptism by fire. My first actual dogfight. I begin to sweat (quite proper—baptism requires sprinkling with water). Then—HERE THEY COME! Singly and in pairs. Dogfights erupt all over the sky.

Flying slightly below Campbell's plane and positioned on his left wing about a wingspan apart, I have to look skyward to stay in formation. Boring down on us are two "bandits." Head-on they look like ME-109s. So I call the break again.

"Trooper Blue Three from Blue Four—break right!"

Campbell does not break. Is my transmitter or his receiver, or both, kaput? Try again. Bandits closing fast. No time for call signs this time. Just time enough to say, "Campbell, break right, NOW!"

Still no reaction. Bill must have his eyes on a Nazi straight ahead and can't hear me. As his wingman, my job is to protect his tail. So, flipping my gun and gunsight switches ON while jamming the throttle full forward, "balls to the wall," with hard right rudder, right aileron and stick back in my gut, I break right into a steep, tight climbing turn to face the two 109s.

Red streaks zing past my cockpit as their tracers pepper A-Train II. Squeezing the trigger on the control stick I answer the attackers with a burst of .50-caliber APIT rounds. The tracers show me that some are hitting home.

The Jerries break off their attack and I exult. Maybe I damaged one or maybe both, or maybe my sudden turn into them scared them off. Whatever it is that caused them to abort their attack, I am glad because for one thing they are not shooting at us anymore. For another, more important reason: I have again faced enemy guns fired at me in anger, with intent to kill, and I have not panicked or turned tail and run. I'm beginning to feel like a combat veteran. But the show goes on.

As the two ME-109s pull up into a climb I see the bellies of their planes. Painted yellow. The distinctive markings of "the boys from Abbeville"! In an earlier briefing our G-2 (intelligence officer), Lieutenant Vincent, had told us about the "boys from Abbeville," with their yellow-bellied planes, who had a reputation of being the cream of Field Marshal Hermann Goering's Luftwaffe.

"Ooooweee!" I whoop, nervously, thinking aloud. "A-Train, we got through that one OK!"

But now I have an immediate problem that must be solved at once. I am alone—by myself in a sky churning with swirling dog-fights everywhere I look. What had Colonel Cochran taught us about being caught by oneself in a combat situation?

"First of all," he had said, "don't, repeat, do *not* let it happen. But if it should happen, for instance if your wingman or element leader is shot down, then you must immediately get into a tight turn. Cut your throttle, hold the nose on the horizon with the stick in your gut until the plane shudders, about to stall. Don't spin, though. If you do you'll be dead meat for any bandit who sees you spinning."

Heeding his advice I crank A-Train II into a tight left turn while craning my head and looking over my left shoulder to "clear my tail." Seeing no bandit on my tail I relax a bit, ease up on the stick, and push the throttle forward. A-Train is back to normal cruise, responding to my slight touch on the controls. Good! No damage from the Abbeville boys' ammo.

Now what? Colonel Cochran's next rule: Find a friendly fighter or formation and tag along until out of enemy territory.

Looking around I see friendlies everywhere slugging it out with bandits. Nearest to me is a lone P-40 about 500 feet below me in a level left turn. "Aha!" I think. "I'll join up with him. Don't know what squadron he's from. Really don't care. All I need to see is the U.S. star painted on his fuselage and he and I are about to become buddies."

As I dive to join up with him I see that he already has company — a pair of 109s behind him, in trail. He seems unaware of his danger, has not cleared his tail, and is not taking any evasive action.

I think: "Here's a chance to save a Yank, get one, maybe two victories and be the first of the 99th to down a Nazi in aerial combat."

Excitedly, aggressiveness fired up, I settle in behind the rearmost 109, A-Train's six .50s blazing. I figure I have the correct deflection lead to hit the front 109 without hitting the oblivious Yank. Squeezing off a short burst I see . . . What's this? My tracers are peppering the rear 109. I'm really not much surprised—I never was much good in aerial gunnery practice before we left the States. "Oh well, what the hell," I think, "two Jerries downed would be better but one down ain't bad."

So fascinated am I with the prospect of a victory, the squadron's first victory, that I forget that A-Train II, too, has a tail. Suddenly a stream of red tracers past my canopy snaps me back to reality. Craning my head around to see where my attacker is, I see what looks like a huge corkscrew, spinning and coming fast as if to bore into A-Train's tail. Jerry is only a couple hundred yards behind me firing his machine guns.

Reacting instantly I reef A-Train into a tight left turn, thinking the while: "If this Nazi is fool enough to try to stay with me in this turn, I will wind up on his tail because Colonel Cochran assured us that the P-40 can outturn 109s." Sure enough, as I tighten the turn and watch over my left shoulder, Jerry disappears from view. But not for long.

After about a half minute, maybe less, he begins to reappear. First the top of his canopy. Then his propeller spinner painted with a spiral design that, when spinning, suggests an ominous cork-screw. Then his belly appears: at least it isn't yellow, so he isn't one of the "b-a-a-a-d boys from Abbeville." That's the good news. The bad news is that he is outturning A-Train. G-2's briefing comes to mind: This must be a Macchi 202! His in-line liquid-cooled engine makes him resemble an ME-109, but he is more dangerous with his tight turning ability. Adding to that bad news, he also brings to the fray a nine-millimeter cannon that fires through the prop spinner. Having checked the range by firing his machine guns and seeing his tracers peppering my fuselage he begins firing his cannon.

Looking back at him over my shoulder I am transfixed with hor-ror as I see what looks like small, dirty gray cotton balls coming out of the nose of his plane. It's like having a nightmare in slow motion. It seems to me that if I could hear any sound above the roar of A-Train's engine, and the trip-hammer pounding of my heart, the cotton balls would sound like: Puff, Puff, Puff. Then . . . BANG! I hear that, above the engine's roar and my pounding pulse. I see it as a cannon shell rips a chunk out of my left wing, and I also feel it as A-Train shudders for a moment. My controls are still OK but I think: "I've got to shake this Jerry somehow, fast! With his next hit I may become a flamer and, instead of being the 99th's first aerial victor, I will be its first KIA [killed in action]."

What to do in such a jam? Pray! And I do: "Oh God, please help me!" That I learned from Brother Rob and Sister Vie, not from Colonel Cochran.

Funny the thoughts that flit through your mind when panic

strikes. Once, in the past, during a "hangar flying" bull session a squadron mate, Lee Rayford, had said jokingly: "If you ever have a Jerry on your tail and can't shake him, just unfasten your safety belt and run around the cockpit hollering, 'Help!' " Then, I laughed along with all the other guys. Now, it is not funny at all.

No. No laughter. Just a fervent prayer punctuated with wild "jinking" (flying erratically with sudden changes of direction and altitude) to affect the Macchi's aim and to help me escape certain death. Scanning the sky frantically for help I see the bomber formation heading home to North Africa airstrips with their fighter escorts, leaving Sicily behind. And me. In trouble! The tail assemblies of the retreating B-26s look like top hats and I'm thinking grimly: "If I don't get some help soon my party's over, forever!"

Just then a miracle happens. As I see the retreating formation, one P-40 pulls up, up, and away from his flight and in a tight diving turn he settles in behind my tormentor, his six .50s blazing. The Macchi breaks off its attack on me and heads back to his base. Or so it seems at first.

My rescuer pulls up beside A-Train II. We exchange OK hand signals and head west toward our airstrips on Cape Bon. However we are not home free yet. We still have to fly that 120 miles across the Mediterranean's pretty, blue deep water. We are still in enemy airspace and Jerry doesn't give up easily, especially with stragglers. Although neither my newfound buddy nor I know who the other guy is, we are now a two-ship element, each man able to protect the other man's tail—the basic defensive unit in aerial combat.

As we cross Sicily's coast, heading out over the water, I see a pair of "bogies" (unknowns—they're too far away to be able to identify them as friend or foe) climbing toward us from about ten o'clock low. Being about five miles away and perhaps 5,000 feet below us, they look like P-40s or Spitfires. As they close in, however, we see the black crosses and identify them: ME-109s. "Bandits"!

Attacked from the rear we begin turning into them to deter their thrusts then turning back toward home. Regrouping, they attack again and we turn into them again. And so it goes—two steps forward, one step back—an aerial *danse macabre*. But slowly and surely we are inching our way home in spite of the fact that my rescuer's guns are not firing. Apparently he has spent all of his ammo in a previous dogfight and chasing the Macchi off my tail.

After about ten minutes of this dogfight with the two 109s, I can't believe what I am seeing—the Macchi 202 rejoins the fight. Twisting and turning, breaking left then right to defend against each pass, then running west "balls to the wall" until the next pass, we finally reach Pantelleria. Probably realizing that they are now in our turf the three Jerries halt their attacks and turn back toward Sicily.

Whew!

About ten minutes later, over the 99th's strip I have an almost irresistible urge to do a victory roll before peeling off to land. I don't really think that I have shot down a Nazi but I am elated just to be alive. However something tells me to be content with a normal landing pattern and get A-Train II on the ground gently and safely. I do just that, then taxi into my revetment and shut down the engine, two long hours after our dawn takeoff. I'm bushed and my inch-thick parachute back cushion is soaked clear through with sweat.

While I am filling out the Form 1, my crew chief, Sergeant Cecil Curl, observes, "A-Train was in a scrap, today, eh Lieutenant?"

"Yeah, Sarge."

"Got a bit banged up too, I see."

"Yep. How bad is it?"

"Come take a look at your left wing, Sir."

Climbing out of the cockpit and jumping off the wing onto the ground my knees are a bit shaky from all the exercise I have had horsing A-Train around since dawn. Then looking through the hole, the size of a grapefruit, I see that only three of the thirty-two strands of the aileron control cable are intact. If I had attempted a victory roll they would have snapped under the stress of the maneuver and I would have "bought the farm." Needless to say, I thank God for my deliverance and for the "something" that had told me: "Just land the plane—don't show off." My rescuer turns out to be Jim Knighten, nicknamed "the Eel," one of the 99th's best pilots in everybody's opinion. Thanking him for coming back into the fray, after already heading home, to rescue me, a comrade in trouble, I jokingly remind him of the old custom that "he who saves someone's life must take care of that person until he dies." The Eel chuckles and says: "Anytime, Hoss, anytime. Glad I was able to help."

While waiting for the operations jeep to pick us up, we sit in the shade under A-Train's wing to escape the scorching sun. It must be over 100 degrees in the shade as we compare notes about the hairy air battle we have just survived. In a few minutes the operations clerk, Sergeant Wendell "Windy" Le Fleur, arrives in the jeep. Minutes later we are in the ops tent for debriefing.

Most of the ten other 99th pilots who were on the mission have already been debriefed by G-2. Now it is our turn to tell our story. All the pilots gather around to hear what happened on the mission that caused us to return to base about a half hour after the rest of the squadron. After telling about our experiences during the mission we learn some good news and some bad, really sad, news.

The good news is that Lieutenant Charlie "Seabuster" Hall has shot down a Focke Wulfe 190 over Sicily. Thus he is the first "Negro American" (quoting a 1943 news article in the *Pittsburgh Courier*) to shoot down an enemy plane in aerial combat—a historical first that earns him a unique place in history. It also wins for him the bottle of Coca-Cola that squadron mate, Lieutenant Louis Purnell, has lugged from the United States to North Africa to reward the first man in the squadron to draw blood.

The bad news is that two of our mates have not yet returned to base: Lieutenants James McCullen of Saint Louis, Missouri, and Sherman White of Montgomery, Alabama. None of the guys on the mission reports seeing either Jim or Sherman bail out or crash, so we are all hoping they are only MIA (missing in action) temporarily. As hours pass with no word from rescue units in the area, hope changes to a growing dread that perhaps they will not return after all. Our first losses in combat?

"No, Lord! Please, no!" I pray.

We have lost squadron mates, all in P-40 crashes at TAAF: McGuiness, Davis, and King. We have already had to try to learn how to live with the empty feeling when a buddy is gone. Airplane accidents have a sobering effect on aviators, reminding them that they themselves are also vulnerable to the forces of nature, machine malfunctions, or their own pilot error. Our first encounters with the death of comrades were rough enough.

Our baptism by fire, in the sky over Sicily, was even more so. More so because it was different. Different because in Sicily our mates were shot down by guns fired in anger. With malice afore-thought and intent to kill. Of course our ground school training as aviation cadets had included viewing the War Department training film, *Kill or Be Killed*. It succeeded in convincing us that in war "it's them or us." Add to that my outrage over Nazi atrocities, generally, plus arrogant Aryan claims of racial superiority, particularly, and I was well motivated to fight Hitler and his gangsters. And to lay my life on the line for my country, if need be.

Some days later McCullen and White are still missing and it be-gins to sink in that they will not return. They are KIA—killed in action. Never again will we see Jim McCullen's tricky moves on a basketball court. Or Sherman White's mischievous smile as he "checks the locks" on some hapless victim at the poker table, then rakes in the loser's money as he apologizes with, "Sorry, Hoss!"

The realization makes me sad. Thinking about our loss, the questions that always seem to follow death, arise: Why? Why them? Why now? Why here? and Will their deaths change anything back home?

For example: With their supreme sacrifice in the cause of preserv-ing democracy, can their remains be buried in any plot in any loca-tion in any cemetery anywhere in their native land?

No.

That answer has appeared in morale-blowing hate stories in newspapers that we receive from the States about Negro service-men killed in action but denied burial in lily-White cemeteries in their own hometowns.

The answer is not only No but, probably, NEVER!

Well then, I muse: Why are we here?

To prove we can fly and are willing, like any other citizens, to fight to defend the United States of America against its enemies, foreign and domestic.

What do we expect to gain if we succeed in helping to defeat foreign enemies, overseas?

We expect to help defeat domestic enemies back home: Jim Crow attitudes and practices in government, schools, jobs, churches—everywhere!

Tall order.

And from what we experienced during our training in Alabama, in the early days of the "Tuskegee Experiment," I have my doubts. But as my thoughts return from such weighty, dubious matters, to the events of the day, one thing is certain: The 99th has survived its baptism by fire in Sicily. No doubt about that!

The date: July 2, 1943.

»»»

That afternoon SHAPE Commander General Dwight D. Eisenhower visited the 99th with congratulations for our first victory and condolences for our losses. So we knew that at least the top man at Supreme Headquarters, Allied Powers, Europe acknowledged our existence and our performance in battle.

We were also visited by RAF Air Marshal Cunningham, who briefed us on British SOPs for aerial combat. His visit clued us that something was afoot. That something was Operation Husky, the invasion of Sicily that was launched on July 10.

It was the first landing by Allied forces on Axis territory during World War II. With more than 2,500 ships bringing ashore 115,000 British and 66,000 American troops, plus 14,000 vehicles, 1,800 guns, and 600 tanks, it was the largest amphibious operation in history up until that time.

For the next week we flew patrol missions over the beachhead, the stretch of the southern coastline between Gela and Licata, to keep enemy airplanes from attacking the invasion fleet and troops on the ground, and then returning to the Fardjouna airstrip. The day after the invasion Lieutenant Dick Bolling had engine trouble and bailed out of his P-40, thus becoming our first combat "caterpillar." After spending the night bobbing about on the Mediterranean in his life raft, he was rescued by an Allied naval vessel and rejoined the squadron a couple of days later.

Our move to Sicily came on July 19. At dawn that day a fleet of about thirty C-47 transport planes landed on our airstrip and were loaded with all our squadron equipment and supplies to relocate us to an airstrip near Licata. Our ground support personnel were airlifted in the "Goony Birds" and our pilots escorted the transports across the 120 miles of the blue waters of the Mediterranean. By midafternoon the move was completed. We had left Africa, with nothing left behind but our mascot "Junior," the little Arab boy.

By the next morning we were launching attacks on German targets all over the island, dive-bombing and strafing in close support of Allied armies on the island. With Hitler's armies retreating to the east, the Allies enjoyed air superiority and our airstrip at Licata did not have to worry about air raids. Between missions we had time to read letters and newspapers sent from home and to write letters. And poetry. J. B. Knighten, "the Eel," borrowed a typewriter from squadron supply and cranked out a ditty to the tune of "Halls of Montezuma":

> From the cotton fields of 'Skegee to the shores of Tripoli,
> We will fight our country's battles in the name of Booker T.
> Booker T. says chop more cotton, Booker T. says hoe more
>   corn.
> We will never leave the cotton fields where old Uncle Tom
>   was born.

And there were some others too raunchy to mention.

Whenever boredom set in between missions there was always pinochle or poker. Poker was usually a low stakes game until our first group of replacement pilots joined us on July 23. Lieutenants Howard Baugh, John Gibson, and John Morgan went along with the game as we had been accustomed to playing, but the fourth man, Ed "Topper" Toppins, changed the poker sessions to high stakes, causing faint-hearted players like me to fold when he charged $75.00 to go to "third street" (draw a third card). "Topper" was as much a daredevil in the air as he was at the poker table.

All four replacements were good pilots who fitted into the ranks of the old-timers with few problems.

The living was easy at Licata. Some lived in pup tents, some like me preferred a lean-to, while some others slept in foxholes that we all had dug after a night air raid on Gela, ten miles east of us. We were bivouacked a short distance from the beach and could get a cool dip in the sea after a hot day in the cockpit. As much a joy as it was, the beach brought sorrow to the squadron on July 27 when Tech Sergeant Edsel A. Jett was caught in the undertow and drowned.

Two weeks later, in a midair collision during a practice mission, we lost Lieutenant Paul Mitchell. The other pilot, Sam Bruce, was able to bail out and survived the collision.

Then came good news about the war: Sicily fell completely under Allied control when Nazis in the city of Messina were defeated. So ended the Sicilian campaign on August 17, five weeks after the invasion at Gela.

Five more replacement pilots arrived from the States in late August: Lieutenants Robert Deiz, Elwood Driver, Herman "Ace" Lawson, Clinton "Beau" Mills, and Henry "Herky" Perry. Like the first group of replacements, the second also fitted into the outfit smoothly.

Come September 2, we lost our CO to the Third Fighter Command in the States, where he testified at a U.S. congressional board of inquiry about the alleged lack of aggressiveness as "evidenced" by the fact that in the four months of our overseas deployment we had downed only one enemy plane. Lieutenant Colonel Davis explained that, first of all, the 99th's missions had been mostly air-ground support missions in which we got few chances to tangle with the enemy in the air and, second, attached to the 33rd Fighter Group for combat missions, the 99th had little to no cooperation from the commanding officer or his staff in operational matters. In fact, in correspondence to his higher headquarters, Colonel William Momyer had been obviously uninformed and patently unfair in evaluating the squadron's performance. Colonel Davis stated his case so well that the War Department decided to go ahead with the activation of the 332nd Fighter Group, plans for which had been tabled because of lack of faith in the combat ability of Negro pilots. Davis was named commanding officer of the 332nd.

Meanwhile back in Sicily, Operations Officer Major Spanky Roberts was left in charge of the 99th as CO. Two days later, on September 4, the squadron moved sixty-two miles north to an airstrip near the town of East Termini on the northern coast of Sicily washed by the Tyrrhenian Sea. The airstrip ran parallel to and was about a half mile from the beach. We pitched our tents on the slope of a low hill about another half mile further inland. The view of the Tyrrhenian Sea, with its deep blue water sparkling in the bright Sicilian sunshine, was spectacular. A perfect setting for a breather from combat missions, which had been flown frequently in the weeks leading up to the fall of Messina. A perfect time for batches of V-mail to catch up with us and for us to catch up with our letter writing.

After a week in our hillside abodes we moved into several cottages right on the beach that had been previously commandeered by Nazi officers who simply evicted the Sicilian owners from their homes and chased them out of the area. The cottages were small but sturdy, one-story buildings with marble floors, indoor plumbing, and sanitary facilities. We moved in, four officers per cottage. I shared a bedroom with Allen Lane, our erstwhile "broken-legged bridegroom." He had discarded his plaster cast way back in Oued N'Ja. He was a prolific letter writer, sending a daily missive, sometimes two letters, to his bride, whose picture he had put up on the wall next to his cot.

I began to label him "the lovesick Lieutenant" because one night, between midnight and dawn, I happened to wake up and saw him with his blanket over his head to avoid disturbing me with the light of his flashlight shining on his wife's picture on the wall and crooning a popular ballad of the time: "You'll Never Know Just How Much I Love You." Allen was really a nice guy and it touched me to discover how very much he loved his Rose.

During the next two weeks the squadron was on standdown while higher headquarters got set for the invasion of Italy. To keep our skills sharp we flew some practice missions and test hops of planes after the completion of periodic inspections. One day while some of us were on the beach, relaxing in the sun and surf, a P-40 came roaring toward us on the deck, so low that its propeller was kicking up sand. We scrambled out of the way—I dove into the surf, just a few feet away. We all knew who it was. Toppins! The daredevil.

He pulled up into a steep chandelle and came around for another pass over the now-empty beach—we all "quit the trail" and dashed into our cottages lickety-split. No one doubted that Ed Toppins was an excellent pilot but, also, none of us was willing to lose his head to prove it. At supper that night we urged "Topper" to refrain from any more such low "buzzing" lest he lose his own head.

After a week or so of this rest camp–like living, the squadron was ordered to move to an airstrip on the coast seventy miles east of East Termini. Each of the pilots ferried his aircraft on the twenty-minute flight carrying only toilet articles in the tiny baggage compartment behind the cockpit. Our cots and duffel bags were to follow in the convoy of trucks bringing the ground echelon to the new location on the outskirts of Barcelona, Sicily. We flew there by flights. With Jamison leading, B-Flight landed there in time for lunch at another unit's mess hall because ours had not yet been set up.

Near dusk we learned that our ground echelon would not leave East Termini until one, maybe two, days later. Some of us, myself included, decided that we would prefer to spend the night back at the old airstrip. So, without bothering to refuel after the day's flying, I took off heading west, following the coastline and flying about two miles offshore with no lights showing on A-Train II to avoid being shot at by shore batteries along the route. Although it was only a twenty-minute flight, I tweaked as my gas gauge needle flirted with the "E" for "empty." Arriving at the airstrip I decided to make a straight-in approach to avoid possibly running out of gas in a peel off approach to landing. Halfway down the runway, after touching down, I saw another P-40 coming toward me out of the dusk! He had just landed in the opposite direction.

"Omigosh, that was too close for comfort!" I murmured as, somehow, the two planes passed each other on the runway. About four of us made that return flight and we all agreed that it was not a very bright thing to do, as we had risked wiping out a chunk of the outfit's pilots and planes. And we agreed not to do any such foolish caper in the future. I felt that my safe passage on that ill-advised flight was a twenty-third birthday gift from the Lord—the date was September 16.

The next day we resumed flying combat missions as part of the invasion force storming the west coast of Italy at Salerno. From our airstrip the Salerno beachhead was 175 miles north across the Tyrrhenian Sea. On that first mission over the Salerno beachhead a flight of eight of us escorted a formation of a dozen medium bombers. It was a good mission in which the bombers hit their targets and all planes returned to base intact. There had been some fairly heavy flak over the target. One of the bombers was hit, trailing smoke from one of his engines, and couldn't keep up with the homeward bound formation. A straggler! Cold meat for any Jerries in the area.

Although we had not seen any enemy planes over the beachhead, we took no chances on losing the straggler, so, with Peepsight Smith flying the bomber's port side and me at starboard, he got back to Sicily safely. That was my first and last combat mission to the Salerno beachhead. During the debriefing Spanky Roberts announced that five of us were being returned to the States to join Colonel Davis in the 332nd at Selfridge Field. There we would help him teach the TAAF graduates what we had learned in combat and then return overseas with the group. The five included from A-Flight: Louis Purnell and Graham Smith, from B-Flight: Charles Dryden and Lee Rayford, and from C-Flight: Walter Lawson. We five were grounded from further flights until our departure from the outfit.

"Hallelujah! I'm going home. Going home to marry my nurse." I was overjoyed that evening and all the next day until the squadron took off headed for the Salerno beachhead. My classmate, Sid Brooks, who was scheduled to fly the mission, had engine trouble when he started up his airplane, nicknamed "El Cid." In order to make the takeoff on time he jumped out of his plane into A-Train II, cranked it up, taxied out to the end of the runway, and took off. As he was turning on course toward Italy we heard A-Train's engine sputtering. Sid turned left onto the downwind leg for an emergency landing, the engine sputtering continually. Turning onto the base leg he lowered the landing gear and then turned onto the final approach. The landing strip was just a meadow that had been bulldozed and leveled, leaving a dirt surface.

The takeoff by the twelve planes had raised a thick cloud of dust that obscured the landing strip. When he was on final approach, Sid must have decided that he was too high and would run into the six-feet-high fence at the far end of the field. In any case, we who were on the ground watching him saw his wheels begin to retract.

"With that engine acting up like that, surely he's not thinking about taking it around for another approach—it might quit altogether. So he must be planning to bellyland it. It will come to a stop much sooner that way. Good thinking, Hoss!"

Those were my thoughts as I watched him, along with a few other guys near the runway. But then, seeing that his belly tank was still hanging under his fuselage, we all starting screaming in desperation: "Drop the tank, Sid! Jettison it! For God's sake, Sid, drop it!"

Of course he couldn't hear us and we weren't near a radio. So we watched, fascinated, as he landed wheels up. On contact with the ground the belly tank sheared off. That was good. After skidding along on its belly for a couple hundred yards, A-Train II came to a halt. But the belly tank didn't. Full to the brim with highly volatile 100-octane petrol, it continued bouncing along crazily, like an oversized football, toward the plane. Suddenly it burst into flame. That was bad. We watched in horror as the fire traveled rapidly toward the plane, following the trail of gasoline vapor, until it caught up with the plane, which then burst into flame. Although it all happened in the twinkling of an eye it seemed to me like a nightmare in slow motion.

Ever the aggressive, never-give-up athlete, Sid shrugged out of his parachute harness, jumped out of the cockpit to the ground, and started running away from A-Train. His flying suit was smoldering. Someone tackled him and forced him to roll over and over to smother the flames. That was good because he suffered no serious burns and walked to the flight line ambulance under his own power, his sense of humor intact as he teased me: "Ole gal," he said, "your A-Train tried to do me in! Sorry I burned up your plane."

"Don't worry about it, Sid. I'm glad you got out OK."

We were told by the ambulance driver that they were going to rush him to a nearby British field hospital where he would probably be kept overnight to make sure he was OK even though he appeared to have suffered no injuries. As the meat wagon drove off, Jamie and I assured him we would visit him that evening after flying operations were over.

After supper we visited him at the hospital. He was sitting up in bed as he told us what his thoughts were during his emergency landing and how he felt fine now, and he fussed the whole time about why he had to be cooped up in a hospital.

"There's nothing wrong with me," he groused. "If you guys can find my clothes I'll leave with you!"

Of course we couldn't, and after a brief visit we left without him but with a promise that "We'll come see you tomorrow and spring you out of here."

Next day, true to our promise, we went to the hospital and got the shock of our lives. Sid Brooks had died during the night! The hospital spokesman told us that secondary shock and smoke inhalation that had seared Sid's lungs took his life. They showed us his body lying on a stretcher. Eyes closed.

My first reaction was denial. "He can't be dead," I thought. "He doesn't look any different from the many times I saw him asleep in the cadet barracks in flight school. Surely he'll get up if I nudge him awake."

Just then a fly lit on his forehead and crawled across his brow. As full of life as I had known him to be—athletic, aggressive, vigorous—I expected him to brush away the pesky fly with a sweep of his hand. When he did not, I realized the truth. He was gone. I had lost a "big brother" from cadet days. I wept.

When Jamie and I returned to the squadron area with the sad news, there were more than a few moist eyes. Sid Brooks had been very popular with everyone. Breaking the news to the men of the 99th was rough enough, but I dreaded telling the details to his widow, Lucille, and his family in Cleveland. My itinerary after leaving the outfit en route to Selfridge Field would take me to New York to visit my family then via train through Cleveland to Detroit.

That dread lay like a heavy stone in my innards and blunted the joy that I would normally have felt at being FIGMO. That was the slang expression used by GIs, whenever someone tried to assign them a long-range task, to indicate that they were about to rotate back to the States. Simply put it meant: "Forget it, I've got my orders!"

I thanked the CO, Captain Spanky Roberts, for those orders sending me home and packed my gear to leave. In my bedroll I had a couple tapestries that I had bought in an Arab marketplace in North Africa. One was a souvenir for Sister Vie. The other was for a friend of Edgar T. Rouzeau, a war correspondent who had joined the squadron in Sicily. He had asked me if I would be kind enough to deliver it to his friend in New York.

"Sure, I'd be glad to," I said as I bade him good-bye. Because I had met Rouzeau only a month or so before, that good-bye was bad enough. But good-bye to all the men who had come over to North Africa on the *Mariposa* was heart wrenching. Especially classmate Jamison, "the Eel" Knighten who had saved my life over Sicily, my crew chief Cecil Curl, armorer Fritz Mayers, Nick Quinones who had been my orderly back at TAAF, and on and on through the roster and ranks of the squadron.

Some had special requests for me. Lieutenant Erwin Lawrence asked me to contact his family as I passed through Cleveland. Knowing how much a fan of Duke Ellington's band I was, Lieutenant Willie Fuller urged me to see the band at the Hurricane Club in New York City, where they were booked at the time, go backstage, and introduce myself to his cousin, Harry Carney, who was the highly touted baritone saxophone star and a longtime pal of Duke. That was an easy mission and I promised to carry it out with pleasure.

So. When all "Be seein' ya's!" had been said there was nothing left to say. Remembering a ditty from World War I that I had heard my Dad hum many times, I packed up my troubles in my old kit bag and smiled, smiled, smiled.

And left, going home.

8   Arrivederci, Sicily!

» September 1943–1944

The next day, September 19, after bidding farewell to our squadron mates—pilots, crew chiefs, and all—we five FIGMOS headed west toward Palermo in a command car driven by one of our motor pool drivers. Arriving late in the afternoon, we had to wait until morning to catch a flight to North Africa.

About midmorning we boarded a C-47 bound for Blida, south of Algiers, with a stop at Telergma, the same airstrip where I had refueled on my solo flight to the war zone three and a half months before. That time there was a lackadaisical air about Telergma. This time it was abuzz with activity. On the ramp a staff car was parked. On each of the front fenders, fluttering in the gentle breeze, was a small red flag emblazoned with the four stars of a full general. Seated on the back seat was Ike—General Dwight D. Eisenhower! As we left the plane to stretch our legs we noted that everyone gave his car a wide berth as they walked into base operations.

Back in the air for about an hour we arrived at Blida where hundreds of troops of all sorts—Yanks, British, Canadians, French, army, air corps, officers, NCOs, enlisted men—were sweating out flights to hither and yon: some going east to war, others FIGMO, like us, going west. Going home.

Before leaving Blida, however, we had to go to the city of Algiers to visit Headquarters NATOUSA. The North African Theater of Operations, USA, was the major command that would issue the orders transferring us back to a stateside assignment. An army shuttle bus from Blida to Algiers took us right to HQ NATOUSA in about an hour. An hour later we had our orders and had some free time for sight-seeing the fabulous, fabled city. But I wasn't interested. All I wanted to do was to get back to the Blida airport and get aboard anything smoking, heading toward the USA.

Back in the terminal I saw several westbound flights load up with GIs, taxi out, and take off. Lee Rayford got lucky and was manifested on one of them. Next to get out was Peepsight Smith. I was getting antsy when I heard the dispatcher's loudspeaker blare out a list of names including, "Dryden, First Lieutenant Charles Dryden!"

"Here!" I shouted above the din of chatter in the terminal, slinging my bedroll on my shoulder and trudging over to the gate leading to the ramp. Heavy rainfall greeted the group of us whose names had been called as we sprinted out to the C-54 transport taking us to Marrakech, French Morocco, the next step on the way home. After takeoff into a dark, glowering cloud bank the plane climbed in the soup for about a half hour before breaking out on top into brilliant sunshine. As the plane's silhouette, circled by a rainbow, moved across the billowy white clouds, I kept repeating to myself: "I'm going home. I'm going home. I'm going to see Pete."

At Marrakech I had an RON layover. The next morning a C-47 flew a handful of us Yanks to an airstrip somewhere out in the middle of the desert, it seemed. I had no idea where it was but I did know that it was hot as the shingles of hades—it was so hot that it was almost impossible to stand on the asphalt ramp very long lest your shoes get stuck in the asphalt muck. A few new passengers got on board for the next leg of the journey, including a native Arab clad in typical desert garb with loose-fitting pantaloons, shirt, and burnoose. He squatted cross-legged on the floor of the cabin with a look of terror on his face when the pilot started the engines. Apparently he had never flown before. I felt sorry for him and tried to settle his fears using my schoolboy French, which he didn't seem to comprehend.

The pilot had informed us passengers that our destination was

Dakar, Senegal, on the west coast of Africa. Several hours later we touched down in that capital city. Little did I know that it would be about a week before I would get out of Dakar and continue my journey home.

The transient BOQ was a large barracks with an open bay and several cots lined up in two rows, each cot fitted with mosquito netting draped over the wooden poles at the ends of the cot. Relaxing on one of the cots was Peepsight Smith, who had left Blida before me.

"Hi, Peep!" I greeted him, dragging my bedroll and setting it down on an empty cot next to his. "What's up?"

"Not much, Hoss. I'm sweating out a hop across the water to South America. Some guys have been here a week or more, so I guess we're going to have to wait our turn."

As we compared notes about what we had experienced since parting company at Blida, he showed me some souvenirs he had bought in a native market in town. Tired from the long, tedious flights in the Goony Bird from Marrakech, I decided to put off any sight-seeing tours until the next day. With Peepsight as my guide, because he had reached Dakar a day ahead of me, I went into town and bought some souvenirs for the folks at home: ivory bracelets and necklaces, fine silk scarves, a dagger with its handle decorated with brightly colored raffia woven into clever designs, a scabbard similarly decorated, and giddy-giddies.

As we wandered through one of the markets out on the street a young merchant I reckoned to be about ten years old walked up to us and spoke in Pidgin English, interspersed with his native French: "Hey Joe! You want buy giddy-giddy?" all the while fingering the many flat rectangular pouches that hung by thin leather strands around his neck.

Continuing his sales pitch, he explained: "You buy giddy-giddy, you no die from bullet. This giddy-giddy, you no die from drown. This one, you no die from curse. This giddy-giddy, you no die from lion" and so on. It seemed he had enough amulets to avoid death altogether, but I figured that the sheer weight of all of them hanging around my neck might break it so I only bought one "giddy-giddy, you no die from drowning" as a hedge against possible ditching in the Atlantic en route to South America.

Dakar was a steamy, humid city in October and I was glad when, after about a week, I was manifested on a flight to Natal, Brazil, nine hours across the Atlantic. Nine hours of NO SMOKING! because, as the pilot explained, the C-87, a converted B-24 "Liberator" heavy bomber, was like a leaking gas tank looking for a spark to explode. That bit of information was somewhat unsettling and I thought, "I should have bought a 'giddy-giddy, you no die from fire'!"

At one point during the flight, about midway across the Atlantic, one of the passengers forgot the pilot's warning and started to reach for a cigarette. As he pulled a pack out of his shirt pocket several pairs of hands flew toward his hand holding the pack and snatched it, crumpling the cigarettes to dust.

"Are you nuts?" everyone chorused.

"Oh, ah, I forgot. I'm sorry," he apologized. I thought: "Whew! That was close."

Finally the green tropical forest of Brazil appeared on the horizon, replacing the blue sea of the ocean that had sparkled at us all the way across. It had been a beautiful flight, CAVU (ceiling and visibility unlimited) all the way. We landed and taxied in to the ramp on a taxiway flanked by dense jungle. In operations I learned that Peepsight had been there and gone on to the next stop: Belem, Brazil. After an RON stay at Natal I was booked on a C-47 for the flight to Belem on the northwest coast of Brazil.

Shortly after takeoff, about ten minutes into the seven-hour flight, I saw the carcass of a large transport-type plane lying crumpled among the tall trees of the dense jungle. Going forward to the cockpit, I asked the pilot about it. He said that the plane had crashed some months before but all attempts to rescue any survivors had failed. The jungle was totally impassable. After hearing that I tweaked the rest of the way to Belem because the terrain along our entire course was covered by the same sort of dense jungle. The steady drone of the Goony Bird's twin engines was of some comfort to this fighter pilot who was accustomed to being in command at the controls of any plane he flew—a fairly typical fighter pilot attitude.

Arriving at Belem at dusk I found two of my squadron mates in the transient BOQ (bachelor officers quarters) sweating out flights for the final leg home. Lawson and Smith had arrived at different times during the previous week and, along with a bunch of home-ward-bound GIs, were anxiously awaiting a flight to Miami. There was nothing going anywhere that night so the three of us went to the U.S. Air Corps Officers Club for dinner. I asked the others about Rayford and Purnell. I hadn't seen or heard anything about them since we had left the Blida airport back in Algiers a couple weeks before. Apparently they had been lucky in getting flights from point to point, keeping one step ahead of the rest of us, and were probably already back in the States.

At dinner we sat with three White American pilots who had completed their combat tour and enjoyed swapping war stories in typical fighter pilot fashion: "There I was at 10,000 feet with the whole Luftwaffe on my tail. . . . " That dinner was great fun with good food spiced with great tales of derring-do shared by comrades-in-arms, Black and White, who also shared a respect for the skill of other birdmen, race notwithstanding.

The officers club was a swanky setup with a beautiful dining room, a cozy bar, and lounge with a souvenir shop where I bought a box of fine cigars for my Dad. Cigars were usually not to my liking but at Lawson's urging I tried one and found it to be really smooth. I knew that Dad would enjoy these mementos of my overseas adventure even though they would go up in smoke!

The waiters and bartender at the club, some Black, some White, were all very cordial and attentive to our requests and interested in our stories about the 99th. They were Brazilian civilian employees who had never heard about the outfit. Some invited us to visit their homes so their families could meet us. They made us feel at ease with never a hint that we might be unwelcome at the club or at their homes. We did not get the chance to accept their invitation because the next morning, at breakfast, we learned that a C-97 Stratocruiser was scheduled to leave at midmorning headed for

Miami with a stop at Borinquen Field, Puerto Rico. It was going to clear out all the troops backed up at Belem awaiting a hop to the States.

We wasted no time getting back to the BOQ, hauling our bedrolls to the flight line, and reporting to the dispatcher to be manifested for the flight. Promptly at the time we had been told the flight would take off, we were rolling down the runway. This was ATC at its best: Air Transport Command had a reputation for being on time. I was glad of that because the closer I got to home the more anxious and excited I became. I had patiently counted down the hours in the flights across North Africa, to West Africa, the days stuck in Dakar, the hours across the blue Atlantic and the green Brazilian jungle. Now I could hardly contain my excitement.

My thoughts ran riot. Thoughts like: "When I get to Miami, should I call Pete, tell her I'm coming to Tuskegee to take her with me and surprise my folks in the Bronx? Or should I go home first, surprise her with a phone call, and tell her to come to New York post haste?" I had plenty of time to mull those questions during the long flight to Puerto Rico. When we took off the weather was, again, CAVU, but not for long. We soon ran into a warm front with cloud decks at several levels and very rough turbulence.

At takeoff I had been humming, "Swing low, sweet chariot, coming for to carry me home." But after a few particularly violent twists and turns of our "chariot" I became a bit nervous. My mind dredged up one of the Dodo verses from aviation cadet days. The one about the Swamp Swivel: "The Swamp Swivel is a bird which, when frightened, flies in circles at ever increasing velocities and ever decreasing radii until it flies up its own anus and disappears." Funny, I mused, what strange things come to mind when one is nervous!

Finally our ordeal ended as the Stratocruiser let down out of a low overcast and landed in a driving rain at Borinquen Field. All passengers disembarked and loaded into buses that took us to base ops while the plane was refueled. I figured that because of the weather we might RON, adding another day's delay. How happy I was to be wrong when the PA system announced: "All passengers on the Stratocruiser to Miami, board the buses in ten minutes. Repeat, ten minutes!"

No one disobeyed that order! About thirty minutes later our chariot poked its nose back up into the soup and climbed on top of the overcast into bright sunshine and smooth air. After a couple of hours the clouds broke up and night fell. Finally, FINALLY, the lights of the resort hotels on the strand at Miami Beach hove into view, followed by the glittering lights of Miami.

What a sight it was! I remembered the thrill of my first night flight at Roosevelt Field during CPT flight training when I saw the lights of New York City. This was even more thrilling because I was home from the war. I had made it through!

At every window of the Stratocruiser guys were eyeballing the beautiful kaleidoscope of lights unfolding below as the pilot flew the traffic pattern to final approach. I never really felt the touchdown, he was that smooth. I did feel a rush of emotion, however, when all of us passengers applauded as our chariot rolled down the runway and turned off onto the taxiway. HOME! Back in the USA!

As we got off the plane some of the GIs got on their knees and kissed the ground. Not me. I ran into base ops and found a phone, put through a person-to-person collect (I had no coins) call to Lieutenant Irma Cameron at Tuskegee Army Air Field. "And please expedite it, Operator," I begged. "My name is Lieutenant Charles Dryden and this is a wartime emergency!"

"OK, Lieutenant, I'll put you right through."

After a few moments I heard music, sweet music to my ears.

"Operator, this is Lieutenant Cameron. Yes, I will accept the charges." Then: "Charlie! Where are you? You sound so clear. Are you calling from overseas?"

"No, Honey, I'm at the Miami airport. I've just landed, about ten minutes ago."

"Wonderful! I'm so happy! Are you coming to Tuskegee?"

"Not right away. I have to report to First Air Force headquarters at Mitchel Field, in Long Island, and then I'll be on leave for about ten days. Do you think you can get Maw Raney to approve a leave for you to join me at my folks' home?"

"Does the sun come up in the morning? She wouldn't dare

turn me down if for no other reason than to keep me from going AWOL!"

"OK, Honey. I'll see you in New York. I gotta run to see about my baggage now. See you soon. Love ya!"

"Love you, too!" she said as I hung up then walked on cloud nine back to the plane to retrieve my bedroll.

There were no flights heading north on the outbound flight board in base ops, but I was manifested on the shuttle to Bolling Field the next morning. So I checked into the transient guest house for a good night's sleep after the grueling ride from Belem trying to snooze cramped in the sling-type seats in the crowded C-97. Tired as I was, sleep was fitful. There was so much on my mind.

After breakfast I boarded a C-54, the shuttle to Bolling Field. My buddies had scattered their separate ways, heading home by the fastest means possible: "Ghost" Lawson to Hampton, Virginia, Lou Purnell to Philadelphia, Lee Rayford to Washington, D.C., and Peepsight Smith to Ahoskie, North Carolina. We would see each other again at Selfridge Field, Michigan, so we wasted no time with maudlin good-byes. "See ya, Hoss! Be good. Take care" was all that we needed to say until we met again.

Once on the ground at Bolling I quickly discovered that there were no flights on the outbound board in base ops and the AO (airdrome officer) said it might be noon the next day before anything would be headed to Mitchel Field. "Phooey!" I thought. "I can ride 'the Pennsy' and be home long before then."

So. To make a short story even shorter, I caught the Pennsylvania Railroad to New York. Four hours later I was on the A-train subway to 155th Street and Saint Nick and then the cross-town trolley to Prospect Avenue where I caught a cab for the last mile to my home sweet, Home Street home. Unannounced. Unexpected.

When I knocked on the door and was asked "Who is it?" my reply, "Charlie," produced pandemonium! The door flew open and my kid sister, Pauline, jumped into my arms squealing: "It's Charlie! Charlie's home!" Mother came to the door with my brother Denis. There were hugs all around. And tears of joy. And Sister Vie saying over and over again: "Thank God! Thank God! Our prayers have been answered!"

Dad was still at work but Mom said, "I must call Rob to tell him the good news." She did and within the hour he was home. The Dryden circle was once again complete.

At suppertime a telegram came. I read it aloud to my family:

FROM LT. IRMA CAMERON, TUSKEGEE ARMY
AIR FIELD STOP
TO LT. C. W. DRYDEN, 800 HOME ST., BRONX, NY
STOP
MEET ME PENN STATION 1800, 29 OCT. STOP

"Good!" Mom said. "Now we'll get to meet Pete. Seems we already know her from your letters about her, Son, and from her letters to us while you were overseas." I was glad that Pete had written to my folks and that they were all looking forward to meeting her. I sensed that there was more than just a little concern about our romance that had blossomed after only one brief meeting and a half year of courtship via V-mail. But I wasn't worried. I was certain that she would charm everyone.

And so she did when I brought her home after meeting her at Penn Station the following evening. Twelve-year-old Pauline was delighted to have a big sister, especially one in the uniform of the Army Nurse Corps with its perky cap and brass-buttoned tunic. Everyone embraced Pete and made her welcome as we all stayed up late getting acquainted, talking about the 99th's exploits, and finally yawning "Good night" just before dawn as Mom made up the divan in the living room for Pete.

About noon the next day Pete tried to call her mother in Belleville, New Jersey, a suburb of Newark, to tell her we were coming to visit with her and Pete's grandmother for a couple of days. No luck; there was no one home. So we decided to surprise her folks. At midafternoon we rode the subway to Penn Station, then under the Hudson River to Journal Square in Newark. As we were boarding the bus to Belleville, we heard a woman's voice saying: "Irma! It's good seeing you. You look nice in your uniform. Too bad your grandmother won't get to see you in it, I'm so sorry to say."

"Oh, but she will, Mrs. Halliwell. This is my fiancé, Lieutenant Charles Dryden, just back from overseas, and we're on our way home now." Irma explained to me that Mrs. Halliwell was an old friend of her mother. Mrs. Halliwell's pale complexion blanched as she realized that Pete had not heard some sad news.

"You poor child," she said. "Haven't you heard about your grandmother?"

"What about my grandmother?" Pete asked anxiously.

"She died yesterday. I thought you were here to help your mother in this sad time."

Thunderstruck, Pete began to weep and buried her face in my chest. She had written me that she was worried about her Granny, whom she loved dearly, and had told me that having met me she felt she would be better able to cope with the loss of her grandmother who was getting frail. With this sad news, what had started out as a joyous trip home to surprise her folks with smiles and laughter was now a tear-stained, heartbroken journey.

We got off the bus and I hailed a cab so I could hold her close as she wept. Arriving at 11 Cleveland Street we went into the tidy, one-story cottage. Pete's mother, Mrs. Charlie Pearl Cameron, was truly surprised to see her. It seemed that Pete's mother had called Captain Della Raney, the chief nurse at the TAAF hospital, to speak to her and had been told that she was on her way to New York. So Mother Pearl assumed that her daughter somehow had learned about Granny's death.

In any case I found myself in an extremely awkward position being introduced to my intended future mother-in-law, the day after her own mother's passing, as the stranger (to her) that her only child intended to marry, immediately. I sensed and, under the circumstances, thoroughly understood Mother Pearl's coolness toward me. However, I was determined to be a bulwark of strength for my beloved in her time of grief no matter what other members of her family, meeting me for the first time, might think about our announcing plans to marry at such a time.

Two days later, during the funeral service, Pete insisted that I be seated beside her on the front pew in the church and that I accompany her in the limousine going to the cemetery. For me the situation was stressful as well as awkward and, although her kinfolk were very cordial to me—especially her two uncles, BJ and MJ—I nevertheless was emotionally drained after the funeral and during the traditional social gathering at the family home following the return from the graveside service. Pete was, too. She said to me: "Honey, please let's go to your home. Too many memories of my grandmother here, and my uncles, BJ and MJ, will look after Mother. I'll explain to her. She'll understand."

I wasn't convinced that Mother Pearl would understand our leaving the next day, but I was beginning to feel sick myself, with symptoms like the grippe, and I did not want to be an additional burden. So we left for the bus and subway trip back to the Bronx. By the time we arrived, about two hours later, I was sick as a dog. It was Sunday and my family were all away at Saint Augustine Presbyterian Church. Using the key Dad had given me, we entered the apartment and I slumped on a bed, shivering with chills although burning with fever. Not knowing what was wrong with me, I felt lucky to have my own personal nurse on my case.

The family was surprised to see us só soon after the funeral. I had called them from Mother Pearl's home with the sad news. And all were worried about my sudden illness. Pete tried treating me for what appeared to be influenza, but after a day of no improvement I became delirious, talking "out of my head" with slurred speech and vomiting frequently. Frightened, Pete called an ambulance. I was whisked to Cedars of Lebanon Hospital in the Bronx where my malady was quickly diagnosed as, not influenza, but MALARIA! It seems that during my stay in Dakar en route home from the war I had been bitten by a mosquito, probably one that had somehow gotten in under my mosquito netting. In any case, during a stay in the hospital for about ten days it was determined that I had the mildest variety of the disease, namely malaria vivax. I was told that it would not recur, as more virulent strains do, but that I must not ever give blood to another person as long as I lived.

Before I fell ill Pete and I had planned to be married while she was on leave in New Jersey, but her leave expired before my discharge from the hospital, so she had to return to Tuskegee. We agreed that as soon as I was released by the medics I would travel to Tuskegee and we would be married on the base. When Mother Pearl heard of our plans she was not too happy about the suddenness of it all and demurred mildly. However, she assented when I declared: "Mother Pearl, if you want to see your only daughter get married, you better pack a bag and use this train ticket I have bought for you because we are going to be married in the chapel at Tuskegee Army Air Field on November 16th. So, please come with me."

"OK, Charlie, I don't want you children getting married without me there, so I will." And she did make the trip to TAAF. So did Pete's Uncle BJ. My Dad and my youngest aunt, Iris, also went to witness the wedding.

Having arrived at the base a couple days before the wedding, our kinfolk were all billeted at a guest house. I discovered that elaborate plans had been made for the gala event uniting in marriage one of the base's angels of mercy with one of its own protégés, the first of the 99th to return to the base. So many of the TAAF family were hungry for firsthand news of their men of the squadron that I had a royal welcome. Colonel Parrish, the base commander, invited me to visit him at post headquarters with my Dad and interrupted his busy schedule to take us on a tour of the base in his staff car. He gave me the keys to the base, in effect, as I found out the day before the wedding.

First of all, he had put at my disposal a staff car to take Pete and Mother Pearl to Montgomery for some shopping. After their return I borrowed the car of a good friend, Weather Officer Lieutenant Johnny Branch, to take Pete on our last date as singles. I had promised to return the car by a certain time and found that I was running late, so I burned rubber trying to keep my promise. After taking Pete to the nurses quarters, I was sitting in the visitors' lounge when I heard a military police radio through the screen door. Walking to the door to see what was happening, I saw an MP with one foot on the front fender of Johnny's car as he was in the act of writing a ticket.

"What's up, Officer?" I asked.

"This vehicle was seen traveling way above the speed limit on the way to the base a few minutes ago and I'm writing it up."

"Well, Officer, don't charge the owner, Lieutenant Branch. He wasn't driving it; I was. So I'm your culprit."

"OK, Lieutenant," he said. "What's your name?"

"Lieutenant Charles W. Dryden."

"You mean you're the 99th pilot who's getting married tomorrow to one of our nurses?"

"That's right, Officer. I'm the lucky guy."

The MP snapped his notebook shut. "Lieutenant," he said, "I can't give you a ticket. Colonel Parrish would have my stripes. But please, Sir, slow down. The whole base is looking for a wedding tomorrow, not a funeral!"

"Thanks, Officer, I've got the message."

Tradition denied me even a glance of my bride-to-be all day November 16. "Bad luck," everyone said. Finally it was time to go to the base chapel with my best man, Lieutenant Cassius A. Harris, one of the pilots who got his wings after my class. The chapel was packed—SRO! Colonel Richard C. Cummings, the base hospital commander, sang "Oh Promise Me" in a beautiful tenor voice and the base chaplain, Major Douglas Robinson, performed the ceremony. Pete's maid of honor was Lieutenant Mary Rickards, one of her buddies who had come to TAAF with her back in April. Uncle BJ gave the bride away and Mother Pearl and Aunt Iris were properly misty eyed. Pronounced man and wife, Pete and I turned and walked swiftly through an arch of sabers toward the back of the sanctuary. It was all so impressive and mostly unforgettable. However, I was certain that a couple of our participants in the ceremony would be glad to forget how fate dealt with them.

First of all, one of the officers holding his saber aloft somehow got it turned around when he tried to slide it into the scabbard when the command "Order arms!" was given after we passed under the arch. So there he was with his arms still raised high when all the rest of the saber detail had returned their weapons to their scabbards and were standing at attention with their hands at their sides. Poor comic, embarrassed figure, I felt sorry for him but I couldn't stop to help him. I had to keep moving toward the exit without pause, again to avoid bad luck, according to those in the know who kept urging us on.

So we avoided bad luck but the photographer didn't. He was unable to get his flash gun to work, and as he was backing up while facing us in our rapid exit he pleaded, "Please stop for just a moment so I can get your picture under the arch of sabers."

On both sides of the aisle folks were saying, "Keep going, don't stop, and don't back up."

As a result we never did get a picture taken under the arch of sabers. However, when we went through the door of the chapel we saw a jeep outfitted with cardboard "wings" and marked on the sides, in large letters, "A-Train." (I learned, later, that a good friend, Sergeant Roy LeGrone of the TAAF Special Services office, had put it together.) Helped aboard, we were driven to the officers club for a reception that lasted for hours.

We were really enjoying the outpouring of love and affection that everyone was expressing and I was especially happy to tell many of the guests up-to-date news about their men of the 99th. Finally, one of the guys said to me: "What are you doing here so late? Ain't you got no home? You're supposed to leave on your honeymoon, so 'git'!"

So Pete and I got out of there, leaving the revelers to their fun and frolic. We spent half of our honeymoon week with our good friends, John and Lil Drew. She was the dietitian in the cadet mess when I was in flight training. The final three days we spent at the home of other dear friends, Medical Officer Captain Charles Pegg and his wife Vivian. Many other TAAF families begged to host the honeymooners but time wouldn't permit. All too soon, the week ended and I had to catch the train at Chehaw headed north to New York. I had an extension to my original leave of absence due to my stay in the hospital but now my time was running out and I had to leave my bride at her duty station.

Upon reporting to duty at First Air Force headquarters, at Mitchel Field, I received orders assigning me to the 553rd RTU (replacement training unit) at Selfridge Field, Michigan. Somehow the orders I had expected assigning me to the 332nd Fighter Group had been changed. In any case, I now had only two days of leave left before my reporting date at Selfridge.

My last night in New York I went to the Hurricane Club to see the Duke Ellington orchestra. During the show I scribbled a note to Duke requesting that the band play "Take the A-Train," signed it "Lt. Charles Dryden, 99th Fighter Squadron," and gave it to one of the ushers. At the end of one of the jazz numbers Duke took the mike and announced that he had just received a request from a member of the 99th in the audience, that "A-Train" was on the program anyway, but that the band would dedicate it especially for the 99th overseas. And they rocked the "A-Train" like I had never heard it before. It was something special!

After the show I was invited backstage and met the members of the orchestra, bringing greetings to baritone saxophonist Harry Carney from his cousin, Lieutenant Willie Fuller, and telling Johnny Hodges, the peerless alto saxist, that I had gone through the Civilian Pilot Training Program with his cousin, Bobby Maxwell, when we were both attending City College in 1940. And, of course, I informed them that I had named my airplane "A-Train" in honor of their jazz gem and not after the subway of the same name. All of the guys in the band and Ivy Anderson, the vocalist, made me feel at home and gave me a photograph of the band for my souvenirs. It was a night to remember, truly a homecoming treat.

After a final RON visit with my family I headed west, stopping in Cleveland for an RON visit with Jamie Jamison's wife, Phyllis, and his family, and Sid Brooks's widow, Lucille, and his family. I had written each family about my itinerary.

When my train arrived at the Cleveland terminal I was met by Lucille and some others of Sidney's kinfolk. Ever since leaving the squadron in Sicily I had dreaded that moment. Had steeled myself to hold back my tears. Seemingly Lucille had gotten over the initial shock during the two months that had elapsed since Sid's death. However, when she caught sight of me and we embraced, the floodgates of our shared grief burst. It was the toughest task I have ever had to perform, before or since.

Just trying to describe the accident and how, although at first it seemed that Sid had survived, we later learned that aftereffects had taken life from a vigorous, full-of-life young man, was rough. One thing I could not bring myself to do was to reveal that his fatal accident was in the "A-Train," my airplane that I had flown just the day before Sid's accident. Within the innermost depths of my being I sensed that Lucille, and others of his family, were agonizing over the unspoken questions: "Why did it have to be Sid? Why not you?"

A natural thought, I felt, for a bereaved person. I prayed for proper words of comfort and solace, but Lucille, whom I had grown to love as my own sister during the months at TAAF after graduation and before shipping out overseas, was distraught when I left to visit my other "sister," Phyllis Jamison, and others of Jamie's family. By day's end I felt totally drained by the emotional storms that had buffeted me all that day. But as unhappy a task as it was, I at least felt at peace with myself knowing that I had faced up to it and had done what duty and decency demanded.

Next day I headed west to Detroit by train, then out to Selfridge by taxi, reporting to duty on my last day of leave.

When I arrived at Selfridge Field in late November, I was in for some surprises. First of all, the weather was colder than I expected. Located on the shore of Lake Saint Clair, which lies between Detroit, Michigan, and Windsor, Canada, Selfridge Field was chilled by offshore winds from the lake.

Second, my 99th buddies who had left the squadron in Sicily with me were already on duty with the 553rd. My reporting date had been delayed by my ten-day stay in the hospital in the Bronx recovering from malaria.

Third, we were checked out in P-39 "Airacobras," a welcome introduction to the tricycle landing gear.

Fourth, we learned that we had been assigned to the 553rd permanently as flight instructors to teach what we had learned about aerial combat tactics, while overseas with the 99th, to graduates of Tuskegee Army Flying School (TAFS). As a new crop got their wings each month, they would come to Selfridge for about three months of training before being sent overseas to the 332nd Fighter Group as replacements. The 332nd, with its three squadrons (100th, 301st, and 302nd), was based at Selfridge Field when we five aerial combat instructors arrived in November 1943. Originally we had been selected and ordered back to the States to join the 332nd and teach its pilots, all TAFS graduates, what we had learned and then return overseas with the group. However, with the change of our orders by Headquarters, First Air Force, we did not have to go back overseas unless we volunteered.

Lieutenant Colonel Benjamin O. Davis, Jr., was commanding officer of the 332nd. He had been our CO when the 99th left Tuskegee eight months earlier to go overseas to North Africa and had returned to the States to take command of the 332nd.

Shortly after I reported to Selfridge, Colonel Davis had a talk with me on the flight line.

"Hello, Dryden. Good to see you."

"Likewise, Colonel," I replied, saluting with real pride as I congratulated him on his new assignment. About three months earlier he had left us, the 99th, in Sicily as a squadron commander. And now: "Group Commander is a good title for you, Sir," I said.

"Thanks, Lieutenant. You and all the men of the 99th helped me earn it. That's a part of what I want to talk about with you. But first, tell me, how was it going with the outfit when you left?"

"Pretty good overall, Sir. As you probably know we were in on the invasion of Italy flying support missions over the Salerno beachhead. That's where my last mission was before leaving the squadron along with Lawson, Purnell, Rayford, and Smith in mid-September. And I'm sure you have read about our losing my classmate, Sid Brooks, on September 18th."

"Yes, Dryden, I read about it in the *Pittsburgh Courier* and was really sad to learn about his death."

After catching up briefly on how each of us had fared since parting company in Sicily, the colonel came straight to the point.

"Lieutenant, I'm sure you are aware that you were sent back to the States to teach the 332nd pilots what you have learned about aerial combat tactics flying with the 99th and then return overseas with the group. With the change in your orders you don't have to return overseas unless you volunteer. I would like to have you on board and if you continue to perform as you have in the past there is a good possibility of a squadron command and major's leaves sometime in the future. Are you interested?"

I choked. What an offer! What an opportunity!—What a dilemma! I had gotten married less than a month before, on November 16. So I declined.

"Thanks, Colonel, for your confidence in me, but I got married at Tuskegee last month while on leave, so I think I'll stay stateside. I hope you understand, Sir."

"Sure, Dryden, I understand. Congratulations to you and best wishes to your bride. Good luck to you both."

"The same to you, Sir, and thanks again."

I felt terrible. I respected Colonel Davis so much—always had and always had wanted to measure up to his West Point standards of performance and excellence. This time, though, I had a stronger motivator: love and marriage and a wife I adored. So I passed up the offer.

So did Lawson and Smith. They, too, had gotten married while home on leave.

Purnell and Rayford volunteered. When the 332nd shipped out from Selfridge Field on Christmas Eve 1943, they joined Colonel Davis as the three 99th veterans returning to combat.

Another surprise awaiting me—certainly the most distressing one—when I first reported to Selfridge Field was the racism evident everywhere in everything at that northern base. Having just returned from overseas where Jim Crow was muted, I was shocked to find it so rampant "back home." In 1943 an incident occurred on base that was widely reported in the Black press, involving the shooting and wounding of a Black soldier by the base commander, who was drunk and insisted that he did not want a "Colored" chauffeur. Although the base commander was eventually court-martialed and retired from military service, the damage had been done. The fires of fury among African Americans at Selfridge Field had been stoked.

Especially odious at Selfridge was the plight of the Black officers and enlisted men of the 477th Medium Bombardment Group. Although I was not assigned to the 477th, their deplorable situation was obvious to everyone on the base.

The 477th had four squadrons equipped with twin-engine, five-man-crew B-25 Mitchell medium bombers: the 616th, 617th,

618th, and 619th. The "trainees" were all graduates of Tuskegee Army Flying School and many had completed B-25 transition training at Mather Field, California. None of them held a command or supervisory position in group headquarters or in any of the squadrons, and none were promoted to any such positions.

Morale at Selfridge was at low ebb when I arrived and remained so continuously. About a month later three more veterans of the 99th arrived and, like the five of us already there, were assigned to the 553rd RTU: Lieutenants William A. Campbell, Herbert V. Clark, and Spann Watson. They too declined to return with the 332nd when it left on Christmas Eve, headed overseas to Italy.

9 "You're Not Ready!"

» 1944–July 1945

"I am ordering you to leave this officers club at once," said Colonel William L. Boyd to three United States Army officers on New Year's Day 1944.

The place was the lobby of Lufberry Hall, the plush officers club at Selfridge Field located on the outskirts of Mount Clemens, Michigan, about twenty-five miles north of Detroit. Colonel Boyd was the base commander of Selfridge Field. The three officers were African Americans.

"Is that a direct order, Colonel?" Lieutenant Milton Henry asked. Lieutenant Henry was a courageous young officer, a graduate of Tuskegee Army Flying School who had challenged segregation and discrimination he encountered during his training there and in the surrounding area.

"That's right, Lieutenant, it is a direct order."

It was also an improper, illegal order that contravened an existing written directive. Army Regulation 210–10, paragraph 19c, stated, in part, that officers clubs and messes had to extend to all officers on duty at the base the right to full membership.

The three officers knew this regulation. They and a large number of African American officers had done their homework as they planned strategies for the elimination of segregated facilities at Selfridge Field. They also knew that disobedience of a direct order from a senior officer could have dire consequences, especially in wartime when such disobedience was tantamount to treason—punishable by death. So they left Lufberry Hall, returned to the BOQ, and reported to the rest of the officers what they had just experienced.

These officers were all were African Americans. All were professional, trained officers, including: *pilots,* all graduates of Tuskegee Army Flying School; six were aerial combat instructors who were veterans of overseas duty with the 99th Fighter Squadron; a large number were aerial combat trainees earmarked as replacements for the 332nd Fighter Group that had left Selfridge Field just one week earlier, on Christmas Eve, en route overseas to Italy. A larger number were assigned to the 477th Medium Bombardment Group, which also had a number of *navigators,* graduates of the training course at Hondo Field, Texas; *bombardiers,* graduates of the training course at Midland, Texas; and *ground officers,* (nonflying) graduates of officer candidate schools (OCS) at various bases.

As one of the six aerial combat veterans, I was an instructor of the fighter pilot trainees. During the Christmas holiday week I had been on leave of absence to celebrate with my wife our first Christmas together. She had come to Detroit, also on leave from her army nurse duties at the base hospital at Tuskegee Army Air Field. Having been away from the base for a week, I did not know of the guys' plans to integrate the officers club.

First thing the next morning, January 2, however, when I returned to flight operations to resume flight instructing, some of the guys briefed me about what had happened the previous night. While I was suiting up in the locker room for an early morning training flight, I heard, "Lieutenant Dryden, I want to talk to you for a minute." It was Lieutenant Colonel Charles Gayle, CO of the 553rd Replacement Training Unit (RTU).

"Yes, Sir," I replied, wondering what he was about to say.

"Lieutenant, you've been on leave, haven't you?"

"Yes, Sir. Just returned to duty this morning."

"Good! We missed you. How were your holidays?"

"Great, Colonel. My wife was on leave from Tuskegee Army Air Field. She's a nurse at the base hospital there, y'know. And how were your holidays?" I asked, thinking, "This is all cordial enough, but what is really on his mind?"

"Fine, Dryden. My holidays were alright, until last night."

"Oh?" "Here it comes," I thought.

"Haven't you heard about the incident at Lufberry Hall last night?"

"No, Sir," I lied, curious to hear his version.

"Well, you know that Lufberry Hall is for use by officers on permanent assignment to Selfridge. Trainees have their officers club in the BOQ. Do you understand, Lieutenant?"

"Yes, Colonel Gayle. I understand."

I understood what he had said and, more important, I understood what he had not said. He had not said that the "club" in the BOQ was the only club to be used by Negro or "Colored" officers. He had not said that Lufberry Hall was off limits to us. But even before he described the incident I knew full well, too well, what he meant.

"Last night three of our 553rd trainees came into Lufberry Hall. Colonel Boyd happened to be in the lobby as they entered and gave them a direct order to leave."

"What did they do, Colonel?" I played dumb. "Did they leave?"

"Not at first. One of them said something about an army regulation that says all officers can belong to the officers club and asked him if he was giving them a direct order. He said 'Yes' and they left.

"Now, Lieutenant Dryden, with your date of rank as a first lieutenant you are the senior officer of your group. As commanding officer of the 553rd I expect you to take the lead in seeing that the rest of the men use the club according to the base policy. Do you understand?"

"Yes, Sir! Clearly, Sir!" I replied, struggling for composure and muttering to myself, angrily, "I understand more than you know."

No point arguing with him, I figured. Better to let my actions speak louder than any words I could possibly muster. Even before this encounter with Colonel Gayle I had made up my mind to join the men planning to visit Lufberry Hall the second night because of the version related by the first-night pioneers.

That day, January 2, it seemed to me that night would never come. The two-hour training flight in the morning, and another one again in the afternoon, seemed to drag on and on. Having flown P-40s in combat, I loved flying the P-39 with its tricycle don't-worry-about-ground-looping landing gear. Every flight was a joy. But that day I was glad when the last flight ended. Nervous tension had been building in my gut all day as I anticipated the coming skirmish at Lufberry Hall: similar to feelings I had experienced before going on strafing missions against heavy flak areas in combat.

After supper in the officers mess, a large number of the guys gathered in the lounge of the BOQ to review our strategy: After the six o'clock movie at the base theater, a number of us would go to Lufberry Hall in random groups—two, five, three, four, and so forth—in order for our visits to appear spontaneous, not a conspiracy.

So. After the movie, at about eight o'clock, I walked the couple of blocks to Lufberry Hall along with two other officers, Second Lieutenants W. H. Johnson and Bob O'Neal. We looked around as we neared the entrance, but none of the other guys were in sight. Nevertheless we pressed on, entered, and saw, just inside the lobby—who else? None other than Lieutenant Colonel Charles Gayle!

Usually sallow of complexion, he turned scarlet as he exclaimed, "Dammit, Dryden, I thought you said you understood when we talked this morning!"

"I did understand what you were really saying, Colonel. However, according to Army Regulation 210–10, paragraph 19c, as officers we are not only encouraged to participate in the officers club, we are in fact obligated to support it. So we are here, Sir, to obey the regulation and join the club."

The colonel looked as though he would explode. He shouted, "You men are to leave this club immediately!"

"Is that a direct order?" we chorused.

"Yes, by God, and you tell the rest of the Negro officers in my command that I will court-martial for inciting a riot the first man who steps into this officers club!"

We turned and left.

The next night some others defied the policy. And the next. Until finally, after about five days of "tests" by different officers, Lufberry Hall was closed. Period. Out of business. Obviously, the base commander, Colonel Boyd, and his cohorts, Lieutenant Colonel Gayle and other White officers, realized the folly of their actions in discriminating against Black officers in the use of the officers club because no court-martial trials were held at Selfridge Field in spite of Gayle's threats.

The closing of the club did not end our anger and disgruntlement over Jim Crow policies at Selfridge. Indeed, from that point in time our situation went downhill rapidly.

A few weeks after the departure of the 332nd and the closing of Lufberry Hall, a team of officers from the U.S. Army inspector general's office visited Selfridge to investigate the causes of the incidents that led to the closing. Heading up the team was Brigadier General Benjamin O. Davis, Sr. He was the first African American to wear a general officer's star, having come up through the ranks from buck private. His son had been my CO in the 99th.

General Davis, Sr., interviewed, one on one, a large number of the officers who had been involved in the Lufberry Hall fiasco. When it came my turn to report to him in a private office in the basement of the base operations building, I was eager to answer his questions.

"Tell me in your own words, Lieutenant, what happened at Lufberry Hall."

I narrated my experiences of January 2, in the morning and that evening, and spent about thirty minutes answering his questions about my impressions of morale at Selfridge and why it was low. I left the interview with the hope that things would change for the better. Not long thereafter Colonel Boyd and Lieutenant Colonel Gayle were relieved of their command of the base and of the 553rd, respectively, and morale improved slightly. But not for long.

The final, crushing blow that killed morale and outraged the Black officers and enlisted men was dealt by Major General Frank O'Driscoll Hunter, commanding general of First Air Force. He visited Selfridge Field in March 1944. Summoning all Black officers present on the base to attend a mandatory officers call, he proclaimed, in effect: You're not ready to fly airplanes in combat. You're not ready to be officers in command of anything. Negroes can't expect to obtain equality in 200 years, probably more. You're just not ready!

He was speaking to us collectively. But I am certain that each of us in that auditorium took his words personally. As a personal insult.

Not ready to fly and fight in combat?

Not ready to be an officer in charge?

Not ready?

After all that we had been through, collectively and as individuals, we were not ready?

After all that I had been through in my twenty-three years of education, training, and fighting, was I not ready?

The general's "indictment" could have been the death knell of my dream of a military career. But I knew he was wrong because as I listened to him trying to kill my dream, I was confident that I was ready. Moreover, I was sure that all of us—officers, NCOs, and enlisted men—were as ready to do our jobs and serve our country as well as any White troops, anywhere!

Two months after his diatribe, General Hunter as commanding general of First Air Force transferred the 553rd RTU squadron from Selfridge. One night in May 1944, all of the Negro personnel of the squadron boarded a troop train headed to—none of us knew where! Neither we six combat veteran–instructor pilots, nor the trainee pilots, nor the ground officers, NCOs, nor enlisted men had any idea about our destination. Neither did the Black newspapers, some of which published their puzzled concern with "Where Are Our Boys?" headlines in their next editions.

During the first few hours as we looked through the windows of the coaches, we saw the names of railroad stations in Canada flash by. Then, down through New York's Mohawk Valley, through Pennsylvania Station, racing along the "Pennsy's" tracks, southbound. New Jersey. Pennsylvania. Delaware. Maryland. Washington, D.C. Still heading south. Virginia. North Carolina. Deeper into Confederate country.

I wondered: Are we going to be interned the way Japanese-Americans/nisei had been interned only recently in California right after the Pearl Harbor "day of infamy"?

Finally at midafternoon the next day, the sealed train slowed and stopped on a railroad spur in a forest of tall pines in the middle of nowhere. There were signs of life but not at all heartening. On both sides of the train, at about 100-foot intervals, there were soldiers with carbines at the ready. My pulse leaped into high gear as I feared the worst. After disembarking from the train we boarded a fleet of six-by-six trucks and were driven to some old, ramshackle one-story barracks that looked to be vintage 1914. They were nothing like the comfortable quarters we had enjoyed at Selfridge Field but, I was thinking, at least we have not been shot or beaten by the carbine-wielding soldiers. Moreover, I didn't see any barbed-wire fences around our area so I guessed that this was not a concentration or internment camp. With that comforting thought I could feel my pulse returning to normal.

But not for long.

After a refreshing shower I changed into class-A summer uniform: tan gabardine short-sleeved shirt; tan gabardine pants with knife-edge sharp crease, girded by a web belt fastened by a gleaming brass buckle that had been polished to a high luster by Blitz cloth and lots of elbow grease; tan leather shoes spit shined to a high gloss by shoe polish, shoe brush, and more elbow grease; all of this regalia topped by a tan garrison cap with polished bill and "fifty mission crush" (that is, the cap was wrinkled and crushed, as if by the rigor of fifty combat missions). Looking at my reflection in the full-view mirror in the latrine, I thought to myself, "I'm as sharp as a Gilette razor and that's sharp on both ends!"

Trying to stay cool in spite of the hot late-afternoon sun, I walked the half mile or so to the base theater at a leisurely pace, keeping in the shade of the pine trees that lined the sandy path. Arriving at the theater I was startled to see about thirty of our men standing in ranks outside the theater with one of our ground officers, Second Lieutenant William Bailous, facing the formation as though assembled for an inspection. Lieutenant Bailous was speaking animatedly to the men, who were standing at parade rest.

" 'Ten-hut!" Bailous barked when he caught sight of me approaching and "popped to" with a snappy salute.

"At ease!" I responded, returning his salute, and asked: "Lieutenant Bailous, what's going on? Why aren't you all in the theater?"

"We were, Lieutenant, but we have been ordered to leave."

"By whom?"

"The officer of the day."

"Why?"

"Because we cut the rope that we saw stretched through the auditorium from front to back with signs for White on one side, Colored on the other. And then the men checker-boarded the seats in random groups—two here, one there, four elsewhere, and so on. The theater manager, a tech sergeant, said, 'Y'all can't do that.' I told him, 'No? You just watch us, Sergeant!' He refused to start the movie and we had sat there for about ten minutes when the next thing I knew the OD came in and ordered us all to leave the theater. I asked him, 'Is that a direct order, Major?' He said, 'You bet it is, Lieutenant.' So I told our men, 'Fall out, on the double!' And we all left and fell into ranks out here in front of the movie."

"Where is the OD now?" I queried.

Before Bailous could answer I heard a voice behind me drawling, "Loo-tenant!"

Turning, I saw a beefy major wearing a black arm band on his left arm. The large white letters "OD" on the arm band identified him as the officer of the day, in charge of all activities on the base whenever the base commander was away. And the .45-caliber automatic pistol on his hip enforced his authority, especially inasmuch as it was probably loaded with seven snub-nosed rounds in the magazine. Also, there was a war going on. Disobeying a direct order, albeit an improper order, during wartime could lead to dire consequences.

With all those factors in mind, I replied, "Yes, Sir!" trying hard to mask my annoyance and to avoid appearing disrespectful, insubordinate to a senior officer.

"Are you in charge of these men?" he asked.

"Not officially by any orders, Major, but I am the senior ranking officer in the group," I replied.

"Well," he said, "the Sergeant in charge of the theater told me that your men cut the rope in there and were sitting all over the place instead of only in the Colored section. Now, that's a violation of this base's policy. I don't know what you boys did up Nawth but down heah we have rules and you boys will just have to obey those rules if you want to stay out of trouble. Y'unnerstand, Loo-tenant?"

"No, Sir. We men don't understand why we cannot sit anywhere we wish since we're paying for our tickets and this is a military base. Is the base commander on base, Major?"

"No, Loo-tenant. It's Sunday afternoon and he's not here. Why do you want to know?"

"Because we want to know more about the base policy and to have him brief us on it so we'll know what the rules are that you mentioned."

"Well, I'm gonna put all this in my report, Loo-tenant, and the Cunnel will call y'all in about these violations. Now I suggest y'all go back to your barracks."

Saluting the major snappily, wordlessly I turned on my heel. Saluted Lieutenant Bailous. As I did so, he and the men in ranks, who had been standing at parade rest through all this, snapped to attention and he returned my salute.

"Attention to orders," I said, loud enough for the men in the rear ranks to hear. "You have all heard the OD's comments. We will hear from the base commander, probably tomorrow. That's when we can tell him how we feel about this situation. Meanwhile let's return to our barracks and get settled in. Any questions?"

"Yes, Sir!" from one of the men in ranks. "Can we get our money back?"

"How about it, Major?" I asked the OD who was still standing nearby.

"Well, uh, I guess so. Yeah," he said, and said something to the theater NCIOC (NCO in charge).

"Fall out," I told the men. Some walked to the ticket window to retrieve their fifteen cents. Most of them grumbled in disgust, saying things like: "They can keep the damn money!" "Welcome to Dixie, ugh!" "Is this what we're fighting for?" as they dispersed.

Next day, Monday, the base commander, Colonel Prince, called a meeting to "welcome" us to Walterboro Army Air Base. Referring to the theater incident, he laid down the law as we had heard it from the OD the day before. No room for discussion. The local customs of segregation would be observed and enforced. Period! I left that meeting downcast but not really surprised, having experienced such rules and policies from another base commander, Colonel Boyd, at Selfridge Field, Michigan, "up Nawth."

The Walterboro "exile" continued with about a week's wait while White flight instructors ferried the thirty or so airplanes of the 553rd RTU from Selfridge to Walterboro: Not one of us six Black combat veterans was used to ferry airplanes, although we all had more flying time than some of the White instructors who made two ferry trips. It was a week during which we, officers and enlisted men, discovered that Jim Crow was total and pervasive on base and in nearby towns and rural areas.

From the day we arrived at this Godforsaken Walterboro Army Air Base in the piney woods of South Carolina, we had seen German prisoners of war, readily identifiable by the letters PW painted on the back of their fatigues in white paint, going into the "White" side of the post exchange cafeteria and WE COULD NOT! We who were American citizens—many of us in training to go overseas to fight Germans, foreign enemies against whom we had sworn to defend our country. Six of us were combat flight instructors, veterans who had already fought Germans overseas and had lost comrades killed by that enemy. WE WERE INSULTED AND HUMILIATED IN OUR OWN NATIVE LAND!

Our mood depressed as tensions heightened. At the "Colored" officers club and in our BOQ we discussed strategies constantly of how best to cope with, and (we hoped) to correct, our situation. Our NCOs and enlisted men did likewise at their "Colored" NCO club and barracks.

Realizing our no-win situation, we resorted to indirect action. First of all we boycotted the theater. Next we launched a massive letter-writing campaign, informal and individual: We wrote personal letters to our kinfolk; to Congressmen William Dawson and Arthur Mitchell; to prominent men and women—Mary McLeod

Bethune, Judge William Hastie, Adam Clayton Powell, A. Philip Randolph, Eleanor Roosevelt, Roy Wilkins. We also wrote to publishers of what were referred to as our "Black Dispatch" newspapers: Carl Murphy (*Afro American*), W. A. Scott (*Atlanta Daily World*), John Sengstacke (*Chicago Defender*), Tom Young, Sr. (*Norfolk Journal and Guide*).

As soon as we found out where we were, we told the world in our letters. Of course we took the precaution of mailing them off base in various mailbox locations to avoid censorship and reprisals.

By the following Saturday the P-39s were ready to resume training flights.

Full of fuel that Saturday morning the airplanes, parked in revetments located around the field, waited for their pilots.

Full of anger and resentment, and smarting over the numerous insults and humiliations since our departure from Selfridge Field, our Black combat flight instructors and our trainees were primed to show that we could fly with the best pilots anywhere. And our ground crewmen, mechanics, armorers, and radiomen were determined to keep 'em flying.

That was my mood on the morning that the 553rd RTU squadron, at its new location, resumed combat flight training. But, again, the question in chapter 2 arises: Why "buzz"—why fly so low?

The answer: ostensibly to demonstrate to the three combat trainees flying formation with me how we returned to our home base after a combat mission. In briefing them prior to the training flight, I told them: "You see, when you return from a mission low on fuel and very likely with ammo zero, you are vulnerable to enemy aircraft. The Luftwaffe loved to stooge around our bases to catch us in the traffic pattern flying low and slow and then attack. For them it's like shooting fish in a barrel. So we must get the flight on the ground and into the sandbagged revetments as quickly as possible. To do that you approach the runway low and fast, peel off in a tight, climbing, 360-degree turn, and at the top of the climb you 'pop' the gear handle to lower the wheels as you reef the ship around and level out with flaps down, airspeed near stalling as you 'kiss-kiss' the runway on the main wheels and taxi to your revetment."

That was what I was trying to demonstrate to my students that Saturday—and that was the basis for the first of two counts of violation of the 96th Article of War for which I was tried.

The second violation happened the next day, Sunday. A typically quiet, peaceful Sabbath in a sleepy southern town. But we had to work. There was a war going on and we had to fly seven days every week to train the JPs in aerial combat tactics. These junior pilots, recent graduates of Tuskegee Army Flying School, were earmarked as replacements for the four squadrons of the 332nd Fighter Group that were overseas in Italy: the 99th, 100th, 301st, and 302nd Fighter Squadrons.

So, bright and early Sunday morning, several four-ship flights took off from Walterboro Army Air Base to perform a variety of training missions. My flight was scheduled for a low-level navigation mission: Walterboro-to-Sumter-to-Orangeburg-to-Walterboro. Total distance: about 160 miles round trip; ETE (estimated time en route): about forty-five minutes at high cruise in the P-39, on the deck (treetop level). That's how you would do it in combat to avoid enemy flak and small arms fire. You zip over enemy ground batteries so fast that you're gone before they can react.

Trouble is, the pilot has a tough job navigating. As he zips over the ground he has little time to recognize any checkpoints and must check his "dead reckoning" time, distance, and heading constantly. Now and then he may have to "climb a tree" (gain altitude) to look around and check his location. When he does, of course, enemy ground troops can get a shot at him. So to show combat trainees how to do it we practiced low-level navigation.

Each of my three trainees got a chance to hone his skill by leading the flight on one of the legs of the triangular course. As we approached the home base I saw an opportunity to demonstrate how to attack a flak tower. In the middle of the town of Walterboro was a water tower, about 100 feet tall, that looked very much like some I had seen overseas in North Africa and Sicily. The enemy liked to install antiaircraft guns in towers where they have a commanding view of the surrounding terrain. The best way to attack such towers was to approach "on the deck" at high speed, pull up to about 100 feet just out of their range, nose down, firing, back to the deck, and hightail away, "jinking" erratically.

So, there we were, four Airacobras approaching the town and the tower, on the deck doing about 250 knots. Allison engines racketing across town, shattering the slumber of the citizenry including, I later discovered, the town mayor, Mayor Sweatt.

Ten minutes or so later we landed, taxied in, shut down, filled out the Form 1s, and strolled into the operations shack. Parachute leg straps loosened and dangling, sweat-soaked flight suits dripping/clinging to skin, helmets and goggles pushed back high on the forehead, with oxygen masks unsnapped and rubber hoses dangling, we were a classic picture of confident, competent, cocky (some a wee bit, others more so) fighter jocks.

I was proud of them. Proud to be their combat tactics instructor because they were good. Damn good! They had navigated their way around the course like homing pigeons. Their formation flying was tight when it was supposed to be. Flight discipline had been flawless. It was as though each of them had read my mind and without putting it into words had determined with simultaneous pride and bitterness "to show these 'crackers' that we are damn good pilots and that anything they can do we can do better" and "that this is our country, too, and don't ever forget it!"

Pride? Bitterness? Strong emotions! But why? Why were such emotions stirred within us? Some of our recent experiences provide clues to the answers.

Pride? Yes! We knew we were good pilots because we had truly earned our wings at Tuskegee Army Flying School (TAFS), located a few miles from the little-known town of Tuskegee, Alabama. We had endured all of the Jim Crow nonsense; overcome the feelings of rejection by the top brass of the War Department and Army Air Corps who really didn't want us and didn't believe "Colored people" (some used the term *niggers* publicly) could fly and be mechanics, armorers, radio technicians, parachute riggers, and so forth. We had survived the rigors of an aviation cadet training program with a quota set to allow only 30 percent of each class to graduate.

Bitterness? Yes! Oh yes! Because of all the humiliations and insults we had to endure. Bitterness so strong and long lasting that even as this book is being written, a half century later, the tears of hurt and rage still flow!

Not long after my weekend of folly and unbridled anger, the boom was lowered. As prescribed by the *Manual for Courts-Martial,* an investigating officer was appointed to determine if my actions warranted a trial by court-martial: Captain B, one of the few "paddy boys" of the 553rd who had earned the respect and friendship of the "brothers," both instructors and trainees. His words, his actions, his attitudes all bespoke his "simpatico" with our situation. Questioning me about what I had done, about my knowledge of existing flying regulations, and about my reasons for my actions, he was scrupulously fair and sympathetic, I must admit. Nevertheless I must also admit that in view of the facts, his investigation revealed his only choice was Hobson's choice—no choice at all. He had to recommend trial by general court-martial.

Two days later, when he filed his report and recommendation, I was grounded. No more flying for me pending the outcome of the trial, which was scheduled for the following week at Walterboro Army Air Field. The upcoming trial became a main topic of conversation among the instructors and trainees, ground crews on the flight line, civilians on and off base. From Blacks I got sympathy and "chin up" encouragement. From Whites, stony silence—except for Captain R, who was heard to say, unwisely, by witnesses, "Dryden is guilty and we've got to throw the book at him!" His comment had an unexpected impact on the ultimate outcome of my trials.

With my wings clipped by the order grounding me, I was assigned to daily duty as runway control officer. That undesirable duty was usually assigned to the instructors on a rotating basis. Whenever flying was in progress the runway control officer was on duty in a vehicle outfitted like a small, mobile control tower complete with VHF radio, Aldis lamp, and flare gun with a supply of red and green flares. And gnats!

The gnats swarmed constantly, making it impossible to doze off when activity slowed down. The runway control truck was driven to a position about 50 yards from the side of the active runway and 100 yards from the landing end. Whenever the wind shifted enough to change the direction of landing, the runway control officer had to move to the new position. His role was to assist pilots with their landing patterns, especially when a pilot was checking out a type of aircraft for his first few flights in it. By radio the runway control officer might assist the pilot with advisory messages such as:

"P-39 turning on base leg, you're high. Drop flaps!"
 or
"You're too low. Pull up and go around!"
 or
"Your wheels are up. Lower your landing gear!"

The pilot was required to acknowledge the call. If he didn't, the runway control officer would use the Aldis lamp beaming an amber light aimed toward the landing plane to caution the pilot to check his aircraft and approach pattern, a green light to continue his approach and land, or a red light to discontinue the approach and go around. If the pilot did not react properly to a red light, a red flare was fired in front of him in a high arc that he couldn't miss seeing.

There were instances when I was able to avert an accident. Now and then a brand new trainee, nervous about flying a high performance fighter plane, forgot to lower his landing gear. Most of the time, however, runway control was uneventful and boring. It was hot out there under the blazing June, South Carolina sun. And the gnats were relentless.

To combat boredom while waiting for training flights to return and land, I read my way through a set of literature classics I had purchased: Shakespeare, Dumas, Balzac, Twain (Clemens), Homer's *Odyssey, The Iliad*, de Tocqueville's *Democracy in America*—a sort of self-improvement program to sharpen my mind.

In addition to being grounded I was also assigned as mess officer of the officers mess. The "Colored" officers mess. There I worked with Second Lieutenant Charles D. Walker, a "brother," former schoolteacher from Indianapolis, who had been the mess officer until I was assigned; he became my assistant. The officers eating there dubbed him "Chop Chop," used as a term of endearment, or scorn, depending on the quality of the meals at the time. We became good friends as I learned much from him about managing a business, employees, supplies inventory, and funds—valuable lessons for an officer who had never been anything other than a "throttle jockey."

So I did gain some benefits from my grounding: a broader exposure to literature and to management, both of which were useful in later years.

But, now, back to my general court-martial trials. There were two.

The first one was at Walterboro Army Air Base as described briefly in chapters 1 and 2. For the record, however, and to understand what followed the first trial, a few more details are necessary.

First of all, at the beginning of the trial and at my request, my defense counsel, First Lieutenant Kelliher (a sympathetic White officer), attempted to have Captain R excused from sitting as a member of the court by my challenge "for cause." The "cause" was his statement, heard by witnesses, that I was guilty: a gross prejudgment in any court. Except this one. The trial judge advocate (TJA), a lawyer on the court, rules on challenges for cause. This TJA ruled that my cause was invalid inasmuch as it was based upon hearsay evidence. So Captain R would remain as a member of the court.

I couldn't accept that. He had to go. Because of his prejudicial statement I felt I couldn't get a fair trial with him on the court. So I told my defense counsel to use my one, and only, peremptory challenge. That was a sure way to get rid of Captain R. With the peremptory challenge no reason is necessary; it can be based upon a reason as frivolous as "I don't like his looks." I had no problem with Captain R's looks. I just didn't like how he sounded. So, he had to go!

After my challenge the court of nine members included five White officers and four Black. The latter were my former squadron mates: Lieutenants Bill Campbell, Herbert "Bud" Clark, Walter "Ghost" Lawson, and Graham "Peepsight" Smith. I was satisfied that I would have a fair trial.

And I did. I was acquitted of the charge of buzzing the town on

Sunday because my explanation of what I was trying to teach my three trainees convinced the court that I should not be held culpable. Not so on the Saturday flight, however. Too many witnesses saw us "cut the grass" on the field in a dangerous manner as alleged. The court had only one possible verdict: "Guilty!" I was sentenced to be dismissed from the service, as reported in chapter 1.

But it never happened. Instead of being dismissed I was granted a new trial by the reviewing authority at higher headquarters. Judging that in my first trial my cause for challenging Captain R was valid, the reviewing authority ruled that my rights as a defendant had been infringed because I had been forced to use my peremptory challenge unnecessarily to get an undesired member removed from the court.

The second trial was held about a month later, in July 1944, somewhere in Charleston, South Carolina, about fifty miles from the base. The court members were total strangers, all White officers who tried me only on the base buzzing incident because I had been acquitted of the town buzzing charge in the first trial. I was found guilty again but this time the sentence was: restricted to the base for three months; fined $110.00 per month for three months; suspended from promotion eligibility for one year.

No dismissal!

Thank God, my career could continue. I had proof positive of the power of prayer: mine, my wife's, my family's, kinfolk's, and friends'. And of the love of my kid sister, Pauline, thirteen years old at time of my trials, who wrote to President Roosevelt: "Please don't put my brother out of the Army Air Corps."

My wife, Second Lieutenant Irma (Cameron) Dryden, U.S. Army Nurse Corps, was still stationed at Tuskegee Army Air Field. Between trials I wished so much to see her. Grounded, I couldn't fly to her. So I decided to go to her by bus.

After arranging for a weekend leave of absence I packed my B-4 bag and hopped a bus into town, arriving about noon on a Friday. The bus terminal waiting rooms were almost empty—Colored and White—when I entered the Colored side, choking with anger at Jim Crow. The next bus to Macon was scheduled to leave at about

1:00 P.M. From Macon it would head for Montgomery, Alabama, passing Tuskegee on the way. By the time the bus was ready to load passengers, both waiting rooms were full. Although many of the Black passengers were early and had arrived before most of the Whites, we were made to wait until they were all on board before we were allowed to board. That did it for me!

"To hell with this!" I swore. "I'll be damned if I'm gonna take this crap!"

I went back to the base stewing in my own juice. Vengeful. Stupefied. Immobilized—at least for several hours.

By about 10:00 P.M. my urge to see my wife was so strong that I was willing to endure the inequities, iniquities, and inconveniences of Jim Crow although still, and forever, unwilling to acquiesce in its doctrine. So I went back to the bus station in time to board the midnight bus to Macon. This time the bus was already there, almost fully loaded. So there was no problem about who boarded ahead of whom.

However, there was a problem, at once ironic and paradoxical. Except for about four Black men and women on the back seat of the bus, all the other passengers were White. Many of them appeared to be college students from colleges up the line, the Carolinas and Virginia, heading home for summer vacation. They were occupying all the other seats including the last row of side-by-side seats, two on each side of the aisle. Another Black man and I boarded and walked to the "Colored" section in the back of the bus where there were no vacant seats. I was startled to hear the bus driver shout as he looked in his rearview mirror: "You kids in the last row of seats gotta move. Those four seats are for Colored passengers. That's the law! So y'all move now, y'hear?"

Four White coeds got out of the seats. The "brother" and I slid into the two pairs of side-by-side seats, he on one side, I across the aisle. We looked at each other and shrugged in disbelief at the unpredictable twists and turns of Jim Crow. I stretched out across the two seats to try to sleep in a cramped fetal position. The four evicted coeds sat or stretched out in the aisle grumbling and probably surprised by the bus driver's decree. I, too, was surprised and had mixed feelings about the situation. As an officer in uniform and, more to the point, having been raised to be a gentleman, custom required that I yield my seat to women and the elderly.

"Oh well, what the hell! That's Jim Crow for you—stupid nonsense!" I thought as I settled down to snooze away the eight or more hours to Macon.

Dawn broke at about 7:00 A.M. As I awakened I noticed that some of the coeds who had been sleeping in the aisle were now in "White" seats. Apparently some passengers had gotten off during the night. Shortly after dawn the bus stopped at a whistle-stop somewhere in Georgia to take on three Black women. My chance to be chivalrous, legally. I stood the remaining two hours to Macon.

In the Macon terminal all passengers got off the bus, including me. I went into the rest room in the Colored waiting room and bought some snacks and a soda for breakfast. Reboarding the empty bus I sat down in a seat about four rows behind the driver, who watched me in his rearview mirror. He didn't say anything at first, but as White passengers approached the bus to board he said softly, menacingly, through clenched teeth, "Sol'jer, you gotta move back to the Colored seats!"

I had seen some red-neck policemen in the bus station. I remembered proverbs I had heard:

> Discretion is the better part of valor.
> He who turns and runs away lives to fight another day.
> A fool and his money (or his life) are soon parted.

I was not a fool—coward maybe—but not a fool. I was determined to live and fight, on my terms, not commit suicide. I did the valorous thing—I was discreet. I moved. I almost retched as I despised myself then. Still do, somewhat, although I realize now that defiance then would have meant . . . Who knows what dire consequences?

The bus took on a few passengers, left after about an hour layover, and arrived at Tuskegee at about 1:00 P.M. Saturday afternoon. Half an hour later a taxi delivered me to the nurses quarters and into the arms of my beloved. We had been married a scant seven months earlier, so our reunion was paradise. But not for long. Paradise was lost the next afternoon when I had to return to Walterboro. I got lucky, however, when one of my buddies, Peepsight Smith, flew over from Walterboro to Tuskegee to fly me back. Bless his heart, Peepsight saved me the horror and hazards of a bus trip back to the base.

Final action on the second trial by the reviewing authority came swiftly. Within a week I was restored to flying status. Hallelujah! No more daily runway control duty—except when my name came up on the roster of instructors. No more mess officer duties either. Every flight instructor was needed. The war in Europe had escalated after the fall of Rome on June 4 and the June 6 D-Day invasion of Normandy by the Allies. Also, as a class of aviation cadets won their wings each month, we had a constant stream of JPs (junior pilots) arriving from Tuskegee Army Flying School to be trained in aerial combat tactics for overseas duty. Training flights seven days every week, from dawn until after dark, sometimes until midnight, was normal routine.

My first flight after being grounded was on August 19, 1944. It was a refresher flight to get reacquainted with the P-47 "Thunderbolt." I had checked out in it at Selfridge Field four months earlier, but I hadn't flown at all since Sunday, May 14, when we buzzed the town. While I was grounded the P-39s were replaced with P-47s.

Certified OK to resume duties as a training flight instructor by the squadron operations officer, I rejoined my former squadron mates from the 99th in teaching the lessons we had learned in aerial combat. There were five of them, all first lieutenants: Bill Campbell, Bud Clark, Ghost Lawson, Peepsight Smith, and Spann Watson. Shortly after my second trial both Campbell and Clark volunteered to return overseas to join the 332nd in Italy.

The stream of JPs coming to us from Tuskegee Army Flying School (TAFS) included a cast of characters, some cocky, almost every one potentially combat competent, all colorful—officers and gentlemen of color. We instructors had excellent materials to work with and mold into aerial warriors. A shared sense of special mission—nay, crusade—among all of us TAFS graduates, instructors and trainees alike, made our task easy. We shared a keen awareness of being regarded by army brass as incapable of flying and fighting as pilots and ground crews, as well as a strong individual and personal vow to make the "Tuskegee Experiment" a success.

So many men came to Walterboro as junior pilots and left about four months later to go overseas as well-trained fighter pilots that I cannot remember all whom I knew while there. However, some scored notable victories in combat and are memorable.

For example, three of them, later flying propeller-driven P-51s with the 332nd overseas, each shot down a German jet-propelled ME-262. They were Lieutenants Charles Brantley, Roscoe Brown, and Earl Lane.

One Walterboro graduate, Lieutenant Clarence "Lucky" Lester, shot down three ME-109s within five minutes!

Some others were memorable because of some unique activity while at Walterboro. For example: One class of JPs upon arrival at Walterboro decided to provide their own transportation rather than depend upon the shuttle bus between the flight line and the BOQ. One of them, Lieutenant Pete Anders, shopped the used car lots for a vehicle that could haul about six of his buddies and bought it. It became the talk of the base. Small wonder—it was a hearse!

Some were cocky. Too cocksure of their flying ability for their own good. To one such braggart, Peepsight Smith delivered a humbling barb by telling him, "Son, I've got more time in the top of a loop than your total flying time!" The braggart got the point, as every aviator knows that in performing acrobatics the time spent at the top of a loop is only a few seconds.

Another show-off managed to embarrass us Army Air Corps pilots at Walterboro AAB in the eyes of U.S. Marine pilots based at Parris Island NAS (Naval Air Station) on the South Carolina coast about thirty miles to the east. Flying P-47 "Thunderbolts" one afternoon, I was leading a flight of four returning to base after completing a practice mission at the ground gunnery range on the coast not far from Parris Island. Cruising along at about 8,000 feet I caught sight of a flight of sixteen F-4U "Corsairs" in a stepped-up echelon dead ahead and slightly above us. Figuring that they were practicing for an upcoming air show, I decided to give them a wide berth. Changing direction slightly to pass to the left of the

Corsairs, I signaled my three trainees to tighten up our formation while calling them on squadron frequency: "Sixteen Corsairs, two o'clock high. Tighten up!"

That was a mistake. One of my self-styled "hot rock" trainees peeled out of formation and made a pass at the Corsairs. Accepting the challenge to a simulated dogfight, the marines peeled off in trail, all sixteen of them. The sky was suddenly filled with deep blue–painted, gull-winged F-4Us outturning, outclimbing, out-speeding, and outmaneuvering our P-47s and, at the same time, outraging our guys on the base who could see our humiliation at the hands of the marines.

We didn't have a chance. Those marines turned us every way but loose! Our Thunderbolts didn't come into their own as fighters until above about 25,000 feet when the supercharger kicks in and gives the 2,800-horsepower engine added power. Down at 8,000 feet, pitted against Corsairs, we were like clumsy, lumbering elephants pestered by pesky swarming mosquitoes. Once on our tail we couldn't shake them—not until they tired of the sport, formed up, and headed back to Parris Island.

Whereupon we formed up and landed. I didn't wait for the debriefing in operations to chew out our brash trainee. Oh, no! I jumped out of my cockpit, ran over to his ship, climbed up on his wing, and lit into him while he was still filling out his Form 1.

"Listen, Dummy," addressing him as if he were still an aviation cadet, "don't you ever, ever, ever break formation like that again! Do you understand?"

"Yes, Sir!"

"Another thing, Mister. Don't ever engage in simulated dogfights without preplanning by all participants. Army Air Corps regulations require such preplanning and you can be court-martialed if you violate that reg. I'm not going to file charges against you, but just remember that with all those planes swirling around up there today we're lucky there were no midair collisions. Do you get the point, Dummy?"

"Yes, Sir!"

We had no more trouble out of him.

We narrowly escaped the demise of the entire "Tuskegee Experiment" because of what happened to one of our trainees when he and his wife went to an amusement park on a Sunday, his day off. Kenny, as I'll call him, was a quiet, reserved, but pleasant fellow and a good pilot, usually unflappable. However, when he reported to operations on Monday morning he seemed agitated and nervous. One of his buddies volunteered the information that the day before, at the amusement park, Kenny and his wife had been insulted, humiliated, denied admission. Full of rage he had been heard to say, "Next time I'm scheduled to go to the ground gunnery range I'm gonna shoot up that goddam place!"

The gunnery range was a mere five miles or so from the amusement park. Fortunately, one of our instructors got wind of Kenny's vendetta and had him grounded for a couple of days until he cooled off. I shuddered to think about what might have happened to all of us if he had carried out his threat.

During their relatively short stay at Walterboro the trainees logged an average of sixty hours in various types of training, including: transition into the fighter aircraft to learn how to make safe takeoffs and landings, formation flying, instrument and night flying, aerial and ground gunnery, aerobatics, and combat tactics. The training flights were flown in P-39s at first, in May 1944. Two months later P-47s replaced the P-39s, which were replaced in turn by P-40s in February 1945. With each change the instructors had to learn the characteristics and peculiarities of the new aircraft:

The P-39 "Airacobra" was unique with its tricycle landing gear; in-line air-cooled engine mounted behind the pilot's cockpit and driving the propeller by means of a long shaft rotating at high speed under the floorboard of the cockpit; and a 37-millimeter cannon in the propeller nose cone. Flying the P-39 was fun because its tricycle landing gear precluded ground loops and afforded straight taxiing—no "S"-ing necessary. Takeoff in the P-39 was tricky because of the angle of attack of its wings on the ground. You had to "unstick" the nose wheel before reaching a certain speed or you would run out of runway. Also, the procedure for recovery from tailspins varied according to the ammunition on board for the .30-caliber machine guns and the 37-millimeter cannon. Use the wrong procedure and you could wind up in a flat spin that was very hard to stop. Perhaps the worst feature of the P-39 was the location of the engine behind the cockpit: On an emergency wheels-up landing, the heavy engine could crush the pilot as its momentum would cause it to continue moving forward after the airframe had stopped.

The P-40 "Kittyhawk" (or "Tomahawk"), a "tail dragger" with narrow landing gear, was a bugbear on landings. Carelessness at touchdown was a sure setup for a ground loop and a scraped wing tip and, maybe, a damaged propeller as well. Because of the long in-line engine you had to "S" from side to side while taxiing. In the air the P-40 was a maneuvering dream. It could turn on a dime. In fact, during that simulated dogfight when the marine Corsairs from Parris Island embarrassed us in our P-47s, I kept wishing we were in P-40s instead. It might have been a different scenario. I had flown combat missions in "Kittyhawks" and knew how maneuverable they were.

The P-47 "Thunderbolt," also referred to affectionately as "the Jug," was also a tail dragger, like the P-40. But there the resemblance ended. The Jug had a big barrel-like fuselage with a big radial engine up front. On takeoff the torque of that big 2,800-horsepower engine could ruin the unwary pilot who failed to compensate by using hard right rudder and right aileron as he applied takeoff power with the throttle. Upon landing, the fourteen-foot-wide landing gear was very forgiving of the careless pilot. At high altitude the supercharger transformed the heavy seven-ton Jug from the lumbering elephant it resembled at low altitude to a swift, agile hawk.

Formation flying at altitude with supercharger boost was hard work, however. The combination of the Jug's weight in motion at high speed produced momentum that, in thin air at high altitude, would cause the pilot trouble holding his position in formation if he didn't anticipate changes of speed by his formation leader.

By mid-September, about six weeks after resuming flying, I had settled into the routine of training flights when my wife Irma, nicknamed "Pete," gave me a birthday present. She called from Tuskegee on "my" day, the sixteenth.

"Hi, Charlie," she said. "Happy birthday!"

"Thanks, Sugar. How are you?"

"Not so good."

"What's wrong?"

"I dunno. I get sick every morning and can't figure out why," she teased. Then, unable to contain her good news any longer, she purred: "We are pregnant, Honey. We are going to be parents!"

"Hallelujah!" I exulted. "That means you'll be discharged from the service and we'll be together again, right?"

"That's right. I'm processing my application for discharge and should be out by October 1st, so you better find a place for us to live, Daddy!"

And I did. I found a Mr. Tracy who had a two-bedroom house for rent in the "Colored" section of Walterboro, next door to his own home and about three blocks from the perimeter fence of the base. He already had one couple in one bedroom and wanted to rent the other. It was wartime, housing was scarce, especially near military bases, and young marrieds like us were more than willing to take anything halfway decent. With indoor plumbing, gas stove, and fairly new albeit rough construction, Mr. Tracy's cottage was a bit better than halfway decent. So I took it.

Pete arrived in early October. We moved into our bedroom, sharing the kitchen, sitting room, and bathroom with the other young marrieds, Lieutenant Everett Bratcher and his wife Helen, a congenial couple, childless like us but with a pet. Herman was a baby squirrel who had the run of their room and delighted everyone who saw him—everyone except Bratcher's boss, who saw Bratcher's shirt pocket moving around one day during a meeting. Asked, "What's that in your pocket, Lieutenant?" Bratcher took Herman out of his shirt pocket and handed him to his boss.

"How cute!" said the boss, setting Herman on his desk. That was a bad mistake! Herman peed all over the papers on the boss's desk.

"Get that varmint outta here!" roared the boss.

"Brat," as Helen called her husband, had a wry sense of humor and we enjoyed sharing the home with them. We were happy anticipating our firstborn until tragedy struck. Pete miscarried. We grieved, of course, but were consoled by the old adage, "If at first you don't succeed, try, try again." Success eluded us for three years.

Meanwhile 1944, the worst year of my life, ended and the constant stream of trainees from Tuskegee continued. Business as usual. Until May 8, 1945: V-E Day. We all wondered if our training program would be terminated.

In January 1945, one of our instructors, Lieutenant Spann Watson, a veteran of the 99th, had gotten into an altercation with Mayor Sweatt of Walterboro. Spann had saved up his gasoline ration stamps for a motor trip to visit kinfolk in North Carolina and New Jersey. He had taken his car to the Ford dealer in town a week in advance. Days passed and it wasn't ready. Finally, the day before his planned departure, he went to get his car. The Ford dealer, who was also the mayor, didn't like his attitude, called him "boy" and slapped him—whereupon Spann punched him in the mouth, sending his glasses flying. Mechanics armed with tire irons rushed Spann, who jumped into his car and hightailed it to the base with a posse in hot pursuit.

He made it to the base, zipping through the gate without stopping. Fortunately for him the posse couldn't pursue him onto a federal reservation and were halted at the gate. Next day he had orders to transfer to Godman Field, near Louisville, Kentucky, and left that very day.

I envied him. I had had it with Walterboro, with the blatant prejudice and the latent violence. I wanted to leave, too.

My chance to escape came in July when Major Bill Campbell came to Walterboro to recruit volunteers for the 99th Fighter Squadron, which had been deactivated in Europe just after V-E Day and reactivated at Godman Field.

After leaving Walterboro the previous year to return overseas, Bill had earned his gold leaves as CO of the 99th. Now here he was, back at Walterboro AAB on official business, asking the three of us Black instructors (Lawson, Smith, and me): "Who wants to go with me as a flight leader in the new 99th to fight in the Pacific? We have spanking new P-47Ns with bubble canopies and equipped for long-range, high-altitude escort missions."

Without hesitation I said, "Take me, p-l-e-a-s-e!"

He did. Within a week I had PCS (permanent change of station) orders to transfer to Godman Field. A few days later, after clearing the base and saying good-bye to friends, Pete and I hit the road to Godman in Black Beauty, the 1938 four-door sedan we had bought shortly after we set up housekeeping.

Thus ended my fourteen-month "exile" in South Carolina.

10 Fighting 99th: Over Here!

>> July 1945–February 1946

For Pete and me the trip from South Carolina to Kentucky was the longest motor trip we had attempted in Black Beauty. The seven-year-old sedan made the trip without a hitch as we were able to meet its needs at any service station along the three-state route. We had no trouble buying gasoline and oil or getting water for the radiator and air for the tires.

We were not so lucky meeting our own needs, however, as we found that in some places restaurant facilities "for Colored people" were either only for takeout or not at all and rest rooms were outdoor, "out back" outhouses. We learned quickly to buy snack foods in large grocery stores in large towns along the way and to ask about rest room facilities before putting any gasoline into the fuel tank.

At dusk we were high up in the mountains of Tennessee and decided to stay overnight in some town if we could find accommodations. As we stopped at a gas station in a fairly large town, I asked the attendant, who was Black, if there was a rooming house or some kind of sleeping facility in town where we could stay. He directed us to a small motel a few miles distant, owned by a relative of his. We found it without any trouble and spent a restful night in one of the tiny cabins, grateful that we did not have to stay on the road and drive through the night simply because of Jim Crow.

With Columbia and Spartanburg, South Carolina, behind us and Knoxville, Tennessee, and Lexington, Kentucky, still up ahead we were about halfway to our new home near Louisville, Kentucky. So early next morning we were on the road again, fighting the early morning fog and the sharp switchbacks climbing up the side of one mountain then down the other; driving slowly and cautiously to stay on roads that seldom had guardrails to keep errant cars from plunging down the steep sides of cliffs on which the narrow shoulders of the road perched precariously.

By midmorning the fog burned off as the sun rose to usher in a warm, beautiful day. By late afternoon Black Beauty had galloped through Knoxville and Lexington and brought us to the outskirts of Louisville. Neither of us had ever been to that town before but something in the air told us that we must be getting close. Something we sniffed that grew stronger with each click of the odometer. "What can that be?" we wondered. Suddenly it dawned on us. Kentucky is the state known for three "B's": bluegrass, blue bloods (horses), and bourbon. Soon after crossing the border with next-door neighbor, Tennessee, we had noted the miles of white picket fences marking the boundaries of horse farms here and there along our route and had seen some beautiful horses grazing the blue (?)—it looked green to us—grass that covered each farm. So the strong odor must be that of sour mash from the whiskey distilleries on the outskirts of Louisville.

Finally reaching the city itself we asked directions to the address where my old squadron mate, Spann Watson, was living. He had been transferred PCS to Godman Field seven months earlier. We found the house in a quiet, old, elegant neighborhood graced with tall oaks and elms shading the lawns of stately looking, rock-solid three-story homes and the streets with canopies of branches in full leaf. A quietly impressive sight. I might have known that Spann would not rest until he had found comfortable quarters for his wife, Edna, and himself where they could live in peace, especially in view of the fact that he had gotten out of South Carolina just one jump ahead of a lynch mob. I hoped that we would be as lucky.

Our first temporary home in Louisville was one room in a private home owned by a friend of my friend, Lieutenant Gordon Southall. Gordon had come through the TAAF experiment and was now stationed at Godman Field in the provost marshal's office.

The contacts we got from him and Spann helped us to find an attic apartment within a couple of days with an elderly couple who "adopted" us as their own "chillun." We were happy to settle down in their home, at least for the time being, but we were hoping to be able to move into quarters on Fort Knox, adjacent to Godman Field.

Commanding officer of Godman Field was my former CO, Colonel B. O. Davis, Jr. After V-E Day, May 7, 1945, the 332nd Fighter Group was deactivated and he was rotated back to the United States assigned as CO of the 477th Composite Group stationed at Godman. On June 21 he assumed command of Godman Field, the first American of color to be in charge of an entire military installation. That fact plus the matchless war record of his 332nd led those of us in his command at Godman to believe that we would have good quarters and free access to various facilities and amenities on both Godman Field and Fort Knox such as post exchange cafeterias, gymnasiums, movie theaters, and so on.

Not so.

In spite of his position, reputation, and rank, Colonel Davis was denied any such courtesies that would normally be extended to a "next-door neighbor" by a commander of a "sister" service. At the time that these segregationist measures were taking place, those of us stationed at Godman Field concluded that the White folks at Fort Knox were just being their usual, typical "mean" selves acting out their mythical notions of their "superiority" versus our "inferiority." Little did I know the depth of the viciousness of the racist scalawags next door who denied us military rights, civil rights, human rights, liberty-equality-and-the-pursuit-of-happiness-rights-as-Americans. While writing and researching for these memoirs I have plumbed the depths of the racism and had my eyes opened to the rancor that our commander faced in trying to deal with the post commander of Fort Knox while seeking fair, decent treatment for his Godman Field troops.

One utterance by Post Commander Colonel John Throckmorton sums it up. Speaking to his superior at higher army headquarters in a recorded telephone conversation, he said: "Well, you know we've got four general officers here at Fort Knox and they sure don't want no goddam coons moving in next door to them!'"

It was probably best for me that I did not know all that "the Old Man" was going through at the time. I had enough problems of my own to cope with in my new assignment to Godman Field. Having arrived on a Sunday and with a couple days remaining from my PCS (permanent change of station) travel time, I had time for Pete and me to get settled into our attic apartment before reporting to duty with the 99th.

From the apartment to Godman was about a thirty-mile drive. On that first day I drove Black Beauty to work, leaving Pete stranded without transportation to get about the city. I fixed that problem the next day by arranging to car pool with some of the other men who also had to cope with the sixty-miles-per-day commute due to the lack of officers quarters available on Godman Field. Before the assignment of the 477th to Godman Field, the officers of units based there, and their families, were billeted at Fort Knox. However, as noted earlier, Colonel Throckmorton "Jim Crowed" the 477th with his refusal to provide housing at Fort Knox.

Reporting to my new commanding officer, Major Bill Campbell, I was assigned as assistant executive officer of the squadron. My immediate boss was Captain Morris Johnson, the executive officer. My old friend, Spann Watson, was squadron operations officer.

The 99th had been deactivated in Europe with the Nazis' defeat and reactivated at Godman Field as the fighter squadron component of the 477th Composite Group, a hybrid, only-one-of-its-kind-in-the-U.S.-Army-Air-Corps, the other component of which was two squadrons of B-25 "Mitchell" medium bombers. The 99th was to be equipped with new P-47N-25 "Thunderbolts" designed for its mission: escort of high-altitude, long-range B-29 bombing raids against targets in the Japanese home islands. Spratmo had it that some missions might last as long as twelve hours!

Our first step on the road to Japan was to get trained on the new "Jugs" when they were delivered. Only a couple were on the ramp when I arrived. The P-47N-25s had features that were certain to endear them even more, to those of us who had flown the "razorback" versions overseas with the 332nd or at Walterboro, as I had done, than the earlier models. For example: more boost at high altitude with water injection to increase engine output; UHF radios for clearer communications; some had autopilots for long overwater flights, all had rudder pedals that could be rotated backwards, once airborne, allowing the pilot to slide his feet through the opening thus created and stretch his legs. And we were told that when we arrived at our Pacific island airstrip we would be equipped with Jugs having "ass massagers," foam rubber seats with parallel tubes that pulsated with air, alternately—like deicing boots on the wings of airplanes—giving the effect of a massage of the gluteus maximus!

In any case, eventually we had about forty-seven Jugs of various models sitting on the flight line, sharing the limited ramp space with about twenty-four B-25s of the 616th and 617th Medium Bombardment Squadrons. The task of training our forty fighter pilots fell to the ops officer, Spann Watson. A buzz bomb of energy, drive, and impact, Spann was a perfect man for the job. An excellent pilot himself, veteran of the 99th's campaigns against Pantelleria, Sicily, and the Salerno beachhead invasion of Italy, and survivor of the civil rights "war" at Walterboro, he had helped train many of the Tuskegee Army Flying School graduates who came through Walterboro for air combat tactics training and who later went overseas and beat the pants off the Luftwaffe's best pilots.

Helping him get the job done were a handful of 332nd veterans assigned as flight leaders. One I already knew: Captain Ed "Topper" Toppins. Some others I had met briefly at Selfridge before they shipped overseas on Christmas Eve 1943: crackerjack fighter jocks like Lieutenants Johnny Briggs, William "Chubby" Green, Weldon K. Groves, Felix Kirkpatrick. And, of course, leading the outfit, "Mr. Fighter Pilot" himself, the commanding officer, Major William Ayers Campbell. "Wild Bill," as some nicknamed him, was the fighter pilot's fighter pilot.

A native of Tuskegee, Bill Campbell was a 1937 graduate of the institute with a degree in business administration. He had earned a private pilot license in the CPT Program and won his silver wings at Tuskegee Army Flying School in aviation cadet class 42-F. He was a member of the original 99th Fighter Squadron and had returned to the States as an aerial combat instructor at Selfridge Field and Walterboro Army Air Base, from which he left to return overseas. Rejoining the 99th in Italy, where it was by then an integral part of the 332nd Fighter Group, he eventually became its commanding officer until the end of the war in Europe. His leadership on the ground as well as in the air led to his being assigned as its CO when it was reactivated at Godman Field, Kentucky, as a component of the 477th Composite Group.

Other officers of the 99th at Godman Field included: Lieutenant J. B. Williams, engineering officer; Lieutenant James J. Johns, adjutant; Lieutenant Walter I. Lawson, supply officer; Lieutenant Ernest Davis (a 1945 West Point graduate who got his wings in class 45-J), tech supply officer; and Lieutenant Richard H. Harris, personal equipment officer.

Supply Officer "Ghost" Lawson was my old buddy from the original 99th and the Walterboro "exile." J. B. Williams and "Rich" Harris were also survivors of the Walterboro "exile."

Our flying training included all the usual elements with emphasis on long-distance navigation because we were earmarked for the escort of long-range, high-altitude bombers across hundreds of miles of trackless Pacific Ocean. A particular restriction on our navigation flights made it difficult to accomplish such training: We were prohibited from landing and RON at any of the numerous military air bases in the United States other than Walterboro Army Air Base, Tuskegee Army Air Field, and Fort Dix, New Jersey. The "problem" with our landing at any other air bases was that transient officers quarters were still not available for Negroes at other bases! Nothing had changed. Just as before going overseas, we had been limited to landing and staying overnight at only a few bases. Our achievements overseas had not changed the status quo stateside.

On July 28, 1945, our entire base complement had a terrible scare. Radio and newspapers were full of reports that a B-25 had flown into New York City's Empire State Building, plowing into the seventy-ninth floor on a foggy day. Thirteen died, including the five-man crew and innocent bystanders in office suites. Our base operations outbound board showed a flight dispatched to McGuire AFB at Fort Dix. Lieutenant Harold Hillery was the aircraft commander.

"Omigod!" I thought when I heard the news about the crash, praying that it was not our crew.

It wasn't. As it turned out, when he was on the ground at McGuire, "Tank" Hillery heard the news, too, and wondered if one of the other B-25 crews had pranged into the Empire State. There was a base-wide sigh of relief when Tank's flight plan for his return to Godman came over the teletype at base operations.

A traditional activity at Godman Field was SMI. Saturday morning inspection in each squadron or unit area was a fixed routine that sometimes was capped by a parade of the entire 477th Composite Group. For me such parades were emotional experiences. Marching with my squadron was always thrilling for me as we passed in review past Colonel Davis and his staff, the band playing a lively Sousa march, the Stars and Stripes and unit pennants flapping snappily in the breeze, unit after unit moving across the parade area responding to "pay attention" commands barked in stentorian voices:

> "Squadr-o-o-o-n!"
> passed down the line.
> "Plat-o-o-o-n!"
> the preparatory command,
> "Column left!"
> echoed by the platoon leader,
> "Column left!"
> Then the command of execution (i.e., the "do it!" command):
> "MARCH!"

And as each unit passed abeam of the reviewing party and the massed colors:

"E-y-e-s RIGHT!" the squadron commander intoned as he lifted a snappy salute while looking sharply to his right at the reviewing party.

After marching the length of the parade ground each unit commander marched his outfit back to its unit area and had a brief meeting before dismissing all hands who had no weekend duty assignments.

Godman Field was the first and only U.S. military post commanded by and operated entirely by African Americans and I was intensely and fiercely proud to be part of it. No matter that although the war in Europe had ended, the war in the Pacific was still raging and we were headed there in a few months. I was just glad to be out of the Walterboro Air Base "exile" where German PWs enjoyed privileges denied American citizens of color.

German PWs were at Fort Knox also. They could be seen at various locations on the fort and at Godman Field performing a variety of tasks.

One Saturday, after SMI, I had arranged to ride to Louisville with a friend who was a lawyer in the base legal office, Captain Jim Redden. Before leaving Godman he stopped at the PX gas station. I remained in the car while Jim got out to supervise the two attendants as they pumped the gas and checked the radiator and the tires. As they went about their work they kept up a constant chatter in German, punctuated with raucous laughter now and then. I was reading a newspaper and paying no particular attention until I heard:

"*Achtung!*" followed by a torrent of German words. Growled, gutteral, angry words spat out in staccato bursts with machine-gun-like impact on anyone within hearing. Although I understood no German, I knew that Captain Redden was chewing out the PWs. I did not know why he was upbraiding them but, obviously, they did because they both straightened up into a ramrod rigid posture and smiles faded from their faces, which turned scarlet. Captain Redden's tirade went on for a couple minutes. He ended with:

"*Verstehen sie?*"

I understood that, and so did the Germans.

"*Ja! Ja! Jawohl mein Kapitan!*" they chorused, visibly shaken.

As Jim slid into the driver's seat and started the motor, I asked him, "What was that all about?"

"Those damned Germans were saying some nasty things, calling us 'niggers' and I gave 'em hell about it. They didn't think that any of us could understand their language. Well, I used to teach German in high school and have been fluent in it as far back as I can remember. Anyway, I'm sure they'll be more careful about what they say and where they say it from now on!"

Every Saturday afternoon saw a big exodus from the base to Louisville. Some made the trip in car pools, others by bus. By whatever means one made the trip, the scenery was, of course, the same: ordinary, unspectacular. However, the trip by bus was extraordinary and gut wrenching because inside Louisville city limits there were no restrictions on seating. Once outside city limits, "niggers to the back of the bus" was the rule enforced by burly Kentucky state troopers.

About ten days after our false alarm about the B-25 that flew into the Empire State Building, the world was shaken and shocked on August 6 when Hiroshima was leveled by the first atomic bomb. Three days later it was Nagasaki's turn. Yet another five days and Japan surrendered on August 14. V-J Day!

It brought wild rejoicing everywhere. World War II was over! Like everyone else I was glad that it was over for all the usual reasons, plus a special reason: I could now tell Pete that I had left Walterboro headed for combat duty overseas with the 477th and not just to remain at Godman as an instructor, as I had done at Walterboro. She was startled to learn that because she had been feeling sorry for the other wives while feeling secure in the belief that her own husband was going to remain at Godman. She had not realized that I was so unhappy at Walterboro that I was willing to volunteer to go back to war, if necessary, just to leave there.

Soon after V-J Day a married officers quarters was made available on Godman Field. Frustrated by the post commander of Fort Knox, in his quest for housing on the fort, and getting no support at all from higher headquarters, Colonel Davis directed the conversion of two barracks to married officers quarters (MOQs). Pete and

I moved into one of them. So my daily sixty-mile round-trip commute came to an end. That was good news.

The bad news was the MOQ itself. With about thirty couples living in the two-story building, each couple's apartment was a one-room cubicle, about twenty feet square, with walls (partitions) that went up only to about a foot from the ceiling. There was no real privacy.

The bathroom facility was more bad news, especially on Saturday mornings when the husbands were rushing to get ready for SMI. The one bathroom for the entire building was an open latrine, on the first floor, with the usual furnishings: a row of about a half dozen face basins each with a mirror above it on the near side of a partial wall that divided the room lengthwise; on the other side of the wall were about four cubicles with commodes and an open bay with a half dozen shower heads and shower boards.

To gain access to the latrine the residents developed a system by mutual agreement. You would knock on the locked door of the latrine. Anyone inside would ask, "Male or female?" If you were the same sex as the occupants of the moment and answered accordingly, the door was unlocked and you entered. If not of the same sex you heard, "Just a minute!" and it could be several minutes before you got in. Oftentimes on Saturday mornings, to make sure they would be showered and shaved in time for SMI, the men would get up at about 4:00 A.M. and take charge of the latrine. By the time the wives began stirring about, the men were dressed, groomed, and gone.

That is how we coped with the worst housing situation I have ever seen anywhere, though no fault of our base commander, Colonel Davis, who tried to rectify it through channels to higher headquarters, and no thanks to higher headquarters all the way to the top brass hats who were determined to maintain segregation at all costs!

An immediate effect of V-J Day was the beginning of the rapid demobilization of the huge military machine that had done its job, defeated the Axis powers, and was now ready to go home. The closing of bases began and one of the first earmarked for closing was Tuskegee Army Air Field. A large number of recent graduates were just marking time there since the war in Europe had ended in May. They were all transferred to Godman Field, and suddenly the 99th had 144 pilots all told, all needing four hours of flying time to earn their flight pay each month. Squadron Ops Officer Lieutenant Spann Watson had the tough job of scheduling the flights for all the pilots utilizing the fleet of P-47s on the flight line.

Our executive officer, Captain Morris Johnson, requested early discharge and I succeeded him in the job. Spann Watson leaned on me, heavily at times, to make sure that the pilots reported to the flight line in time to take off precisely on time on a tight schedule. Anyone who missed his scheduled takeoff time or, once airborne, was late returning exactly four hours later, missed his flight pay for that month or the next.

As Christmas approached and many men were discharged, either voluntarily or otherwise, the overall future of the 477th Composite Group looked gloomy. Then just after the holiday season ended we heard some very good news. Spratmo had it that the entire organization at Godman was going to move to Lockbourne Army Air Base, about ten miles south of Columbus, Ohio.

Soon spratmo became fact when my CO, Bill Campbell, sent me to Lockbourne as an advance party for our squadron to make arrangements for its PCS move in early March. Pete and I loaded Black Beauty with all our worldly possessions and hit the road to Ohio one beautiful, sunny morning.

We were glad to go. The Jim Crow rampant at all the facilities on Fort Knox coupled with the miserable billets at Godman had become unbearable. And besides, when we crossed the Ohio River into Cincinnati en route to Columbus, we were shaking the dust of the South from our boots. That fact in itself made the move worthwhile. We were on our way to another place on the map and another level in the social scheme of things. We thought of Lockbourne, in Ohio, as a sort of heaven on earth. Writing now, with the hindsight of the Kennedy years, I have another name for it: Camelot!

11 Camelot!

» February 1946–June 1949

The five-hour trip from Godman Field to Columbus, Ohio, went without a hitch. Coming out of the mountains of Kentucky onto the broad plains of Ohio, our eight-year-old '38 Buick, Black Beauty, galloped along like a frisky colt gobbling up the miles in between. It was late afternoon when we saw the sign on the outskirts of the city with its insignia of Kiwanis, Rotary, Lions, Chamber of Commerce, and the like proclaiming "Welcome to Columbus."

Before leaving Godman Field I had checked with a couple of my buddies who had kinfolk in Columbus and had obtained addresses and telephone numbers. I knew that such advance planning was necessary because Lockbourne was a vacant base with no billets available and, although it was in "the Nawth," Columbus, Ohio, was no haven of unrestricted housing or hotel accommodations. Therefore, I had to plan ahead so that Pete and I would have a place to lay our heads when we first arrived in town.

We were indebted to Lieutenants James E. Harris and Lewis Lynch for steering us to their relatives, who helped us find temporary quarters in the city. Jim's Aunt Edith was a kindly "little old lady" who took us in the first night of our move to Ohio. Then we were able to secure a room with an in-law of Lewis's where we stayed for a few weeks. Mrs. Geraldine Hamilton was as congenial a landlady as could be found anywhere. Her home was a two-story cottage with living room, dining room, and kitchen downstairs and two bedrooms upstairs. It was spick-and-span, neat as a pin, and yet had the ambiance of being "lived in." BB, a Chinese Chow, was Gerry's watchdog and was the most "human" animal I had ever seen—or been evaluated by.

"You must be good people," Gerry said, when BB's tail began to wag as we patted her head. "She's very choosy and doesn't take to everybody. So we'll be glad to have you folks live with us here as long as you like."

With our living accommodations all set for the time being, I was ready to tackle the task I was sent to Lockbourne to do. Pete and Gerry hit it off fine right from the start so I had no worries in that regard.

On Monday morning I drove to Lockbourne and found base headquarters where some officers of the 477th advance party were getting set up. I was shown a map of the base and where the 99th's squadron area, with orderly room, supply room, and enlisted men's barracks, was located. Also where the BOQs were located.

Prior to the 477th's move to Lockbourne, a B-17 combat crew training center and the Army Air Corps all-weather flying school had been stationed there. In some of the buildings earmarked for the 99th I found literally hundreds of spare parts, like roller bearings and various metal gizmos, in cabinets and closets that had simply been left behind when the B-17 training outfit moved out. I had not the slightest clue as to their use or purpose. Or how to dispose of them. One of the officers in the headquarters advance party knew how to go about salvaging all of the surplus materials, which were now superfluous because of the end of the war, and took the spare parts off my hands by moving them out of our area.

Within the week some others from the 99th came to Lockbourne to complete the setup of the squadron area and facilities before the entire complement of men and planes moved in. All over the base other units were busy setting up and settling in. From March 13, 1946, when Colonel Benjamin O. Davis, Jr., assumed command of Lockbourne Army Air Base, it wasn't long before all units and facilities were in full operation with Colonel Davis, his staff, unit commanders, and personnel, all Americans of color, in full control of the entire base.

Variously referred to by the men and women of Lockbourne as

"the Colonel," "B.O. the C.O.," "Bo the Co," and "the Old Man," or just "the Man," he was very clearly in charge. From the very beginning Lockbourne Army Air Base bore the stamp of Colonel Benjamin O. Davis, Jr., graduate of West Point, son of a brigadier. From the boom of the cannon and the bugle sounding reveille at daybreak until the strains of the national anthem at retreat as the Stars and Stripes were lowered at the end of the day, all activities were conducted with precision and pride. Not to say "perfection" because there were goofs and gaffes as could be expected with any operation involving over three thousand people.

One humorous goof happened one morning shortly after we moved to Lockbourne. Because it was still dark one morning when Old Glory was raised on the flagpole outside base headquarters, the flag-raising detail did not note carefully what they had done. However, on my way to the flight line for an early morning briefing, I saw the flag and got on the phone to the officer of the day.

"Hey, OD," I said, "how come the base is in distress?"

"What are you talking about?" he asked, somewhat peevishly.

"Well, I think you might want to take a look at the flag before 'the Old Man' sees it 'cause it's upside down," I chuckled.

"Omigosh!" the OD exclaimed. "Thanks, Dryden. I'm sure glad you told me in time. I'll have it fixed right away."

Except for an occasional lapse like that, everywhere on the base there was evidence of striving for perfection as units moved in and participated in a base-wide beautification program by sprucing up their own area. Keen competition occurred between units to be rated the best during SMI. And during parades. And in the air.

During the first few months at Lockbourne, flying activities were somewhat spotty and restricted for both the bomber and the fighter pilots of the 477th. That was because demobilization of the U.S. armed forces was in full swing, and with the large surplus of pilots in each unit, flying time was limited to the bare four hours per month required to earn flying pay. In the 99th a good number of pilots volunteered for separation and relieved the pressure a bit. However, there were more who wanted to remain on active duty than the T/O (table of organization) authorized, so a large number had to be discharged involuntarily. This was a sticky problem solved by the squadron commander, Major Bill Campbell, acting on the recommendations of his operations and executive officers, Spann Watson and Charles Dryden, respectively.

When the squadron was finally whittled down to the proper size, normal flying training resumed.

Daytime flying included formation flying, navigation cross-country flights, air show demonstrations and aerobatics, and under-the-hood simulated instrument flying practice in the P-47s. Night flying consisted of taking off at dusk, climbing up into an assigned zone above the field, and droning around for four hours. The area around the base was divided into twelve zones: the northeast, southeast, southwest, and northwest quadrants each had three levels at which planes were assigned for night flying, that is, at 3,000, 5,000, and 7,000 feet. By that scheme, adequate flight separation was maintained among all the twelve planes aloft.

Because it was boring to stay in the local night-flying traffic pattern and just orbit in a zone for four hours, oftentimes the pilots scheduled for night flying would team up to go on a round robin cross country, with no landing anywhere except back at Lockbourne after four hours aloft. Whenever night flying was in progress, one of the 99th's pilots had to be on duty in the control tower. One night while on tower duty I heard over the squadron frequency:

"Hey, Harvey! This is Butler. Why are we flying upside down?"

Lieutenant Jim Harvey, C-Flight leader, had a flight of four Jugs up on a night cross country and was inbound to land after about three hours aloft. I heard him reply: "Butler, we're not upside down. We're just in a diving turn and it just seems that we are inverted."

"Aw, c'mon, quit clowning!" Butler insisted. "Keep this up and I'm gonna have a bad case of vertigo, Harve, so let's get right side up!"

It was a moonless night with the darkness aloft relieved only by scattered twinkling stars above and scattered farmhouse lights below making it difficult to tell up from down, especially when you have been flying formation on another plane for three hours. Knowing this phenomenon, Jim Harvey said: "Just fly tight on me,

Butler; we're in a diving turn now. I'll roll us into straight and level flight and then you can spread out, look around, and get your bearings. Trust me, Hoss, you're OK."

"Roger," Butler replied.

About ten minutes later Harvey called the tower for landing instructions, brought his flight over the field, peeled off, and landed without further incident. In operations, during debriefing of the flight, Lieutenant Jewell Butler described his sensation of being inverted while actually being upright:

"I have heard how vertigo can happen and how it can affect a pilot but I would never have believed that I could be mistaken about being right side up or upside down. It was weird! It's a good thing that Harvey knew what was happening and how to straighten me out or I might have crashed. I didn't even want to believe my instruments!"

Another evening, just at twilight, night flying was about to begin. After briefing in the 99th ready room by Ops Officer Spann Watson, the twelve of us scheduled to fly that night trooped out to our Jugs. Preflight walk-around completed, cockpit checklist reviewed, and engine started up and purring with a muffled roar, I signaled the standby crew chief to pull the chocks. Taxiing out to the end of the active runway, I was about number seven in the lineup awaiting takeoff clearance as we all ran through the standard pretakeoff engine run-up. As each plane ahead of me lined up on the runway and took off, I moved ahead until, finally, I was next to go.

Watching the plane ahead of mine rolling down the runway, gathering speed, and lifting off well before the far end of the runway, I lined up on the center line, pressed the mike button, and called: "Lockbourne Tower, Air Force 619, ready to roll."

Before the tower operator could answer I heard an excited voice saying: "You're trailing smoke. I think you're on fire!"

It was one of the pilots already airborne reporting what he was seeing on one of the other planes that was also aloft. His sharp eyes and alertness were commendable. The only problem was that he failed to identify himself and the identity and location of the smoking Jug. Consequently all of the pilots checked their engine gauges and swung around in their cockpit seats to see if they were smoking. All except one: the pilot in the Jug just ahead of mine. He was at about 1,000 feet when the "you're on fire!" message was broadcast. Taking no chances, he bailed out.

Still poised for takeoff, I was looking down the runway when I saw his parachute blossom as he went over the side and then his Jug nosed over and plunged straight down, crashing a scant couple miles off the end of the runway. Fire trucks with sirens screaming and an ambulance from the flight line headed toward the crash scene. The tower instructed: "All P-47s awaiting takeoff clearance, return to the ramp."

We did, and within about an hour our CO, Bill Campbell, and the hapless pilot, unhurt and carrying the voluminous folds of his parachute, came into squadron ops. As Bill read the riot act to the pilot about reacting to a general emergency message without first determining if it was addressed to him, I felt sorry for the poor guy and will not mention his name. He suffered enough from Bill's tongue-lashing and the knowledge that he had foolishly pranged a $100,000 airplane and blemished the squadron's flying safety record.

So, at "Camelot" we had some goofs. But mostly we had glory, in our professional lives and in our personal lives, too.

For Pete and me the arrival of our firstborn, Charles Walter, Jr., on October 30, 1946, was a glory day, a day of joy. Early during Pete's pregnancy we had been able to rent a small two-bedroom cottage in Hanford Village, a development of brand new houses located about ten miles from the base. The owner, Tech Sergeant Leroy Robertson, was a member of the 99th and, as a landlord, a prince of a man.

We moved into 870 Lyman Avenue in late September along with Mother Pearl, who had come west from New Jersey to help her only child birth her first grandchild. All went well and after less than a week Pete brought "Thumper" home from Grant Hospital in midtown Columbus. Nicknamed for Thumper the rabbit in Disney's movie, *Bambi,* because of the way he kicked against my hand laid on Pete's swollen abdomen before he was born, our son might have been better nicknamed "Screamer." He spent many of his waking hours hollering and writhing in pain.

Poor guy, he had colic. Bad. And it was some time, and several meal types—mother's milk, cow's milk, Orolac, Similac, Biolac—before we discovered that the only food he could tolerate was goat's milk. His first days at home brought sleepless nights for us as we were up all night rocking him to sleep. However, we had worked out a routine schedule for his feedings and thought we had things under control when my CO upset our routine.

At squadron ops one day in early November, Major Campbell announced that the 477th Composite Group was committed to a joint army-navy war games exercise in California. The 99th's P-47s and the 617th's B-25s were scheduled to be staged at Blythe Air Base, out near the Mojave Desert, for about three weeks beginning November 8. Hearing his announcement, I wasn't worried about going away on TDY because I knew that he knew that we had a brand new infant at home and was sure that Bill would let me remain at Lockbourne. After all, only about a dozen of our pilots were needed to fly the missions and it seemed logical to leave me behind.

I was wrong. Bill felt it more logical for me to go west with the squadron because, he declared: "You did your bit nine months ago. Pete doesn't need you now!"

So on November 8 a dozen P-47s headed west to Blythe AAB (army air base) with RON stopovers at Tinker AAB, Oklahoma City, and Biggs AAB near El Paso, Texas, where some of us crossed the border into Mexico to sample the nightlife in Juarez. The next day we flew the final leg to Blythe, landing in the blistering heat of midafternoon. Close to 100 degrees when we landed, the temperature plunged to near freezing after sunset. The daily temperature swings made our stay there most unpleasant.

Flying the missions was fun as we engaged in tactical air-ground support of a simulated amphibious assault on "enemy invaders" who had "captured" San Clemente Island about ten miles off the California coast just west of Los Angeles. Our P-47s also escorted our B-25s, of the 617th, and bombers of other units simulating attacks on "enemy" positions along the coast. And we conducted high-altitude patrol missions over "friendly" areas. It was on one such mission that I learned at firsthand how serious hypoxia could be.

Leading a flight of four Jugs on a patrol mission at 25,000 feet late one sunshiny afternoon, I had set my oxygen regulator on automatic position, which was designed to supply oxygen on demand. That meant that as I breathed the regulator metered the flow to provide just the amount I needed with each inhaled breath. For the first half hour or so of our patrol assignment everything was normal as my equipment worked properly. Then, all of a sudden, as I looked around at my flight I saw two Jugs on my right wing, four on my left—twice as many as had taken off with me.

Shaking my head in disbelief and rubbing my eyes, figuring that perhaps the bright reflection of the sunshine on the ocean had caused an illusion, I looked again. The doubled images were still there. Then my high-altitude pressure chamber training came to my rescue, reminding me that oxygen starvation is very subtle and can be very sudden. Quickly I flipped my oxygen regulator to the 100 percent oxygen position, which sent a constant flow of the life-sustaining gas through my mask. Instantly the number of wingmen returned to normal—one on my right wing, two on my left. Just to verify what I had deduced, I flipped the regulator lever to automatic again while looking at my right wingman and was amazed to see the image of his plane split into two planes. Finally convinced that my oxygen regulator had begun to malfunction in automatic, I left the lever in the 100 percent oxygen position for the rest of the patrol mission. Luckily for me we only had about fifteen minutes to remain on station before descending to return to base because the oxygen tank empties rapidly in the 100 percent mode.

I remembered hearing the story of one of the Red Tails—the pilots of the 332nd Fighter Group painted the tails of their P-51s red—who was on a high-altitude escort mission in Europe during WWII. Suddenly his P-51 nosed over, went into a shallow dive, and never recovered. Others in the flight kept calling the pilot trying to rouse him, to no avail. He crashed without ever recovering, apparently victim of anoxia. I considered myself blessed to have come to my senses in time and remembered to switch to 100 percent oxygen before it was too late.

One weekend during our TDY in California, Peepsight Smith, Ghost Lawson, and I rode a bus into Los Angeles to see the town and visit some of Peepsight's kinfolk living there. We also got to meet movie actress Louise Beavers, celebrated for her roles in *Imitation of Life* (with Claudette Colbert), *She Done Him Wrong* (with Mae West), and many others. We were truly charmed by that gracious lady, who seemed pleased to meet us and to hear something about the Tuskegee Airmen who were participating in the war games in progress at the time. She had read articles in local newspapers about the squadrons of Negro pilots involved in the war games and extended a warm invitation to visit her whenever we were in Los Angeles.

Finally, the "war" ended with the "enemy" routed and San Clemente Island reclaimed. Not a day too soon for me. Life on the edge of the desert held no charm for me, what with the sweltering heat of the day and shivering cold after sundown. So I was happy to break ground on December 1 and head east to Lockbourne in the 99th's formation with Bill Campbell in the lead. His departing message to the control tower at Blythe Army Air Base, "99th Squadron, on course, on time!" was music to my ears.

When we had formed up into the widespread formation for the flight home and settled down to normal cruise airspeed, I had time to reflect about what we had experienced at Blythe. It was the first time that our fighters of the 99th and bombers of the 617th had participated in simulated war exercises. And we had done so with a minimum of snafus.

It was only natural that there was constant rivalry between the B-25 twin-engine bomber pilots and the P-47 single-engine fighter pilots as to who were the best pilots, the "hottest rocks." Sometimes discussions at the mess hall or on the flight line got pretty heated. The moments of truth came in the air when the 477th Composite Group was engaged in joint training exercises, giving the bomber pilots and the fighter pilots a chance to show off their skills.

It was important to get the squadrons off the ground at the times prescribed by the operations officer during mission briefings and to make good all other planned times such as: time on course; time of rendezvous with other units (if required); time over target; time to head for home. In peacetime training missions, as well as in combat, time was of the essence; so, for me, it was always a thrill to hear the formation leader declare to the control tower: "On course, on time!"

Whether we were just a flight of four or the entire group of perhaps more than seventy airplanes, those few words represented the culmination of hours of hard work: by the operations staff who had planned the particular mission; by the ground crews who readied the airplanes for flight, with engines and all systems working properly, fuel tanks topped off, oxygen tanks filled, guns and ordnance as required, and radio frequencies all "five by five"; by the pilots who checked their route maps and S-2 information, visually inspected their aircraft, and started engines at the prescribed time in order to taxi out to the runway with their particular flight, take off in their proper sequence, join up swiftly, smoothly with the group formation into a beautiful, tight formation that the leader maneuvered to fly directly over the base to the delight of the troops on the ground who noted that the group was "on course, on time!"

In my opinion, in the California war games the bomber and fighter pilots of the 477th Composite had proven that they could work efficiently and effectively as a team, so we could return to our "Camelot" with a keen sense of satisfaction. Mission accomplished! As we approached Lockbourne AAB we tightened up from a widespread, cross-country formation to a tight, tight air show formation. Bill Campbell, skipper of the 99th, and C. I. Williams of the 617th didn't have to call their P-47 and B-25 pilots, respectively, to tighten up. We were returning home from "war" and were bound to show off for our folks on the ground.

My folks were in town and I wasted no time getting home after landing and being debriefed in squadron ops. All was as well as could be expected, what with Thumper still plagued with colic and Pete trying to cope with his problem. Mother Pearl had returned to her home in New Jersey the day before to resume her post office job in time to get ready for the Christmas rush. With only three weeks to go before Thumper's first Christmas ever and our first in a house with no other occupants, just us, we had to hustle to get the house ready and gifts bought and wrapped.

The house in Hanford Village had a basement with a hand-fired coal furnace that required little attention and kept the cottage cozy in spite of "the hawk" blowing icy blasts outside. So in spite of Thumper's continuing discomfort we enjoyed a fairly merry Christmas. But then the base daily bulletin was published with the roster of OGs (officers of the guard) for the coming week. Scanning my copy in the 99th orderly room I saw that the beginning of my new year was not going to be very happy because I was scheduled to "wear the gun" on New Year's Eve.

What a blow! To be the "sheriff" on duty on New Year's Eve was no honor and certainly was no fun because everyone else on the compound would be partying and having fun while the OD (officer of the day) and his assistant, the OG, were responsible for maintaining order and proper decorum among the troops. The OD was always senior to the OG and therefore could pull rank on the OG and direct him to take over.

My duty as OG started at noon on New Year's Eve when I reported to the provost marshal's office to pick up my "piece" and the arm band. The new OD, whom I knew (and who will be Major Mudd for this narrative), also reported to begin his tour of duty. As a first lieutenant I was obliged to follow his orders while we shared the tour of duty. He had no particular orders for me until around midnight. By then we had toured the key checkpoints on the base—main gate, base ops, hospital, finance office, base headquarters, guardhouse, and the enlisted men's, NCOs', and officers clubs. At all the clubs parties to greet the new year were in full swing. At about half past eleven Major Mudd and I were at the officers club observing the crowd when he said to me, "Lieutenant, I'm going to leave you with it and go to my quarters to greet the new year with my wife and my new baby. I know you can handle it. If you need me just call me at my quarters. OK?"

"OK, Major," I said. I thought, "What else could I say except, perhaps, 'If all hell breaks loose somewhere on this base tonight and I can't get to you right away, your name will be mud.' " He left the club headed home and I braced myself for I knew not what as the clock ticked toward midnight.

With about fifteen minutes to go I heard myself paged over the club public address system: "Lieutenant Dryden, phone call in the club office."

"Uh, oh!" I thought, "it's started already. What kind of ruckus and where is it happening?" I wondered as I wound my way through the crowd of dancers and revelers toward the club office. Picking up the phone I said: "Officer of the guard, here. What's up?"

I heard a familiar voice, the strictly business, no-nonsense voice of the base commander: "Lieutenant Dryden?"

I thought: "Oh, crap! What's happened now to cause the 'Old Man' to call me instead of the OD?"

I said: "Yes, Sir, this is Lieutenant Dryden, officer of the guard."

"Lieutenant, this is Colonel Davis. I want you to find Lieutenant Green, the alternate officer of the guard for today, and have him relieve you of the duty immediately. You are to leave the base and repair to your home. Your wife called me moments ago. It seems she is having an emergency with your baby. Tell Lieutenant Green to call me at my quarters when he has assumed the duty. Clear?"

"Yes, Sir," I replied. Colonel Davis hung up and I set about looking for Lieutenant "Chubby" Green, my hapless alternate. "Chubby" was a fighter pilot, nonpareil, who had distinguished himself during the war by fighting alongside Yugoslav partisans, after being shot down on a combat mission, with such bravery that he was awarded the Red Star of Yugoslavia.

I had seen him at the club earlier that evening when he said to me, "I sure am glad to see you're wearing the gun 'cause now I can relax and have some fun without worrying about going on duty as OG."

Now I had to find him and spoil his fun. Finding him in the lounge, I broke the news to him.

"Aw, c'mon, Dryden," he said. "You gotta be kidding, man!"

"No, Hoss, I'm not kidding. C'mon to the office and let's call B.O. to verify, OK?"

It took some needling to get Chubby to agree even to go to the club office and watch me dial Colonel Davis's number. When the colonel's voice came on the line I handed the phone to Chubby and watched his facial expressions change as he said a series of Yessirs, ending with "Very well, Sir," and hung up the phone.

Turning to me, Chubby said: "I'm sorry your kid is sick, Hoss, but damn! Why on New Year's Eve of all times?"

"I'm sorry, too, Chubby, but I'll take the gun for you next time you're scheduled as OG. Meanwhile I've gotta go see about my gang. Before I leave I'll call the OD in his quarters and notify him about the switch. OK?"

"OK, Dryden. See ya!"

I left the club just as the party horns began blaring, the noise-makers started a racket, and hugs and kisses ushered in the new year. Driving home over the ten miles of icy, snow-covered roads was slow going because a snowstorm had moved into the Columbus area. Thick, fat snowflakes, heavy with water, splattered against the windshield of Black Beauty, reducing visibility to near zero straight ahead. Crawling along at about 15 mph it took about an hour to reach home. Pete was still awake, waiting for me. And so was Thumper, still crying as if to continue his own greeting of the new year.

Pete greeted me with: "Happy New Year, Honey. I'm so glad you're home. I was so tired staying awake to make Thumper comfortable that I called Colonel Davis in desperation. I hope it didn't cause you any kind of embarrassment."

"No, Baby, you did the right thing because it was sort of an emergency. Anyway, Chubby Green was on tap as the OG supernumerary, so he relieved me just before midnight and I've spent the last hour on the road trying to get home."

After toasting the new year and sharing a wee drop of sherry with Thumper, hoping that he might get looped and drop off to sleep, we finally fell asleep as well. But not for long. The traditional New Year's Day officers call to greet the base commander at his office in base headquarters was scheduled to begin at 0900 hours. So I was up at about 0700 to allow plenty of time to get back to Lockbourne safely over the icy roads.

The snowstorm had ended but not before dumping several inches of slushy stuff everywhere. About halfway to the base I saw one of the guys' almost-brand-new Packard lying upside down in a ditch, and I said a silent prayer that Lieutenant Henri Fletcher, one of our bomber pilots, had escaped without injury. Arriving at base headquarters I learned that he had gotten out of the car without a scratch, nothing bruised but his ego. He took a lot of ribbing about trying to "fly" his car like a B-25.

At headquarters each of the officers visited with Colonel Davis in his office for a minute or two to exchange greetings of the new year. When my turn came I was glad for the opportunity to thank him for having been considerate the night before, heeding Pete's plea, and to report that our son was much better now.

Chubby Green was also at headquarters during the officers call and I thanked him for taking over "the duty" for me. Some of the guys ribbed me about the "convenient emergency" that had gotten me relieved from OG duty on New Year's Eve, but one of them had heard about a "down home" remedy for colic and told me: "See if you can find some goat's milk on some of these farms around here. That might help."

He was right. Upon returning home from the base I told Pete about the "goat's milk" cure. We scouted the city by telephone and finally located a goat farm a few miles north of Columbus. Off we went to visit the farm and bring home some of the elixir. At seventy-five cents per quart it was three times as costly as cow's milk but, for us, price was no object if it worked.

It did. Thumper's writhing in pain, and squirming while sleeping fitfully, and crying almost constantly when awake, stopped. With these changes in our son's days and nights the new year began to be a truly happy one as 879 Lyman Avenue became one of the quietest houses on the block. We really began to enjoy our rented cottage, so much so that we began thinking seriously about buying one of the houses on Clay Court, still under construction in the Hanford

Village development. The more we talked about it the more we wanted to invest in our first home.

In February we took the plunge with a $6,500 mortgage on 817 Clay Court, a two-bedroom cottage with unfinished attic and basement. And unfinished backyard full of weeds. But we were happy to be in our own home. My situation overall seemed like "Camelot":

At home, all was very well.

At work, almost all was unbelievably well. Only "almost all," not completely "all," because in our segregated situation we were not able to expect promotions, training, or assignments commensurate with our increasing experience the way airmen, officers, and NCOs in the Army Air Corps at large could. Apart from that major drawback, however, Lockbourne was a model air base run completely by Americans of color. Referred to variously from time to time, and from place to place, as Colored, Negro (with dialect distortions of the word), Black, Afro-American, African American, the men and women assigned to Lockbourne operated one of the most, if not the most, efficiently run air bases in the Army Air Corps. So I have been told in later years by people from other places and other bases who landed there just to refuel and go on their way or to RON or to conduct inspections.

Just about one year after moving to Lockbourne the 477th was ordered to participate in "Operation Combine," an air-ground exercise at Fort Benning, Georgia, located adjacent to Lawson Field. The exercise was designed to demonstrate the close support of ground troops in a simulated combat situation with fighter aircraft strafing, dive-bombing, dropping napalm, and firing five-inch HVAR (high velocity aerial rockets) at buildings, tanks, and vehicles in a simulated target area on Fort Benning. Medium bombers and heavy bombers attacked the "enemy" ground targets as well, while friendly ground troops maneuvered at short distances from the target area. At a further, safer, distance away, observers from U.S. Army, Navy, Marines, and Air Corps, as well foreign allies, watched the action from the grandstands.

The air-ground firepower demonstration was conducted most

Friday afternoons for about three months. The scenario required the participation of other types of airplanes, from several other bases, such as P-51s and B-29s. Eighteen B-25s of the 477th were tasked to drop 500-pound bombs in level bombing attacks. Twelve P-47s of the 99th Fighter Squadron were divided into four-ship flights to strafe the target building and vehicles, drop napalm, and fire five-inch HVAR into the targets. I was leader of the rocket flight.

During the three-month schedule of air-ground firepower demonstrations, the 477th staged out of Myrtle Beach AAB, South Carolina, on TDY from our home base at Lockbourne. While at Myrtle Beach, from Saturday through Wednesday all of the pilots assigned to the firepower demonstration practiced the route and timing of their particular roles in the scenario by flying with their "specialist" flight over a route that mirrored the exercise flight path at Fort Benning. The timing of takeoffs, time over IP (initial point), target time, spacing between attacking aircraft, and altitudes at the initiation of attack and over the target itself were practiced again and again to ensure that each attacking fighter pulled up from the target within no more than five seconds, plus or minus, of his scheduled time.

On Thursday afternoons the pilots assigned to the upcoming mission flew the two-hour flight from Myrtle Beach to Lawson Field where we remained overnight to be ready for the demonstration on Friday afternoon. On Friday mornings our planes were refueled, armed with appropriate ordnance, and readied for the mission. At precisely the prescribed time each specialist flight started engines, taxied to the runway, took off, and proceeded to the assembly area a few miles out of sight of the spectators in the grandstands and orbited until time to fly to the IP. En route to the IP the leader spread out his flight in string formation, armed his ordnance, and started his attack approach at the prescribed time, plus or minus five seconds, and each member of his flight followed suit. All of the planes in all of the units that were part of the demonstration were on similar tight schedules that had to be made good to avoid injuries to ground troops maneuvering near the target area.

After completing the attack on the target each flight was free to leave the demonstration area and fly directly to their staging base, provided that none of the planes had any unexpended ordnance still hanging under the wings or fuselage. Flying cross country with such dangerous weapons that might fall off and kill or injure persons, or damage property, was too risky. Therefore, the operations SOP mandated that anyone with "hung ordnance" after pulling up from the target must fly to the jettison area a few miles away and try to get rid of his ordnance, whatever it was: bombs, napalm, machine gun rounds, or rockets. Failing that, he must return to Lawson Field to have the ordnance removed by ground crews.

One Friday afternoon one of my flight members, Lieutenant Ed Drummond, had a five-inch HVAR hung up after his target run. At the jettison area his one remaining rocket still would not drop off despite his making several dives and sharp pullups while pressing the trigger on the control stick. That meant our flight had to return to Lawson Field for his plane to be disarmed rather than heading straight to Myrtle Beach without landing. I was upset and annoyed at the turn of events but, as it turned out, it saved my life.

The week before that particular mission I had applied for a cross-country flight in my Jug, number 619, to Mitchel Field, New York. Ops Officer Watson and the CO, Bill Campbell, had approved my request. Then, about midweek, one of our pilots going up for an instrument check ride in an AT-6 training plane taxied too close behind a flight of about four B-25s that were on the taxiway running up their engines before taking off on a practice mission. Their combined propwash flipped the AT-6 up on its nose and destroyed the propeller. That did it! Major Campbell canceled all cross-country flights for the coming weekend. No amount of pleading my case could budge him. Because I had told my family to expect me that Saturday, I tried to find some other way to get to New York.

At base operations I learned that the pilot of a B-26 based at Myrtle Beach was scheduled to take off to Mitchel Field early Saturday morning. I looked up the pilot and signed on to hitch a ride to New York, fully expecting to be back from the Operation Combine mission by Friday night.

After landing at Lawson Field to have Drummond's rocket removed, my flight had to RON there because night had fallen and our SOP prohibited night flights while we were committed to Operation Combine. Still hoping to get back to Myrtle Beach in time to board the B-26 flight to New York, I told my flight that I wanted to have "wheels in the well" at daybreak and that we were going to fly the return trip to Myrtle Beach flat out, "balls to the wall" all the way.

Next morning we saw the first rays of the sun as we broke ground and formed up heading east. In record time we reached Myrtle Beach and were entering the traffic pattern to peel off for landing when I saw a B-26 taxiing out to the end of the runway. I heard the control tower giving the pilot departure instructions and his flight clearance. After the pilot had acknowledged his clearance I called him, saying:

"B-26 on the runway, this is Lieutenant Dryden with a flight of four Jugs overhead, peeling off. I've been manifested on your flight since Wednesday. I'll be on the ground in a couple minutes. Can you delay takeoff for about ten minutes? I'd appreciate it."

"Sorry, Lieutenant, I've got my ATC clearance and it's IFR to D.C., so I gotta go right now or I'll lose it. Sorry! Maybe next time."

I was crushed, disappointed. But tragically there was no next time for him. A few hours later we learned from ATC that the B-26 had crashed in bad weather in Virginia. There were no survivors!

Operation Combine ended in May. We wasted no time clearing out of Myrtle Beach AAB and returning home to Lockbourne, landing on the fifth. I found peace and harmony at 817 Clay Court. Pete informed me that Thumper cried very seldom anymore, to which I replied, "Thank God for goats!" Pete looked more rested than when I left on TDY three months earlier, but she had a pesky cough that she could not get rid of. She pooh-poohed my worrying about it, saying: "Not to worry, I'll shake it off. It just takes time." But I worried anyway. And with good reason as it turned out.

One day, a few weeks after the 99th's return from Operation Combine, I was up on a routine training flight in my Jug when I heard, in my headset: "Air Force 619, this is Lockbourne tower. Over!"

"Roger, Lockbourne, this is 619. Over."

"619, return to base and land. Repeat, return to base and land. Over."

"Lockbourne, 619. Wilco."

Upon landing and walking into 99th operations, I found a telephone message to report to Major Bryce Anthony's office at the base hospital. Bryce was an old friend from my old neighborhood on Sugar Hill in New York City. We had been in the same class all the way through junior high school, had dated girls together, and had competed building model airplanes. When I went off to Tuskegee Army Flying School to win my wings, he went off to medical school and earned his M.D. degree. We were both delighted to find our paths recrossing at Lockbourne. We were good buddies, and I could tell from the look on Bryce's face as I entered his office that he had some bad news for me. Worried, I tried bravado:

"What's up, Doc?" I bantered.

Leading me over to a lab table on which he had a large medical book opened to a page of illustrations, he told me to look at one that was a color photograph of a specimen slide. Then he said: "Come, look into this microscope. Does what you see look like the picture in the book?"

"Looks identical, Bryce, but so what?" I quavered, afraid to hear his answer.

"Charlie," he said, his eyes misting slightly, "the picture is of tuberculosis bacilli. The slide is a specimen of Pete's sputum."

"Oh God! Omigod!" I breathed, as I felt my heart begin to race. In 1947, tuberculosis was still a killer and I felt my bright Camelot fading to black despair. I scarcely heard Bryce's voice explaining that Pete had been suspicious of the persistent cough and had consulted with him. She remembered that while assigned to the base hospital at TAAF she had had a similar cough that had been diagnosed as pleurisy, erroneously as it turned out. In any case, that was history. We had to deal with the here and now as well as with the future.

I thanked Bryce for having notified me in such a thoughtful way, making sure that I was on the ground and in his office before giving me any hint that anything was wrong. Although it was a bright, sun-filled day, I drove home in a fog. Walked into the house and took Pete into my arms and just held her for long moments. And fought the tears. Then we laid plans to cope with our problem.

First, call Mother Pearl: "Come quickly, Mom. We need you to take care of Thumper."

"I'll be there day after tomorrow, Charlie," Mom said. She made it sound so easy. All she had to do was take a leave of absence from her post office job.

Next, get Pete admitted to a hospital to begin treatment immediately in hopes of a long shot at recovery. At first blush that seemed easy because Franklin County Sanitarium, which specialized in treatment of tuberculosis, was only two miles from our home on the way to the base. The problem was the long waiting list for admittance. That problem was resolved with the kind help of Major Vance Marchbanks, commanding officer of the base hospital at Lockbourne, who expedited the retrieval of Pete's military medical records from the War Department, and through the good offices of a dear friend, Dr. Maurine Redden, a physician on the staff at the sanitarium and the wife of Captain Jim Redden—the same Captain Redden who had shocked the two German PWs at the gas station at Godman Field, Kentucky, with his fluent German.

On Sunday morning Mother Pearl arrived at the railroad station in downtown Columbus and I drove her to 817 Clay Court, which she had never seen. She liked its looks and location but vowed to help us complete the furnishings and right away began settling in for a stay of however long it took to get her daughter well. By midweek Dr. Redden had arranged for Pete to be admitted to the hospital. We all drove there, the four of us, with Mother Pearl holding Thumper on the back seat. Pete had begun wearing a surgical mask to avoid any infection of others as she was seriously concerned about infecting her mother, husband, or infant son.

When we arrived at the hospital parking lot Mom stayed in the car with Thumper while I went into the admissions office with Pete. Within the hour she was settled in her private room on the third floor overlooking the parking lot. That's when the realization of what was happening really hit me. I was about to leave my wife in a hospital with what was then regarded as a terminal disease! To add to the sorrow, she was being torn away from her first (perhaps her last?) child!

She was much stronger about facing the problem than I. After embracing she told me in no uncertain terms: "I'm going to get well and I'm starting right now, so—shooo, Honey! I need all the bed rest I can get."

Downstairs at the car I held Thumper up high above my head so that she could see him and wave good-bye. That day in June 1947 was one of the most poignant moments of my life.

A series of tests at a local clinic revealed that neither Mom, Thumper, nor I had been infected. I hastened to tell Pete to stop her from worrying about us. For the next several months my days ended with a visit with Pete on the way home from the base, except when I was away on TDY somewhere.

On July 1, 1947, a major change took place at Lockbourne. Apparently, the top brass of the air corps decided that a composite group comprising bomber and fighter planes was no longer needed. The 477th Composite Group was deactivated and the 332nd Fighter Group was reactivated with three squadrons: the 99th, 100th, and 301st. The immediate effect of that action was that the bomber pilots had to check out in the P-47Ns. Also, and regrettably, the bombardier-navigators were out of a job. And the B-25 mechanics, armorers, and radiomen had to make the transition to different equipment.

Most of the bomber pilots welcomed the changeover to a single-engine fighter airplane because it gave them an opportunity to fly another type of aircraft. Likewise, the ground crews were able to add experience with another type of aircraft to their résumés. Some of the suddenly unemployed bombardier-navigators were absorbed into nonflying jobs on the base. However, many of them became surplus to the needs of the segregated base and, because transfer to other bomber units was not possible, they returned to civilian life, bitter at the sudden end of their military career.

Those of us who survived the changeover, both officers and enlisted men and women, became acutely aware of how tenuous our individual futures were as long as segregation severely limited our assignment to only one base.

In the reorganization Major Bill Campbell was named CO of the 332nd Fighter Group and Captains Melvin "Red" Jackson, Elwood Driver, and Richard Pulliam were commanding officers of the 99th, 100th, and 301st Fighter Squadrons, respectively. When fully equipped with their complement of airplanes, the 332nd could put seventy-five Jugs in the air! Never called to launch all the airplanes, the group nevertheless was often called upon to put on air shows at various locations.

One such memorable mission was the opening of Idlewild Airport, later renamed J. F. Kennedy Airport, in the New York City area when several air force units took part in the flyover. The 332nd's P-47s were staged from Stewart Air Force Base, near the U.S. Military Academy at West Point, New York, from which we flew south down the Hudson River to the tip of Manhattan, then east to the tip of Long Island, then swooped down northward to fly over the new airport in tight formation with Bill Campbell leading. Swarms of airplanes from other participating units of the U.S. Army, Navy, and Marines filled the skies of New York that day. I felt that we were helping to make history and, as we climbed back up to altitude after completing our pass over Idlewild, we passed over Roosevelt Field where I had first learned to fly in the CPT Program eight years earlier. And I thought, "Bill Pyhota [my CPT instructor] would be proud to see how far I've come from the Piper Cub in which he soloed me!"

Another mission was a series of air shows from takeoff at Lockbourne, to a flyover at Beckley, West Virginia, and a couple other small towns along the route to Washington, D.C., finally landing at Andrews AFB after a flyover there. The day was Armed Forces Day, 1948, and the 332nd had been ordered to dispatch twelve P-47s to participate in the observances at those locations. The weather was CAVU all the way: There wasn't a cloud in the sky, no cloud deck to shield us from the bright sunshine pouring into our cockpits through the bubble canopies of our Jugs. By the time we landed at Andrews, some four hours after takeoff, I was bushed and was glad to park number 619 on the grassy edge of one of the taxiways where the 99th was directed to remain until refueled for the return trip. While seated on the ground in the shade of the wing, just killing time with other guys in the flight, I saw a squadron of F-80s roll past us on the taxiway. One of the jet jockeys saw us and began waving wildly. Because of his crash helmet and oxygen mask we couldn't recognize him at first. But then he doffed his helmet and mask and I saw that he was my old advanced phase instructor in flight school, Clay "Buckwheat" Albright! After parking his bird he walked over to where we were and there were handshakes all around, as some of the rest of the guys had been his students also and he had been one of the favorite White instructors at Tuskegee—a good pilot and a good friend. It was good seeing him again and to congratulate him on his change from the major's gold leaves on his collar that he wore the last time I had seen him, in 1943, to the silver leaves of a lieutenant colonel that now gleamed on his collar. By the time all of our planes were refueled, we had swapped war stories to a fare-thee-well. Then it was time to go. Our Jugs got cranked up and onto the runway before Albright's. Forming up after takeoff, we swept across Andrews in as tight a formation as I had ever seen.

"Just to show old 'Buckwheat' what good formation flying looks like," I thought as we headed west toward Lockbourne, "on course, on time." Our air shows for the day were behind us. All we had to do was fly a direct route, dodging a few scattered, late afternoon "thunderbumpers" along the way. So I had time to reflect about some things that welled up in my mind.

First of all, I thought how nice it had been to see Clay Albright and to remember that in spite of his Arkansas roots he was "colorblind" in his relationship with us Tuskegee Airmen. My next thought was how glad I was that we only landed at Andrews and did not have to go into the city. The nation's capital held no charm or allure for me, especially after my encounter with Jim Crow there just four months earlier during the inauguration of President Harry S Truman.

Lockbourne AFB had been directed to participate in Truman's inaugural parade with a contingent of troops. The day before the parade a couple of C-47 transport planes flew several officers, NCOs, enlisted men, and WAFs from Lockbourne to Andrews, where they were billeted in airplane hangars along with troops from numerous other armed forces units from around the country. I was lucky enough to copilot one of the Goony Birds hauling the troops, with Captain Jim Wiley as pilot.

Jim was one of the original pilots who had gone overseas with the 99th Fighter Squadron. Always interested in checking out every airplane he could get his hands on, Jim had found a downed Italian-built, open-cockpit biplane in Sicily, had gotten it into flyable shape with the help of some of the squadron mechanics, and tried to ship it to the States as "his" airplane. That didn't work, but at Lockbourne he had been able to get checked out in twin-engine planes—B-25s and C-47s—an opportunity that many of us fighter pilots coveted but were unable to arrange. This flight to Andrews was a chance for me to wrangle some twin-engine flying time.

Once at Andrews and having seen to our troops' billets in the hangars, where the vast floor was covered with army cots, we repaired to our quarters in a barracks. Inauguration day dawned fair and clear, a cold day in January. Glad that as a member of the air crew I did not have to march in the parade, I rode a bus into D.C. to watch the ceremony from the second-floor balcony on the south side of the Senate building. By the end of the parade I was shivering with cold and decided to ride a trolley uptown to the Howard University area to lunch on a bowl of soup and a sandwich. Seeing a small cozy-looking drugstore/soda fountain up ahead of the trolley car, I got off, crossed the street, and entered, still shivering from the cold, brisk breeze but warm inside from a feeling of patriotic fervor. After all, I had just witnessed the kind of miracle that happens only in America—underdog Harry Truman had just been sworn in as president after having beaten "shoo-in" Tom Dewey. Truman's liberal record as a senator from Missouri gave promise of perhaps a new day in civil rights for minorities in the nation. That thought warmed my insides. But not for long. As I entered the store the counter clerk watched me walk over to the row of stools, then announced, "We don't serve niggers in here!"

Shocked! Stunned! Standing there in tailored, full-length officer's overcoat with silver bars gleaming and garrison cap with the eagle insignia, having just participated in the installation of my commander in chief, I could not believe that this affront would happen in the nation's capital. But there it was, with the clerk's hostility mirrored in the faces of other customers at the counter and elsewhere in the store. My instant reaction was to protest his stand, invoke the "liberty and justice for all" shibboleth, and insist on being served. My second thought was: "Dryden, how stupid can you be? What if you get him to serve you somehow? How will you know that he won't foul up your food with spit or rat poison or who knows what?" A sobering thought. So I retreated with my health intact, my dignity bruised, and with a sour memory of Washington. I had no desire to go into town the day we landed at Andrews for the Armed Forces Day air show.

Halfway home between Andrews and Lockbourne that day my thoughts turned to Pete and Thumper. He was still with his grandmother, Mother Pearl, at her home in Belleville, New Jersey. Pete was still in Franklin County Sanitarium. Almost a year had dragged by since her treatment had begun. Some new medications, Aureomycin and Terramycin, seemed to be helping in battling the disease but some side effects were disturbing. One of her fellow patients became deaf after a series of Terramycin treatments. So, Pete had told me just before the air show mission, her physician was hinting at need for some minor surgery to assure her recovery. The rest of the flight home my mind dwelt on that possibility as I was anxious to get on the ground, rush to the hospital, and find out the latest news.

As I entered her room she greeted me with, "Hi, Hon, you must be tired after all that flying today." I had briefed her about the 99th's air show itinerary the previous day.

"Yeah, Babe, I guess I got about seven hours in the hot sun under the bubble canopy but I'm OK now. How 'bout you? What's the latest spratmo about your condition?"

"Umh, hmm," she chuckled, "I can see that my warrior has gotten a couple shades darker from all that sun. Looks good on you, Charlie. As for me, my doctor wants to nip off a bit of the tip of my right lung and I'll be good as new."

"What does Dr. Redden say?"

"She agrees."

"Then let's do it and get you out of here as soon as possible, Honey! What do I need to do to expedite the procedure?"

"Well, I'm going to have to have some pints of blood for transfusion during the operation. You can't donate blood because of your bout with malaria on your way home from overseas, so we'll have to find some donors. Think you can find some in the next couple days?"

"I don't think I'll have any problem, Honey."

And I didn't. When I mentioned our situation to the squadron adjutant, Lieutenant Jimmy Johns, a fine man and a good friend, he spread the word throughout the outfit and I had a flood of volunteers, including himself. Another good friend insisted on being one of the donors—Lieutenant Johnny "Skyhawk" Porter, who had been one of my protégés at Walterboro AAB. Thanks to the donors, the skill of the surgeon, and the grace of God, Pete's surgery was a success and she beat the odds. She was on the road to recovery from tuberculosis and only needed a few months of bed rest to assure the medical staff that she was indeed healed.

The summer of 1948 passed with the three squadrons of the 332nd Fighter Group going to Eglin Field, Florida, for gunnery, taking turns at operating Eglin's Auxiliary Field Number 6 completely, that is, flight operations, aircraft maintenance, armament, ordnance, mess hall, field hospital, motor pool—the works. The gunnery TDYs gave the squadrons the opportunity to hone their skills in all areas of their activities as an independent fighting unit. Of course the main object was for the pilots to sharpen their skills in aerial and ground gunnery. In attacking targets on the ground with machine guns, rockets, and napalm, I could hold my own—but about my aerial gunnery, the less said the better!

However, enough cannot be said about some of the pilots' aerial gunnery skills. Three of them represented the 332nd Fighter Group at the very first U.S. Air Force–wide aerial gunnery meet at Las Vegas AFB (later renamed Nellis AFB), May 2–12, 1949. Officially known as the Continental Air Gunnery Meet, the competition included propeller-driven and jet fighter airplanes. Five fighter groups each fielded a four-man team in the "conventional" (propeller-driven) competition, which included firing .50-caliber machine guns at aerial and ground targets, dive-bombing, skip bombing, and firing rockets at ground targets.

The 332nd's team of four included Captain Alva Temple and First Lieutenants Jim Harvey and Harry Stewart of the 301st, 99th, and 100th Fighter Squadrons, respectively, with First Lieutenant Halbert L. Alexander of the 99th as a spare. Posting the best overall team score for all events, the 332nd's team won the coveted Frank Luke Trophy. Of the fifteen pilots flying conventional airplanes in the meet, Captain Alva Temple placed second in individual overall score. Unquestionably, Lockbourne's reps were among the best top guns of the United States Air Force. A fitting climax to our stay at Lockbourne and to our existence as a segregated, separate and unequally treated, air force unit.

Our stay was indeed coming to an end: President Harry S Truman, by his Executive Order Number 9981, July 26, 1948, had mandated the desegregation of the armed forces. It had taken almost a year for the fledgling U.S. Air Force, which had become an independent service only the year before, in 1947, to get its wheels in motion to comply with the directive of the commander in chief. Some of the top-level air force commanders balked and dragged their feet, hankering for the status quo ante. Others implemented their chief's order with orders of their own. A case in point was Major General Laurence S. Kuter, commanding general of Military Air Transport Service, who made no bones about his position on the matter by issuing each MATS commander a MATS Headquarters Letter Number 9, dated May 1, 1949, that read, in part: "Integration of Negroes into Formerly White Air Force Units: Selected and qualified Negro Officers and Men will be assigned to duty throughout the Air Force without regard to race. Direct attention to this changed condition is required throughout the command. Judgment, leadership and ingenuity are demanded. Commanders who cannot cope with the integration of Negroes into formerly white units or activities will have no place in the Air Force structure."

The first concrete evidence I had that Lockbourne was being phased out came while I was on leave of absence in New Jersey.

"TOP GUNS OF 1949" (left to right): Team Leader Capt.
Alva N. Temple, 1st Lts. Harry Stewart, James H. Harvey, and
Halbert L. Alexander.

During the Christmas holidays of 1948, Pete had been released from Franklin County Sanitarium on her own initiative, completely healed. Knowing about President Truman's executive order, we figured that sometime soon I would be transferred to another base and, because Pete had not seen her baby for almost a year, she would do best by moving to Mother Pearl's home until my assignment was set. So in early spring we drove to Belleville, New Jersey, for a brief but happy reunion with Thumper and Mother Pearl. While there I received a TWX (telegram) from my 99th CO, Captain Marion "Tojo" Rodgers, ordering me to: RETURN TO BASE, SOONEST STOP INTERVIEWS SCHEDULED STOP ACKNOWLEDGE.

Calling Captain Rodgers at Lockbourne, I learned that a team of officers from the Pentagon was at the base interviewing all the troops to ascertain each person's preference for the next assignment and/or career field. Promising him that I would be back to duty by the following evening, I headed west in the 1948 Hudson four-door sedan with which I had surprised Pete by replacing Black Beauty, our venerable and weary Buick, while she was still in the hospital. The Hudson was a real "going machine" that the company touted as having won the Mexican rally races several years running. Unfortunately, I took the hype too seriously and, "flying low" in my haste to get back to the base, I blew a piston rod right through the engine block just about a mile short of the Pennsylvania Turnpike and had to have the Hudson towed to Harrisburg for major repairs. Continuing to Columbus by train, I arrived at squadron headquarters in time to be interviewed.

"What kind of assignment do you want, Lieutenant?" the Pentagon interviewer asked me.

Like everyone at Lockbourne I had been mulling over that question for some time. I had decided that this was a rare opportunity to ask for an assignment and stand a good chance of getting it. I figured that with eight years of just fighter jockey experience, with a little management as a mess officer at Walterboro and squadron executive officer at Godman Field and Lockbourne, it was time for me to acquire some military schooling in a technical specialty. So I replied: "Communication Officer School is my first choice. Second would be to go to a jet fighter outfit."

"OK, Lieutenant. Those are good choices, and I can tell you right now that you will most likely get your first choice."

He was right. My orders came through in mid-June to report to Scott Field by NLT (not later than) July 1, 1949. All over the base people were receiving orders to transfer to hither and yon, in the USA, in Europe, the Far East. Our Camelot was fast fading into history.

I pondered why I had thought of Lockbourne as Camelot. It was because Lockbourne had been "our" base, run, from top to bottom and all in between, by "us." "We" had commanded all units on the station: from the commanding officer of the 332nd Fighter Wing, Colonel Benjamin O. Davis, Jr., and his headquarters staff, to the COs of the four component groups: Fighter Group, Major William A. Campbell; Maintenance Group, Lieutenant Colonel Nelson Brooks; Air Base Group, Major George Webb; Hospital Group, Major Vance Marchbanks; and down through all the ranks and levels of command.

Transient aircrews passing through base operations encountered the "by the book" efficiency of Captain Dudley "Fearless Fosdick" Watson, whose combat exploits as a Red Tail earned him the nickname of the intrepid cartoon detective, Dick Tracy. I had never flown a combat mission with Dudley because I had returned from overseas before he went over to Italy with the 332nd. However, on one occasion while stationed at Lockbourne, I rode as a passenger in a C-47 that he piloted. The trip included a stop at Olmstead AAB near Harrisburg, Pennsylvania. When he took off that night the weather was, as pilots would describe it, "stinko": heavy rain, gusty winds, low visibility, and low ceiling.

Personally, I would have preferred to RON and proceed the next day. "Fearless Fosdick" would have none of that. He had a green instrument card, which he had earned by logging the required number of hours flying on instruments in actual weather, and which authorized him to fly in the prevailing weather conditions that night. And he was "hot to trot" to get back home. For my part I had read enough flying accident reports to be leery of the aviator's malady known as "get-home-itis," which caused many a pilot to take unnecessary risks. But when Captain Watson said, "Let's go home, mates," I boarded the Goony Bird along with about six other souls all beset with varying degrees of nervousness.

It seemed an eternity, after the engines cranked up and we taxied to the end of the runway for takeoff, before we began rolling. It was really only about a fifteen-minute delay while air traffic control was finalizing the clearance for our flight along the airways, but it was plenty long enough for nervous tension to build. Then we began rolling down the runway into the pitch black night that, just after lift-off, was illuminated on my side of the cabin by a huge electric-light sign hung on a row of steel mill smokestacks at the far end of the runway that proclaimed, in large red letters: "IF YOU CAN READ THIS SIGN, YOU ARE TOO CLOSE!"

Undaunted, "Fearless Fosdick" got us home safely with no mishaps and won my admiration with his cool, unflappable response to my thanks for a safe flight through very rough weather. He said: "No sweat, mate. It was a piece of cake!"

Another Dudley was the "sheriff" at "Camelot." As provost marshal, Captain Dudley Stevenson was responsible for all security measures on base. All MPs (military policemen) were under his command, the guardhouse was part of his domain, and each day the officer of the day and the officer of the guard were issued their specific instructions by him. "Steve," as everyone called him, informally, was one of the original six officers of the 99th who had applied for aviation cadet training back in 1941. Assigned to the Air Corps Technical School at Chanute Field in Rantoul, Illinois, each of them began technical training as aviation cadets in a particular specialty, including: William Thompson and William Towns, armament; Nelson Brooks and Dudley Stevenson, communications; and James L. Johnson and Elmer Jones, engineering.

They were expecting to go through flight training also. However, when the United States was plunged into World War II by the Japanese attack on Pearl Harbor, five of them were commissioned immediately in their particular specialties (Towns had been washed out), thus becoming the first Blacks commissioned in the U.S. Army Air Corps. However, they were thus deprived of the chance to be commissioned as flying officers and the 99th was deprived of five potentially fine pilots: Two of them, Elmer Jones and William Thompson, had completed the Civilian Pilot Training Program. In any case, all five saw service overseas with the 99th or the 332nd, helped to achieve the outstanding records of those units, and continued to do so at Lockbourne.

All across the base, in all units there were highly qualified non-commissioned officers and enlisted men and women who formed the backbone of the base, as is the case in every military organization. From the moment of entering the main gate and observing the impeccable uniforms of the MPs on duty, their military bearing and snappy salutes, and throughout a tour of various offices and squadron areas one sensed a pride in "our" base. Being assigned to the 99th I was most acquainted with our NCOs and enlisted men: the likes of our topkick, First Sergeant Herbert Davis, who was short in physical stature but stood tall in the respect of everyone in the squadron as he directed the orderly room staff of NCOs (Staff Sergeant Melvin Robinson, the finance clerk, and Sergeant Russell Meade, the personnel records clerk, and others) in running the day-to-day affairs of the outfit; Master Sergeant Calvin Hobbs, flight line chief, who supervised our mechanics in keeping our F-47s in the air with minimum down times; Master Sergeant Fred Archer, a veteran of the 99th's combat tour in North Africa, Sicily, and Italy, who was a walking encyclopedia on armament and ordnance; Sergeant Caver, operations clerk, who kept the pilots' Form 5s complete with accurate postings of all flying time in the various categories of day, night, instruments, weather, type of mission, number of landings, and so forth. There are too many to list; it is difficult to recall, five decades later, the names of all who made Lockburne AAB, "Camelot."

Also an integral part of the base complement was a detachment of WAACs (Women in the Army Air Corps) whose name was changed to WAFs (Women in the Air Force) when the air force became independent in 1947. First Lieutenant Oleta Crain and Second Lieutenant Verdia Higginbotham were commanding officer and adjutant, respectively. With nearly 200 women in their squadron, the WAFs were assigned to various units on base such as the hospital, headquarters, operations, supply, message center, maintenance hangar—performing every type of task except flying.

To me, Lockbourne Army Air Base was "Camelot" because "we," African Americans, were in charge. We were operating all the usual activities of an air base. We were doing so in outstanding fashion, as some inspection reports from higher headquarters indicated. And, what's more, we had fun doing so—especially with the recreational facilities on base and in the city of Columbus. Although not very hospitable to us at first, the White townspeople of Columbus came to be more cordial as time passed and the impact of our spending in shops and stores was felt—and as our air shows and participation in Fourth of July parades and Armed Forces Day "open house" shows brought favorable publicity to our presence in the community.

We enjoyed reams of favorable publicity from the traveling troupe dubbed "Operation Happiness" created by Special Services Officer Lieutenant Alvin Downing and with Lieutenant Daniel "Chappie" James as master of ceremonies. A variety show of singers, dancers, musicians in a big band, and soloists, "Operation Happiness" showcased the talents of entertainers like soft shoe tap dancer Private First Class Calvin Manuel; singers Private First Class Evelyn Matthews and the show's emcee, "Chappie" James; magician Staff Sergeant George Crawley; and classical/jazz pianist Private First Class Dwight "Ivory" Mitchell, who teamed with virtuoso pianist/producer Al Downing on duets that thrilled audiences at several air bases as well as Lockbourne. The troupe included a number of other outstanding performers who spread happiness and goodwill as they traveled to a number of bases around the United States in a C-47 piloted by Lieutenant James. And it sent a message to all and sundry that it would not toady to Jim Crow, as "Chappie" refused to have the troupe perform before segregated audiences.

Taken altogether the stage was set for desegregation with President Truman's edict that, to some degree, grew out of the wartime exploits of the 332nd, the peacetime performance of the African Americans at Lockbourne, and the widening knowledge about such exploits and performance throughout the armed forces and the public at large.

Professionally, I dare say, everyone at Lockbourne was ready to perform and do well on a desegregated stage and looked forward eagerly to being integrated into the mainstream. For too long, for eight long years, we had been isolated from opportunities for promotions, training, and varied assignments in the United States and overseas that were SOP (standing operating procedure) for White airmen. Now the barriers were gone; only the sky was the limit, and we were ready to reach for it, having no doubts that we could compete with anyone in our particular AFSC (air force specialty code) anywhere in the U.S. Air Force.

Emotionally, however (and here I speak only for myself, although I suspect that many felt the same pangs of regret), I was not really ready to be desegregated. I was not ready to leave the supportive cocoon in which I had been nurtured for those eight years. Desegregation meant that I was going to be in the inhospitable White world, without the close support, the next-door-in-the-BOQ/ flying-tight-formation-every-day/share-the-laughter-and-tears kind of close support that had been welded during those eight years that we Black Eagles had been together. Now we were about to become Lonely Eagles scattered to the far corners of the globe.

As the days of our Camelot dwindled down, so did the number of troops on base. Each day saw more leaving with their PCS orders for a permanent change of station to faraway places. The mood of those leaving and those waiting to leave was a mixture of excitement and gloom. Excitement came from the anticipation of new opportunities at new places elsewhere in the United States, Europe, the Far East. Gloom was the Shakespearean variety: "Parting was such sweet sorrow." One of the 99th guys expressed it best as he stood on the steps of the BOQ just before climbing into his car, packed with all his worldly belongings, on his way to his new billet with a jet squadron in Germany. Lieutenant Earl "Flaps" Williams said, eyes brimming, "I hate to leave you guys!"

My sentiments exactly! I personally was going to miss so many with whom such strong bonds of friendship had been welded during those eight years since the "Tuskegee Experiment" began: Major Bryce Anthony, M.D., my boyhood friend from my old neighborhood in New York, for whom I had stood as best man when he was married the year before and who had broken the news of Pete's illness to me so gently in his office; Captain Clarence "Jamie Boy" Jamison, my 42-D classmate in aviation cadet training; officers, NCOs, enlisted men and women in various units with whom, in official and social contacts, I had grown firm in the conviction that "we" were making history by demonstrating our competence on the job.

And I was going to miss our commander: "the Man," "Bo the Co," "B.O. the C.O.," Colonel Benjamin Oliver Davis, Jr., base and wing commander, Lockbourne Air Force Base, Columbus, Ohio. We had never been close friends, had never been "buddy-buddies": I did not play bridge and therefore was not in his card-playing circle; his four levels of rank above mine created a pecking-order distance between us that had existed from my first meeting him as a captain and I as an aviation cadet. I had gone overseas as a member of his 99th Fighter Squadron and had chafed and groused along with all the other guys at his insistence on "spit and polish" SOP in the boondocks of North Africa and Sicily; and I had marveled at the compassion he showed by responding to my wife's desperate plea on New Year's Eve, relieving me from OG duty that night when our baby was sick.

Overall I admired Ben Davis, the man, who had survived the four years of "silence" at West Point, and I respected Colonel Davis, the officer, who had endured the eight years of segregation that had prohibited him from being a commander of, and an advocate for, his troops in all respects. I was going to miss being in his command.

And I was going to miss Camelot's "first lady," Mrs. Agatha Davis. I would never forget how gracious she had been one Sunday afternoon during a social gathering at their home on the base to which I had been invited along with a number of other officers and their wives. While chatting with some of the other guests I was holding a bottle of beer that was wet on the outside and was beginning to slip from my grasp. Instead of setting the bottle on a table to get a firmer grip I attempted to shift it upward slightly and catch it. I failed. The bottle slipped through my hand, fell to the terrazzo floor, and EXPLODED, splattering beer on guests within ten feet of ground zero! I expected Mrs. Davis to be as furious as I was embarrassed. She wasn't. Instead she tried to put me at ease by stooping to wipe up the mess with paper towels and saying, "Don't worry about it, Lieutenant, it's alright." I still wanted the earth to swallow me but her graciousness helped me to live through my most embarrassing moment.

Yes, indeed, I would miss the Davises.

As if to dot the last *i* and cross the last *t* of my Camelot chapter, while awaiting the issuance of my PCS orders fate arranged for the issuance of another type of order for which I had been waiting seven years—promotion to captain, effective May 23, 1949! I was so elated that I wanted to take old number 619 up, fly over the base, and do my signature "hallelujah" peeloff one last time. But I couldn't. All of our Jugs had been grounded while being prepared for flyaway to other units or to storage sites. My last flight at Lockbourne was in a T-6 on June 4.

Two weeks later my turn came to leave for my new assignment to the 3310th Technical Training Wing at Scott AFB, near Belleville, Illinois, about twenty miles east of Saint Louis, Missouri. After the usual round of brave farewells—"See ya around, Hoss!" "Watch your airspeed on final!" "Let's keep in touch"—I got into my loaded car and drove to the main gate from the BOQ. On the way, as I passed the old cemetery, I thought of our guys, none of whom were buried there, but whom we had lost while at Lockbourne. I felt sad that they had not lived to see what we all had been dreaming of, hoping for, fighting for—overseas and at home—from the very beginning of the "Tuskegee Experiment." They had all been good friends, comrades in arms, and in my mind I saluted them silently:

Lieutenant Milton "Baby" Hall,
Lieutenant Allen Gaston Lane,
Lieutenant Lincoln W. Nelson,
Lieutenant Harvey "Mr. Cool" Pinkney,

Captain Edward "Topper" Toppins,
Major Andrew "Jug" Turner.

That done, there was nothing left to do but return the snappy salute given me by the MP at the gate and turn left heading west, away from Camelot. And away from an outmoded way of life in the United States Air Force, forever.

Part II

After Desegregation

12 Lonely Eagles

>>   June 1949–July 1950

"Go West, young man!" Horace Greeley once told a protégé who asked his advice on how best to seek his fortune, quoting John Soule's article in the *Terre Haute Express,* 1851. Terre Haute was on my route as I drove through Indiana heading west to Scott Field and a new assignment, but I wasn't thinking at all about my fortune. My mind was full of thoughts about my immediate future. The eight hours it took to cover the nearly 500 miles from Lockbourne to Scott Air Force Base allowed me plenty of time to ponder a host of questions:

About the new base where I was going to spend the next eleven months: What kind of quarters would I have? Would my room be in the BOQ along with other student officers, as Truman's edict led me to expect? How about meals? Would I be able to use the officers club and mess without hassle? Could I get a haircut in the PX barber shop without worrying about having my hair chopped up, at the least, or my throat cut, at the worst?

About my monthly flying time to earn my flight pay: What kind of planes would I be flying? I had never checked out in anything but single-engine trainers and fighters, so would I now get a chance to qualify for a multiengine rating? And would I thus be able to log instrument-weather flying time, enough to earn a green instrument card? Some of the former B-25 pilots at Lockbourne already had their green cards because they had logged *beaucoup* weather time in their bomber craft. Would I be able to fly cross-country trips on weekends to see my family in the New York area?

How about the new subject matter I was going to have to master? I knew that communications involved some math, and I wasn't worried about that as that had been one of my strong suits in school. But I also knew that principles of electricity were basic to most phases of communications, and in my electrical engineering courses at CCNY I had struggled mightily, mainly because of problems with Ohm's law applications to circuit analysis. So I began to worry about that even before arriving at Scott.

I worried because I figured that I would probably be the only Black in the class and that my classmates might possibly already have had a background in communications, making it well nigh impossible for me to come out at the top of the class. To be "top banana" wherever we ended up in our new assignments was a goal that all of us who were dispersed from Lockbourne harbored secretly in our hearts and minds, I am sure. Our trophy-winning top guns had set the pace at the air force gunnery meet, and that was a standard that each of us had inbred from our isolated, insulated experience.

As the miles and hours moved along, I thought about what my White classmates would be like. Would they be of the same mold as the bigots I had encountered at Selfridge Field and Walterboro AAB? Those who had caused me to be leery of "White folks"? I hoped not.

On the other hand, I had plenty of reason, from some of my past acquaintances, to hope that they would be decent, fair, and friendly as we learned and worked together. After all, I reflected, some of my best friends of the past were "White folks": Mary Elizabeth Sullivan in elementary school, algebra teacher Agnes Louise Mackin in junior high, and drafting professor Mario Carbone in college; Roy Matthews, Max Rappaport, Ethel Verbeek, Bill Pyhota, Charlie Gregson, and Frank O'Brien in the CPT Program; Colonel Noel F. Parrish, Major Robert R. Rowland, and Captain Clay Albright at Tuskegee Army Flying School.

By the time I rolled through the main gate at Scott Field at just about dusk, my fond memories of friendly Whites had far outweighed my bitter memories of hostile bigots. My worries faded away and I was ready to face my new assignment with renewed confidence.

I reported to the 3310th Technical Training Wing headquarters and was given a folder containing a clearance form for incoming students and an assignment to a student BOQ that turned out to be integrated. As I was unloading my car one of the guys from Lockbourne came down the hall from his room and gave me a hand. I was delighted to see Lieutenant Samuel Lynn, most recently an F-47 pilot of the 99th, a B-25 pilot of the 617th, and cadet captain of his class at TAFS. A fine officer and good friend. He had left Lockbourne about two weeks before and was that far ahead of me in the "Comm" (communications officer) school.

During dinner at the officers mess, Sam answered most of the questions I had pondered during the long drive. I had already noted that both living quarters and eating facilities were integrated. But I still wondered:

"What about the barber shop?"

"Well, theoretically," Sam said, "the barbers are bound to cut your hair, according to the regulations. But do you really want to risk injury or looking like a plucked chicken with a barber who can't cut good hair like ours?"

"No," I chuckled. "But what about flying time? What kind of birds do you fly here? And how much time can we get per month? And how about cross countries on weekends?"

"You'll be checked out in the Goony Bird and you'll be scheduled for night flying and weekends to fulfill your 60–16 [air force regulations] criteria and to log your monthly four-hour minimums for flight pay. Once you're OK'd for cross countries you can probably get a 'bird' every weekend if you really want to. There's usually some student who needs a pilot or copilot to fly somewhere on the weekend. In fact I'm planning a trip to Mitchel Field soon to spend a weekend with Polly and Storme and our folks out in Long Island. Would you like to go?"

"You betcha!" I exclaimed. "Pete and Thumper are in New Jersey with her Mom. I drove them there almost four months ago before leaving Lockbourne, so I sure would like to fly copilot with you on that trip to go see them."

"By the way, Charlie, Spann Watson is also here in Comm school but I think he's gone for the weekend."

"So I'll see him on Monday when he gets back on base. That's great! It'll be good to see our old ops officer here. You know we go back a long way to cadet training and the 99th overseas. I sure am glad to see you here, too, Sam, ole buddy!"

"Likewise, Charlie. Any way I can help you get settled, just let me know."

"OK, Hoss. Thanks!"

Monday morning I reported to a large auditorium where about thirty officers were assembled for orientation about the eleven-month course. Handouts included a course syllabus that described briefly the many subjects we would be required to learn in order to graduate as fully qualified communications officers. I got the impression that the course would have to move at a rapid pace in order to cover, in less than a year, such subjects as: principles of electricity; radios; antennae arrays; wire systems: telephones, teletypes, outside plant, cables; cryptography; management: certification, federal ICC (Interstate Commerce Commission) regulations, international protocol.

Concurrent with classroom instruction, much time was scheduled for laboratory work, using various types of equipment, learning how to work with electricity safely, and how to climb poles to install telephone lines in outside plant sites. "A lot to learn in a short time," I mused.

After the general orientation the students were assigned to classes and I met my seven classmates. They were a pleasant, friendly bunch whose backgrounds represented a cross section of experience in communications—from zero knowledge of the subject, to lengthy experience in one or more aspects. None of them had experience in *all* aspects of communications; therefore, every one of us was going to have to learn something new. They were all company grade officers: Captains Eldridge Faulkner and Joe E. Lewis, First Lieutenants Ernie Banks and Kenny Willard, Second Lieutenant Joe Evola, Chief Warrant Officer Robert Reese, and Warrant Officer Junior Grade Clarence Meyen.

Captain Faulkner was our class leader by virtue of his date of rank. By virtue of mine, I was the junior captain of the class. However, we all formed bonds of friendship from the first day in class, with those who knew a lot about communications helping the novices, like me, to grasp the subject matter in class and in the lab.

Capt. Charles Dryden (extreme left) poses in this 1949 photo with his classmates at Communications Officers School at Scott AFB, Illinois—his first assignment after desegregation of the armed forces. Left to right: Capt. Dryden of New York, 2nd Lt. Joe P. Evola of Illinois, 1st Lt. Ernest S. Banks of Georgia, CWO Robert Reese of Florida, Capt. Joe E. Lewis of California, Capt. Eldridge Faulkner of California, WOJG Clarence Meyen of Wisconsin; 1st Lt. Kenneth R. Willard of Oklahoma.

As I had feared, my biggest bugbear stumped me early on. Ohm's law as applied in circuit analysis had caused me grief in electrical engineering problems at City College and there it was again, ten years later, still "blowing my fuses." Unfortunately I had never had anyone explain circuit analysis in a way that I really understood how to do it. Until one night in the student BOQ at Scott.

It was after dinner at the student officers mess one evening about two weeks after starting the first phase of the course, "Principles of Electricity." One of the students in a class about halfway through the course stopped by my room with an invitation I hated to refuse. I was hunched over my desk, agonizing over a knotty problem trying to analyze a complex circuit of resistances, coils, condensers in combinations of series, and parallel circuits.

His invitation was: "C'mon, Charlie, let's go to the ball game in Saint Louis. The Cards are playing the Dodgers, and it ought to be a great game."

"Sorry, Goose, I can't make it tonight. I've got a bunch of homework to do and it's giving me a fit."

"Goose" was Captain William Goosherst, whom I had first met on the flight line when I was checking out the C-47. He was a flight instructor who introduced me to the world of twin-engine airplanes and taught me, as a rank fighter jockey, how to handle single-engine procedures, feathering propellers, and a host of emergency procedures that I had never had to worry about before.

He proved to be as good an instructor in academics as in the airplane when he asked me, "What's the problem?" and then proceeded to explain how to break down a circuit diagram, component by component, then apply Ohm's law, step by step, and finally compute the unknown quantity, whether it was the current or voltage in the circuit. He made it clear as crystal. For me it was as if someone had flipped a switch and turned on the lights! What a joy it was to have someone help me understand circuit analysis as thoroughly as Miss Mackin had helped me understand algebra way back in junior high school!

To make sure that I could solve any kind of such problem, Goose had me do the ten or so problems of my homework assignment plus a few more for good measure. Then we took off to the ball game. Playing on their turf before their hometown crowd, Stan "the Man" Musial, Enos "Country" Slaughter, Marty "Mr. Shortstop" Marion, and the rest of the Cards humbled my hometown Brooklyn Dodgers that night. But it didn't get me down because I had my own win—over my old "adversary," Ohm's law—and I had a new, amiable friend in the BOQ, Captain Goosherst.

Most of the other White officers in the BOQ were at least civil, if not as amiable as "Goose." One particular exception was a redheaded captain who was in an advanced phase of the course with only a few months remaining before graduation. Our paths crossed only when washing up and shaving at the sinks in the latrine each morning and sometimes in the hallway of the BOQ after dinner. In our first encounter he had totally ignored my "good morning" greeting at the sinks, and his dour facial expression led me to interpret his attitude toward me as being hostile. Later when I heard his thick drawl as he conversed with one of the other students in the BOQ hallway, I felt even more strongly that he resented my presence in the building. And when I learned that he was from Mississippi, I thought, "He's a stone 'cracker'!"

But then, for some strange reason—just plain curiosity, I suppose—I decided to study him, to observe him, his traits, idiosyncrasies, habits. To my surprise I observed that he spoke to no one at the sinks in the morning! He was closemouthed with everyone, not just me.

So. Having gotten over the notion that he was aloof only with me I decided to make a conscious, intentional effort to befriend him simply by the courtesy of a "good morning," every morning. After a couple of weeks it began to work, as he began by grunting a reply, and after another week or so he allowed himself a "how're ya doin'?" By the time of his graduation he had told me something of his air force career so far and about his new assignment.

I never did know his name—he didn't volunteer it, and I didn't ask—just called him "Red," like everyone else. But I learned a valuable lesson from our brief encounter, a lesson about judging a person on the basis of first impressions and scanty information.

Flying at Scott AFB was fun—not as exciting as zipping through the air at the high speed and high altitude that fighter aircraft could achieve, but fun nevertheless.

"Let's go up and smash some bugs" is the way pilots would suggest taking off in a Goony Bird to log their four hours of flying time to earn their flight pay for the month. Such flights, just droning along with no special mission to perform or particular place to go, were truly boring. I preferred to log my time on cross-country trips with some hours at night, others in actual weather. Sometimes the latter could be exciting in the extreme.

Sam Lynn and I made a trip to Mitchel Field as planned, around Easter 1951. We had a full load of passengers, about thirty GIs from the base who wanted a hop to the New York area to celebrate Passover with their families. The trip east was "a piece of cake." The weather was CAVU all the way that Friday. Upon arriving at

Mitchel our passengers hurried to reach their homes before sundown. Sam headed out on Long Island and I subwayed and bused to New Jersey to spend all day Saturday with my family.

Come Sunday everyone hurried back to Mitchel for the return to Scott. The weather officer at Mitchel had bad news for us. About one hour west of Mitchel we were going to run into a weather front with strong headwinds. The AO (airdrome officer) showed us some PIREPS (pilot reports) that indicated heavy turbulence and icing along Airway Green Five, our route home, and asked, "Do you guys really plan to fly in this mess?"

Having flown a lot of actual weather time when he was in B-25s, Sam Lynn was a very competent instrument pilot. More so than I.

"What do you think, Sam?" I asked. It looked like a rough trip but not an unsafe one with competent pilots at the controls. Besides, we had a planeload of students who had to be in class on Monday morning. So we filed an instrument flight plan, Mitchel AFB to Wright-Patterson AFB via Airway Green Five at 8,000 feet, out of the reported icing level.

After loading our passengers we took off heading west, climbing in the clear to our assigned altitude. By the time we crossed the New Jersey–Pennsylvania state line we were in the soup and stayed in it all the way to Wright-Patterson. Heavy turbulence tossed the plane about from time to time and we took turns at the wheel. Each time the bumps subsided, one of us went aft into the passenger compartment to check on the troops. Many had upchucked—some into paper bags, others into caps, handkerchiefs, or onto themselves or on the floor—giving a foul, sour odor to the cabin. All had expressions of some degree of terror on their faces.

After a few hours we reached Wright-Pat; Sam made an instrument approach to the field, breaking out of the overcast at just above the published minimum ceiling for the field and landing in a heavy rainfall. Night had fallen and the "Follow Me" jeep was a blessing as it met us at the far end of the runway and led us to the brightly lit ramp. A couple buses took our passengers into the base operations building. After filling out the Form 1, Sam and I went in also to close out our flight plan and to see about filing for the final leg to Scott Field.

"Nothing doing!" said the AO. "Neither of you pilots has a green card and I'm not about to sign off on a clearance for you to break ground from here tonight. Not with what the forecast says about the weather between here and there. And don't try to tell me that you've got to get these troops back to duty by reveille. Some of them have already told me that, but I'm telling you to cool your heels 'til morning. The tail end of the warm front will still be in your way but you shouldn't have much turbulence. Just strong headwinds. Now we'll put your passengers up in a nearby barracks and you officers can RON in the flight line transient BOQ. And we'll get on intercom with Scott operations to notify them about why you are delayed. Fair enough?"

"OK, Major," I said. "That will also give us a chance to have our troops clean up the cabin where several tossed their cookies when we hit some bumps along the way."

The next morning we got the passengers on board, filed an IFR (instrument flight rules) clearance on Green Five at 6,000 feet, and took off at about 0900. As forecast, headwinds were strong—at one point we had a ground speed of only about 75 mph! And during the flight of about three hours we heard only one other airplane giving a position report on Green Five. It seemed that even the birds were standing down that day. When we finally reached the Scott radio beacon it was about noon. I made an instrument letdown through about a 1,000-foot ceiling, landed, and taxied in to the ramp behind the Follow Me jeep.

The passengers were glad to tumble out of the funky cabin and hustle off to their barracks to clean up and report to their units. Before leaving the plane, however, almost every one thanked us for having flown them home for their Passover holiday and for getting them back safely through all the rough weather.

Sam and I closed out the flight plan, reported to the training squadron as being back to duty, but repaired to the BOQ rather than to class. We were too bushed to sit in any classroom the rest of that day!

I lived in the BOQ at the base for about the first three months of school. During that time I met some friendly folks in Saint Louis. The "Gateway to the West" on the Mississippi River had sent a fair number of young men to Tuskegee Army Flying School and over-seas: Charles Brantley, one of the three Red Tails who, flying an F-51, shot down a German jet fighter over Berlin; Johnny Briggs, whose always-natty appearance marked him as one of the "sharp-est" officers at Lockbourne; Lewis Lynch, whose mother-in-law, Gerry Hamilton, had boarded us for a few weeks when Pete and I first moved to Lockbourne; Wendell O. Pruitt, one of the top pilots of the Red Tails; Charlie White; Hugh White; and Chris "Hummer" Newman.

From some of them I got names and addresses of friends and neighbors in Saint Louis before I left Lockbourne. One particular family that I visited sort of "adopted" me: Mr. and Mrs. Thomas Rector, their preteen daughter Tommie Lee, and their schoolteacher daughter Mildred ("Rickie"), whose fiancé, Henry Twigg, Esquire, was an up and coming attorney who later became a judge. There were many memorable, pleasant Sunday afternoons spent with that circle of warm, hospitable friends. And when my family came west by train to be with me during the remaining eight months of my schooling, the Rectors insisted that I bring Pete and Thumper to their home in Saint Louis to meet them before driving out to the farmhouse in Belleville, Illinois, where I had arranged for us to live.

That was an invitation for which I was deeply grateful, because when I met Pete and Thumper at the depot I learned that he had gotten sick on the train—nothing serious that a three-year-old could not shake off with a little rest and some good hot soup. When I called the Rectors from the station and described our problem, Ma Rector said: "Sure, Son, bring your family here 'cause I've got just what your baby needs to feel better. Besides, you know we want to meet your wife and tell her how you've been misbehaving here in Saint Louis," chuckling as she hung up.

Within the half hour we arrived at the Rectors' home. Only brief introductions were necessary because I had told my family and my "family" so much about each other that they felt a ready-made kinship. So Pete and Ma Rector went right to work bringing Thumper's low-grade fever and diarrhea under control and soon he was sleeping peacefully.

Henry Twigg came by to meet Pete and to join in the joshing

about my carousing ways—all in good fun as they teased and "taunted" me. But then the talk got serious as lawyer Henry and schoolteacher Mildred gave us some insights into the ways and meanness of Jim Crow in the "show me" state. Missouri projected a lot of images, from the past and the then-present:

Having come into the Union as a slave state, with free state Maine, as a counterbalance in the 1820 Missouri Compromise, it was the site of the Dred Scott decision by the Supreme Court in 1857. "In fact," Henry informed us, "the courthouse in which the case was held is just a couple miles from here."

And, of course, Missouri was the home state of President Truman, whose executive order had desegregated the U.S. armed forces just months before.

Nevertheless, in Saint Louis's hotels, restaurants, schools, and so forth, Jim Crow was very much alive and kicking—so much so that Blacks needing medical care were barred from hospitals that served Whites and were limited to all-Black-staffed Homer G. Phillips Hospital, Peoples Hospital with its only-one Black doctor on its staff, and Saint Mary's (Catholic) Hospital with its lily-White staff. "The White folks' Barnes Hospital was an exception to the Jim Crow pattern," said Mildred. "My uncle was treated there once, but they put him into the basement, among the pipes!"

Strangely enough, Blacks could sit anywhere, drink at any water fountain, and use any rest room at the indoor sports arena, at Sportsmen's Park (baseball stadium that was home to the National League Saint Louis Cardinals and the American League Saint Louis Browns), and at Forest Park, the outdoor theater-in-the-park. Exceedingly strange, the etiquette of Jim Crow!

From the lengthy discussion with the Rectors and attorney Henry Twigg we "learned the ropes" about life for Black folks in Saint Louis, such as where we could go and what we could do without risking life or limb at the end of a rope.

After a pleasant evening in their midst Pete and I thanked them for their warm hospitality, awakened Thumper, and, with promises to visit again, drove off to our farmhouse home in Belleville, about twenty-five miles east of Saint Louis and across the Mississippi River.

It was late, about 10:00 P.M., when we arrived. That was late for farm folks, but Uncle Willie and Aunt Callie Dotson were still up waiting for us. I had called them from the Rectors' to expect us at about that time. It wasn't really necessary to alert them by phone, however, because Uncle Willie's hunting dogs gave the alarm when we drove up to the farmhouse. Both blue ticks, "Ole Blue" was old—could hardly see but could howl and could hunt; "Trailer" was a puppy—frisky and lovable, but dumb. That dog couldn't hunt. But he had a lively tail that wagged him when he got excited.

We lived with the Dotsons for the next eight months until my graduation from Comm school. Uncle Willie taught me, a city boy from New York, how to hunt rabbit, possum, raccoon, and quail in the woods around his farm. Thumper wanted to hunt, too, so we gave him a popgun for Christmas and he went out into the woods with Trailer.

For Christmas Uncle Willie slaughtered a hog. It was a memorable experience for us city kids accustomed to shopping at the local butcher or supermarket for our food. We learned a lot about country living at the Dotsons' small farm and enjoyed our stay with them even though winter in Illinois brought bitter cold and snowstorms now and then. Spring came late to Belleville but summer rushed in early with its high temperatures. I had always heard that Saint Louis in summer was one of the hottest cities in the United States, but I wasn't prepared for Fahrenheit 90s in June. So, much as we were enjoying life in the country, and I was going through the Comm course with relative ease, we were glad when graduation day came.

By then my classmates and I had become close friends. We had a ball at a farewell party at the home of our class leader, Captain Faulkner. We exchanged home addresses and vowed to keep in touch through the years as our military careers progressed. We were being assigned to air force bases all over the world. I got lucky and drew an assignment to an idyllic locale, the part of the world to which all servicemen and their families wanted to go at that point in time: the Far East—JAPAN!—General Douglas MacArthur's domain where, I was told by GIs who had returned from there since V-J Day, the living was easy and pleasant.

The document that officially terminated our status as students contained a bit of armed forces folklore as administrative officials wrestled with the problem of identifying Negro personnel—for "statistical tracking," it was said. Special Orders Number 108, issued by Headquarters, 3310th Technical Training Group, 3310th Technical Training Wing, Scott Air Force Base, dated June 5, 1950, announced in paragraphs 12 and especially 13 that the "Following Officers (Race as indicated) having completed Comm Officers Course . . . are . . . graduated and relieved from duty as students effective 6 June 50." Next to the name of each of my classmates was typed the symbol (W). Next to mine there was (N).

Sometimes written orders indicated Negro personnel with an asterisk. In other instances I saw orders on which (1) was used to indicate White personnel and (2) for Negroes. In conversation among ourselves we Blacks adopted a system to describe someone nonverbally without Whites nearby knowing what we were doing: As we mentioned a person we would, very casually, display the back of the hand if we were talking about a Black person, the palm if referring to a White one.

With my PCS orders in hand plus my diploma indicating I had completed the course, rated third of the eight in my class, I was satisfied with the way my first integrated assignment had turned out. And I was happy to have acquired the new AFSC (air force specialty code) of communications officer, a bundle of flying hours in the twin-engine C-47, including a lot of actual weather instrument time, and last, but certainly not least, seven new friends, genuine friends as our eleven months together had proven. Bidding them farewell wasn't easy.

Good-byes to Uncle Willie and Aunt Callie, on the farm, and the Rectors and Henry Twigg, in the city, weren't any easier. But promises to keep in touch masked the pain of parting.

My orders granted me a thirty-day leave of absence before my July 6 reporting date at the POE (port of embarkation) at Camp Stoneman, California. So, after leaving Scott Field for the last time we headed east toward New Jersey, where we would spend the thirty days of my leave at Mother Pearl's apartment on the second floor of the new house built by Pete's Uncle BJ in Nutley.

The first three weeks were a nice vacation of carefree days and fun-filled nights visiting friends and family, hers in New Jersey and mine in New York. Everywhere we went we were objects of instant envy when people found out that we were going to Japan for at least three years. Admittedly, I began to feel smug, as well as blessed by good fortune, and sorry for everyone not in my shoes. Then fate took a turn that put the shoe on the other foot and I felt sorry for myself: With about a week to go before leaving home to report to Camp Stoneman, I heard that North Korean armies had invaded South Korea and attacked U.S. troops stationed there on June 25. So now, instead of going overseas for an idyllic tour of peacetime duty, I was heading into war again. My second war—and I wasn't even thirty yet!

Now, before leaving for California, I had to try to calm everyone's fears and worries about me. I wasn't sure how good a job I did for others but I, myself, wasn't too worried about surviving this war as I had World War II. Sister Vie's prayers had brought me through shot and shell before and she would do it again. With that confidence in my mother's direct line to heaven, I boarded a Super-Connie at Newark Airport to San Francisco. Then on to Camp Stoneman, some distance north of Frisco, by bus.

Stoneman was a huge "repple depple" (replacement depot) where troops leaving or returning to the States were processed. Normally operating at a civilized pace, it had become frenetic with the sudden surge of troops being deployed to Japan for further moves to Korea. Among the thousands there awaiting shipment I found two of my buddies from Lockbourne: Captain Theodore "Brute" Wilson and Lieutenant Harold "Buick" Brown, whose nickname distinguished him from another Harold Brown there, nicknamed "Oldsmobile" Brown. The cars they drove earned the nicknames.

"Buick," "Brute," and I were together at Stoneman for about two weeks. We rented a car and explored the Bay Area a couple times, taking in the usual tourist traps: Fisherman's Wharf, Chinatown, marveling at the Golden Gate Bridge, and astonished by the sudden, rapid drop in temperature at dusk and the swiftness of the fog rolling in covering the entire bay.

Every day large groups of troops moved out of Camp Stoneman. Both Brown and Wilson left before I did, but finally my name came up on the shipment manifest. Along with scores of others I boarded a U.S. Army bus and rode a few miles to a dock where the USNS *General Howze* rode at anchor. Up the gangplank to the deck I struggled with my B-4 bag loaded with personal effects, enough to survive a long sea journey. I figured that crossing the Pacific would take much longer than the nine days the USS *Mariposa* had taken to cross the Atlantic seven years earlier.

Thirteen days after going under the Golden Gate Bridge we made landfall in Japan on August 8, 1950. During the voyage I discovered that among my hundreds of shipmates was a former Lockbourneite who had also been a squadron mate in the 99th: Lieutenant Alvin "Marryin' " Johnson, whose nickname derived from his few trips down the nuptial aisle. As the ship crossed the international dateline, all hands who had never done so before were doused with seawater by "King Neptune," one of the ship's crew with a mop head for Neptune's locks and a pitchfork for his scepter.

The crossing was smooth sailing all the way to the dock on which the 289th U.S. Army Band serenaded us and welcomed us to Yokohama on the Japanese island of Honshu. As I stepped off the gangplank onto foreign soil I couldn't help thinking: "Here I am, 'Over There'—AGAIN! But, going to war this time, I am more mature: I have thirty combat missions under my belt, 2,049 hours flying time in my log, including enough instrument flying in actual weather to feel confident in all conditions, nine years of military experience, and a wife and son to return to."

The army band was playing lively Sousa marches, but inwardly, privately, as I contemplated my uncertain future, I was humming the words of a spiritual I had learned from Tuskegee's chapel choir during my cadet days:

> "Precious Lord, take my hand
> Lead me on, let me stand. . . . "

13   Over There—Again!

» July 1950–February 1952

The shooting war in Korea was only forty-four days old, but casualties among U.S. and ROK (Republic of Korea) troops were mounting rapidly. Eighty-nine thousand Soviet-armed North Korean troops had moved swiftly south of the 38th parallel, the dividing line separating the People's Republic of Korea (north of the parallel) and the Republic of Korea, which was nominally under United Nations control. Greatly outnumbered and hopelessly outgunned, the defending U.N. troops, mostly U.S. Army infantrymen alongside ROK Army soldiers, were squeezed into the "Pusan Perimeter," an area about one-tenth of the territory of the Republic of (South) Korea, with Taegu at the northwestern corner of the perimeter and the seaport of Pusan at the southeastern corner.

To ease the precarious situation of the ground troops in the Pusan Perimeter until more troops could be deployed from the United States, air force units began flying air-ground support missions.

At first the only fighter-bomber aircraft available in the theater were jet-propelled F-80 "Shooting Stars" and propeller-driven F-51 "Mustangs" of World War II vintage. ROKAF (the Republic of Korea Air Force) had some F-51s on bases within the perimeter; however, in the early weeks of the war air support was provided mostly by USAF squadrons based in Japan. Combat missions were launched from such bases, flown across the Sea of Japan, with strikes against North Korean ground targets, then returned back across the Japan Sea to home bases. Takeoff-to-landing time of missions, and fuel consumption, were excessive and time over targets was too short to make such missions feasible. Air operations planners had to cope with the situation until airstrips with runways long enough to handle heavily loaded fighter-bombers became available.

Initially, U.N. forces enjoyed air superiority—the North Koreans simply did not employ much air power for several weeks. However, their small-arms fire and antiaircraft artillery were taking a toll of low-flying Allied aircraft.

That was the war situation when the USNS *General Howze* docked at Yokohama. Along with several hundred other *Howze* passengers I was transported by bus a few miles from dockside to a "repple depple" (replacement depot) where newcomers to Japan were processed. A young captain at one of the interview cubicles welcomed me to "the Land of the Rising Sun," scanned my 201 file, and said: "Captain Dryden, I see you have two critical AFSCS: one as a fighter pilot, the other as a communications officer. Our people in Korea need both skills badly now to fight the war, so you have a choice. In which one would you prefer to be assigned?"

It was lunchtime and my gut was growling, "Feed me, now!" So I said: "That's a good question, Captain, but may I think it over and let you know after chow? I don't think too clearly on an empty belly."

"Sure thing, Captain. Let's meet back here at 1300 and I'll get you on your way to your new outfit by sundown."

"Good deal," I replied and headed for the mess hall in another part of the building.

Munching through a good meal, I had time to think my way through a train of thoughts, such as: "Although I am fresh out of Comm school where I scored fairly high on classroom and lab exams, I don't feel ready to put my 'book' knowledge, plus lack of communications experience, to the test in the field in combat. On the other hand, although I haven't flown a fighter aircraft in over a year since I left Lockbourne, I won't have any trouble 'retreading'—refreshing my fighter jockey skills. Besides, I have heard that the aircraft carrier USS *Boxer* has brought a flight deck covered with F-51s taken out of mothballs to be used in missions against the North Koreans.

"I have regretted missing the chance to fly the Mustang in combat during World War II. When I left the 99th in Sicily in 1943 we were still flying P-40s. The 332nd did not get into the Mustangs until long after I had returned stateside, and all of the Red Tails I have ever met said it is the 'Cadillac' of prop-driven fighters. I did get to check out in the F-51 during the 1948 Christmas holiday season when about a half dozen pilots of the 99th went TDY from Lockbourne to Newark Airport, New Jersey, to ferry some F-51s to a base somewhere in Texas. The three hours of transition time that I logged then whetted my appetite and I was looking forward to logging about ten more hours in it on the cross-country flight. Unfortunately, the weather punked out with conditions below the minimums prescribed for ferry flights, so the trip was canceled and we returned to Lockbourne.

"However, the prospect of another chance to fly the Mustang in combat almost makes me drool. I can hardly wait for the clock to strike 1300 and announce to the good Captain, 'I want to fly a combat tour in fighters, especially 51s.' "

"OK, Captain Dryden, that's what you want, that's what you've got. And I'm not surprised that you want a combat tour. I have seldom met a fighter jock who wasn't like an old fire horse—sound the alarm and he's ready to go. Now there's an outfit at Yokota Air Base, close to Tokyo, where fighter jockey 'retreads' like you are being transitioned in F-51s to be assigned to squadrons here in Japan. So I'm going to cut orders sending you to Yokota and arrange for a vehicle to run you over there this afternoon. It's only a little over an hour from here. OK?"

"Yeah, sounds good to me. Thanks, Captain, I appreciate your help in getting squared away in my first assignment over here. See ya!"

"You're welcome, Captain Dryden. Good luck, and have a good war!"

Outside the replacement depot building the bright afternoon sun combined with the heavy humidity to make the atmosphere steamy, muggy. Big, puffy cumulus clouds sucked up tons of moisture from the Pacific with the pull of the sun's heat, swelled miles high above the earth, adding nimbus to their names, then dumped tons of rain in torrents, soaking everything unroofed. On the way to Yokota in an open-sided weapons carrier, I got soaked and figured it would be the next day before I dried out. However, after about fifteen minutes of downpour, the sun came out and shone with such intensity that I was practically dry again by the time we drove through the gate at Yokota, the "Friendliest Air Base in the World," according to the sign at the gate.

As we pulled up in front of the transient officers quarters (TOQ) the skies opened again and drenched me and the Japanese porter who helped me unload my footlocker and B-4 bag from the weapons carrier and haul them into the building.

The porter, or "houseboy" as others in the building referred to him, was a wizened, old man who looked to be about sixty. Short (he couldn't have been more than about an even five feet tall), lean, and wiry, but he hefted my 100-plus-pound footlocker up upon his shoulders, waddled with a bowlegged gait rapidly through the doorway into the Quonset hut, and deposited the trunk at the foot of one of the cots in the open bay where about a dozen cots were placed. I marveled at the ease with which he had lifted the heavy trunk and thought that in hand-to-hand combat he would be a tough opponent. I had needed help at the repple depple to lift the footlocker onto the weapons carrier and I felt glad that he was a "friendly" and not an enemy.

He declined the tip of a few yen that I offered him, but my tourist-book-learned phrase of thanks, "Domo arregato, gozai-mas," spoken with my Yankee accent, brought a broad, toothy smile and a "Doi tachi maste" in reply. I knew I had a new friend in Nippon.

None of the other occupants of the room were there when I arrived, so I stowed my gear on and under an empty cot, changed into a dry, summer uniform, and walked to headquarters to sign in and begin clearing in on the base. By suppertime I had walked a few miles, going from place to place on the clearing-in itinerary, and had been soaked by rain then scorched by sun a couple times in the process.

Returning to the TOQ I found all the other occupants already there and met them. All were White, all were former fighter pilots being "retreaded" like me; most were cordial, offering their names and a firm handshake as I offered mine. Others grunted their names, unintelligibly, and gave a "dead fish" handshake bringing to mind my initial reaction to "Red," from Mississippi, back at Scott Field. I decided to wait to see if, like "Red," they might become civil after some time.

A group of the "friendlies" urged me to join them for supper at the mess hall and spent the hour briefing me about the transition flying program, some general information about Yokota, and the latest scuttlebutt about the war that they had heard from some of the pilots stationed there who were flying combat missions every day. Most dramatic was the story about the jet pilot on a strafing run whose F-80 was hit by a barrage of small-arms fire as he pulled up from the target, causing his turbo to quit, cold. He had two viable options. His wingman bellowed one at him over the radio:

"Punch out, Colonel! I'll cover you."

The other option was to ride his crippled bird to the ground and land wheels up.

Lieutenant Colonel Brown rejected both viable options. He had gotten the word that the North Koreans were taking no prisoners, so he created his own option as he was heard to growl over the radio, "If I've gotta go, I'm gonna take some of these SOBs with me!" He dove his powerless but ammo-loaded plane into the midst of enemy troops on the ground and died with them as his plane exploded.

"Rough way to go!" one of the guys exclaimed.

"Yeah, but I hear that the action over there is kinda rough, generally, because the North Koreans are torturing prisoners of war, then killing them." That gave all of us something to think about.

The next morning I reported to the flight line and found the operations shack of the fighter transition outfit. After scanning my Form 5 and noting my total fighter time, including a handful of hours in the F-51, the operations officer asked, "Captain Dryden, how much time do you think you need to be ready to fight in the Mustang?"

Figuring that I needed about five hours transition with touch-

and-go landings plus a menu of aerobatics to "wring it out" with various configurations of fuel in the tanks (especially in the auxiliary tank just behind the cockpit), instrument flying "under the hood," and some ground gunnery familiarization, I replied, "Oh, about ten hours."

"OK, Captain. Go see the personal equipment officer about getting fitted with a chute and I'll schedule you for a couple flights tomorrow afternoon. This afternoon I want you to absorb these tech orders on the '51': Get to know all the systems, emergency SOPs—the works. Then when you pass a cockpit check we'll turn you loose. OK?"

"Roger, Major."

The next afternoon I climbed aboard a de-mothballed F-51 and had a ball getting reacquainted with the "Cadillac of fighters" and with the f-r-e-e-d-o-m of the fighter pilot aloft in his element. The day was bright and sunny, the sky splotched with billowy cumulus clouds, and off to the north, Fujiyama rose majestically from the plains around Tokyo to its snow-capped peak, more than 12,000 feet above sea level. It was the kind of day that the joy of flying was hard to describe. The kind that inspired the aviator-poet, John Magee, to write, "Oh I have slipped the surly bonds of earth. . . . " The kind that tempted me to try all kinds of aerobatics on that first retread flight after a year away from fighters. And I couldn't resist temptation; after I had emptied the seventy-five-gallon auxiliary tank aft of the cockpit, as I had been cautioned to do, Mustang and I gamboled all over the sky.

Landing after a couple of hours aloft I went into operations for debriefing and learned that one of our airplanes had been sent as a replacement to an outfit flying combat missions in Korea. It seemed that one of their pilots had "bought the farm" on a strafing run that afternoon. So now our fleet was down to five.

The next day and the next and the next, the pattern was the same. We retreads flew a training flight or two during the day and by nightfall another of our birds was sent off to war. By the end of a week we had no more airplanes! Which meant that Far East Air Force (FEAF) had about twenty "half-baked" retreads who were almost, but not quite, ready to wage war astride a Mustang. Like fish out of water we wondered what we would do next. A day or two later we heard that some of us were going to be transferred to a Mosquito outfit.

"A Mosquito outfit!" I yelped when I heard the scuttlebutt. I should have known that the scuttlebutt of the air force at-large was as unreliable as the spratmo of my segregated air corps days. "Mosquito" to me meant the De Haviland Mosquito, a British-built, twin-engine "going machine," vintage World War II. I had seen one swoosh by overhead at the airport at Blida, south of Algiers, the day, seven years before, when five of us 99th pilots were sweating out seats on flights heading west toward the United States. Its speed was awesome—having wings and fuselage built of plywood, it had to be swift to survive enemy fighter attacks. Just the thought of flying the Mosquito got my juices flowing.

The reality of what Headquarters FEAF meant by "Mosquito outfit" was enough to stem the flow. "Mosquito outfit" referred to the 6147th Tactical Control Squadron, based at K-2 airstrip adjacent to Taegu, Korea. Its mission was to locate enemy ground targets and direct Allied fighter-bombers to such targets to destroy them.

In official jargon its pilots were forward air controllers who worked closely in coordination with ground controllers attached to front-line army units and under the control of central ground control, code named Mellow Control. Unofficially the tactical air controllers were nicknamed "Mosquitoes" because of the way they harried the enemy ground operations by searching out lucrative targets and calling in fighter-bombers to destroy them. Although the North Koreans were expert at the art of camouflage, the "Mosquito" pilots, flying low and slow in their AT-6 "Texan" two-seater trainer airplanes, unarmed except for smoke flares to mark targets, were able literally to look in the window of a mud hut and see a tank or truck that had been stashed there for future use.

With orders to report to the 6147th at K-2 without delay, I hitched a ride on a C-46 from Yokota to Itazuke. Then, on a C-47 loaded with artillery shells, across the Korea strait to K-3 airstrip at Pohang, on the east coast of South Korea. K-3 was under fire as the airplane landed and the pilot had to cut short his landing roll to stay out of small-arms range of enemy troops in the nearby hills. Quickly offloading some matériel earmarked for K-3, the pilot took off again, headed out to sea to climb above the small-arms fire, then headed west and landed at K-2 airstrip, about fifty miles away.

As we taxied in to the parking area I noted a B-17 parked across the field from the operations shack and the control tower. To my question, "What is that old relic doing here?" the pilot replied: "That's General Partridge's plane. Scuttlebutt has it that if you don't see that Flying Fortress parked there, it's time to bug out because the 'Old Man' is long gone!"

The "Old Man," Major General Earle E. Partridge, was at the time commanding general of Fifth Air Force, headquartered at Taegu.

That was interesting trivia, to me, at that time. However, I was more concerned about my personal role in the war. A jeep took me from base operations to the 6147th ops shack where I checked in and met the CO, Major Merrill Carlton, and the operations officer, Captain John Planinac. Major Carlton welcomed me aboard and briefed me about the outfit's mission. Captain Planinac had the personal equipment officer issue me a parachute, flak vest, and .45 automatic pistol. The flak vest was like a miniature general store with all sorts of survival gear in its many pockets—first aid kit, halazone tablets, matches in a metal tube, fishing line and hook, flashlight, compass, signaling mirror. "Dressed to kill" with my new wardrobe *de* combat, I rode over, in a jeep that Captain Planinac let me use, to the Tent City where the troops of the 6147th lived.

I was billeted in an eight-man pyramidal tent with about five other guys at the time. The weather was hot and muggy and the tent flaps were rolled up and securely tied along the edge of each side of the tent to allow a cross breeze to waft through. As I approached my Mosquito "home" I saw two guys stretched out on their cots, taking it easy between missions.

"Howdy!" one greeted me. "I'm Ed Hawes."

"And I'm John Thompson," the other chimed in.

"Glad to meet you," I responded. "I'm Chuck Dryden."

Then began a marathon mutual briefing in which they asked where I had come from, my last assignment, and so on. I asked

MOSQUITO PILOT. Standing in front of his trusty AT-6, a "state of the art" machine (at least for tactical air controllers), Capt. Charles Dryden scans the Korean sky at K-2 airstrip, Taegu, in September 1950. His survival vest is a sort of "general store" with .45 automatic pistol holster under the left armpit and pockets for first aid kit, flares, signaling mirror, matches, compass, extra bullets, mosquito headnet, rations, water bag, halazone water purification tablets, fishing line and hooks—everything but the kitchen sink!

questions about what Mosquito missions were like, how long was the average mission, how many missions constituted a combat tour, how many each of them had already, and so on, until supper at the mess hall and later into the late hours. By the next morning I felt ready to be a Mosquito pilot; no refresher flying time was necessary because the AT-6 was a training plane that was easy to fly and I had *beaucoup* hours in it from cadet days and instrument check rides through the years.

September is my birth month. Two weeks and two days before my thirtieth birthday I wondered if I was going to live to see it because early on the morning of September 1 I was sitting in a combat briefing getting ready to take off in an unarmed plane and fly low and slow over strange territory infested with enemy troops eager to shoot me out of the sky. Along with five other pilots I was learning about the latest enemy activities in our assigned patrol areas from the squadron S-2 (intelligence officer). My area, designated "Hammer," was a sector of enemy territory due west of Taegu and across the Naktong River, covering about ten miles along the arc of the Pusan Perimeter and all land westward to a distance of about fifty miles. Every pilot was assigned to a particular sector and each sector was constantly patrolled during daylight hours by one of the half dozen or so pilots assigned to it.

In the back seat of his T-6 each pilot had a U.S. Army officer whose job was to note on a map marked with the grid coordinates of his sector all significant enemy activities observed during the flight. The observers assigned to the 6147th on TDY for about two weeks were from various branches of the U.S. Army: infantry, artillery, mechanized cavalry, engineers, and so forth. I was to learn a lot from the different observers who rode in my back seat.

On my first mission an infantryman first lieutenant nicknamed "Steve" rode my back seat. He had been in action from the very first day of the war, had been wounded, recovered, and insisted on getting back into action. He had been on a number of missions with other Mosquito pilots in the Hammer sector so he knew what to look for to determine enemy actions taking place or that had taken place since his previous patrol.

We took off into the sun just peeping over the horizon. As I climbed I turned right, rather than to the left, which is the usual direction for leaving the traffic pattern, with good reason— enemy ground troops were not very far from K-2 and there was no point in giving them a shot at us. As I turned our plane 180 degrees to head west toward the Hammer sector, it was comforting to see General Partridge's B-17 parked in its accustomed spot.

Leveling off at 3,000 feet, I followed a paved road that had once connected Taegu and Taejon, about eighty miles north, which was now an enemy stronghold. The bridge across the Naktong River had been bombed and dropped into the river to halt North Korean troops in hot pursuit of South Korean and American troops during the early days of the surprise invasion. I continued our patrol along the road to Kumchon, about twelve miles from the river, crisscrossing back and forth to become familiar with the terrain of the sector; all the while "Steve" was giving me a running commentary about previous missions and pointing out where "goddam gooks" had been killed by F-51s or F-80s dropping napalm or firing rockets or just plain strafing.

The sector was quiet during the entire two-hour patrol with nothing moving anywhere. Steve was fit to be tied because we could hear radio chatter from Lieutenant John Thompson in the sector to the east of ours calling: "Mellow Control, from Mosquito Wild West: I've got four tanks moving on a road heading south. Gimme some fighters, quick!" The Wild West sector was also known as "the bowling alley," so nicknamed by our infantry, according to Steve, because the rolling barrages of artillery, ours and theirs, sounded like a bowling alley with fifty lanes all in play at the same time.

We were relieved by the next Mosquito Hammer patrol as we were crossing the Naktong heading home to K-2. In the ops shack the S-2 (intelligence staff officer) was disappointed that we had little of interest to report about activity in Hammer sector, but I was glad that my first patrol had been quiet, allowing me to become familiar with the terrain and enemy strongholds that Steve had shown me: Those would be good targets of opportunity to which we could direct fighters when, at some near future time, there were enough Allied fighter-bombers to service all the sectors simultaneously.

The main problem faced by the battle planners holding on to the small area of the Pusan Perimeter was the scarcity of war materials with which to repel the enemy. The long supply lines from the States were taking a long time filling up.

The main problem faced by me was people like Steve. By all accounts he was a good officer, a fearless warrior—I had it on good authority that he was in line for a Silver Star for bravery under fire with his outfit in the "bowling alley." But I was leery of his language and the attitude it expressed. I had the feeling that his "goddam gook" slur easily changed to "goddam nigger" behind my back. After our debriefing and while we were waiting for our next mission, I called him outside the ops shack, out of earshot of the other guys, and did something I seldom did—threw rank on him, with:

"Steve, that was a good mission, the first one of my second war, and I want to thank you for teaching me so much that I need to know about the sector. But, Lieutenant, let me tell you something. I don't appreciate your referring to the Koreans as 'gooks,' because you give me the impression that you just as easily call me a nigger behind my back. Now I believe we can be a good team flushing out the enemy, but if I have to fly you thinking all the time that you disrespect me, then we won't make it. Just remember, Lieutenant, that when you're in my back seat, your butt is in a sling and you have to depend on me to get back on the ground. So. Don't you ever, repeat ever, let me hear you refer to Koreans, North or South, as 'gooks,' again! And if you have a problem with that then let's just tell the ops officer not to ever schedule us to fly together again. Is that clear?"

Brash, brave, and bold though he was, the lieutenant was astute enough to get my point and acknowledged with: "Yes, Sir, Captain. I have no problem with flying with you and you will not hear me use that word again."

Whether he meant merely that he would continue to use the slur but not within my hearing or that he would scrub it from his vocabulary entirely, I was not sure, but I felt that I had at least made him aware of his bias and how I felt about it.

We did fly again, several times during my fifty-mission tour. The next time was the day before my birthday. By then I was about halfway through my tour and was up on a late afternoon mission. The war had not been going well for the U.N. forces on the ground, and North Korean armies were on the move toward the Pusan Perimeter from all salients. Scuttlebutt had it that Allied troops were getting ready to bug out from the Pusan Perimeter and retreat to Japan.

As I rolled down the runway and broke ground, there was something about K-2 that wasn't right, was different than what I was accustomed to. "What is it?" I wondered. Then it hit me, just as Steve called me on the intercom: "Say, Cap'n, the 'Old Man's' bird has flown the coop. The Partridge has gone!"

"Uh, oh," I thought. "That's bad news. I guess the 'bug out' scuttlebutt is right after all."

Then, about an hour into the patrol Steve called my attention to a column of enemy tanks moving up a narrow road that wound around the face of a steep hill; they were heading toward K-2, about ten miles away.

"Mellow Control, Mellow Control, Mosquito Hammer here. We've got four enemy tanks heading in. What've you got for us? Over."

"Hammer, Mellow here. No fighters available for you right now. They're busy all over the place. Sorry. Over."

"Roger, Mellow. But keep trying 'cause they're getting close to Taegu. Over and out."

All during that dialogue I was circling above the tank column at about 1,000 feet, just keeping an eye on them in case Mellow Control got some fighters for us to direct an attack. From our vantage point above the tanks we could see something that the tank crews could not. As the column approached a bend in the road, a platoon of about eight GIs, well camouflaged, rose up from concealed cover a few yards down the slope from the road bed and aimed bazookas at the lead tank. Puffs of gray-white smoke on the tank indicated "bullseye!" and it stopped dead in its tracks. So did the three tanks following. The road was too narrow for them to turn around and the slope was too steep to make a run for it. So the bazookas picked them off one by one. As the hatches were flung open by the tank crews, the GIs moved in and took prisoner those who dismounted, hands in the air. Those who tried to escape on foot were mowed down.

From our aerial grandstand the whole scenario looked like a re-run of a World War II movie. We still had another hour on patrol before landing. When we did and related what we had observed, S-2 told us that the North Korean tank column commander had been captured. Interrogated, he had declared that K-2 was targeted for attacks that very night by suicide squads whose mission was to murder as many persons as possible while they slept. I wondered, seriously, whether I would live to see my birthday, the next day!

With the unsettling information about suicide squads spreading throughout the airstrip, the security status was raised to "yellow alert." For us living in Tent City, several changes in our activities occurred. Normally, in order to maintain a modicum of civiliza-tion, we groomed ourselves, before hitting the sack, with a bird bath and a shave using a helmetful of water; then some guys donned pajamas before climbing into their bedrolls and hung their flak vest and shoulder holster, with .45 firmly in place, on the cross-bar at the foot of their cot and unfurled their mosquito nets to keep out the bugs. The tent itself was normally "buttoned up" at night with the side flaps fastened to stakes on the ground.

That night everything was different: Tent flaps were left un-staked and mosquito nets rolled up out of the way; everyone retired in flying suit with boots on; flak vests were at the head of the cots, and .45s were under pillows. Tension in the tent was palpable. Sleep was slow in coming but eventually we all fell asleep, tired from the two or three missions each of us had flown. I slept fitfully until awakened by nature's urge to empty my tank. As I lay on my cot for a moment to get my bearings in the dark, I could hear the even breathing of my tent mates. A fair breeze was whipping the un-staked tent flaps about, producing soft slapping sounds. Then, sud-denly, a strong gust slapped one of the flaps down hard with a loud "POW!"

Instantly the sounds of even breathing stopped. Then I heard rapid, excited breathing. And then a series of more ominous sounds: CLICKUP! as each of the guys jacked a round into the chamber of his .45. With everyone in that pitch-black tent uptight about possible suicide squads moving about, it was no time to be going outside to the latrine. So my steel helmet had to double as a potty that night—I wasn't about to risk being gunned down by a trigger-happy tent mate.

Scheduled for the dawn patrol in the Hammer sector, I was up early on my birthday. On the way to the mess hall I thought, "Well, I've made it to thirty and if I 'buy the farm today' they'll have to carve September 16 on my tombstone only once, for both birth and death date"—a somber thought, but that was the mood we all shared. The mood engulfed me—until I reached operations and was briefed by S-2. On the situation map he showed many arrows heading north from Pusan to Taegu and said that the Allies were gearing up for a massive thrust to break out of the Pusan Perimeter that very day. The threatened suicide attacks had not occurred and K-2 was secure as Allied armies were about to go on the offensive.

Before leaving ops I met my back seat observer whose name has escaped me. It wasn't Steve. Gung ho Steve had gotten wind of something about to happen and had requested relief from Mosquito duty to return to his outfit at the front. So I had a young shavetail, an engineer, with me. We took off to the east just at dawn, and as I made the customary right turn out of traffic I was thunderstruck to see the road from Pusan, south of Taegu, choked with vehicles. There was a rush hour, Times Square–kind of traffic jam that was moving toward the area surrounding K-2.

As I flew west following the Taegu-Taejon road, I crossed the Naktong River and looked at the old bombed-out iron bridge with its girders and spans sticking up out of the water grotesquely. See-ing no replacement bridge, I wondered aloud on the intercom to my young engineer in the back seat, "How are our troops going to cross the river?" As he was describing to me the bridging technique that would be used, I had to cut him short to report our arrival on station in the sector:

"Mellow Control from Mosquito Hammer. Over."

"Mosquito Hammer from Mellow. Go ahead."

"Mosquito Hammer on station. Over."

"Roger, Hammer."

On the west bank of the Naktong the road to Taejon ran west across flat open country for about two miles then curved sharply toward the north as it passed through a defile between two steep hills. Parked in the bend of the road and between the steep hills was a Russian-built T-34 tank. Not firing at the moment that we spotted it, it was just sitting there as though daring anything or anyone to attempt to cross the river from the Taegu side.

"Mellow from Hammer. Over."

"Hammer from Mellow Control. Over"

"Mellow, Hammer here with an enemy tank facing the Naktong. What have you got for me? Over."

"Hammer from Mellow. That's the guy who has been holding up the show. A flight of four 'Stangs coming to you. Over."

"Roger, Mellow. Hammer out."

Using the call sign of the incoming flight of F-51s that Mellow gave me, I was able to contact the flight leader and give him the grid coordinates of the tank's location and my position. In a couple of minutes the flight arrived in the area where I was orbiting the tank. After making a simulated dive-bombing run at the tank, with the flight leader watching, I moved off to one side to watch his flight destroy the tank with their five-inch HVAR. Unfortunately they had no luck, splattering rockets all over the sides of the hill. The problem was that the steepness of the hillsides plus the sharp bend in the road made it difficult to bore in for an effective approach and pull up in time to avoid crashing into the hills.

Another flight reported to me after the first one had failed to dislodge the tank. Mellow Control was growing shrill with orders to "Get that tank."

The next flight had napalm, which they proceeded to try to drop on the tank but succeeded only in setting the hills afire. By the time they had dropped their napalm tanks it was time for me to be relieved from sector patrol to return to K-2. I was unhappy to report, as I checked out of the area, "Mellow Control from Mosquito Hammer. Checking out. No joy!"

After lunch my young back seat shavetail and I took off on the afternoon patrol and found the situation of the enemy tank unchanged. He was still there, an ominous monster belching fire at anyone and anything that tried to cross over. Mellow Control was beside itself, frustrated by the unsuccessful attacks. I detected desperation in the voice of the Mellow speaker when he called: "Mosquito Hammer from Mellow Control. I have a flight of four F-51s for you, call sign, 'Gashouse Willie.' You know the target. Over."

"Roger, Mellow. Hammer out."

Then I began calling: "Gashouse Willie, Gashouse Willie, Mosquito Hammer here. Do you read me? Over." I made three or four calls like that before I heard in my headset:

"Mosquito Hammer, this is Gashouse Willie with four F-51s hauling rockets. What've you got for us? Over."

The voice sounded familiar. Like someone from "Camelot." So I took a chance and asked, "Chappie, is that you?"

"Roger," he replied and must have heard a voice that sounded familiar as he guessed, "Chuck, is that you?"

Chappie James and I had not seen or spoken to each other for over a year since leaving Lockbourne, but here we were joining forces to wage war in the skies over Korea.

"Roger, Chappie. What's your position? Over."

From the grid coordinates he named I knew he was almost directly overhead at 8,000 feet.

"You're right above me, Gashouse Willie, so come on down to Angels 2 [2,000 feet]. I've got a juicy target for you. I'm orbiting it. Over."

"Roger, Hammer."

In a couple of minutes the four Mustangs whizzed by me in a right-echelon formation. "Mosquito Hammer from Gashouse Willie. I have you in sight. Where is my target? Over."

"Gashouse Willie, Hammer here. I'll make a dry run on a tank that is parked on the road between the hills. Just watch me."

After diving on the tank in a simulated rocket attack, I heard:

"OK, Hammer, I see it. Let's go to work. Just move out of the way and we'll wax that guy."

"Roger. He's all yours."

Chappie spread out his flight in string and flew a gunnery pattern on the tank—blew it to smithereens and opened up the road to Taejon for the breakthrough at that point of the perimeter. Allied troops and equipment poured across the river, quickly linking up with other units that had breached the perimeter in other thrusts. Within a couple days of fierce battles, Allied troops captured the high ground atop many of the hills on the west bank of the Naktong. The bomb line was "fluid" and some of the hills were still owned by the North Koreans. That situation led to a mission that caught me and a couple of fighter pilots in the midst of what turned out to be an international incident.

During an afternoon patrol about a week after the breakthrough I was checking out the hills just west of the river to see which side held what real estate. At the very peak of one hill I saw a large dugout in which a couple of bare-waisted GIs wearing steel helmets were securing their position digging foxholes and placing branches for camouflage over their stronghold. Flying low enough above them to see what appeared to be dogtags hung around their necks, glinting in the sun as they worked, I waggled my wings in response to them waving their hands as we flew by. My back seat observer noted their position on his grid coordinates map in order to update our S-2 about this new location of Allied troops when we landed and were debriefed.

No sooner had he done so, and I had headed away from that spot to patrol the rest of the sector, than our headsets crackled with:

"Mosquito Hammer, this is Mellow Control. I have a hot target for you in your sector. Are you ready to copy grid location? Over."

"Roger, Mellow. Hammer here. Over."

Copying the grid coordinates he cited and finding the spot on the map, my observer and I were both dumbfounded. It was the same spot we had just flown over and had seen, close up, what we were sure were friendly troops. So I called:

"Mellow, this is Hammer. Those are friendlies. Over."

"Negative, Mosquito Hammer. That's an enemy position and I'm assigning a flight to you to hit it. Clear? Over."

"Mellow Control, Hammer here. Not clear. Say again position of target. We just buzzed that location you gave us and the troops there are ours, repeat, friendlies. Over."

By this time Mellow Control's tone became shrill with anger. "When your fighters arrive, you put them on that target!"

Before I could reply a flight of two F-51s, with napalm tanks hung under their wings, flew about 500 feet above us and began orbiting left around our plane as the flight leader checked in with his call sign and asking: "Mosquito Hammer, where is our target? I've got the coordinates but I want to cross-check with you."

Cross-checking was often done because moving at over 400 mph the fighter-bombers liked to have the slow-moving "Mosquitoes" pinpoint the target by making a dry run on it. So with the flight leader watching me I simulated a diving attack on the hilltop, and as I pulled up I said to the flight leader: "Mosquito Hammer here. We think those are Allies in the dugout. What do you think?"

"I'll check 'em out," the fighter leader replied as he made a dry run on the hilltop with his wingman following in trail while I orbited above. "Yep, I believe they're ours," he said.

Mellow Control went berserk. Although located on the east bank of the Naktong and several miles from the bomb line, Mellow was somehow convinced that the hilltop was in enemy hands and broadcast a direct order: "Hit that target, NOW!"

Complying with the direct order, the fighter leader dropped a napalm tank on the hilltop. Immediately, as he was pulling up from the attack, a red flare arched upward from the area of the dugout. The wingman broke off his attack run and rejoined his leader. For a moment or two I pondered the best course of action when I heard a calmer, but somber, voice over the radio saying: "Mosquito Hammer from Mellow Control. Return to base. Repeat, return to base."

"Mellow Control, Mosquito Hammer here. Wilco."

K-2 was less than ten minutes away, and as I turned toward it I saw the two Mustangs headed toward their airstrip. They, too, had been ordered to return to base.

As I taxied up to the ramp, I was met by the ops officer in his jeep. Before I had cut the engine he jumped up on the wing and said: "Captain Dryden, we've got a call from Fifth Air Force headquarters for you to report to General Partridge as soon as you can change into class-A uniform. Come on, I'll drive you over to your tent so you can make a quick change, then I'll drive you into Taegu, to his office."

After about fifteen minutes to freshen up and don a summer uniform, I was ready to go on my "last mile." On the way into town I wondered if I was about to be slaughtered like a sacrificial lamb, a scapegoat for someone else's snafu. The closer we got to headquarters, the more nervous I became. Once inside the building I felt that this was my doomsday and feared the worst, sure that I was going to be blamed for botching a mission. After about fifteen minutes in General Partridge's outer office I was joined by another pilot, a major who introduced himself as "Moon" Mullins. He was the leader of the two-ship flight that had been ordered to attack the hilltop by Mellow Control.

He and I reviewed what had happened and agreed that because Mellow Control was so far away from the bomb line it should not have ordered a strike in such a fluid situation. We wondered, though, if General Partridge would also agree when he heard our version of what had happened. I had seen pictures of the general in which he appeared tall and stern, but I had never seen him in person.

When he came into the room from his office I saw that I was right in one respect. He was tall, over six feet. But his manner dispelled my notion that he was stern. Returning our salute, he put us at ease by inviting us to be seated and to tell him our version of the mission that had just been performed in the Hammer sector. After hearing us out, General Partridge revealed that he had been informed that a number of ground stations and air crews airborne in various locations during the mission had reported that Mosquito Hammer and the fighter flight leader had disputed with Mellow Control until given the direct order to "Hit that target, NOW!" The general assured us that he was convinced that we had done our job and that we need not worry about any repercussions that might occur—he would bear the brunt. Urging us to continue doing a good job in our squadrons, he dismissed each of us with a handshake and a salute.

Whew! I was so relieved I could have jumped for joy. Feeling like we had been reprieved from the hangman's noose, Major Mullins and I shook hands, exchanged salutes outside headquarters, and returned to our units. Captain Planinac had waited for me and gave me a lift back to the field. In the ready room that evening all the Mosquito pilots were glad to hear how fair and understanding our commanding general had been. Sometimes, in close support work with ground troops in a fluid situation, intelligence information lagged behind swiftly advancing friendly troops. The results could range from embarrassing to disastrous. In the Hammer sector incident it was a bit of both, as an article in the *Stars and Stripes* a few days later noted that an exchange of diplomatic notes between the United States and the United Kingdom took place following an unfortunate drop of napalm on some Scottish Argyle soldiers who had captured Hill 282 from North Korean troops, unbeknownst to Mellow Control, causing almost 100 casualties.

The breakout from the Pusan Perimeter gained momentum as Allied troops raced with their armored vehicles northward toward Seoul, the capital of South Korea, to link up with General Douglas MacArthur's forces that had landed at Inchon on the same day as the breakout at Taegu and at other points on the perimeter. Along the road from Taegu to Taejon the North Koreans had stashed a number of tanks and trucks, many of them camouflaged in mud huts.

One morning, about four days after the breakout by the Allied ground forces, as I was flying low and slow and practically looking through the windows of a number of huts alongside the road, my back seat observer and I discovered a number of tanks just waiting to be used by enemy troops who had been bypassed by our swiftly advancing armies. Calling for fighter support I was able to direct the destruction of four tanks and five trucks by fighter bombers that morning and reported that information to the S-2 in debriefing.

The word got around the front about the many tanks and trucks "killed" that morning on the Taegu-Taejon road in a short stretch between Waegwan, just on the west bank of the Naktong River, and Kumchon, a few miles north. At lunch, the CO introduced me to a war correspondent who wanted to ride my back seat on my afternoon patrol to see the carcasses for himself. Extending a hand in greeting, the reporter said: "Captain Dryden, I'm Ben Price. I hear you had a good show this morning and I'd like to do a story about it."

Seeing the puzzled look on my face, Major Carlton said, "He's been cleared to ride with you, Chuck, and it's got the boss's blessing." That's all I needed to know. "The boss" was General Partridge, and after the way he had handled the Hammer sector incident without any backlash on my hide, I was glad to fly the mission just the way he wanted it.

After getting Ben fitted with a parachute and settled into the back seat, I took off on the afternoon patrol. Heading north I flew low over each of the dead tanks and trucks, doing "S's" across the road as we looked each one over. Then, as I was looking in the window of one of the huts, a tank that had been driven into the side of the hut and camouflaged suddenly roared into life and swung around, headed for the road to make a run for Kumchon, about five miles to the north.

"Mellow Control," I squawked, "Mosquito Hammer here. I've got a tank on the run toward Kumchon. Send fighters, NOW! Over."

Before Mellow could answer, I heard: "Roger, old boy, Aussies here. We'll get the bloody bastards. We're at seven o'clock to you, Angels 2. We see him. We'll get 'im."

Looking over my left shoulder I saw three Mustangs in trail, diving straight toward the tank. It was in full flight as the lead Mustang fired a rocket that stopped it dead in its tracks. Then as the hatch flew open and the tank crews jumped out they were strafed by number two and number three Mustangs. Meanwhile two other tanks had decided to try to make a run for it on the road to Kumchon and suffered the same fate. In his grandstand seat in the back of the T-6, Ben Price saw it all and had a lot to write about already. But the show wasn't over yet.

With no more movement on the road and no more camouflaged tanks that I could detect, I flew toward Kumchon, which was still in enemy hands. North Korean artillery emplaced on the sugar loaf–shaped hill on the outskirts of the town was giving our ground troops fits as they advanced toward the town. A forward ground controller in his radio-equipped jeep called: "Mosquito Hammer, there's a gun up there on the mountain that's got us pinned down here. See if you can find it. Over."

"Hammer here. We'll give it a try. Out."

When we reached the hill that rose a couple hundred feet above the level of the town, I told Ben to make sure his safety belt was fastened and snug and that his equipment was firmly in hand. Then I made a series of steep dives at a number of areas on the back side of the hill, jinking erratically while pulling up sharply after each dive.

"What the devil are you doing that for?" Ben asked on the intercom. Watching his expression in the rearview mirror mounted at the top of the windshield in the front cockpit, I saw him blanch slightly when I replied, "I'm looking for the gun and I'm trying to draw his fire so I can see his muzzle flash."

"Good Lord!" Ben exclaimed. "Do you do this often?"

"Yeah, Ben. Whenever necessary we Mosquitoes do this sort of thing to find the enemy and help direct firepower on him to destroy him."

Apparently Ben was impressed, because an article appeared in some newspapers back in the States. My wife, Pete, sent me an article clipped from the Newark, New Jersey, *Sunday News*, dated September 24, 1950, under Ben Price's byline and headlined: "N.J. Pilot Aids Record Attack: 15 Tanks Destroyed on 14-Mile Korea Road." The article read, in part:

> IN THE AIR OVER KUMCHON (Delayed)(AP)—U.S. Fifth Air Force fighters today set some kind of record for this beat-up war by destroying 15 tanks on a 14-mile stretch of road.
>
> The road runs from Waegwan to Kumchon, west of the Naktong River. I know they were destroyed because I saw six go up in flames and counted the still smoking hulks of the others.

Capt. Charles W. Dryden of New York and Nutley, N.J., found 10 of the tanks plus five trucks.

Nowhere on the Kumchon road or in Kumchon itself could any large body of enemy forces be seen.

Even the flak tower on the hill just back of Kumchon to the west was silent. Dryden flew over it deliberately in an effort to draw fire. I was his observer. . . .

One tank was spotted by Dryden in the open, racing down the road in a gun battle with the lead tank of the advancing U.S. 24th Division.

Dryden, a 30-year-old ex-fighter pilot and veteran of the all-Negro 99th in World War II, led a flight of three Australians in F-51s into the scrap.

Pete enclosed the news clipping with a letter in which she described a paradox involving herself and our son, Thumper, who was then almost four years old. On Monday, September 25, the day after Ben Price's article appeared in several newspapers, she had learned from a maid at the nursery school where Thumper was enrolled that he was being treated unfairly. The maid, a neighborhood friend, told her that Thumper was being made to sit apart from the other children, was not being given the same kind and quantity of food for lunch as the others, and was generally being treated harshly and unkindly.

Furious, Pete took Thumper out of the school and planned her next move. Taking pen in hand she wrote to several newspapers apprising them of what had happened. Editorial comments published in the next few days lamented the sad situation in which the son of an American fighting man was made the victim of racial bias even as his father was risking the supreme sacrifice for his country.

Shamed, the school called Pete with apologies and an invitation to bring Thumper back. She declined, realizing that his life would be made even more miserable by overt and covert acts done by school officials smarting from the unfavorable publicity. Learning about what had happened to my family back home, in their skirmish with domestic enemies in our native land, certainly did nothing to help my morale in my war with foreign enemies overseas.

Nevertheless I continued racking up two, sometimes three, missions every day until by October 2, thirty-two days after my first Mosquito mission, I had logged fifty missions and 149 hours of combat flying time. I was tired and ready to rotate back to Japan.

On October 5 the 6147th moved out of K-2 and flew north to K-16, just outside of Seoul. As the squadron's planes were cranking up for the flight north, I was taxiing out to take off and head south to Japan across the Korea strait ferrying a T-6 to "Tachi" (Tachikawa Air Base), outside of Tokyo, for depot maintenance. I had PCS orders in my pocket transferring me to the 6161st Air Base Group at Yokota Air Base, and I thanked the Lord for sparing me in my second war.

The trip to Tachi was pleasant, especially once I had crossed the 150 miles of deep water in the Korea strait. I had been a bit apprehensive about flying a war-weary bird in need of engine overhaul across the drink, but it purred all the way with nary a cough or a sputter. The skies were cloudless and sunny, CAVU, and I had a lot of time to think about what I had experienced in the Land of the Morning Calm.

During the thirty-two days we had lost only one Mosquito pilot. While flying low and slow looking for targets, he had flown into a cable that had been strung across a road by the North Koreans. Allied troops found the wreckage in his sector a few days after the breakout from the Pusan Perimeter. The bodies of both the pilot and the observer were found in the plane, riddled with bullets.

As a counterbalance to that sad event, I had the pleasure of seeing some of my old buddies from Lockbourne during my stint at K-2. "Marryin' " Johnson, who had been a shipmate on the voyage to Japan, had been assigned to the Mosquito squadron about halfway through my tour and we both were glad to have a buddy in the outfit.

One day, after completing a mission, I was sitting in the cockpit busily filling out the Form 1 when the control stick began beating a rat-a-tat on my knees. "What the hell's going on?" I hollered, looking over my shoulder and ready to fight my tormentor. Standing behind the airplane and fanning the rudder back and forth, rapidly, was "the Eel," James Bernard Knighten, the former 99th fighter jockey who had saved my life over Sicily during World War II. Grinning from ear to ear, he teased me with, "Hey, Dryden, what're you doin' fighting a war in a trainer?"

I hadn't seen Knighten since WWII and was so glad to see him that I couldn't get angry. He told me that he was flying supply missions in C-46s and just happened to land at K-2 that day.

Other Tuskegee Airmen who came through K-2 at one time or another were Captain Melvin "Red" Jackson, who had been my CO in the 99th at Lockbourne and who was flying F-51s with the ROK (Republic of Korea) Air Force; Lieutenant Harold "Tank" Hillery, also an F-51 jockey with the 39th Fighter Squadron, 35th Fighter Group. Tank had been overrun by North Korean soldiers while he was on duty as a forward controller, on the ground with U.S. Army units in Taejon, in late July, and he was the last person to see Major General William Dean alive in that battle. General Dean was commanding general of the 24th U.S. Army Division that had taken the brunt of the North Korean attack when hostilities began on June 25. After being overrun, the general escaped and evaded enemy troops for several weeks before being captured and held prisoner until the war ended. Tank Hillery also had to evade enemy troops for a couple weeks before he was able to find his way back to friendly forces.

My first touchdown after crossing the Korea strait was at Itazuke Air Base. When I went into the weather station there to file my flight plan to my next stop at Nagoya, I found that another former Lockbourneite was in charge—Captain Weldon K. Groves. He had been the chief instrument instructor of the 99th at Lockbourne and had taught me how to fly instruments on many a check ride. It was good seeing old "Flattop," as the guys used to call him.

The next leg of the trip was to Komaki Air Base at Nagoya where I RON'ed. I was in no particular hurry to end the very pleasant cross country to Tachikawa. Nagoya to Tokyo was the final leg of the trip, and I took off about midmorning the next day, arriving at the Tachi traffic pattern at about noon, just in time to hear another familiar voice from the days at "Camelot," saying over the radio: "Tachikawa tower, Air Force C-46 three miles south. Request landing instructions. Over." It was Captain Fitzroy "Buck" Newsum.

It had to be Buck—no one else at Camelot had the mellifluous lilt of West Indian rhythm in his speech and, because of my Jamaican roots, my ears were tuned to the slight accent. After I landed and went into base operations to close out my flight plan, I found out I was right. Buck was already there and we spent some time catching up on what each of us had been doing since leaving Lockbourne more than a year before.

By delivering my airplane to the maintenance people at Tachi, my ferry mission was complete and I was free to proceed to Yokota Air Base, which was a few miles distant. A shuttle bus made the trip in about a half hour, delivering me back to the "Friendliest Air Base in the World." I was glad to be back to my "home away from home" with a combat tour behind me.

Checking in at base headquarters I received orders assigning me to the 6161st Communications Squadron with additional duty as the base A&R (athletics and recreation) officer. The latter duty placed me in charge of the base gymnasium with all of its athletic teams and activities. That suited me just fine as I enjoyed sports both as a participant and as a spectator.

At the billeting office I got my quarters assignment to a three-bedroom cottage shared with two other officers who were married and awaiting the resumption of family travel from the States so that their families could join them. One was my CO in the Comm Squadron, Captain Jerry Moore. The other, Major Ted Miller, was a personnel officer on the base commander's staff. Both were very cordial, and I felt that Yokota was going to live up to its "Friendliest Air Base" billing.

It probably was one of the busiest air bases anywhere with the 20th Heavy Bombardment Group of Strategic Air Command deployed there. My first morning in my room at the cottage was startling for me. I had become accustomed to the morning sounds of aircraft being preflighted on other bases in the past. But they were trainers and fighters. These were heavy bombers with the heavy voices of four engines on each plane roaring out its greeting to the dawn. They were B-29s, the pride of General Curtis Le May, that daily flew raids deep into North Korea to destroy strategic targets.

My duties at the Comm Squadron were easy to handle because a crew of highly qualified technicians, GI noncoms and Japanese nationals, knew their business and needed only support from the squadron officers in obtaining whatever supplies and equipment the unit's mission required. Highly motivated, they operated efficiently with minimum direction. I was pleased because, with no problems in my primary duty, I was able to focus on the A&R programs at the gymnasium.

I was also able to enjoy a pleasant social life on the weekends. At Yokota I found a number of former "Camelot" folks. The home of Captain Harold "Tank" Hillery and his wife, Virginia, was a weekend mecca for a number of former Lockbourneites who were now stationed at Yokota: my doctor friend from junior high school and growing up on Sugar Hill, now a lieutenant colonel, Bryce Anthony; Lieutenant Leroy "Tweedy" Roberts and his wife, Ann; Major Joe "Jodie" Elsberry; Lieutenant Robert King. Add to the Yokotans the many who were stationed at nearby bases—Johnson Field, Tachikawa, Ashiya—or at faraway bases—Misawa, Itazuke, the K-fields of Korea—and the weekend soiree at the "Hillery House" was the venue to see and be seen by old friends from Camelot: guys like Johnny Briggs; Virgil Daniels, brother of renowned entertainer, Billy Daniels, and his wife, Inez; Chappie James, later to become the first African American four-star general; Sam Lynn, my buddy from Comm school at Scott Field, and his wife, Polly; Lieutenant Colonels Bill Campbell, former CO of the 332nd at Lockbourne, and Hubert L. "Hooks" Jones, both assigned to FEAF headquarters in the Meiji Building, near General MacArthur's headquarters in Tokyo.

Fun time at the "Hillery House" was in forming teams to play charades, trying to stump each other with words and phrases that defied interpretation by mimicry. The Hillery youngsters, Skipper and Sharon, five and three years old, respectively, were pretty clever at charades. And so were the adults, especially the women: some wives of Tank's squadron mates, some U.S. Civil Service employees on overseas assignments, some Red Cross ladies—all delighted in beating the guys in games. Esther Case from Lambertville, New

Jersey, used to convulse the gang with anecdotes about her small nephews, Denny and Kenny; Elvira Turner and Wilma Bradley added their graciousness and quiet good humor to the company, helping to keep spirits up when the news from the front across the strait got scary as the North Korean juggernaut rolled south.

At charades, only once was everyone totally stumped: by the phrase "Punting on the Thames" posed by Chappie, who roared with delight when no one on the opposing team was able to act out the phrase. Pokeno, tonk, dirty hearts, canasta—all provided relaxation, and diversion, but marathon monopoly matches were the favorite pastime.

On the surface, such activities might have seemed frivolous, but they served a vital purpose. They helped relieve tension at Yokota—tension that, although sub rosa, was almost palpable because of the news that filtered back from the war front about atrocities done by the North Koreans; news now and then about one of the guys in an outfit who had "bought the farm." When Tank Hillery was missing for several days while he was evading the enemy after being overrun, along with General Dean, at Taejon, it was nail-biting time for all who knew him and Ginny and the kids. And it was time for a rip-roaring celebration when he showed up at home and told us about his adventure.

With Tokyo only thirty miles from Yokota, it was easy to get into that huge, bustling capital city to see the sights and shop for bargains at big department stores like Takashimiya, or the PX on the Ginza, or haggle for souvenirs in quaint shops off the beaten path. The Ginza was a broad street with lots of traffic, vehicular and pedestrian, at all times of day. In more ways than one it was like New York's Times Square where, it has been said, if one stood in one spot for a few minutes one would be sure to see a familiar face in the crowds passing by.

One Sunday I saw "Peepsight" Smith, an old buddy from the 99th during World War II. I hadn't seen Peepsight in five years—the last time was when I escaped from "exile" in Walterboro, South Carolina. Now here we were, halfway around the world fighting another war after having survived the big one. He told me he had just arrived recently in Japan and was on his way to Korea for a combat tour in P-51s. Before year's end I got the sad news that on a strafing mission he had been brought down by antiaircraft fire and was killed in action.

In spite of the war raging in Korea, life at Yokota was pleasant and "peaceful." I looked forward to having Pete and Thumper join me as soon as dependent travel from the States was resumed. (It had been halted with the outbreak of the war.) The situation in Japan seemed secure enough to the powers that be during spring 1951 and the ban on dependent travel was lifted. By then I was fairly high up on the priority list for family quarters, so I wrote Pete to begin making plans to join me at Yokota. Her reply was that our families were worried about the war situation and were imploring me to return stateside. Letters from other kinfolk had similar comments, and I decided to do so as soon as possible.

With the rotation point system in effect at the time, I could accrue only one point per month while stationed in the rear area at Yokota. In the combat zone, rotation points accrued at the rate of one and a half per month. So I decided to volunteer to return to Korea as a communications officer, my other critical AFSC.

In April 1951 I joined the 934th Signal Battalion in Taegu. Its personnel were air force, its organizational structure was army, its mission was to work in conjunction with army communications units in Korea to ensure continuous, uninterrupted radio and landline links between Eighth Army and Fifth Air Force headquarters and units in the field. My specific assignment was as a duty officer in the teletype communications center. My boss, Major Julian I. Salzstein, an old hand at multiple communications systems, was in charge of a comm center with more than fifty TTY circuits linking numerous units and headquarters, as well as radio networks handling voice and Morse code, plus a cryptographic facility.

After a few days spent learning the ropes, I eased into the routine of the TTY center, which was a "pressure cooker" with constant heavy volume of message traffic, especially around midnight when lengthy "frag" orders were being transmitted down the line to fighter units, bomber units, rescue units. That was when the duty officer was busiest coordinating the activities of the TTY, radio, and crypto sections. It was interesting, vital, never-a-dull-moment work. The only aspect that I did not enjoy was the shift schedule that rotated among the four duty officers: 0800–1600 was the best shift, of course; 1600–2400 was tolerable; midnight–0800 was the bane of my life with the 934th because I could not sleep in the daytime.

That situation was short-lived, however, because the 934th received orders to move from Taegu to Seoul. In the capital city of the Republic of Korea we were billeted in buildings on the campus of Seoul University. The medieval architecture of the sturdy, stone buildings sitting atop a hill on the outskirts of the city earned them the nickname of "the Castle." A shower room on the ground floor of the officers building provided the luxury of hot and cold running showers. We were assigned two to a room on the first and second floors. An auditorium on the second floor served as our movie theater, and the third floor housed the officers club.

Supply officer for the 934th was a Tuskegee Airman I was proud to know, Lieutenant Fred Samuels. "Sam," as he was nicknamed, was one of the "Famous 101" officers who had been placed in arrest in quarters at Freeman Field, Indiana, in 1944 for the "crime" of entering the segregated White officers club. I felt a special kinship with Sam because of my expulsion from Lufberry Hall at Selfridge Field, Michigan, just weeks before the Freeman Field incident. We provided mutual moral support whenever Jim Crow tried to raise its ugly head in the 934th.

A few weeks after moving into "the Castle," scuttlebutt had it that the 934th was being deactivated and reorganized with an air force TO&E (table of organization and equipment) and redesignated the Fifth Communications Group. No official announcement was made to the personnel in any unit meetings or by means of notices on bulletin boards. But the rumors persisted.

One day while visiting the orderly room to check my mail I saw an organization chart on the adjutant's desk. It was titled "Fifth Communications Group Organization Chart." So the rumor was true! Studying the boxes drawn on the chart, I discovered some disturbing features. There were some new slots for majors that showed the names of two captains junior to me who had joined the 934th after I had!

I was not about to take that discrimination lying down. So, I borrowed the chart from the adjutant, took it to my room, laid it flat on the floor, stood on a chair, and took a picture of it. Next, after dinner that evening in the officers mess followed by the usual sessions of "liar's dice" and "horses" on the bar at the club, some of the officers were "oiled," especially the CO, Colonel John M. Maersch. I was cold sober because I was about to do battle for my career. As he was about to enter his room to retire, I greeted him with: "Good evening, Colonel. May I have a word with you for a moment?"

"Sure, Chuck, come on in," he said, ushering me into his room. "What's on your mind?"

"Well, Colonel, today I learned that the rumors about the reorganization of the 934th are true."

"That's right, Chuck. We will become the Fifth Communications Group supporting Fifth Air Force headquarters. And we'll have the TO&E of an air force unit. That's a real plus, don't you think?"

"I suppose so, Sir, but I see a negative in the TO&E."

"What's that?"

"Well, as you know, Colonel, as of this moment I am your senior-ranking captain, and yet on the new organization chart that I saw today the two new major slots are to be filled by captains who are junior to me. I can't figure out why, for the life of me, because I know I'm eligible for a combat spot promotion."

Flustered, the Old Man sputtered: "Well, uh, Captain, uh, we'll have to look into that in the morning. Not now. Anything else?"

"No, Sir. That's what's on my mind right now and I'll appreciate your looking into it. Thank you, Sir."

I didn't leave it at that because I knew from past experience that sometimes promises made were not kept. I figured that a gentle, subtle nudge might help my cause. So I wrote a letter, a very innocuous letter, to a friend in the Pentagon and urged him to reply by return mail using an official Department of the Air Force envelope. Just over a week after I mailed my letter, his came bouncing into our mail room. The adjutant handed it to me personally. I smiled inwardly as I took it, knowing full well that the CO would be informed that Captain Dryden had received a communiqué from someone in the Pentagon shortly after our conversation.

When the organization chart of the Fifth Communications Group was posted on the bulletin board, it showed Major Charles W. Dryden in charge of training. Official orders for my spot promotion to major were published by Headquarters, Fifth Air Force in September. At the rate I was accruing rotation points, I expected to return to the States in February 1952 so I would be able to wear the gold leaves on my shoulder for at least four months before reverting to the rank of captain upon leaving the Far East. Even though it was only a temporary promotion, I felt especially exhilarated about it because I had been able to win a battle in the continuing war against Jim Crow!

As training officer I had to develop materials for training some of our NCOs and enlisted men in their skill areas as applicable under combat conditions. I was fortunate to have available the input and expertise of senior, experienced NCOs who helped me put together standard materials in short order. Then the CO gave me the task of creating an I & E (information and education) program and sent me off to Tokyo to attend an I & E conference at FEAF headquarters.

There I ran into one of the old crowd, Major John Suggs, who told me that he was assigned to Johnson Air Base, about ten miles from Yokota, as an education officer. During the conference I learned that the youngest of the U.S. armed forces, the air force, had the lowest percentage of officers with college degrees. The top-ranking "blue suiters" were determined to raise USAF's status to surpass the army and the navy and were putting much emphasis and pressure on the subject by urging all air force officers lacking a college degree to earn one as soon as possible.

Returning to "the Castle" at Seoul with all the literature acquired at the conference, I was able to convince Colonel Maersch, the CO, that we had to set up an effective I & E program at once. He agreed and directed that a Quonset hut be earmarked for it. An NCO, Airman First Class Green, who described himself as a "hillbilly from Tennessee" and who had worked closely with me on the training materials, helped me set up the Quonset hut as a sort of library stocked with a variety of reading and study materials as an encouragement for all the unit's personnel to further their education. I made sure that Airman Green knew all the procedures, reports, and other requirements for conducting an I & E program in compliance with directives from higher headquarters. In addition to wanting to help him become fully qualified in his AFSC, I had a selfish motive that grew out of the situation involving the replacement of personnel in Korea at that time.

Oftentimes replacements were slow in coming out of the pipeline from the States, causing some veterans who had the required number of rotation points to be held in place "until your replacement arrives from the States." I did not want that to happen to me.

In the week before Christmas I invited the CO to attend a briefing by Airman Green about the I & E program and a walk-through of the I & E center. Colonel Maersch was so impressed by Green's presentation that he teased me with: "I don't see why we need a major to do this job. Looks like a noncom can handle it." Turning serious, he continued: "Your replacement is due in here about mid-February, so I'll let you leave on time when your eighteen months are up at the end of January. How's that sound, Dryden?"

"Just fine, Colonel. I'm going to Tachikawa on Christmas Eve on a three-day R & R, as you have already approved, Sir, to spend Christmas with friends. When I return I will start winding down my affairs here."

"Fair enough, Major."

So, that was that. My plan to leave Korea on time was going to work. I couldn't have asked for a better Christmas present. On the morning before Christmas I got a ride to Kimpo airport, where I got on the manifest of a C-46 headed for Tachikawa. On the way out to the airplane I saw one of the old gang from Camelot as he was walking into the terminal with some other pilots. Glad to see him, I broke out into a broad grin and locked on his eyes with mine as I greeted him with: "Hey, Hoss! How're ya doin'?"

His steely blue eyes looked right through me, past me, as he and his buddies passed by. His fair complexion, ruddy from the cold, December wind blanched for a fleeting moment. I thought to myself: "You know me. And I know you. And I know that you know that I know who you are. I am sorry you have crossed over to pass as White and deny all your old friends. How sad it is that *you* don't know who you are!"

Spending Christmas with my old friends, Captain Sam Lynn, his wife Polly, and their three-year-old daughter Storme, in their quarters at Tachi was pretty close to spending it with my own family. While on R & R I also got to visit with the Hillerys and a host of other friends at Christmas parties, all of which made my last few weeks in the Far East memorable.

Returning to "the Castle" after R & R, I greeted the new year, 1952, with the guys of the Fifth Comm Group. We had a rip-snorting party in the officers club up on the third floor, a fitting way to begin the year in which my second war would end—with joy and laughter.

In the first week of February my PCS orders were issued, transferring me to Mitchel Field, New York, to report to duty about mid-March after a thirty-day leave. My long journey home began on February 9 when I signed out from the Fifth Comm Group and was driven to Kimpo by Staff Sergeant Green. He had been promoted and, as we parted company, he thanked me for having had confidence in him. I countered with thanks for his having been such a top-flight noncommissioned officer. And a friend.

My chariot to Tachikawa was a C-47. The flight was long and would have been boring except that I was going home. Once on the ground at Tachi I reported to the POE (port of embarkation) office and was given the option of crossing the Pacific by air or by sea. By air would take about a full day with a refueling stop at Hawaii. The sea voyage required thirteen to fifteen days and I would have to pay for my meals.

I opted for airlift mainly because I could not afford the cost of meals for two weeks on a ship—I had spent almost all my spare cash on souvenirs for the folks at home: Noritake china, service for eight, was such a bargain at the PX that I shipped sets home to Pete and to my sister Pauline; handwrought silver jewelry and ornaments were so reasonable in Japanese shops that I spent a prince's ransom on gifts bought mainly from a shop in Tokyo, the Oriental Bazaar, owned by a middle-aged couple with whom I became quite friendly, charmed by their graciousness and courtly manners.

Having elected to go by air I was put on a waiting list of active duty troops and dependents heading to the States. It was a long list that took three days of two or three flights a day to get to me. During the wait I was billeted in a transient officers quarters at Tachikawa. While there I saw an old friend from way back at Tuskegee Army Air Field, one of the first two men there promoted to the rank of master sergeant—Jim Reed. He told me that he was maintenance chief with an outfit in Korea and was only visiting Tachikawa for a few days on TDY.

Another morning, as I woke up and got ready to roll out of my sack in the lower bunk, I saw a brown arm hanging down over the side of the top bunk. The guy was still asleep with his face to the wall and I couldn't see if it was someone I knew. "Oh well," I thought, "I'll find out who he is after I've been to breakfast and checked the passenger manifest over at operations. Surely he'll be up by then."

Indeed he was up and getting dressed as I returned to the room.

"George Haley, you old rascal!" I blurted out. "When did you get in, Hoss?"

"Charlie Dryden!" George exclaimed. "I got in after midnight and didn't want to disturb you with the light as I didn't know who you were. But tell me, what are you doing here?"

"Man, I'm goin' home. I've had two tours in Korea, one as a Mosquito pilot, the second as a comm officer, so I'm ready to rotate. What's your story, George?"

"Well, Charlie, I'm with the Fourth Fighter Group in Korea. I'm the group intelligence officer, and I've been in the Far East since November '51. I'm here at Tachi on TDY for just a couple of days."

We spent a short while more catching up on where we had been since integration and whom we had seen lately. All the while I was packing my gear, getting ready to check out of the TOQ, because I had gone to base operations and had seen MY NAME ON THE PASSENGER MANIFEST! My C-54 flight to Hawaii was posted for an 1100 takeoff.

So. With a firm handshake to an old friend, I bade George and the Land of the Rising Sun:

Sayonara!

14 Sayonara!

» February 1952–September 1957

First stop on the way home: beautiful Hawaii! Some tourists plan for years to get there and spend days or weeks or maybe a lifetime in "paradise." I was impressed with the mild temperature when we arrived; a brief, pleasant shower cooled things off and heightened the fragrance of the gorgeous flowers that abounded everywhere. But I was not impressed enough to want to interrupt my eastward flight. At the passenger terminal at Haneda airport, near Tokyo, I had been assured by the dispatcher that I was booked straight through to Travis AFB, near Sacramento, California, and that I didn't have to worry about being "bumped" along the way. So when I checked at the dispatcher's desk at Hickam Field about the takeoff time for the final leg to Travis, and learned that my name had been scrubbed from the manifest, I was shocked. And upset. And let him know it.

"Sergeant!" I fumed. "What in hell's going on? How come I'm not on the manifest for the flight that just came in from Tokyo? Have you checked my priority?"

"Yes, Major." (I was still wearing the gold leaves of my spot promotion, reluctant to give them up until I set foot in the USA. And besides, the effective date of rescission of the spot promotion was February 15, 1952.)

"But I have orders to remove you from the manifest."

"Sez who?" I growled.

"I got the word from the ATC office in the terminal, Sir, and I have arranged for your gear to be offloaded. It will be over in the baggage room. Maybe you can find out what's going on over in the ATC office. It's right next to the snack bar near the main entrance. Sorry 'bout that, Sir. Good luck!"

"Thanks, Sarge, for the tip." Although he was not the culprit, I was still ticked off. Stomping through the terminal with a full head of steam as I weaved in and around the clusters of passengers, some GIs, some dependents, some coming east, some going west, I arrived at the ATC office ready to lock horns with whatever knucklehead had messed up my flight. The office had large windows shuttered with venetian blinds that were partially open and I saw a familiar face seated at a desk inside. "Great!" I thought. "At least I'll have a friend in court when I make my plea to be put back on the manifest in time for takeoff in about an hour."

As I entered the office, Captain Paul Adams, an old buddy from Lockbourne AFB, rose to greet me.

"Hi, Charlie, uh, Major! Good to see you."

"Good to see you too, Paul, but I won't have much time because I'm here to get back on the flight to the States that just came in from Tokyo."

"Yeah, Hoss, I know. I saw your name on the incoming manifest and had you bumped so you could spend a few days here and some of the other guys here in Hawaii could get to see you."

"You WHAT?" I roared. "You mean to tell me YOU had me bumped? Here I am on my way home to my family and you had me bumped?"

Paul looked hurt. "Well, yeah, man. After all, it's been almost three years since we all left Lockbourne and I try to see all the guys who come through here, going either way. For old times' sake."

"Look, Paul, I appreciate your sentiments and I really am glad to see you. But I have to be honest with you: I'd really prefer to see my wife and son. So, since you claim you can have anyone bumped, let's see if you can get me back on that flight."

"If you insist, I can get you out tomorrow on the first thing smoking, but your flight is about to taxi and it's too late. So since you're going to be here, RON, why not relax and enjoy Hawaii? I'll show you around, if you'd like."

"Thanks for the offer, Paul, but I'm beat from that long haul from Japan, so I think I'd just as soon check into the TOQ and maybe see the movie at the base theater, then hit the sack early."

"OK, Charlie. I'll make sure you're manifested out tomorrow, first thing. And I'm sorry you won't stay awhile on my tropical isle."

Paul was as good as his word. His assignment at Hickam had him in a position to shuffle passengers, and he got me out the next morning at dawn's early light. Several hours, and miles of Pacific Ocean, later my chariot swung low and touched down at Travis AFB.

"Hallelujah!" I exulted. "I've done it again. Another war behind me, with nary a scratch. Thank you, Jesus!"

Now to find a telephone to tell Pete I was back in the States, dead broke from buying last-minute souvenirs, and to wire me some money to continue homeward bound on a commercial flight. The outbound flight schedule board at Travis AFB operations was showing no flights heading east all the way to the coast and I didn't want to hedgehop all the way across the country, perhaps taking days to get home. So I elected to fly commercial, leaving as soon as possible. Pete's response came within a couple of hours with enough bucks for airfare, plus.

Next, a bus ride to the airport at San Francisco and a nonstop flight to La Guardia airport in New York, and I was home again, the same day—the date on which I had been striving so hard to arrive: February 14, Valentine's Day. A fitting day for a reunion. Pete was at the gate in the terminal as I strode up the passenger ramp and into her arms. She had left Thumper at home, with Mother Pearl, so we could have the hour or so alone together during the drive across the George Washington Bridge to catch up on the latest news about her side of the family and mine. And to surprise Thumper when he came home from nursery school and found me at home.

Homecoming from my second war was joyful for me and a relief for my kinfolk as the Korean "hostilities" had long since escalated into a full-blown war with the entrance of the People's Republic of China into the conflict in November 1950. So, as Pete had written me when I suggested that she and Thumper join me at Yokota after I had completed my combat tour with the Mosquitoes, everyone preferred that I return to the States. And everyone affirmed that opinion with phone calls, visits, invitations to visit, and welcome home parties.

With thirty days' leave of absence I had plenty time to bask in the warmth of "welcome home." But I was more than ready to report to duty at my new assignment at Mitchel Field when the leave ended. The main reason was that I had become accustomed to being addressed as "Major" while holding that spot-promotion rank in Japan and was a bit miffed when I had to revert to captain upon leaving FEAF. I had good reason to believe that the USAF promotion board would be elevating a number of captains by midsummer, and I was anxious to get to work in my new job and earn the kind of ER (effectiveness report) that would warrant promotion to major. Having held the rank, even though for only a few months, with a spot promotion, I felt that I would have a leg up on other captains who had never held the rank. As it turned out I was right.

My first assignment at Mitchel Field was to the 34th Communications Squadron attached to First Air Force. The CO, Captain Antonio Federico, was a veteran "communicator" who knew the business and was easy to get along with, easing me into the routines of his outfit. However, I remained in his command for little more than a month before moving laterally to another career field and upward to a higher command level. This move took four months to complete and began one evening at dinner at the officers mess.

While dining with a couple of newfound friends one evening in early May, another Black officer, Major Ted Draughn, joined us and informed us that he had learned of a slot for attendance at the Associate Intelligence Course at the Air University at Maxwell AFB near Montgomery, Alabama. "Anyone interested?" he asked.

Without hesitating one second I declared, "I am!"

My reasoning was that successful completion of any Air University course was a step up the ladder, careerwise. Moreover, by adding another AFSC to my 201 file I would increase my value to the air force, to say nothing about the increased scope of knowledge in my own noggin.

"Well, OK, Dryden," Major Draughn said. "I'll put your name in for the slot tomorrow. CONAC [Continental Air Command] will cut orders for you to attend the class beginning around the end of April. It's about a sixteen-week course and you will be reassigned back here at Mitchel when you finish, but you will be at CONAC headquarters because that's where there's a vacancy for an S-2 officer. Understand?"

"Yes, Sir. Sounds good to me."

Within the week I had my orders and after another week I was headed south to Maxwell AFB driving our Hudson Hornet. Although the armed forces had been desegregated by President Truman's order, civilians were not yet ready to remove restrictions on hotel/motel/restaurant/rest room/recreation facilities for use by "Colored" or "Negro" or, as many Whites mispronounced, "Nigra" patrons. So, in preparation for such a cross-country motor trip, one would be wise to obtain a copy of "the Green Book": This was the Black traveler's guidebook that listed the rooming houses, boardinghouses, and private homes in various cities where one could find a place to stay that was run by Blacks.

Unfortunately I was unable to find a copy of a Green Book and had to rely on luck in finding a place to stay in some town when I had driven as far as I could before fatigue caught up with me. My "survival kit" included a thermos of hot coffee, several sandwiches, and some candy bars so that I would not have to risk being threatened with loss of limb, or life, in some backwoods place where the local slogan might be "The South shall rise again" and where the Stars and Bars replaced Old Glory.

After several hours on the road, driving in bright, hot sunshine, I decided against trying to drive straight through to Montgomery, nonstop, for fear of falling asleep at the wheel. By then I was somewhere in South Carolina, which in my mind was second only to Mississippi in southern inhospitality to Blacks. Stopping for gas at a filling station in a fairly large town, I asked a Black porter at the station if he knew of any place where I might find a room to rest until morning. Following his directions I found a little old widow lady whose warm greeting reminded me of the "Grandma" who had been so kind to me on my first trip into the South on my way to Tuskegee to begin flight training.

This lady showed me into her guest room, tiny and overcrowded with a large four-poster bed that had an overstuffed mattress covered with a thick quilt. It was much too much cover for a hot, humid night but I could have cared less—I could sleep uncovered. But I couldn't sleep very well on the mattress that had lumps on top of lumps and felt like one large washboard. However, I managed to make it through the night sleeping fitfully and, at least, was not as tired when I hit the road again in the morning as I had been when I had hit the sack the night before.

Sometime that afternoon I drove through the gate at Maxwell and reported to Air University headquarters to sign in and receive my orders assigning me to my particular class and my room in the student officers quarters. I had arrived on a Saturday afternoon and there was not much activity going on the base. So, after unloading my car and stowing my gear in my room, I showered, donned some casual clothes, and meandered over to the officers club. The club swimming pool was fairly well crowded with people, mostly kids, having a splashing good time swimming and diving off the low and high boards while adults, mostly moms, lounged on chaises around poolside, soaking up the sun and, I supposed, gossiping.

As I walked onto the grassy lounging area I saw, without looking directly at anyone in particular, that heads turned in my direction and eyes stared. Facial expressions seemed to challenge: "Surely, you don't plan to use the pool!"

Because I was dressed in casual street clothes, my unspoken response to the unspoken challenge was: "No, not at the moment. But after dinner, when it's cooler, I'll be back to join you in the pool."

And so I did return. And swan-dived into the cool water. And swam a couple laps. And was amazed how quickly I became sole occupant!

The next day, Sunday, I sallied into Montgomery to rekindle an old friendship. Richard H. "Rich" Harris was a Tuskegee Airman who had graduated in cadet class 43-F. One of his classmates was a cousin of mine, Lieutenant Walter Palmer, who had flown 158 missions with the Red Tails in Europe as a member of the 100th Fighter Squadron. Harris had left the service shortly after V-E Day, got his degree in pharmacy at Xavier University, and was operating Dean's Drugstore in Montgomery, as his father had done before him. Richard and his wife, Vera, were special people to Pete and me because during our "exile" in Walterboro the four of us often frolicked on the sands of the "Colored" section at Myrtle Beach. And later, in Louisville, Kentucky, while we were stationed at Godman Field, Richard and Vera married with Pete and me standing in as matron of honor and best man. They were one of the friendliest couples we knew and we thoroughly enjoyed being in their company. I knew that my stint at the Air University was going to be memorable for the many times they would say, "Come on by the house."

"Rich" Harris was as jovial as I remembered him. He was ever the perfectionist, a trait that served him well when he was personal equipment officer at Godman Field because all the pilots felt confident that their oxygen masks, parachutes, "Mae West" life jackets, life raft dinghies, and so on were always in good working order. And those traits of his assured the prosperity of Dean's Drugstore. Most everyone in the Black community in Montgomery knew and loved "Doc" Harris and patronized Dean's. For my part, I was glad to have some good friends in town whom I could visit while in school.

Classes began Monday morning with get-acquainted-with-your-classmates-and-your-instructors sessions. With more than 100 student intelligence officers going through the course, we were divided into eight-man cubicles for class sessions. By various methods of instruction—lectures, seminars, research projects, briefings by "cloak and dagger" veterans—we learned the basic elements of intelligence: collection, collation, analysis, production, dissemination. Each element was a specialized discipline in itself, and in our sixteen weeks at Air University we barely scratched the surface even though we spent a lot time in the excellent library and burned a lot midnight oil studying. It was hard work and I had to learn it by the sweat of my brow—literally, because Alabama in the summer is HOT!

Weekends, after the homework assignment was completed, at least gave me a chance to relax and cool off in the pool at the officers club. And I was delighted at the opportunity to host some friends from town who had never been inside the club—especially one couple whose eight-year-old daughter, Toni, was shy about jumping into the pool while other kids, all White, were in it. It saddened me to see how timid she was and how programmed to kowtow. So I took her, piggyback, into the pool and reassured her, "Toni, Honey, you are as good as any other children and you can have a good time in the pool like anyone else." It wasn't long before some of the other kids began playing with her and her shyness vanished. I was glad that President Truman's executive order desegregating the armed forces had made it possible.

In the city itself, of course, the "Cradle of the Confederacy" was far from ready to desegregate anything.

Early on in my TDY at Maxwell, May 8 to be exact, my promotion to major came through. This time it was not a spot promotion—it was the real thing. I was delighted to pin on the gold leaves again and happy to note that the names of many of the old gang from Lockbourne were also on the promotion list.

After graduation from the course in late August, I returned to Mitchel Field with a new rank, a new AFSC, and a new assignment. That meant a new boss in a new office. Lieutenant Colonel Arthur Clark, my new boss, was director of intelligence for Headquarters, Continental Air Command (CONAC).

The commanding general of CONAC was Lieutenant General Leon Johnson, who had led B-24 bombing raids on the Ploesti oil fields of Rumania during World War II. As one of the major commands of the U.S. Air Force, CONAC's role was to train air force reservists, often referred to as "weekend warriors," in the numerous skill areas needed by USAF in peacetime as well as during wartime mobilization.

Colonel Clark's mission was to develop and maintain the skills of reservist intelligence officers with training materials and activities to be used and conducted by CONAC units throughout the

United States. The primary vehicle used to fulfill that mission was a monthly magazine, the *AITB*, the *Air Intelligence Training Bulletin*. An unclassified publication designed to keep intelligence reservists up to date on developments in their military profession, the *AITB* was an oxymoron to a large extent: Most intelligence information was so sensitive that it had to be given a security classification, from the low status of RESTRICTED up through TOP SECRET to EYES ONLY and, as we used to joke in intelligence school, information so sensitive that it was classified BBR, that is, BURN BEFORE READING. The problem with the *AITB* was that it was created to be published monthly, to contain useful intelligence information, and yet to be disseminated through the mail, which meant that it had to be UNCLASSIFIED. The editor of the *AITB* was faced with the challenge of producing every month a magazine with articles of keen interest to intelligence reservists, articles sent to them through the mail.

"Major Dryden, I need an editor for the *AITB*," Colonel Clark said, "and you're it."

I had first met my new boss in his office on the third floor of the Continental Air Command headquarters building located across the street from base operations on the flight line at Mitchel AFB. With his easygoing manner, I took a liking to him straight off. He put me at ease, somehow sensing that I was awed by being assigned to a major command headquarters with a three-star general's office on the second floor, a couple of major generals elsewhere on that floor, a brigadier as deputy for operations in an office down the hall from the commanding general, and a flock of bird colonels all around the building. After hearing my answers to his questions about my previous assignments and reviewing my records from the intelligence school, Colonel Clark gave me the first of many gems of advice offered during the four years of our association: He said, "Major Dryden, this is your first staff position and it is at a pretty high level up the ladder, but just remember one thing about all these people wearing all this rank—they put their pants on one leg at a time, just like you!"

I knew that this was a boss for whom I was going to enjoy working.

So when he named me editor of the *AITB*, I vowed privately to do my best to meet the challenge of publishing an unclassified intelligence periodical. *AITB* had been in existence for more than ten years before I came to the scene, and numerous back issues gave me insights into certain kinds of articles that were appropriate and acceptable. More important, Colonel Clark had a crew in his office who had been putting the "guts" of *AITB* together for years, so I did not have to start from scratch.

Colonel Clark's staff numbered seventeen, including five officers, four NCOs, and eight civilians. As his highest ranking officer, I acted as his staff chief with responsibility to process all correspondence and reports received or generated in the directorate—all of which forced me to learn quickly how to deal with bureaucratic red tape and how to keep things moving smoothly. My first on-the-job training project was to compose a reply to a letter that had been addressed to the commanding general and referred by his chief of staff to the director of intelligence. My predecessor had not been able to compose a reply that satisfied the chief of staff and the letter had been bounced back to Colonel Clark for action. He bucked it to me to see what I would do with it.

I produced a first draft containing what I regarded, pridefully, as deathless prose and clever composition, and I submitted it to my boss. He OK'd it and forwarded it to the chief of staff, downstairs on the second floor of the CONAC headquarters building, and we figured that it was a completed project as I congratulated myself on having passed my first hurdle as a staff officer. It wasn't, and I hadn't. It was bounced back up to the third floor with a sharp comment criticizing its lack of clarity and completeness. So my boss said, "Try again, Major."

I did. Five more times, each time submitting a revised version that I thought would be approved by the chief of staff. By the sixth rejection I was at my wit's end and felt that my career as a staff officer was going to end abruptly. Fortunately I had kept a copy of each version and, in desperation and despair, I decided to submit, as my seventh attempt, the very first version. This time, to my utter amazement, it was approved and our file copy of the indorsement (i.e., reply) that was finally sent to the original writer was sent upstairs to us with a cryptic note proclaiming, "Major Dryden: Why didn't you say that in the first place?"

"*Merde!*" I swore.

Another project mystified me even more. This time it was a letter from an army general complaining about our having reprinted in the *AITB* an article that had first appeared in an army publication. The general had fussed about our failure to go through proper channels to obtain permission to reprint it, and his letter had been bucked upstairs to our office for reply. When showing it to Colonel Clark to prepare a draft reply, I expected him to tell me to get on it right away. Instead, after reading it he opened the large center drawer of his desk, tossed the letter into the drawer on top of a small pile of other papers already in there, and said, "Don't worry about it, Major."

Flabbergasted, I stuttered, "But, Colonel, we'll get some flak about it if we don't RBI [reply by indorsement] within a week."

"Don't worry about it, Major," he repeated. "Let's just let it simmer on the back burner for a few days before doing anything with it. The problem might just go away."

And, somehow, it did. I never found out why, but Colonel Clark taught me that unless a project demands immediate action, put it on a back burner and just think about it for awhile—in the shower, while driving, wherever. That delay gives you a chance to mull over possible approaches, to choose the best one, and take action by the deadline. Better still, by delaying the start of action you just might be told by your boss: "You know that project that everyone was hot to trot on? Well, just forget it; it's been scrubbed." The trick for the successful staff officer was to know which projects demanded immediate attention and which could be left on the back burner to simmer and, perhaps, disappear!

My training as a staff officer was going well under Colonel Clark's tutelage, but I had a personal need that demanded attention. I needed to complete my college education and earn a degree. In my last assignment in Korea, as an information and education officer, I had become convinced that a college degree was going to be mandatory for a career in the air force of the future. Considering the fact that there were a number of colleges in the New York area,

I had no excuse not to earn a degree. One, Hofstra College, was just across a highway from Mitchel Field and offered night classes that fit my working schedule.

Another factor that prompted me to resume my college education, which had been interrupted by World War II, was the fact that I was commuting to my home only on weekends. Nutley, New Jersey, was a two-hour drive from Mitchel. The daily four-hour round trip through New York City traffic, as well as freeways in Long Island and New Jersey, was more driving than I could cope with.

I was living in the BOQ rather than in family quarters on the base because Pete had secured a position with a bioanalytical laboratory, Riverton Laboratories, in Newark, New Jersey, while I was in the Far East, and she wanted to grow with the fledgling company, owned and operated by Blacks. It seemed more feasible for us to maintain our home where she had a short commute, so we bought a home in East Orange, adjacent to Newark. I agreed with the arrangement and proceeded to enroll at Hofstra to pursue a bachelor of arts degree in political science. Encouraged by my boss, Colonel Clark, I pitched into the rigor of night classes with determination.

By transfer of some of my credits from classes taken at City College fifteen years earlier, I was able to arrange a program of twenty-one courses that would earn my degree. Beginning in the fall semester of 1952, I enrolled in two courses each semester and four each summer until the fall semester of 1954. Colonel Clark and the top brass of CONAC headquarters really supported my efforts by allowing me to take my thirty days of annual leave as sixty half days of leave. Thus I was able to take two courses in each of the two sessions of summer school at Hofstra College, during the summers of 1953 and 1954. By the fall semester of 1954 I was within five courses of my degree.

By applying for and being approved for the air force's "Operation Bootstrap," I was able to complete those five courses under the auspices of the so-called final semester TDY program. Under "Bootstrap," for six months I had no military duties except to fly four hours every month for my flying pay. By January I had completed my twenty-one-course program with nineteen A's and two B's, and

I received my diploma in June with the class of Hofstra-'55, on the Dean's List—and at the advanced age of almost 35. My autograph on my graduation picture that I gave my parents reads: "At last!"

During the three years of my going to night school and summer school, many persons in the CONAC headquarters building and all of our staff in the directorate of intelligence urged me to stick with it. Some others were taking night classes, too, and there existed an attitude that was strongly supportive of efforts to further one's education. One ambitious young airman first class, Fisher, who was a clerk in the directorate, also was attending night school, and we used to discuss the various air force education programs. One that was especially interesting was the AFIT (Air Force Institute of Technology) program. Under AFIT a lucky applicant would be placed on TDY at one of a number of participating universities, with no military duties for a whole year, to pursue a graduate degree.

When I completed my B.A. studies under "Operation Bootstrap," I returned to full duty at the directorate and found that Fisher had been transferred to the Pentagon. I learned that he had been "moonlighting" at the officers club as a waiter and that his courteous service had so impressed a party of visiting officials from the Pentagon that he had been offered a job as a waiter in the VIP dining room at the "head shed" in Washington. It was an offer he couldn't refuse.

Several weeks later, after my return to full duty, I had to visit the directorate of intelligence in the Pentagon. While waiting in an outer office for a conference, I saw Staff Sergeant Fisher enter with an armload of documents. He had been promoted and was now a messenger. As we exchanged comments about how our plans for higher education were working out, he congratulated me on my graduation from Hofstra and asked, "Major Dryden, have you applied for AFIT?"

"No, Sergeant Fisher, I haven't. I figure that because I just had six months TDY under 'Bootstrap,' there's no way I would be approved for a year's TDY under AFIT so soon."

"Well, Major," Fisher said, "all you have to do is submit the application and I'll arrange for it to be approved."

"YOU will have it approved?" I asked in disbelief.

"No, not I, but I can arrange for it to be placed on the top of the pile of applications that my boss, Lieutenant Colonel Black, handles every day. He's the person here in the Pentagon who OKs them, and I'm the one who processes them as they come in. So just send it in, Major, and I'll make sure he sees it. Compared to a lot of the applications I've seen come through the pipeline, I'm sure he will OK yours."

"OK, Sergeant Fisher, I'll take you up on that."

As soon as I returned to my office at Mitchel I filled out an application requesting graduate study at Columbia University to pursue a master of arts degree in international relations, got Colonel Clark's enthusiastic indorsement on it, and submitted it through channels. Then I prepared to wait several months for a reply.

Meanwhile I looked about for every opportunity to attend some school to enhance my professional background as an intelligence officer.

In October I attended a nine-day course at Southern Pines, North Carolina, in which I learned techniques of joint military operations with U.S. Army ground forces. And, coming home by train, I learned something, new to me, about the mores of the SWM (southern White male). In my class there were only about a dozen officers, including one other Black. During the nine days we all got to be quite friendly and cordial: Yankees and "good old boys," Blacks and Whites, all together in uniform, in the service of our country, and each man, regardless of race, religion, or national origin, having proclaimed his pledge of allegiance, many times, to "one nation . . . indivisible, with liberty and justice for all." I truly, and naively, thought that we were all brothers in arms, especially since Commander-in-Chief Harry Truman's desegregation order seven years previously. And, with the Earl Warren Supreme Court's decision the year before in *Brown v. Topeka Board of Education,* I thought the walls of Jim Crow were tumbling down.

Major James Burns, one of my classmates at Southern Pines, taught me how foolish and naive I was. He was a Georgia boy stationed at Fort Devens, Massachusetts. We caught the same train going north. By the time we reached my station, Newark, New Jersey, we were both bushed and tacky, needing a shave and shower, after the long overnight train ride. He faced several more hours on the train before reaching his station and I took pity on him by saying:

"Burns, why don't you get off with me in Newark and lay over at my home in East Orange? We can have a home-cooked breakfast, you can shower, put on a fresh uniform, and rest awhile before continuing on to Massachusetts. How about it?"

"Thanks, Dryden, but I can't do that."

"Why not, for heaven's sake?"

"Because it just isn't done."

"Waddayuhmean, it just isn't done?"

"Where I come from, White people just don't ever socialize with Colored people."

For just a moment I was speechless. Thunderstruck. I couldn't believe my ears. I thought: 'Well, I'll be damned! No, better yet, YOU be damned!"

Finally, after a moment of pregnant silence, I managed to growl: "OK, Mister, suffer! No better for you and your funky self. I hope you starve to death!"

And I got off the train—wiser, but sadder.

Upon returning to my office at CONAC I found a set of orders placing me on thirteen weeks' TDY to attend the Strategic Intelligence School (SIS) at the Main Navy Building in Washington, D.C., to report NLT (no later than) November 4, 1955. SIS was the training ground for military attachés and I had ambitions for such an assignment somewhere in the world, but preferably in Jamaica or the U.K. I had applied for the school shortly after graduation from Hofstra College.

"Hallelujah!" I exulted when I read the orders. "I'm on my way to a cushy assignment and this is the first step."

SIS proved to be a real asset in my professional education as I was taught the intricacies and techniques of gathering intelligence about other countries and utilizing it for the benefit of our own. However, I regretted the timing of my assignment to SIS somewhat because it kept me from "going to the Dogs." "The Dog" was the nickname for the F-86D, an all-weather fighter plane that was a modification of the famed F-86 fighter-interceptor that had bested the Migs during the Korean War. Shortly after my orders were cut to attend sis, a levy to train seventy-five fighter jockeys as "Dog" pilots was issued by Headquarters usaf to all major commands. conac's personnel office wanted to list my name but I had been "frozen" by the sis assignment and so missed the chance to fly the "Dog." Perhaps it was just as well because some buddies who flew it averred that the "Dog" was indeed a "dog" as compared to other jets, because it had very short time-aloft endurance.

In any case, after graduating from sis in late January 1956, I returned to conac and resumed editing and publishing the *AITB*.

My flying activities, from the time I first arrived at Mitchel from the Far East, had been in multiengine transports and trainers: the C-47 "Goony Bird" and C-45 "Twin Beech." Because I was at the base weeknights, rather than at home, I volunteered to fly administrative missions for base operations whenever they needed a pilot on those nights that I was not in class. Very soon after arriving at Mitchel I earned a reputation of being available and eager to fly in all kinds of weather to any destination. I became a sort of workhorse and built up my total time and instrument time rapidly, which enabled me to acquire a green instrument card on January 5, 1953. The green card authorized me to fly in the worst type of weather conditions imaginable; obtaining the card was the last hurdle I faced to earn a senior pilot rating. I had already held the aeronautical rating of pilot for four years more than the seven required by air force regulations, and I had already logged the 2,000 hours of total flying time required. So, on January 9, Headquarters, Continental Air Command issued Personnel Order Number 2 designating me as a senior pilot.

With a copy of my orders in my hand I hurried over to the post exchange and bought two pairs of wings with the star above the shield. Almost eleven years had passed since I first pinned on the silver wings of a military pilot.

The next rating after senior pilot required 3,000 hours of total flying time. It took me a few months more than four years to log the additional 1,000 hours—four years of hustling to fly every chance I could get between work and school. I finally achieved my goal on May 15, 1957, when Headquarters, Air Force Institute of Technology (AFIT) issued Aeronautical Order Number 20, which designated me as a command pilot—the top aeronautical rating, symbolized by the star on the wings encircled by a wreath. How proud I was to pin the command pilot wings on my blouse and proclaim to all the world that "I am a seasoned aviator!"

As well as being a symbol of achievement of the highest air force aeronautical rating, the command pilot wings were evidence that I was keeping up with the old crowd of flyboys from Tuskegee. Many were already proudly displaying their stars-and-wreaths-on-the-wing, especially those who had been flying a lot in transports and bombers in which flights might last more than twelve hours—far more than flights in fighters—since being integrated into the air force at large. So now I had joined the club of African Americans who caused eyebrows to be raised whenever they walked into a base operations anywhere, with their command pilot wings gleaming, signed their own flight clearance, without need of the airdrome officer's signature, then stalked out to their plane, cranked it up, and leaped off into the gray soup yonder. Ceiling and visibility might be zero-zero but we knew we could hack it because we had overcome so many obstacles along the way.

At Mitchel Field there were a number who were already in the command pilots "club" or were close to gaining admission—men who had been my buddies from way back in the early days at Tuskegee. Some were assigned to units at the base itself, others to air force outfits in the vicinity. They included such stalwarts as: Majors Lee Archer, who had downed three Jerries on one mission during WWII, and J. B. "the Eel" Knighten, who had saved my life during my baptism of fire over Sicily in July 1943; Knighten's 43-D aviation cadet classmates, Major Lee Rayford and Lieutenant Colonel George Knox; Majors Fitzroy "Buck" Newsum, one of the early B-25 pilots who transitioned into fighters at Lockbourne AFB, and Spann Watson, who was an original member of the 99th Fighter Squadron when it deployed to North Africa in 1943 and who was its operations officer during the last four years before integration.

Also assigned to units at and nearby Mitchel Field were some of the "old-timer" nonflying officers, men and women who had helped to keep us flying, including: Majors Ruth Faulkner, one of the original Army Nurse Corps officers at the TAAF Hospital when Pete was stationed there; Bill Phears, a civil engineer by profession; Eldredge Williams, an outstanding, outspoken officer with strong convictions about morality and fairness and the courage to stand by his convictions as well as being a peerless athlete who had been a PT (physical training) officer at Tuskegee; and Colonel George Webb, one of the original Black officers assigned to TAAF to get it started, and former CO of the Air Base Group at Lockbourne.

During my long stay at Mitchel I also met a number of Black officers I had not met before. They were not the trailblazers of the TAAF era but were certainly the torchbearers of the post-TAAF present. One was a pilot, an intrepid aviator who had the skill, and guts, to file an IFR clearance at base operations one day at Mitchel to take off into a low overcast with icing in the clouds and fly a cross-country mission in an A-26 "Invader," a plane that had no wing deicing system: Lieutenant Marlon Green later showed more guts when he left the air force, applied for a job as airline pilot with Continental Airlines, took them to court when his application was rejected on no reasonable grounds, and won his suit, thus opening the doors to cockpit jobs for African Americans that had been hitherto tightly shut by all commercial airlines.

There were some other "newcomers" at the base hospital, as well: doctors—Captains Lorenzo Harris and George I. Lythcott—and air force nurses—Captain Elizabeth Brittain and Lieutenant Mervel Winzer. And more than holding their own in administrative positions on the base were Major Ruth Lucas and Lieutenant Jane Cotton.

So, overall, there was a fair representation of African American officers at Mitchel Field with whom I had associated during my tour of duty there, assigned to CONAC on Colonel Clark's staff.

At the end of March 1956, Colonel Clark was retired from the air force for medical reasons and I was named acting director of intelligence for a short time. It was with mixed feelings that I took over the reins of the directorate, for although I was pleased at the prospect of being the top banana in the S-2 shop, I was sad to see Colonel Clark leave. He had been a wise mentor, a staunch supporter of my pursuit of college education, and, best of all, a true friend.

After a month or so he was replaced by Lieutenant Colonel James Hickman. He was my boss for only a couple months before I was transferred from Headquarters, Continental Air Command to Headquarters, Air Force Institute of Technology (AFIT) with TDY for one year at Columbia University to pursue a graduate degree. Sergeant Fisher had done it, after all! True to his promise, he had shepherded my application through the bureaucratic maze and made it possible for me to live with my family in East Orange while commuting to Columbia in Manhattan and doing nothing but study and learn—and fly four hours once per month for my flying pay. It was the best of all possible worlds!

From mid-September 1956 until mid-August 1957 I was a student, spending many hours in Columbia's huge Butler Hall library in which millions of books were available. In my first semester I disposed of almost all the credit courses required for the master's degree in public law and government. Happily I passed the French exam for the second language requirement, after having spent the Christmas holidays reading through several issues of *Le Monde* bought from newsstands near the public library at 42nd Street and 5th Avenue in order to buttress the *petit peu* French I had absorbed in Stuyvesant High School twenty years before.

My second semester included mostly courses for which I needed only a "registration" grade; that is, no final exam was required. A quality grade was required in only one of the five courses, a sociology course in which the teacher, Professor Leland Goodrich, required a final exam and a term paper for the final grade. With his approval I chose to write a paper on the subject of human rights in the Union of South Africa. He liked it so well he suggested that I expand its scope and submit it as my master's thesis. I liked the idea, especially inasmuch as Professor Goodrich was the mentor who would review my thesis for award of the degree.

By the end of April all my term papers in my other courses were completed and submitted and my decks were clear to begin work on my thesis: "The United Nations Declaration on Human Rights vs. South Africa." I set a timetable for myself, planning to do all of the research in May and all of the writing in June. My deadline for submission to Professor Goodrich was July 1 because he was going on vacation in mid-July and I had to allow two weeks for a thesis typist near the campus to type it in the classic format, with every *ibid.* and *supra* in its proper place in the footnotes.

So on May 1 I began my reading odyssey by following the example of a fellow student I had befriended: Abe Ashkenasi was a doctoral candidate who urged me to "read a book a day" to cover the ground. So I did, and by May 30 I had read and made copious notes from thirty books, some pencil thin, some pound heavy, some factual like United Nations documents, some fictional like *Cry, the Beloved Country.*

With research completed right on schedule, I began writing on June 1. My writing room, on the third floor of our home in East Orange, was declared off limits to everyone but me, and there I scribbled, like a monk in a monastery, from 6:00 A.M. until midnight, every day for thirty days, wearing out a bushel of pencils, pads, and erasers. When I crossed the last *t* and dotted the last *i* on June 30, I felt as though writer's cramp would cripple my right hand for the rest of my life. But I was ecstatic that I had made good my boast to my classmates that I would complete my thesis in sixty days from start to finish, whereas some planned to take as much as a year to do theirs. What they did not realize was that I did not have the luxury of more time to complete it—AFIT allowed only one year to complete *all* requirements for the graduate degree. And my military career depended on my successful completion within the allotted time.

Approval of my thesis by Professor Goodrich ended my quest for the master of arts degree with all requirements completed in July. However, my TDY orders from Headquarters, AFIT did not expire until the end of August, so I took an additional graduate course to broaden my background. It was a course on the politics of the Middle East taught by a Jewish scholar who had a daily verbal skirmish with an Arab student—from which I was able to infer much of the animosity between the warring factions in that part of the world. The course ended with hot tempers flaring between the Arab and the Jew, the student and the teacher, and I couldn't help wondering what kind of grade the student got after all.

JET PILOT. Maj. Charles Dryden posed on wing of T-33 jet trainer at Mitchel AFB, New York, in 1955.

To tell the truth, it really didn't matter to me because I was FIGMO. I had received my orders for PCS to an overseas base in Germany, near Kaiserslautern, West Germany. I was due to report there NLT September 17, the day after my birthday. Packing to leave for overseas after five and a half years in the United States was easy.

I had no complaints about the upcoming assignment. Ramstein Air Base was just about the most wanted spot in Germany among GIs going overseas. And, thanks to Major Thomas J. Money in the personnel office in the Pentagon, who was an "old-timer" from the early days at Tuskegee, I had been assigned to Mitchel Field when I left the Far East. The tour of duty at Mitchel Field had been the most fruitful of my career so far. While there I had earned two college degrees, achieved two higher aeronautical ratings, attended three professional military schools, added over 2,000 flying hours to my Form 5 flight log, including some time in the T-33 jet trainer, and achieved certification as an instrument flight instructor pilot—to say nothing about the many pleasant years I had been able to spend with my family and friends in my old neighborhoods nearby. Indeed I had enjoyed and profited from the tour of duty there and I was ready to move on to the third overseas tour of my career.

After farewells to Pete, Thumper, Mother Pearl, Mom and Dad, sister Pauline and brother-in-law Artie, and a host of friends at an *auf Wiedersehen* party, I went to the aerial POE. At McGuire Air Force Base in New Jersey I boarded a C-54 bound for Frankfort, Germany, on the day after my birthday and prayed that this deployment, unlike the previous one to the Far East, would not turn out to be the prelude to another tour of combat duty. Two wars were enough at my tender age of thirty-seven.

15 Guten Tag, West Germany

>> September 1957–May 1959

Ramstein Air Base, the home of 12th Air Force, was across the autobahn from Landstuhl, a small country town next to which Ramstein's airfield, hangars, and runways were located, and a few miles from Kaiserslautern, a slightly larger but still small country town in central West Germany. In preparing myself for the upcoming tour of duty in Deutschland, I had read some materials available at the personnel office at Headquarters, CONAC that were given to troops going overseas. Most helpful, however, was an issue of *Life* magazine that featured West Germany and the various festivals celebrated there during a year's time. I was most impressed with the vivid description, accompanied by colorful pictures, of Oktoberfest and Fasching, a pre-Lenten festival that seemed like Mardi Gras a la Allemagne. It sounded interesting and exciting and helped to counterbalance the apprehension I felt when I first received my PCS orders to go to Germany.

Memories die hard. Especially memories that carry pain. Like memories of the German PWs going into the PX cafeteria at Walterboro in 1944 when I couldn't; the German PWs at the gas station at Godman Field who were chewed out by my German-fluent friend, Captain Jim Redden, when he heard them insulting us with ethnic slurs, in German, in 1945; the loss of sixty-six of my 'Skegee buddies fighting the Germans during WWII; the "Mein Kampf" Aryan superiority arrogance—I wondered if it had survived the war and was still to be confronted in postwar Germany.

Arriving at Ramstein Air Base the day after my birthday, I was pleasantly surprised to find that it was a lot like Yokota had been during my tour in the Far East eight years before: a friendly place. From the men and women in uniform, some officers and enlisted men and women from other nations—Canadians, French, West Germans—but mostly Americans, to the local German civilians working in various jobs on the base, almost all were congenial.

Ramstein was the home of Headquarters, 12th Air Force, USAFE (United States Air Force, Europe). Major General Gabriel P. Disosway was commanding general. My former squadron commander, now Brigadier General Benjamin O. Davis, Jr., was his deputy chief of staff for operations (DCS/O). That was an especially pleasant surprise for me because my duty assignment was to the staff of the director of intelligence who reported to the DCS/O. Thus I would be working for "the Old Man" again, albeit indirectly. However, now it would be more appropriate to refer to him as "General Ben," as many at Ramstein had taken to doing.

I did not get to meet him again until I had been at Ramstein for about a week. Meanwhile, once I had cleared in on base—assigned to a two-room suite in the BOQ, sharing an interconnecting bathroom with another officer, and squared away with the base operations people for my regular flying proficiency activities—I found that there were a fair number of "old-timers" from the Tuskegee-Godman-Lockbourne era: Majors Bill Kelley and Bob King were both in the communications directorate at the headquarters, Dudley "Fearless Fosdick" Watson was in operations, and Harold Hayes was plying his professional skills in meteorology on the headquarters staff.

The director of intelligence at 12th Air Force headquarters was Colonel Bill Adams, an old intelligence hand who had cut his S-2 eyeteeth during World War II and who knew his business. When I reported for duty a command-wide exercise was in progress and all of the staff sections of the headquarters had only a skeleton staff on duty in the headquarters building at Ramstein. The bulk of their people were at "the Cave" conducting simulated war operations around the clock.

"The Cave" was the popular nickname for the Combat Operations Center, or COC, where, in the event of war in Europe, air operations involving NATO (North Atlantic Treaty Organization) forces would be controlled and monitored. Dug out of the side of a small mountain about ten miles from Ramstein, "the Cave" had once served Nazi army units as an ammo dump during World War II, a storage warehouse for medical supplies by British occupying forces after the war, and currently as the Combat Operations Center.

After a couple days of orientation at the intelligence directorate at the headquarters building at Ramstein, I was detailed to the COC by Colonel Adams. One morning he called me into his office and briefed me: "Major Dryden, our headquarters staff sections and units in the field are almost constantly engaged in one kind of exercise or another to test our war plans and preparations. The one going on now will be a good opportunity for you to get your feet wet with what we do and how our intelligence input fits in with everything else going on at the COC. You will be assigned to the Combat Intelligence Section out there, headed up by Lieutenant Colonel John C. Shumate, and you will report directly to Major Jim Truscott. I have alerted them to expect you at 0800 tomorrow morning when the day shift begins. And because this will be your first trip to the Cave you might want to ride the shuttle bus. Any questions?"

"No, Sir," I replied, "not now, but I'm sure I'll have lots of 'em by this time tomorrow."

Dull and early the next morning I boarded the shuttle bus to the COC. Seldom could one say "bright and early" in Germany. It seemed that oftentimes the skies over Ramstein were overcast, as they were the first time I entered the Cave. Once inside, the sky conditions didn't matter because the COC was windowless.

The main entrance to the COC was divided by a tall fence of barbed wire into two walkways, one for entrance into the COC, the other for exit from it. This division facilitated the movement of the few hundred people entering and leaving at the times of shift changes.

As I was moving along with the throng of people entering the COC for the day shift, I noticed a Renault staff car on the exit side of the fence. Just as I glanced at it, the back door opened, a tall officer uncoiled himself from the back seat, extended his hand to me through the fence, and said: "Major Dryden, it's good to see you. I had heard that you were coming to Ramstein and I am glad to have you aboard."

"Thank you, General," I responded, pleased and flattered that my former CO had remembered me and had taken time to get out of his staff car and greet me so warmly. Eight years and another war had passed into history since we had left "Camelot" at Lockbourne Air Force Base in Ohio. He looked well, ramrod straight as ever, every inch the West Point graduate as I had always observed him, but somehow friendlier, less tense than he had seemed in past years. In any case I was glad to see him and looked forward to being on a base where his brand of efficiency was the order of the day.

Once inside I saw that the Cave comprised three long parallel tunnels with hemispheric walls and ceilings that resembled the inside of Quonset huts, connected by three or four shorter tunnels crossing the main tunnels at right angles. The offices of the various functional units of the COC were located in the long tunnels. The heart of the COC was the command post, a fairly large room in which the status and movements of NATO and potentially hostile armed forces were tracked on a tote board, much like the large vertical display board in the modern-day NORAD (North American Air Defense Command) command post at Colorado Springs, Colorado, that has been pictured so often in news articles.

After reporting to Colonel Shumate, I was taken on a tour of the COC by my boss, Major James C. Truscott. Jim and I quickly became good friends: We were both veterans of air combat in World War II (he was in the Pacific) and Korea, and we shared a love of the profession of intelligence, especially the analysis aspect. It was the task of the Combat Intelligence Branch to monitor all available information about the capabilities and deployments of potential hostile forces, analyze the information to determine the likely intentions of the enemy, and make recommendations for appropriate actions to the commander of the Combat Operations Center.

Colonel Robert Newberry, the COC commander, relied heavily on combat intelligence for "threat intelligence."

Much of the "threat intelligence" was derived from constant radar surveillance of flying activity of Warsaw Pact air forces. At all times, every hour of every day, an intelligence officer was on duty in the COC command post. I was placed in charge of the Intelligence Duty Officer (IDO) Section, which comprised three other IDOs and me. While on duty in the command post we were required to monitor air activity displayed on the tote board and alert the COC commander whenever observed air activity deviated from the norm without some logical explanation.

As deputy chief of staff for operations, General Davis held weekly staff meetings that were attended by the heads of staff sections, mostly full colonels. Occasionally, however, he called an ad hoc staff meeting to address a particular situation. On one such occasion the Combat Intelligence Branch of the COC had made a proposal for a new communication facility and the staff gathered to review the proposal and determine appropriate action. Before leaving the COC and going to the headquarters building at Ramstein, a meeting was held to agree upon "the party line" for the proposal.

I had a problem with "the party line." I did not agree with the proposal at all. I was convinced that if implemented it would cause all manner of repercussions with the Soviet bloc. In the wide-ranging discussion of the proposal at the COC, I was invited to express my opinion. It was contrary to the majority and, more important, was vetoed by Colonel Shumate, chief of the Combat Intelligence Branch. Nevertheless he invited me to attend the staff meeting at headquarters.

"Knowing that I am strongly opposed to this proposal, Colonel, do you still want me to go to the headquarters staff meeting?" I asked him.

"That's right, Major Dryden."

"Well then, I take it that you won't be expecting me to make any presentation or statement about it, is that right?"

"Right again, Major."

"OK, Colonel," I responded, and we left the Cave headed for the head shed: Lieutenant Colonel Shumate and me from Combat Intelligence and some representatives from other units at the COC. My immediate boss, Jim Truscott, was on TDY in the States.

When we arrived at the headquarters conference room we settled into the comfortable swivel chairs, awaiting General Davis's entrance. Promptly, at the appointed time, he entered, announced by the "Atten'-hut!" barked out by one of the assembled officers who was seated by the door. As we scrambled to our feet the general put us at ease with, "Please be seated, Gentlemen." And the discussions began with a briefing about the overall proposal by a team of COC staff officers followed by attempts to answer questions posed by General Davis.

As the discussions swirled around and about me, I felt almost as though I was not a part of it all because I had been told, in effect, that I was there only to be seen, not heard. And so I was practically wool-gathering, thinking about what I had to do back at the COC when the meeting ended. Suddenly I heard a familiar, firm voice asking, "Major Dryden, what do you think about all this?"

Flustered for a fleeting moment, my mind came back into focus. I knew, of course, that "the party line" was all in favor of the proposal. However, I also knew that General Davis knew me and that, because I was a product of his military upbringing, he could read me "five by five." More important, he could trust me to say what I really believed and not parrot what someone else might want me to say. Most important, there was a strong thread of loyalty to a former-commander/comrade-in-arms/veteran of foreign and domestic (i.e., Jim Crow) wars that would never allow me to misstate my true opinion. So I replied, "General, in my personal opinion, this proposal will get us into a lot of trouble."

"Why so?" he asked, riveting gaze upon me.

During my brief explanation, focusing on security aspects of the proposal, he listened intently until I had concluded.

"Thank you, Major Dryden. I appreciate your candor," the general said.

About what the lieutenant colonel said back at the Cave, after the meeting at headquarters, the less said the better. In any case, I felt better about having given an honest answer than I would have had I lied. I remembered how welcome both of the Davises had made me feel at Ramstein when I first arrived at the base. How General Ben had greeted me warmly at the entrance to the COC. And how gracious Mrs. Davis had been when she spied me in the lobby of the Ramstein officers club.

She was in the lobby with a group of other ladies about to leave the club after a meeting of the Officers' Wives Club, just as I was entering. Catching sight of me, Mrs. Davis left the group and came toward me with her hand extended and a greeting: "Why, Major Dryden, it is so nice to see you here at Ramstein. Welcome to Germany!"

After eight years she remembered my name! I thought: "How nice to be remembered, considering the literally hundreds of people the Davises have met in the interim." And then I thought, "Perhaps Mrs. Davis remembers me because of the beer bottle I dropped on her terrazzo floor during a luncheon at their quarters one Sunday afternoon at Lockbourne!" Whatever the reason, I appreciated their friendship.

Being overseas on a solo tour of duty (i.e., without my family), I missed the environment of a "together" family and tried to fill the void by frequently visiting old friends who took pity on me with invitations to dinner, picnics, parties, and outings. We "old-timers" from Lockbourne shared fairly close ties that led to mostly happy times. But we were all shocked and saddened when we lost Major Dudley Watson in the crash of a T-33 on a night landing in bad weather conditions: "Fearless Fosdick" was one of our top-flight pilots. Visiting his widow, Bernice, as she prepared to leave Ramstein and return to the States tore me up, just as visiting Lucille, the widow of my classmate Sid Brooks, had done fifteen years before.

My own flying activities at Ramstein were most enjoyable. With long stretches of days and nights with low ceilings and low visibility in the area, the opportunities for logging bad-weather flying time were unlimited. Because I had acquired a command pilot aeronautical rating while at Mitchel Field, as well as hundreds of hours as an instrument instructor pilot in the C-47, I could practically "write my own ticket" at base operations. I was fortunate in getting an airplane for cross-country flights practically whenever I requested one.

The liberal policy about cross-country flights was a real morale booster for the troops at Ramstein and the various U.S. Army units in the vicinity because it gave GIs an opportunity to visit many faraway places with strange-sounding names that they perhaps might not have otherwise been able to visit. My flight log shows trips to Athens, London, Madrid, Naples, Paris, Rome, Tripoli. My diary records that:

In Athens I visited the Parthenon and other ruins like the cave where Socrates drank the hemlock.

On the visit to London I was able to meet my Uncle Wilmot face to face in his home in Kenton Harrow; I also caught a train to Cambridge University where my cousin Gerald "Bunny" Lalor from Jamaica, West Indies, was pursuing his doctorate in chemistry. I was thoroughly delighted to tour the beautiful grounds that seemed so serene with a pond in one area in which a pair of regal swans preened and paraded along the gently sloping banks, and the quadrangle, a patch of exquisitely manicured grass on which only certain members of the faculty possessing a particular academic rank were privileged to walk. While we sat on a bench at the edge of the quadrangle just chatting and catching up on family doings, he drew my attention to a professor wearing a flowing black gown exercising his privilege on the grass patch, and I commented, "Cousin, yonder professor looks like the swans, preening and parading out there on the quadrangle."

"Yes, Charlie," Bunny said, "some of the professors are snobbish about it. But come, let me show you where I live while here."

A short stroll across the campus grounds brought us to his dormitory. Emmanuel College's hall (dormitory) was over 400 years old. The electric wiring and plumbing were obviously much-later additions to the venerable structure that had housed generations of scholars. I was much impressed, nay, awed by the mystique of Cambridge and very proud that a kinsman of mine would be one of its alumni. (At this writing he is Professor the Honorable Gerald

Lalor, Vice Chancellor, University of the West Indies, Kingston, Jamaica.)

Poor timing had me land at Madrid the day after the end of the corrida and I missed seeing a bullfight. However, I did observe the siesta custom of Madrilenos whose shops close at about noon, while most of the populace goes home for a rejuvenating nap during the heat of the day, then reopen at about 7:00 P.M. Dinner at many restaurants was not served until 10:00 P.M. and movie theaters began showing films at 11:00 P.M. At 2:00 A.M. the streets and avenues of Madrid looked like New York's Times Square at rush hour! All of this was new to me and to my copilot, a self-professed hillbilly, who whooped with delight when he discovered a bidet in the bathroom of the hotel room we shared: "Hey, Chuck, look at this nifty foot washer they got in here!" It was all I could do to keep from laughing out loud, to keep from embarrassing him, as I explained what it was really for.

In Paris a good friend from the old days at Tuskegee and Mitchel Field, Major Lee "Buddy" Archer, was protocol officer at Orly Field, and he took pride in showing me around "his" city. As it happened, jazz pianist Hazel Scott and my favorite bandleader, Duke Ellington, were in town attending a reception at an office of the U.S. Embassy where I was able to meet them.

The usually clamorous streets of Paris were strangely quiet: because of an ordinance recently enacted in an attempt to decrease the noise level, there was no honking of the taxicabs—a sound that was traditionally part of the ambiance of Paris. Instead, every now and then, there was the tinkling of glass falling on the pavement as the bumper of one automobile crashed the headlights or taillights of another.

In Rome I was astounded by the rat race of motor scooters, Fiats, Alfa Romeos, and so forth around the outside of the Coliseum with apparent disregard for life or limb. Incredibly there were few accidents. Inside the Coliseum I had an eerie feeling as I contemplated the fact that unknown numbers of Christians had been thrown to the lions there.

The Tripoli trip was really one to remember, for a number of reasons. First of all, it was a weekend trip for a full passenger load of GIs who had never been to the African continent, and the landing at Wheelus Air Base, near Tripoli in Libya, gave them the opportunity. For me, personally, it was a chance to visit my one surviving cadet classmate, Major Clarence "Jamie" Jamison, and his family. Also stationed at Wheelus was Captain Ed "Bulldog" Drummond, who had been in my flight in the 99th Fighter Squadron back at Lockbourne.

In planning the trip I decided that for both flights, to Tripoli and the return to Ramstein, the most convenient refueling stop was the airport at Marseilles, on the Mediterranean coast of France. Although I would not have enough time to visit the famous city I would, at least, be able to say "I've been to Marseilles."

The flight to Tripoli was uneventful: from early morning takeoff at Ramstein and flying west across Germany, crossing the border at Saarbrucken, west across *la belle* France past Metz, Nancy, Chaumont, to the Marne River, then south above the Rhone River valley past Lyon, Dijon, Montelimar, Avignon. Along the route there were just a few scattered clouds here and there, not enough to obscure the magnificent snowcapped Alps way off to our left. The GIs in the back of the plane came forward to the pilots' cabin, one by one, to look out through the front windows, oohing and ahhing at the beautiful scenery unfolding below us as we flew down the Rhone River valley and busily snapping pictures for scrapbooks and letters to the folks back home.

Finally, at the water's edge of the sparkling blue Mediterranean—Marseilles! Refueling took little time with the flight engineer seeing to it while the copilot and I filed our flight plan for the final leg to Tripoli. Weather over the Mediterranean was forecast to be CAVU and we were itching to get back into the air. However, filling out the documents required by the French customs and immigration officials took a bit longer.

The flight to Tripoli was all over water except for a short stretch over the southern tip of Sardinia and a passing glance at "Panty" (Pantelleria), the island footnoted in history books as the only military objective that had surrendered to air power alone. My first World War II combat mission in "A-Train" had been on a dive-bombing "Panty raid" along with seven other pilots of the 99th. As I described to the copilot how I felt on that first mission and how the round-the-clock bombing of the island had demoralized the German troops there into surrendering, he remarked, "It sure looks peaceful now." But for me it brought back memories of friends lost and of survival through my first war.

About three hours after takeoff from Marseilles we touched down at Wheelus Air Base located right on the coast. As we taxied behind the Follow Me jeep to the ramp in front of base operations, we could feel the hot breath of the desertlike terrain wafting in through the windows of the pilots' cabin. Fortunately there was a sea breeze blowing in from the sea that helped to keep the temperature bearable during the day.

When we had parked the Goony Bird, filled out the Form 1, and reminded our passengers about the departure time for the return flight to Ramstein on Sunday, two days hence, the copilot and I split up, each of us going to visit friends who were stationed at Wheelus Air Base.

Because of its year-round good flying weather and wide expanses of unpopulated areas, Wheelus played host to U.S. fighter units stationed at bases in Europe and the U.K. that deployed there for gunnery training and practice.

Major "Jamie" Jamison, my old classmate, was the base finance officer. He and his wife, Phyllis, and their kids, Michal and Clifford, Jr., had been at Wheelus for two years and were looking forward to their return to the States after another year. My visit with them in their comfortable quarters was a joyful reunion.

Likewise I was glad to see Captain Ed Drummond, my old flight mate from the days at Lockbourne. I remembered how reliable he had been on navigation training flights when, with me leading a flight of four Jugs flying in formation, I would fly a circuitous route for about an hour to get the guys "lost" and then radio, on squadron frequency, "Drummond, take us home!" Whereupon Ed would take over the lead as I fell back to "tail-end Charlie" position and watched him turn to the course heading home and lead us back to Lockbourne like a homing pigeon.

At the time of my visit to Wheelus Air Base, Ed's squadron,

the 513th Fighter Interceptor Squadron, was there on TDY to practice gunnery in their F-86D "Dogs"; their permanent base was at Phalsburg, France. I bent the elbow with him in the officers club, reminiscing about a lot of the "good old days" at "Camelot" in Ohio. All of ten years had gone by since desegregation broke up Lockbourne, and we hadn't seen each other since then. In the interim Ed and Jim Harvey, one of the "top guns" on the Lockbourne gunnery team that won the air force trophy in 1949, had fought their war in Korea flying F-80s with the 49th Fighter Group. Having lost good friends—Peepsight Smith, Ghost Lawson, E. J. Williams, and others—to the Korean War, I was especially glad to see Ed Drummond and know that he had survived that war with flying colors.

My weekend of reminiscing and camaraderie ended at noon Sunday when we took off on the return flight to Ramstein by way of Marseilles. The first leg to Marseilles was routine with fair skies and few clouds, which covered Pantelleria as we passed over it. I was glad that I had been able to see "Panty" on the way down to Tripoli.

When we landed at Marseilles airport to refuel we breezed through the customs and immigration officials because they had checked us out just two days before and processed our papers, as one of them remarked, proudly, "C'est finis. Vite! Vite!"

Filing our flight plan took a bit longer this time because the weather maps and forecast spelled bad news. The Rhone Valley was covered by a stationary front, with all kinds of foreboding conditions aloft, north of Montelimar. We could expect icing in some clouds, heavy turbulence through some stretches of the route, lightning, and heavy precipitation (sometimes rain, sometimes snow, sometimes sleet) from time to time. The forecast was almost enough to make a pilot say: "Enough, already! I'm standing down." Almost, but not quite enough. I felt that the good old Goony Bird was a stable enough instrument-flying bird to make it OK, so we filed an IFR flight plan to Ramstein Air Base with London's Heathrow airport as an alternate.

Although we took off into bright afternoon sunshine, the weather forecaster was right as rain. And sleet. And snow. And ice. And turbulence. Turbulence forced us to abandon any thought of turning on "George," the autopilot. The copilot and I had to manually manhandle the controls, the wheel, and rudder pedals—at times both of us together—straining to keep the plane in a straight and level attitude.

Fighting our way up the Rhone Valley through the teeth of the storm we were constantly mindful of the Alps off to the right of our route and were careful to stay right on course as we flew from radio beacon to radio beacon, adjusting our heading each time the reading on the "bird dog" (radio compass) indicated that wind direction in the clouds had shifted, causing us to drift off course.

After we had been in the soup for about two hours we had seen everything the weatherman at Marseilles had forecast, except ice. Avignon and Montelimar were already behind us and the "bird dog" needle was just beginning to fluctuate from left to right of the straight-ahead position at the top of the radio compass instrument, indicating our passing over Lyon, when it happened. It sounded like large pebbles rattling around an empty tin can being shaken vigorously. With my eyes glued to the instrument panel and wrestling the controls to keep on even keel, I couldn't even sneak a peek out of the window but said to the copilot: "What's making that racket? Sounds like golf balls banging against the fuselage."

"That's because there are golf balls out there—hailstones as big as golf balls, seems like," he said. "And look at that," he continued, beginning to look a bit scared, his ruddy complexion turning pallid. "What is that? I've never seen anything like that before!"

"Here, take over for a moment," I said. "Let me check it out."

My copilot was a young first lieutenant, with just a few hundred hours, total, and very little actual weather time. I knew that fact because I had checked him out in the Goony Bird within the past month and he was on this trip to build up his proficiency in it.

Relieved for a moment from wrestling with the plane, which was pitching and tossing in the tumultuous clouds, I glanced out through my window and saw what he had seen. Like him I had never seen it in flight before. It was at once beautiful, fascinating—and scary. It was like miniature flashes of lightning dancing along the leading edges of the wings, leaping to the fuselage and racing around and around the frame of the window, lighting it up with a soft green glow. I had read about Saint Elmo's fire in books about phenomena of flight in clouds, but this was new to me. Fortunately my reading about it had indicated that it was seldom harmful to modern airplanes in which all parts were electrically bonded, so I was able to remain calm and to reassure the copilot.

To keep him busy, and to keep his mind off our nail-biting situation, I had him turn on the wing deicer boots and keep track of how well they were shedding any ice that built up on the leading edges of the wings. If the boots did not keep our wings free of ice I would have to call air traffic control for clearance to another altitude where ice formation was not a problem. I didn't think ATC would have a problem assigning us another altitude on the airway because I had not heard any of the chatter on the radio that is usually heard when there is normal to heavy traffic flying the airway. It seemed to me that all other aviators, including birds, had sense enough to stand down in such weather and that we were the only ship of fools trying to buck it.

Eventually we flew out of the icing and turbulence and out of the clouds at 9,000 feet as we made our turn eastward and crossed the French-German border at Saarbrucken. It was dusk as I continued to navigate by the "bird dog's" indicator needle because we were "500 on top" of a thick overcast. The sun had already sunk below the horizon. Night was falling fast.

I made a position report by radio to the air traffic control ground station, saying: "This is Air Force C-47, en route Marseilles to Ramstein, over Saarbrucken, one five past the hour at Angels niner. ETA Ramstein at three two past the hour. Request Ramstein weather. Over." In response, I heard: "Weather at Ramstein rapidly deteriorating, expecting near minimums, your ETA. All Europe going below minimums. Your London alternate expected to go below minimums in about two hours. Proceed at pilot's discretion. What are your intentions? Over."

"ATC, this is Air Force C-47, proceeding as flight planned. Request let down clearance starting now and GCA assistance over the outer marker. Over."

"Roger, C-47. You are clear to begin your let down. No other traffic in the area. Report passing through each thousand-foot level. Upon reaching Angels 2, maintain altitude and inbound heading. Read back. Over."

As the copilot repeated the let down instructions, I began the gradual descent through the clouds, 500 feet per minute, strictly "on the gauges," concentrating on the attitude indicator (otherwise known as the artificial horizon) to ensure a gentle descent straight ahead with the wings level and airspeed above stalling.

After continuous descent for about fifteen minutes we arrived at 2,000 feet. I leveled off, reported, "ATC, this is Air Force C-47, level at Angels 2, inbound to Ramstein," and continued following the "bird dog" needle that indicated Ramstein was dead ahead.

"Roger, Air Force C-47," ATC responded. "Switch now to Ramstein GCA frequency. Good night."

I nodded assent to the copilot's question, "Shall I switch now?" and asked the crew chief to go into the back and tell the passengers to buckle themselves in their seats and prepare for landing. Ramstein GCA came in loud and clear: "Air Force C-47, Ramstein GCA here. How do you read me? Over."

"Five by five, Ramstein. How me? Over."

"Likewise, five by five. Turn left ninety degrees, NOW. Over."

"Roger, GCA. Turning left ninety degrees. Over."

After a pause, we heard, "OK, Air Force C-47, we've got you on the scope. Turn back right heading zero eight five. Prepare for landing. Begin standard descent to one thousand feet, NOW. Over."

"Roger, GCA. Leaving two thousand now. Over."

"Roger, C-47. Just keep on coming. Be advised that weather here at Ramstein is expected to be below minimums within about fifteen minutes, with light snow falling and some buildup on the active runway. Do you read? Over."

"Roger, Ramstein. C-47 continuing approach. Now level at one thousand. Over."

"Roger, C-47. You're approaching the glide path. Turn left ten degrees."

"Wilco, GCA."

Then after about a half minute GCA announced, "C-47, you're on the glide path, aligned with the active runway. Resume standard descent. Ramstein operations advises that in about five minutes this base will be closed to all arrivals, so let's make this a good run. You need not acknowledge any further transmissions until on the ground."

Relieved from transmissions to GCA, I turned my attention to the copilot, giving him the thumbs down signal and asking for, "Gear down!" He pushed the landing gear activating lever down and into the locked position. With the gear extended I had to adjust the throttle setting to maintain the proper airspeed for descent on the glide path and trim tabs to help keep the nose up in the correct attitude for landing.

The GCA controller kept up a running commentary, advising me: "You're on the glide path, lined up with the runway. Looking good. Just hold what you've got and you'll beat this weather."

"I'm sure glad to hear you say that," I thought, "because I darn sure don't want to shoot a missed approach procedure and fly another couple hours to our alternate, Heathrow airport at London."

Just as the GCA controller advised, "C-47, you're over the boundary. Take over visually," the copilot announced excitedly: "I see the runway! I see the runway straight ahead!"

Raising my eyes from the instruments swiftly, I looked through the windshield in front of me and past the windshield wipers that were oscillating rapidly, back and forth, trying to keep up with the fat, fluffy, feathery flakes falling furiously from the storm clouds blanketing Ramstein, and much of Europe, with a white shroud. Joyously, I echoed, "I got it! I see it too!" and called on the radio: "GCA, C-47 with visual contact. Over."

Before GCA could respond, the copilot blurted excitedly, "Major, Number Two is running away!"—whereby he was alerting me to a possible malfunction of the starboard (right) engine. I noted the high reading on the right engine tachometer as I pushed the propeller pitch controls full forward, preparing for touchdown.

"Shall I feather it?" he asked, his voice rising excitedly.

Ordinarily I would have had him shut down the engine by feathering the propeller (that is, increasing the angle of the blades until they were parallel to the direction of flight and stopped rotating) to keep them from "windmilling," which would create drag and, in turn, make the control of the plane more difficult. Under the circumstances, being just about fifty feet above the runway, my only thought was to get on the ground—on terra firma!

"Hell, no, Lieutenant," I roared, slapping his hand away from the red feathering button on the console of switches on the ceiling of the cockpit, just above our heads, that he had begun to reach for. "I'm going to put this beast on the ground NOW, with or without Number Two. So you just hang on, Sonny, and don't touch nothing!"

In about ten seconds we touched down. About ten seconds later visibility on the runway dropped to zero. The glare of the landing lights reflecting back from the wall of snow that was now falling heavily caused a "whiteout" making it virtually impossible to taxi in to the ramp safely. As often as I had landed and taxied at Ramstein's airfield, across the autobahn at Landstuhl, and as familiar as I was with the taxiways, I dared not try to taxi in on my own. After having flown the plane and passengers safely through all the four hours or so of nasty weather, with the grace of God, I wasn't about to goof up and taxi into a ditch. So we waited for the Follow Me jeep to find us and lead us in. I was bushed from the nearly nine hours that had elapsed since I had cranked up the engines of the Goony Bird for takeoff from Wheelus, including the hour on the ground while refueling at Marseilles. But I was in no hurry to spoil an otherwise good trip with an unhappy ending.

When I finally parked the plane on the snow-covered ramp I saw a fleet of private vehicles, as well as an air force bus, in front of base operations. Spouses, children, girl friends, and buddies of the GI passengers were awaiting our arrival. They had been sweating us out for the past few hours as broadcast reports of the monstrous front were heard and discussed. As the passengers gathered up their baggage containing the souvenirs they had bought in Tripoli, almost every one came forward to the pilots' cabin with expressions of appreciation for the flight, like: "Thanks, Major, for getting us back safely through the bad weather. You did a helluva job!"

My response was: "Don't thank me. Thank God, because I was praying right along with you all the way home, and He heard us."

After filling out the Form 1 and bidding good-bye to copilot and all the passengers, there was nothing for me to do but go into the base operations office and close out my flight plan, thus confirming our safe arrival and precluding any unnecessary searches by air-sea rescue units for a "missing" aircraft. Mission accomplished!

But there was something missing for me as I walked slowly to my snow-covered Volkswagen in the base ops parking lot. Everyone on that airplane had someone there to greet him or her, except me. I felt sorry for myself and a deep sorrow for being alone and for having been alone on solo tours of duty ever since leaving Lockbourne. Except for the year that I lived at home in East Orange while studying for my master's degree at Columbia, for seven years I had either been far away from my wife and son (as in Japan and in Germany) or had been commuting on weekends from New Jersey to Long Island. And as I drove slowly through the heavy snowfall, alone, I thought, for the first time in my fifteen-year-old marriage: "This is no good. This is not working."

I was a lonely man who filled the void by visiting friends and their families living at Ramstein or in its environs and at Wiesbaden. Early on after arriving I had bought a third- or maybe fourth-hand Volkswagen from a GI who was returning to the States. Thus I had wheels to visit my old friends from the memorable days at Yokota, Major "Tank" and Virginia Hillery. In addition to their first son, Skipper, and daughter, Sharon, whom I had gotten to know and love in Japan, they now had another daughter, Cathy, and another son, Scotty or "Fat Buddy." The Hillery "band of angels" became my kinfolk and kids away from home and I was labeled forever with the title "Uncle Charlie."

Major Nancy Leftenant, sister of Sam Leftenant (one of our Tuskegee Airmen killed in action [KIA] in combat during WWII) and the first African American woman commissioned as a U.S. Air Force flight nurse, was also stationed at Wiesbaden.

At Ramstein, there were African American families who "adopted" me in my lonely, enforced bachelorhood. Some I had known before, at Godman Field or Lockbourne: Major Haldane King and his wife Jean and their kids were especially cordial and dear to me, as were Major Bill Kelley and wife Mary, Major Harold Hayes and wife Ruth, and Captain Jim Warren and his family. Others I met at

Ramstein for the first time also made me feel at home in their home—dental officer, Captain Carlie Hicks, and his wife Leah became my good friends.

My boss, Jim Truscott, and his wife Jean were special friends also. Many a Sunday afternoon, when I was not on duty at the COC or off on a flight or sight-seeing junket somewhere in Europe, I spent pleasant hours with them. They had a young adult daughter going to school back in the States. With them at Ramstein they had a French poodle named Bismark, an otherwise intelligent animal that seemed to believe his master whenever I was visiting and Jim said to him, "Ah, Bizzy, here's your lunch!" whereupon the dog would look at me and begin salivating. Whereupon Jim would crack up and roar with laughter as he commanded: "Down, Bizzy! Down, boy!"

In my VW I got around the outlying areas of Ramstein fairly well at first. However, the heating system left a lot to be desired and the first chance I got I traded it in for a brand new Ford Taunus, built in Germany. That's when I really began to get around Europe, my first trip being to Switzerland.

The grandeur of the Alps is what impressed me most about that landlocked country; the natural beauty of the land took my breath away. I was also mightily impressed by the cleanliness of the streets of the first city that I visited, Basel, near the Swiss-German border: No trash or garbage littered the gutters or sidewalks; trees, shrubs, and grassy areas looked manicured. And the people—how friendly they were!

Near the center of town was a round, sunken, open pit ringed by a waist-high, iron picket fence, about forty feet in diameter and about twenty feet deep in which a large brown bear danced and pranced for passersby who threw him carrots and other goodies that could be bought from a nearby fruit stand. The day I stopped by to watch him for a moment was a misty, gloomy day and his only other audience was a young couple, obviously American. After a few minutes of watching the bear's antics and sharing laughter at his tricks, the couple walked around the railing to where I was standing. The young man asked, "Are you an American?"

I was wearing civvies, rather than my uniform, and I suppose he felt that I was obviously, or at least, presumably American because Black people are scarce in Switzerland. In any case, when I replied "Yes, I am," he extended his hand in greeting and introduced himself and his bride. "We're from Mobile, Alabama, and we're on our honeymoon. We're glad to see another American 'cause there aren't any in this town."

I thought: "I wonder how you feel being a sort of minority for a change."

I said: "I'm Chuck Dryden from New Jersey. I just drove into Basel this morning from Ramstein Air Base near Kaiserslautern. If you're looking for Americans there are a lot of them in that area."

I remembered: Major Burns, the Georgia "good ole boy," who had declined the hospitality of my home when we were tired on the train trip from Southern Pines, South Carolina, proclaiming that "Where I come from, White people just don't ever socialize with Colored people."

I thought: "I wonder if you would be as cordial to me if we were back in Alabama where you come from."

After some trivial chitchat we parted company and I continued my weekend junket in Switzerland in my new Taunus. As I drove along admiring the scenery, stopping now and then to note the history of a particular place, I thought about the couple from Alabama and wondered if they were as provincial as many of the Americans on duty in Europe; many, especially wives of servicemen, lamented being overseas in a foreign country, moaned about being bored "with nothing to do," and forever hankered to get back to the States. I was always amazed to hear such tales of woe. There was so much to see in Europe and I was happy to be able, at Uncle Sam's expense, to enjoy a "grande tour" of sorts on my weekends off, somewhat like private citizens pay thousands of dollars to do.

Every chance I got I was off exploring, experiencing the "Old World." When the Special Services office at Ramstein announced a weekend bus trip to Brussels to see the 1958 World's Fair, I signed up posthaste. In addition to going to the fair, I also wanted to visit Belgium because it was there that my Dad was wounded during World War I.

The bus was an ordinary metropolitan type, not a cross-country coach with reclining, cushioned seats. The long overnight trip was an ordeal, but the sights I saw at the fair made it worthwhile. Along with throngs of visitors from all over the world I stood in line to get into the Soviet Union's pavilion to get a glimpse of the star of their exhibit—a model of sputnik, the first man-made satellite that the Soviets had launched on October 4, 1957. Just two weeks after I had arrived at Ramstein, Americans were shaken by the news that sputnik (acronym for the Russian name of the satellite, "Fellow traveler from earth") was in orbit. Exhibits in other nations' pavilions paled beside the Soviets' beeping, hollow steel ball.

While in Brussels I was able to see many interesting sights. One was especially popular with tourists because it provoked laughter in most although it offended some Pollyanna types. It was the fountain of the "Mannequin Pis." The "once upon a time" legend was that a young prince was lost—had disappeared from the palace. The distraught king offered a reward and vowed that wherever his son was found, on that spot he would have a statue made depicting his son doing exactly whatever he was doing at the moment he was found. His majesty was true to his word and so, on one of Brussels's busy streets, there is a fountain with a life-size statue of a small boy taking a leak. Souvenir shops all over town do a brisk business selling tie pins, rings, post cards showing the "Mannequin Pis." The tie pin I bought turned out to be an instant conversation piece whenever I got up enough nerve to wear it.

I had to get up a lot of nerve to make another trip—this time by train, to West Berlin, the victorious Allied powers' enclave in East Germany. The train had to travel through 110 miles of the Communist-bloc nation and because, sometimes, trains or motor vehicles on the autobahn to West Berlin were halted and hassled by East German authorities, there was usually a feeling of uneasiness among travelers from "the West." Being warned, strictly, by the conductor not to take any pictures of the countryside or towns while the train was in East Germany did a lot to increase the uneasiness. But it did nothing to deter my snapping pictures surreptitiously through the window of my one-person compartment. After having the pictures developed I weighed whether the risk I had taken of being taken off the train and jailed in East Germany was worth what I gained—a set of snapshots of very drab, uninviting landscapes and villages.

West Berlin itself was everything but drab. Quite the contrary, it was a glittering jewel of a city that sparkled always, especially at night when shops, *brauhauses,* and clubs along the many bustling streets, like the main drag "Kurfustendamm," lit up like Christmas trees. Sight-seeing, I went to the Brandenburg Gate, took pictures, and peeked through its columns to see the drab street in East Berlin on the other side. I stayed some distance away from the gate because every now and then there were tales of Allied military persons being abducted, whisked behind the Iron Curtain and never heard from again.

For the same reason I obeyed strictly the orders I had been given back at Ramstein when I requested permission to visit West Berlin: "Don't, repeat, DO NOT go down into the subway because its route takes it into East Berlin and, therefore, all persons with certain types of security clearances are absolutely prohibited from riding the subway." Although I was curious to see how Berlin's underground compared with New York's, which I had ridden for years going to school there, I remembered the old saw that says, "curiosity killed the cat," and I stayed aboveground.

My travels while in Germany included two trips to the United States. One of the personnel policies of Headquarters, 12th Air Force was that, except for an emergency, trips to the States on ordinary leave would not be approved until the individual had been overseas for six months. Accordingly, I applied for a stateside leave in March 1958. It was approved and I got a hop from Ramstein to the Rhein-Main airport at Frankfort and then on a MATS (Military Air Transport Service) transport plane to McGuire Air Force Base, New Jersey.

Some of my friends at Ramstein asked me to bring back some items that they could not get in Germany. One of the pint-size guys in headquarters wanted some dress shirts in a small size that was not available anywhere in Germany; another asked for a particular men's cologne he couldn't find in the PXs anywhere. My boss, Jim Truscott, needed particular parts for his Cadillac. I took a list of the requests but, mindful of how much I wanted to do with my family and friends at home, I made no promises to fill the orders.

I took something with me that I had bought in Germany for a friend from my college classes at Hofstra College. Professor Herbert Rosenbaum, a Jew, had been a teenager in Germany during Hitler's Third Reich, enduring the horrors of Nazi brutality. Herb was a superb teacher, a brilliant scholar who knew how to get his students to focus on the essential essence of a course of study. For instance, the day of the final exam of his course in "Fundamentals of Political Science," he walked into the examination room that was crammed full with his students who were crammed full of facts gleaned from his class lectures, and he wrote the entire exam on the chalkboard. There was just one question:

"Design a question based upon what you consider to be the most important thing you learned in this course, then answer the question."

And he walked out of the room. Students were in varying stages of shock for a few minutes. The toughest part of the question was designing the question to be answered: too trivial a question and Professor Rosenbaum would know that the student had missed the essence of the course. From that experience I learned how to study and to prepare for examinations in any subject by designing "heart-of-the-matter" questions and then answering them fully. By so doing I was able to anticipate exam questions in later courses about nine times out of ten.

Professor Rosenbaum and I became good friends, and before leaving to go to Germany I had visited him for advice about important places to visit and things to see, and I asked him if there was anything that I could bring back for him. "Yes," he said. "I play the recorder, a wooden fifelike musical instrument, and I really would appreciate one brought from Germany."

"Sure thing, Professor," I replied. "I'll be delighted to bring one for you the first chance I get back to the States."

So, on this first return trip I was happy to see his joy at receiving the recorder from Germany. I was also happy to see my family in East Orange and took a number of souvenirs from Germany to them. The ten-day leave was over before I could really get to feeling at home—I spent a good bit of time finding and purchasing the items that my friends in Germany had requested and was glad to be able to pack all the things in my B-4 bag when I went back to McGuire for the flight to Rhein-Main, Germany.

I got manifested with no trouble and was on my way in a MATS C-54 transport plane that landed at Prestwyck, Scotland, to refuel. Some kind of maintenance problem with the airplane cropped up while we were in the terminal at Prestwyck but, after about a four-hour delay, we were on our way again heading for Germany. The entire return trip to Deutschland had been pleasant for me, except the end of it. When I went to the baggage claim area my B-4 bag was nowhere to be found!

"*Rass!*" (a Jamaican bad word) I exclaimed, when the baggage clerk told me that it had probably been offloaded in Scotland during the temporary layover. He gave me a claim form to fill out and submit to the operations office. After doing so, fuming and fussing all the while, I caught a hop to Ramstein and reported back to duty. The guys who had requested items from the States were as disappointed as I over the loss of my luggage, especially my boss whose Cadillac was sadly in need of the parts he had requested. About three weeks later I received a TWX notifying me that my bag had indeed been offloaded, inadvertently, at Prestwyck and was en route to me from there. It arrived at Ramstein a couple days later. And so ended my first leave to the States.

The second return trip to the United States was in December, the week of Christmas–New Year holidays. I had not been eligible to spend the previous Christmas with my family in the States because I had not yet been overseas the required six months. This Christmas of 1958, however, I was ready to go stateside. I had bought a set of Rosenthal china, service for eight, and a set of exquisite lead crystalware, also service for eight, and had them shipped home in time for Christmas. And I carried with me a number of gifts for Pete, Thumper, and Sister Vie and Brother Rob (Mom and Dad), but I didn't tell any of them that I was going to be home for Christmas. It was to be my supreme surprise. My special present to my family.

As it turned out I was the one surprised because when I burst into the house with a "Ho! Ho! Ho!" my wife responded with "Oh! Oh!

Oh! I'm just about to leave on a trip to Mexico. I've been working so hard at the lab the past several months that I decided I need a vacation. I only wish you had let me know you were going to be home for the holidays, I would have changed my plans. I'll cancel the trip now if you want me to."

Although disappointed by her words I nevertheless said: "No, Pete, you go on to Mexico and enjoy your vacation. I'll hang around here with Thumper and Mom and Dad, and visit Mother Pearl while I'm home. And then, come May when my eighteen months' solo tour is over, I'll be back home for good, anyway."

So she flew off to Mexico. And for the second time I had a thought like the one after the grueling flight from Marseilles to Ramstein, when everyone aboard had someone there to meet them:

"This is not working!"

Everyone at home did everything to make my Christmas leave pleasant and I was able to relax more than during the visit home in March because I didn't have any things to look for and take back to friends at Ramstein. The holiday week passed swiftly and after ushering in the new year in the bosom of my family, sans wife, I rode a bus to McGuire to board a flight to Germany. Getting manifested was no problem because there were few troops willing to travel on New Year's Day, what with all the bowl games on television. After uneventful flights over the Atlantic and across Germany, I arrived at Ramstein, this time with my B-4 bag in hand.

Back to duty in the COC, I also resumed my flying activities. Sometimes my job schedule got in the way of my flying and I had to pass up a cross-country trip taking GIs someplace. One such conflict probably saved my life.

I had been asked by base operations if I was willing to take a planeload of GIs on a trip to Athens, with a stop at Naples. Two other pilots were going along. Both were current in the C-47 and needed the flying time that they would log on the long round trip. However, because I was an IP (instructor pilot) in the airplane, I would be able to log every hour flown, as an IP, rather than having to split the time with the other pilots. It sounded OK so I signed on to make the flight as the AC (aircraft commander).

Two days before the scheduled flight an exercise involving COC personnel began and I had to withdraw from the crew for the trip to Athens. Another pilot took my place and the flight took off as planned. The next day base operations got a message that the plane had crashed into Mount Vesuvius, outside of Naples. There were no survivors. It seemed that the pilots took off on an IFR clearance into a low ceiling and a thick cloud bank and while climbing to their en route altitude they turned toward the mountain instead away from it and crashed fairly close to its summit, 3,981 feet above sea level.

The base was devastated by the awful tragedy that took so many lives. I shuddered to realize how close I had come to being one of the victims—although I was certain that if I had been aboard, and at the controls, I would never have turned toward the mountain on the climb out from the airport at Naples's Capodichino airport. I had landed there and taken off from there and was familiar with the terrain. However, had I been on the flight I probably would have piloted the plane on the first leg from Ramstein to Naples and let one of the other pilots be in charge on the Naples-to-Athens leg while I snoozed in the passenger cabin. So I would have been a goner, too. That was the second time in my flying career that I had missed an encounter with the grim reaper by missing an airplane flight!

Sobered by my second "near miss," I nevertheless continued my exploring by air. I had learned that my old squadron mate, and engineering officer of the 99th Fighter Squadron during World War II, Major Gene "Pepe" Carter was stationed at Erding Air Base, near Munich. I had a hankering to see my old friend and his lovely wife, Mildred, and their kids. So, one weekend in October I flew down to Munich and spent a pleasant day with them. I was intrigued by Gene's descriptions of his duties as deputy director of the MAAG (Military Air Advisory Group) working with the West German Air Force. I was even more enthralled by Oktoberfest, the nationwide celebration of the harvest. All over Germany, fun and frolic were the order of the day during Oktoberfest, but Munich was the place to be. And I was there!

Gene and Mildred took their kids and me to an amusement park to see how some of the local citizens had fun during Oktoberfest. I had a really good time that was marred only by my wishing that my family could have been there, too, to join in the fun. Again, while visiting nearby Oberammergau, where the Passion play depicting the crucifixion of Jesus Christ is performed at the beginning of every decade, I hankered for my family. With my solo tour in Germany about two-thirds over, I was really looking forward to being FIGMO.

In my year in Deutschland so far, I had traveled around Europe by airplane, bus, car, and train. Only a trip by boat remained. I took care of that by riding a river steamer down the Rhine River as far as Cologne. It was an overnight trip highlighted by the fantastic scenery of the vineyards on the sloping banks of the Rhine; ancient castles perched on the ridgetops along the river's course; the steady traffic of large flat-bottom barges, going in both directions, hauling cargo and serving as home for whole families;—and the Lorelei.

The Lorelei was an outcropping of rock at a bend of the river upon which, legend has it, a voluptuous damsel sang her siren song to lure unwary sailors to their death on the rocks. Tradition has it that when boats pass by the Lorelei rock, the passengers join in singing the song of that name, with much gusto. At the far end of the trip down the Rhine River was the city of Cologne with its ancient, magnificent cathedral in which I stood marveling at the soaring spires and the medieval architecture, inside and out.

As a boy growing up in New York City I had been on many a trip up the Hudson River on excursion steamers, but I cannot remember ever having enjoyed the scenery and the boat ride itself as much as I did that day on the Rhine.

Soon after that voyage on the Rhine I received PCS (permanent change of station) orders to return stateside and report, on May 15, to the Air Force ROTC Detachment 130 at Howard University, Washington, D.C., as an assistant professor of air science. So, with only two months remaining of my tour in Deutschland, I was FIGMO.

In my waning days at Ramstein more friends from the past came through from time to time. One was my "birthdate twin" who was born on the same date as I, September 16, 1920—he in Blakey, Georgia, and I in New York City—Major Freddie Hutchins. He was flying jet fighters at Nouasseur Air Base, Morocco, and flew into Ramstein every now and then. Another friend from the dim past, way back to my teenage years on Sugar Hill in New York, was Major Jack Warrick, U.S. Army, stationed at Pirmasens, a few "clicks" (kilometers) from Ramstein. A few years older than I, Jack had been like a big brother to me back in the old neighborhood. Now here we were meeting in the Ramstein O Club, strictly by chance, halfway around the world from where we grew up together and a quarter century since our last meeting. It was good to see my "brother" Jack.

The first week of May brought me authorization orders to ship my car to the United States. I was directed to deliver it to the U.S. Army quartermaster at the port of embarkation (POE) at Bremen, West Germany. The drive from Ramstein took about six hours and covered some pretty country scenery reminiscent of the midwestern USA. After completing all the paperwork and leaving the Taunus in the hands of the POE officials, I returned to Ramstein by train.

There wasn't much left to do other than bend the elbows with friends and well-wishers who insisted on the traditional farewell parties, going-away gifts, and trite teasings about what the returnee was going to face in his, or her, next assignment back in "the land of the round door knobs." (Door handles throughout Germany, and in most all of Europe, were crank levers rather round knobs.)

At my farewell party at the officers club I was presented with a German beer stein complete with hinged lid and etching of a nude *fraulein* in the bottom that you could see only after drinking all the beer in the stein. I also received a lacquered wooden plate with the insignia of the COC and with a good luck inscription around the edge.

One of my well-wishers was Abe Ashkenasi, whom I had first met at Columbia University in 1956 when he was working on his Ph.D. and I on my master's. It was Abe who had urged me to follow his example by reading "a book a day" in doing research for my thesis, just as he was doing for his dissertation. He was a Jew whose family had suffered Nazi atrocities in their native Germany. We had become good friends at Ramstein and I was pleased to hear him salute me at a farewell party, raising a glass of wine in a toast to my health and future with the word, "*Lehayim!*"

Another of my well-wishers, a Colonel Taylor, who had been in an Air Force ROTC assignment in the past, teased me with a parting shot: "You know, Chuck, you'll know you're over the hill when you're strolling across the campus, thinking you're still relatively young, still 'hot stuff,' and you overhear some cute young coed say about you, 'Who is that distinguished OLD gentleman over there?'"

That did it! It was time to go. Time to say *auf Wiedersehen!*

With a hop from Ramstein to the Rhein-Main airport, at Frankfort, then a quick dinner in the airport snack bar before boarding a MATS "Connie" (Lockheed Constellation transport plane), I was on my way back home to the USA.

16 Auf Wiedersehen!

»   May 1959–January 1962

It was well after sundown before the Connie lifted off from Rhein-Main's runway, which was glistening with puddles of rain falling steadily but gently from a low overcast. A twenty-minute or so climb brought us through the tops of the clouds into a world of a full moon and twinkling stars as the pilot headed west toward his refueling stop in the Azores.

I had had a long day clearing Ramstein, riding up to Frankfort, and sweating out being manifested on "anything smoking" heading west. I was bushed, and having "monitored" the pilot's climb out of the clouds, I was glad to settle down into the comfortable, cushioned reclining seat, smiling to myself at my fighter pilot's syndrome: the lingering unease whenever in an airplane being flown by someone else. There was no doubt in my mind whatsoever that the pilots up front knew what they were doing and were as competent as any pilots anywhere because, after all, they were MATS (Military Air Transport Service) pilots and had to meet the highest standards in frequent proficiency flight checks. Nevertheless, I breathed easier when we broke out on top of the overcast into the moonlit night.

For the first hour or so I looked out the window watching the shadow of Connie racing along the top of the clouds below and pondered what I had accomplished during the third overseas tour of my eighteen-year career in the air force. My mind totted up the score: Apparently, I had done a creditable job with my duties at the Combat Operations Center—the effectiveness report that my boss, recently promoted Lieutenant Colonel Jim Truscott, had written on my performance attested to that; I had visited twelve major cities in nine countries; had added 253 hours of flying time as a command pilot, much of it in actual weather; had taken courses in typing and speed reading offered by the I & E (information and education) office at Ramstein when I learned that I was going to be assigned to teach on a college campus. Also, in order to gain some teaching experience OJT (on-the-job training), I had taught courses in U.S. military history to off-duty GIs who enrolled in the University of Maryland extension program at Ramstein Air Base.

And, most cherished of my memories of my tour in Germany were the friendships, some new, some renewed, that I had enjoyed. A group of noncommissioned officers and enlisted men and women had made an impact on my life. All African Americans, they were in their early twenties and, relative to my thirty-seven years, were almost just kids. But they were mature for their age and competent on their jobs. They took to treating me as a big brother, sometimes seeking my advice about some problem on their job, sometimes sharing the humor, or anger, of some ironic experience that had stemmed from an encounter with Jim Crow, American style, that some "cracker" had imported from the States. Within the group were a couple of couples who were dating and were serious about their future lives together. Ben Dotson and Marguerite Davis were talking seriously about getting married. And before I left Ramstein I had the honor of standing in as the father of Irene Danzy, "giving her away" as she married Al Augustine. She was from Detroit, he was from New Orleans, and I was deeply moved at their invitation to be a part of their wedding party. Ann Barr and Marianna "Tweety Bird" Crabtree, both members of the WAF Squadron at Ramstein, were bridesmaids, and I remember how closely knit all of the group were as they stuck together to "make it" in a foreign land.

With such fond memories of the past I drifted off to sleep. It was still dark when I awakened as the Connie landed at Lajes Field, the Azores. By the time we passengers had gotten off to stretch our legs, sniff the fresh air, and grab a snack in the flight line snack bar, the sun had begun to peek over the horizon. We took off into a brightening dawn and clear skies. Refreshed by the sleep and ener-gized by the light breakfast, I resumed my musings but in a differ-ent direction. Last night I was preoccupied with the past. Today my thoughts were full of what the future held for me in this final as-signment of my military career.

I had been on active duty for just two months shy of eighteen years. My original goal at the start of my career had been to re-main on active duty for thirty years or more. However, the general court-martial on my record that stemmed from my reaction to the stresses of Jim Crow at Selfridge Field and Walterboro AAB, four-teen years earlier, ruled out any hopes I had about obtaining a Regular Air Force commission and a long-term career. Indeed, all through the ensuing years I had considered myself lucky to survive the RIFS (reductions in force) that hit the armed forces every now and then, due to budget cuts, and hoped that I would at least be able to remain in uniform for twenty years, then retire.

With that revised game plan in mind, this next assignment to an Air Force ROTC unit would be my last before retirement. I was really delighted at the prospect of ending my military career in the civilian environment of a college campus. I reasoned that I would acquire some teaching ability, which might be salable in the job market. Moreover, I would be able to take some courses in business administration that should help equip me for a career in industry. And, also important, by being stationed in the nation's capital I would get to meet key people in government, in industry, and in academia.

Perhaps the thing that provided the "icing on the cake" was the fact that my boss at Howard was going to be Lieutenant Colonel Thomas J. Money—the same Tom Money who had been "through the mill" at Tuskegee and who had been in the personnel director-ate at the Pentagon when I was ready for rotation back to the States from Korea in 1952. I had requested assignment to a base close to my home in East Orange, New Jersey, and he had made the arrange-ments for my assignment to Mitchel Field.

With all of these pluses in mind, I couldn't wait to start my new duties at Howard University. But first there was the pleasant task of reunion with my family and spending a ten-day leave at home with Pete, Thumper, Sister Vie, and Brother Rob. They were all living in the three-story home to which Pete and I had mortgaged ourselves back in 1953, while I was stationed at Mitchel Field. Also living under the same roof at 228 North Oraton Parkway was my sister, Pauline, my brother-in-law, Arthur Miles, and their daughter, Wendi, a pretty toddler. Each family unit occupied a separate apartment on one of the three floors. So I was blessed to be living under the same roof with many of the people I loved most in all the world.

Mother Pearl, Pete's mother, had her own apartment in a senior citizens' high-rise apartment house in Newark. We visited her, as well as many kinfolk and friends whom I had missed while away in Germany. The week of visits and "welcome home, Charlie!" parties passed swiftly and before I knew it I was on my way to Washington, D.C., to begin the home stretch of my career. Thumper, almost a teenager and attending junior high school, could not go with me as the spring term still had a few weeks to go before the summer vacation. Pete, more busy than ever at Riverton Laboratories, would not go because of the workload there. So off I went alone to a new assignment, a new station. Alone. Again!

While at home I had received a notice to pick up my Taunus at the dock in Brooklyn where automobiles shipped from overseas to the East Coast were held until their owners claimed them. The Taunus had traveled well and arrived in mint condition. And it ran like a sewing machine, smooth as silk, on the four-hour drive to Washington.

During my first week in D.C. I lived in the BOQ at Bolling Field, commuting from there to the Howard University campus. When I reported for duty I met Colonel Money again, ten years after we all had left Lockbourne. I was glad to see him and two other "auld acquaintances" from the Tuskegee Experiment who were on his staff: Major Clarence "Lucky" Lester and Captain Clarence L. Shivers.

New acquaintances were Captains Dayton Ragland and Eugene Terry and three noncommissioned officers: Master Sergeant Matthews (topkick of the detachment), Tech Sergeant Stinnett (administrative chief), and Staff Sergeant Harley (supply sergeant).

Harley had the monumental task of keeping the 300- to 400-man cadet corps outfitted with the proper uniforms and equipment during the fall semester, then retrieving everything after the school year ended in June, and having uniforms cleaned and repaired as necessary in time to issue all items again in September. The civilian secretary of the Air Force ROTC Detachment 130 was Mrs. Clyde Woolridge, who was one of the fastest typists I had ever seen in action on the typewriter and who, as one of the nation's leading contract bridge players, had so many master points that she had stopped counting them as she topped the field in many bridge tournaments around the country.

That was the competent staff that was turning out trained air force officers, from raw college freshmen, over a period of four years.

To begin my orientation briefing on the role of the air force detachment on campus, how—as a unit of Air University Command—it went about training air force officers, and how I would fit into the staff, Colonel Money interviewed me, one on one, in his office. He had already looked through my 201 file (personnel records) to get up to date on my past duty assignments and how I had performed in them. Thus there was no need to ask me a lot of questions about myself.

Instead, after greeting me with, "Hi, Major Dryden, welcome aboard. We're glad to have you here," he asked: "You've just come back from Ramstein where General Davis is, right? How is he?"

"Doin' fine, Colonel. As I was leaving, spratmo had it that he was up for his second star. Know anything about that?"

"Yeah, we've been hearing the same rumor here in Washington, and it is quite likely true. I hope it is because he certainly deserves it."

"I hope so, too," I agreed.

"Well, Dryden, let's talk about your assignment here. What do you know about Air Force ROTC programs and what do you want to know?"

"Very little, in answer to your first question, Colonel, and everything, in answer to your second."

"No need for you to worry about lack of knowledge about the

ROTC program in general and what we do here because you will be going to the Air University at Maxwell Field, in Alabama, in a couple weeks to take the six-week Academic Instructor Course [AIC]. There you will be taught how to teach and prepare lesson plans and examinations. Your instructors will be officers and noncoms who have taught ROTC classes before. From them you will learn various techniques of teaching, including the 'do's' and 'don'ts' of teaching.

"As for your duties here, I have you slotted to teach sophomores this fall semester after you have completed the AIC. Depending on the number of last year's freshmen who return for their sophomore year, you will likely have two full classes, about thirty cadets each, to deal with. And I might add, because sophomores are traditionally the 'know-it-alls' of college campuses, you'll have your hands full conducting two class sessions per week for each group.

"In addition to classroom instruction and keeping records to track each of your cadets' progress, you will join me and the rest of the staff in supervising the cadet officers as they conduct drill and parades every Thursday afternoon, from 1300 to 1600. Major Lester is the commandant of cadets for our detachment and he has molded our corps of cadets into one of the finest in the United States. Because he is a flying officer and I am not, I will leave your briefing about flying activities here in the Washington area to him. I'll just say that I hope you still love to fly as much as you did back at Lockbourne because you will get a lot of flying time taking the cadets on orientation flights and field trips to other air force bases. Do you have any questions about what I have said so far?"

"No, Sir. But I am wondering about how we, as military personnel, relate to the civilian college faculty. And where do we fit into the college hierarchy?"

"Tactfully, in answer to your first question, and as assistant professors of air science, in answer to the second. For the most part your direction in academic matters, for what and how to teach your cadets, will come to you through the usual channels, that is, from the Air University through me. In addition to my direct connection to the Air University, I have a sort of adjunct linkage with Howard University. As head of this department I am accorded the status of professor of air science [PAS] with a staff of assistant professors of air science, like you and the others."

"Begging your pardon, Sir," I interrupted. "How do we relate to the university faculty and administration? By that I mean, how much contact do we have with them?"

"You have read my mind, Dryden. I was coming to that. You won't have a whole lot of contact, officially. Oh, you will be expected to attend the monthly faculty meetings and, of course, convocation ceremony at the beginning of the school year and graduation at the end. Other than that, how much you become involved in the university's activities is strictly up to you. And, of course, as a member of the faculty you can take courses free of charge. Now, to get you off on the right foot I have made an appointment with the university president, Dr. Mordecai Johnson, to introduce you to him. We'll do that after lunch. Do you have any more questions at this time?"

"A few, Colonel, but they're nuts and bolts kinds of questions and I figure I'll get the answers at the Academic Instructor Course at Maxwell, so I'll make a list of them and check them out when I get there."

"Fair enough. Well, then, let me call in the rest of the staff and introduce you formally."

We left his office and repaired to the conference room. Within minutes the staff filed in, took seats around the conference table, and looked me over. Colonel Money began with, "Lady and Gentlemen, I want you to meet the new addition to our detachment staff, Major Charles Dryden, just back from a tour in Germany. He was at Ramstein Air Base where our former commanding officer, General Davis, is now stationed. Major Dryden is one of the original pilots of the 99th Fighter Squadron who went overseas to North Africa with General Davis back in 1943. He will be going to Maxwell in a couple weeks to attend the Academic Instructor Course, at the same time that Captain Ragland is scheduled to go. So," he continued, looking at Ragland, then at me, "maybe you men will want to travel together. In any case, let's go around the table and introduce ourselves to Major Charlie Dryden."

"Correction, Colonel," I interrupted. "I picked up a nickname in Korea. I now answer to 'Chuck.'"

"OK, Major, Chuck it is, from now on."

As the rest of the staff members introduced themselves, I gathered some tidbits of information about my colleagues: Major Clarence Lester was, of course, the "Lucky" Lester who had shot down three German fighters within five minutes as a Red Tail, member of the 332nd Fighter Group in Italy during World War II—he was the senior cadets' instructor as well as the commandant of cadets; Captain Dayton Ragland, the freshmen's instructor, had flown F-86s in the Korean War; Captain Clarence Shivers, the sophomores' instructor, had also been a Red Tail during WWII and was an accomplished artist—his murals of aviation scenes lined the walls of the conference room; Captain Eugene Terry, instructor of the juniors, was a jet pilot with *beaucoup* hours in the F-100. As the PAS (professor of air science), and head of the Department of Air Science, Colonel Money had a full slate of tasks to do, however he often pitched in to help out with teaching the senior cadets.

The next step in my orientation was a visit to the office of Howard University's president, Dr. Mordecai Johnson. Dr. Johnson was a world-renowned educator whom I had always admired in a manner similar to the way I had admired Dr. George Washington Carver in my youth. Upon meeting Dr. Johnson I was thrilled as I had been upon meeting Dr. Carver and felt privileged to have an opportunity to teach classes on the university campus.

Colonel Money began the formal introduction with: "Dr. Johnson, I'm pleased to present to you Major Charles W. Dryden, who has joined my staff at the Air Force ROTC Detachment. Major Dryden was one of the original members of the 99th Fighter Squadron who went overseas with General Benjamin O. Davis, Jr., and has just returned from Germany where he served again on General Davis's staff."

Extending his hand in greeting and with a firm handshake, Dr. Johnson said: "Welcome to Howard, Major Dryden. From what we have heard and read about you, we are pleased to have you join us at the university. We have a unique challenge here to educate students, some of whom come to us from not-so-strong backgrounds, and graduate them four years later fully qualified in their chosen fields. We are proud of the success that our faculty has had in turning out outstanding graduates in the past, and we look forward to your helping us to continue doing so."

Although some acquaintances had warned me that Dr. Johnson was a formidable figure, I found him to be gracious, and I was grateful for his cordial welcome.

Next on my introduction to the powers-that-be at Howard was Dr. Frank Snowden, dean of the College of Liberal Arts, of which the Air Force and Army ROTC Departments were a part. He, too, was gracious in his welcome, making me feel at ease in my new, civilian/quasi-military environment.

Finally, winding up the rounds of introductions, Colonel Money took me to the Army ROTC office where I met his U.S. Army counterpart, Lieutenant Colonel Hyman Y. Chase. Gruff and rough on his own staff of officers and noncoms and on his cadets, Colonel Chase was cordial enough with me and assured me that he would be glad to provide any information I might need about the army program. "All you have to do is ask," he said.

"Thank you, Colonel. After I return from the Air University in July I'll take you up on that offer."

I had arrived at Howard just a few days before graduation ceremonies and marched with the faculty in the grand procession. I was pleased to be rubbing shoulders with so many scholars clad in their academic robes, each with a stole draped over the shoulder made in a color distinctive of his or her alma mater, most with a mortar board for a hat, some with a soft pillow-type hat, all with a stride of pride—at least that is how I perceived them.

One professor in particular caught my eye. Not only because he was tall and stocky, a veritable "bear" of a man. Nor because his hair was carrot colored and his fair complexion was sprinkled with freckles. But because he looked vaguely familiar. Small wonder. He was Oliver "Red" Morse, one of the guys with whom I had grown up in the Bronx. Back then he was a skinny kid, "a string bean," who, like most of us in the neighborhood, had dreams and ambitions but were doubtful that "White folks" would ever allow us to reach the heights we dreamed of achieving.

When I approached him to ask, "Don't I know you?" he exclaimed, before I could get my words out, "Charlie Dryden, you old rascal, what are you doing here?"

"I've just checked into the Air Force ROTC Department a couple days ago, after eighteen months in Germany. When I saw you in the procession I recognized your face and hair but you're not the same skinny 'Red' Morse that I knew back on Union Avenue and 166th Street. Tell me, what are you doing here at Howard?"

"Yeah, Charlie, I've changed a bit with many more pounds here and there, and I have been here at Howard on the Law School faculty for several years now."

"Sure is good to see you, Red, after all these years—how many years since we last saw each other? It must be almost twenty, because I left the Bronx to go to Tuskegee in '41 and here it is '59. We'll have to get together and compare notes about what's been happening to each other in all the years since then."

"Sure thing," Red said. And our paths did cross often after that, in faculty meetings and various ceremonies.

Meanwhile my orders came through for me to proceed to the Air University at Maxwell Field, on the outskirts of Montgomery, Alabama, the self-proclaimed "Cradle of the Confederacy." Captain Ragland also received orders to attend the six-week Academic Instructor Course (AIC) from May 31 to July 14. Because I had been a student at the Air University back in 1952 when I took the Associate Intelligence Course, I knew something about the base and the school setup there. However, some things had changed radically in the seven years since then.

First and foremost, in 1954 the momentous U.S. Supreme Court decision in the case of *Brown v. Topeka Board of Education* declared that "in the field of public education the doctrine of 'separate but equal' has no place." This benchmark decision sounded the death knell of other forms of discrimination in American society. The following year, Rosa Parks refused to give up her seat to a White man in a public bus in Montgomery and move to the "Colored" section in the back of the bus as ordered by the bus driver.

Thus was born the bus boycott by Montgomery's Black citizens that lasted for a year and so diminished the bus company's profits that it was about to go bankrupt. However, in November 1956 the federal courts ordered the end of segregation on the Montgomery bus line. Actions like these by the U.S. Supreme Court justices heralded the beginning of the end of de jure discrimination in the nation. Sadly, however, de facto injustices were still alive and well as a number of incidents across the country demonstrated that Jim Crow was not dead by any means. It was just such a social and political climate into which Captain Ragland and I plunged as we headed south to Maxwell Air Force Base in late May 1959.

For the sake of the convenience of having a car available during the six weeks of TDY at the Academic Instructor Course, we each decided to drive our own car. For the sake of personal safety during the long drive through the possibly hostile southland, we agreed to make the trip in convoy fashion, thus providing mutual support, very much in the manner that leaders and wingmen support each other in aerial combat. Once on the road we took turns leading. And, as we had agreed when planning the trip, whoever was leading would observe speed limits strictly, especially when approaching towns. From past experiences we had learned that as the speed limits decreased progressively, in 10-mph increments, from highway speed limits to the limit in local country towns, oftentimes a local policeman in a squad car would be lurking near one of the lower speed limit signs, waiting to pounce on the hapless driver who didn't slow down fast enough. Many towns were notorious for their "speed traps" in which, if caught exceeding the posted speed limit, the motorist would be hauled before the local justice of the peace (JP) and fined whatever the JP thought the traffic would bear. Failure to pay cash on the spot meant doing time in the local pokey—or, as in some extreme cases that had happened in the past, doing time on a chain gang.

Needless to say "Rags" (Captain Ragland) and I were careful to avoid being "speed trapped." We had planned the trip carefully. Figuring that the trip of more than 800 miles would take fourteen hours to reach Maxwell Field, we decided to leave Washington, D.C., at dawn and drive all the way to Greenville, South Carolina, passing up Charlotte, North Carolina, the halfway point, to RON and get some sleep. Although that meant nine hours behind the wheel, we preferred remaining overnight in Greenville because Donaldson Air Force Base was located nearby and we figured on getting two rooms in the Transient Officers Quarters. By leaving D.C. at 0800 and allowing an hour for pit stops (to refuel and for rest room visits) our ETA (estimated time of arrival) at Donaldson AFB would be 1800, a couple hours before nightfall.

We made good on our ETA when we drove through the main gate at Donaldson at just after 1830 hours. Bushed after more than nine hours of driving in the hot sun, we wished for nothing more than a sack to flop into after a shower and a hot meal—we had been surviving on sandwiches and soda all day to avoid Jim Crow at restaurants in country towns along the way. Our hopes were dashed at the billeting office where the sergeant on duty at the desk asked, "Do you have a reservation, Major?"

"No, Sergeant," I replied, "but Captain Ragland and I are passing through on TDY orders, from Washington, D.C., to Maxwell, and we need to RON here and rest up for the last five hours' drive to Maxwell tomorrow."

"Well, I'm sorry, Major, but all of the rooms are booked and there are no vacancies now and for the next three days. Y' see, Sir, we've got a command-wide exercise starting tomorrow and there are aircrews that are staging out of Donaldson. Some are already here, others are due in tonight. So I really have nothing available, Sir. I'm sorry."

The sergeant was properly respectful but I had a sense that even if what he had said were true, he was gloating over his opportunity to deny us Black officers something we needed and had requested. So I asked to use the base telephone and called the officer of the day. When the OD came to the billeting office I told him of our situation and requested his assistance in finding us a bed somewhere on Donaldson to spend the night and get some sleep. His suggestion was that we go into Greenville and check into a hotel.

Hearing that, I thought: "I am not about to try to get a hotel room in Greenville, South Carolina, of all places. I remember too well that it was at Pickens, just a mere twenty miles or so west of

Greenville, that back in about 1946 while we were all still at Lock-bourne, a Black sailor had his eyes gouged out by a local police-man who used the end of a billy club. I learned about it from a Sunday afternoon broadcast by Orson Welles who bought radio time to discuss social issues and trumpet the needs for action by the citizenry. Orson Welles had described how the Black sailor, Isaac Woodard, in uniform, while riding in a seat near the front of a bus in Pickens, was told by the driver to get up and move to a seat in the rear. Woodard refused. A short while later the driver stopped the bus next to a policeman walking his beat, hailed the cop, and told him about the 'uppity nigger' who refused to move to the back. Whereupon, Orson Welles related, the policeman boarded the bus and ordered Woodard to get off the bus. As Woodard was going down the steps of the bus the policeman hit him a sharp blow to the head, knocking him to the ground. And while Woodard lay there semiconscious, the policeman gouged out his eyeballs! Orson Welles expressed his outrage at the atrocity, which had little notice in the newspapers, and vowed over the airwaves, 'I don't know who the culprit is but I will find you out and expose you.' I remember that Orson Welles did discover the identity of the policeman, but as far as I know nothing was ever done to prosecute or punish him. However, with that 'intelligence information' about that part of the country, I am not going to run the risk of encountering such a thug. No way!" Those were my thoughts.

Responding to the OD's suggestion about checking into a hotel in Greenville, I countered with: "I tell you what, Captain. As fa-tigued as we are after driving almost half a day, we would be acci-dents waiting to happen if we go back on the road without some sleep. Furthermore, we are so tired that we are really ill, so I would appreciate it if you would call the base hospital to send an ambu-lance over here to take us to the emergency ward so we can go on sick call."

The OD blanched. I guessed that he was thinking of what the base commander and the base hospital commander would say if they were disturbed on a Saturday night to deal with a request such as ours. In any case, the OD had a hurried, whispered conference with the sergeant desk clerk, who announced: "Major, we can put both you and Captain up in a general officers' VIP suite. One of the generals that we were expecting to check in yesterday has not shown up yet, so we can let you use that suite. Is that OK, Sir?"

"That's just fine, Sergeant," I said. "Thank you for solving your problem." Turning to the OD, I said, "And thank you, too, Captain, for your help."

The VIP suite was very comfortable. Rags and I showered and had dinner at the officers club, where we noted that the dining room was crowded with pilots in flight suits, apparently the air-crews involved in the exercise that the sergeant in the billeting office had spoken about. We hit the sack early in order to get an early start on the final, five-hour leg to Maxwell.

Bright and early Sunday morning we hit the road. The rest of the trip was uneventful except that we stopped in Tuskegee, which was right on our route, to have lunch and allow me time to see some old friends there. Finally, late Sunday night we rolled through the main gate of Maxwell Field. Mission accomplished! We had run the gauntlet through the southland without accident or incident. I silently thanked God for safe passage throughout the journey.

Monday morning, when we reported to the AIC administrative office, Captain Ragland and I were assigned to different cubicles and instructors. Each instructor was assigned to a specific class-room ("cubicle") in the school building with a group of eight to ten students, all of whom were in training to be Air Force ROTC in-structors at various colleges and universities across the country.

During the six weeks we learned techniques of different teaching methods: straight lecture; demonstration-performance; seminar; with or without visual aids. We were also required to teach a les-son on any subject of our choice using one of the techniques. We learned tips about public speaking as well; with my years of expe-rience giving intelligence briefings, using the techniques I had learned seven years before, right there at the Air University, I had an easy time of it in the classroom sessions.

To maintain our flying proficiency while at Maxwell, all the rated officers were assigned to base operations, where we were checked out in the two kinds of airplanes available: C-47 "Goony Birds" and C-45 "Twin Beeches." Because my Form 5 showed hundreds of hours in each type, I had no trouble at all putting my IP status to good use by flying navigation cross-country flights almost every weekend.

The six weeks sped by so fast that I had precious little time to enjoy the social life among Montgomery's Black citizens. However, there was one couple I was bound and determined to visit: "Rich" Harris and his wife Vera, the couple for whom Pete and I had served as best man and matron of honor when they married in Louisville back in 1945. After leaving active duty at the end of World War II, "Rich" had gotten a degree in pharmacy at Xavier University in New Orleans in order to take over Dean's Drugstore, which his father had established many years before. So now, to all his faithful, admiring customers, he was "Doc."

"Doc" Harris was one of the most amiable persons I had ever known—almost always smiling pleasantly, unflappable, and a perfectionist. And a champion of civil rights actions. In fact, during the Montgomery bus boycott, Dean's Drugstore was one of the pickup points where the boycotters assembled to board the private cars and station wagons to go to and from work. Doc Harris was a highly respected and a much loved man, and his "Miz Vera" was a charming lady from Charleston, South Carolina.

As we spent several hours reminiscing about old times, Doc asked me where my last assignment was before going to Howard University. I told him that I was fresh from Germany, where I had the pleasure of serving under "the Old Man" who was a brigadier when I left Ramstein Air Base. "However, Doc," I said, "when I arrived at Maxwell I learned that he's now wearing two stars—he was promoted to major general on May 22nd."

"Gee, Charlie, that's great! B.O. is the first of our race to reach that rank. F-a-n-t-a-s-t-i-c!"

"Yeah, Doc, I whooped and hollered when I heard the news, too."

That news, like a pebble dropped in a pool of water, had a widening effect beyond the circle in which General Davis moved. At least I can attest to my experience in which fellow officers paid respect to "our general" with complimentary remarks about what a "helluva officer" they had heard he was. Some of the White AIC instructors had served under him in other assignments, and they described him as "a perfectionist and tough, but fair, disciplinarian." I said "Amen!" to that.

Perhaps it was General Davis's achievement, widely publicized in the *Air Force Times*, or perhaps the reputation of the Red Tails wrought in WWII combat and becoming more widely known among air force veterans of the great war, or yet perhaps it was the trauma that Montgomery had suffered during the bus boycott— whatever the real reason, I found the social climate on the base, to a far greater extent than in town, to be more relaxed, less tense, less charged with hostility than when I was there in 1952 attending the Intelligence Officers Course. There seemed to be more genuine camaraderie among the officer students when celebrating "happy hour" at the O Club, the White officers inviting, nay insisting, that we Black officers join them in round after round of "liar's dice" or "horses" and "chug-a-lugs" at the bar.

I had hoped things would be somewhat changed for the better because, after all, integration of African Americans into the armed forces at large was only a four-year-old toddler then. By now, at ten years old, integration should be commonplace, and it was pretty much so on the base. However, I still could not stay at the Jefferson Davis Hotel in the vaunted "Cradle of the Confederacy," even if I had wanted to, which I didn't! Indeed, the White natives were so hostile that they had bombed the Reverend Martin Luther King Jr.'s home on South Jackson Street just a few doors from the home of my friends, Doc and Vera Harris, on December 23, 1956, two days after Montgomery's buses were desegregated. Scary though that was, my gutsy friends had no thought of moving away. They and their civil rights comrades all over Montgomery were determined, more than ever, that "We shall not be, we shall not be moved!"

Swiftly our six weeks came and went and Captain Ragland and I, through with the Air University, moved on up the road without incident to Washington, D.C., back to duty at Howard University. It was only mid-July and there were no cadet classes during summer school, so both of the ROTC staffs, air force and army, were busily getting ready for the fall semester. My first task was to shadow Major Clarence "Lucky" Lester as he set up procedures for registration of all the cadets in the various classes they were required to take, especially the juniors and seniors whose successful completion of the four-year curriculum would earn a commission as a second lieutenant. There was no "luck" to Major Lester's smooth operation when registration day arrived. It was the result of excellent planning and hard work by all hands of the detachment staff, and I learned a lot from him as he earned my respect for his administrative ability—I already knew he was a helluva fighter pilot from his three aerial victories in less than five minutes during the war!

In the few weeks remaining before the cadets began arriving to begin the fall semester, "Lucky" drove me out to Bolling Field to introduce me to the base operations people and get me started on checking out the C-47s that were available for all the legions of pilots assigned to units in the D.C. area: in offices of the Department of the Air Force, some located in the Pentagon, others scattered around the city; in Air Force ROTC Detachments like ours at Howard—for example, at the University of Maryland and at Georgetown University. There was a lot of demand for the airplanes and, therefore, I again found that my IP rating gave me a leg up on other pilots who, although many were command pilots, not as many were instructor pilots. Thus, being able to log every hour that I flew, without having to split the time with other pilots on a flight, I was able to accumulate flying time rapidly.

Another pleasantry about flying out of Bolling Field was the fact that, in addition to having the good old Goony Birds available for taking thirty or so cadets on field trips, there were Cessna U-3A type airplanes on the flight line for use in orientation flights for three cadets at a time. The sleek aircraft with a tricycle landing gear was a four-seater set up for flight by one pilot—no copilot necessary. However, the cabin was so cramped that there wasn't enough room for seat-pack parachutes. Instead we used backpacks, which allowed enough room for medium-size occupants to sit in the cabin but, I wondered, "How difficult would it be to get out of it to bail out if necessary?"

Fortunately I never had to learn the answer to that question. The

"Blue Birds," as the U-3As with their air force–blue paint jobs came to be nicknamed, were very reliable airplanes that never gave me any reason to think about bailing out. I really enjoyed flying the "Blue Birds." And so did the cadets, who got a kick out of handling the controls and discovering that flying was fun. Of all the hundreds I flew on orientation flights only one became airsick in the U-3A: that happened when I allowed one of the other cadets to make some turns and he got into a steep spiral. The hapless cadet, sitting on the back seat, upchucked. He used his flight cap, the only receptacle available, to hold his vomit. I returned to Bolling Field immediately to land and let him out of his misery—and to air out the cabin! Poor guy—the other cadets ribbed him mercilessly.

Besides introducing me to the operations folks out at Bolling Field to get me squared away with my flying activities, "Lucky" also introduced me to an older couple who sort of "adopted" me and provided me room and board during my tour of duty in D.C. inasmuch as my family was not going to move from New Jersey. They were Mr. and Mrs. "Sonny" Gray, mother and stepfather of another Tuskegee Airman, my good friend Major Chuck Cooper. At that time Chuck was an air force test pilot with Republic Aircraft Corporation at Farmingdale, Long Island, on the outskirts of New York City. His folks really made me feel at home in their comfortable home located a mere fifteen-minute drive from the university. With a comfy place to lay my head during my weekdays in Washington and a convenient base from which to spread my wings, I was all set to start earning my living as a college professor.

As he had briefed me at the outset, Colonel Money assigned me to teach two classes of sophomores, a total of about sixty students, almost all of them, as he had forewarned me, "know-it-alls." However, by using some of the techniques I had learned in the Academic Instructor Course, plus some advice from Captain Shivers, who had been teaching sophomores, I was able to weather the first skirmishes with each of my two groups of mavericks and convince them that I wasn't a complete dunderhead as some freshmen-cum-sophomores seem inclined to think about all teachers.

My weeks, during the three months of the fall semester, were hectic what with teaching classes to my two groups, flying a couple afternoons, and helping supervise the cadet corps activities and close-order drill in the university stadium on Thursday afternoons. By the end of the Monday to Friday routine, I was ready to declare TGIF (thank God it's Friday)!

More often than not I spent my weekends, for the first three months, in Washington preparing lesson plans for the coming week in order to stay at least two lessons ahead of my students. On those weekends that I felt caught up enough to go home to East Orange, I either drove the four-hour trip or caught Pennsylvania Railroad's Congressional Express, nicknamed "the Congo," which made the run to Newark in three hours. Those six hours of the round trip on the train gave me a chance to work on lesson plans and keep abreast of world events by reading news magazines—*Newsweek* and *Time*—from cover to cover.

By the time of the Christmas break I felt caught up enough to begin exploring the nation's capital. I was still leery of the natives— the White ones; still haunted by my experience the day that Harry Truman was inaugurated and I was told by the soda fountain attendant on Georgia Avenue, "We don't serve niggers in here!"

An old friend from my boyhood days on Sugar Hill in Manhattan, Teddy Richardson, was in Washington where he was employed in some government agency. I looked him up and we reminisced at length about "the good old days" on Saint Nicholas Place. He took me to visit his aunt, Mrs. Maxine Dargans Fleming, who was a sort of "major domo" to Congressman Adam Clayton Powell. Maxine had been like a big sister to Teddy and his buddies as we were growing up. I hadn't seen her since leaving New York to begin flight training at Tuskegee, almost twenty years before! I was delighted to see her and to meet her husband, Bob. And I had the privilege of meeting Congressman Powell in his office as well. "Adam," as the people liked to call him, was very cordial and hospitable, and I was impressed by the deference that people accorded him.

With classes suspended during the Christmas break, I spent about three weeks at home with my family. It was a welcome respite from the routine at the university. More important, the time was ripe for Pete to give birth to our second son. Great with child though she was, we went to a formal affair during the Christmas holidays: Pete danced and danced in hopes of inducing labor and birthing a child during the holy season—as well as an income tax exemption for 1959.

It didn't work. Keith Cameron Dryden waited until January 6 to make his appearance. We were delighted to have a second son, a healthy six pounds, seven ounces, born just over thirteen years after Charles, Jr. And, as speculated by my former boss in Germany, Jim Truscott, when I wrote him about our good news, Keith was born "exactly nine months and one minute after my return to the States!" Pete and I chuckled at Jim's wise-guy remark in his congratulations card.

Keith's birth was a great way to begin the new year. When classes resumed about mid-January I returned to Howard with new vim and vigor. The spring semester started out "business as usual" with classes, ROTC drill on Thursdays, and flying frequently. Until February 1. That day, in Greensboro, North Carolina, four Black students of North Carolina A&T College took seats at the lunch counter at a Woolworth's store, defying Jim Crow segregationist practices of the southland. Ignored by the store attendants and physically attacked by local bullies, the students were joined in the following few days by friends from the college. As the news of the "sit-in" raced throughout the country, the A&T students were joined by Black students from other colleges. One such "outsider" was one of my sophomores, a Mister Diamond, who turned up absent from class. When he returned a few days later and described his experiences in Greensboro, he was saluted for his courage by his classmates in the cadet corps, and his absences were forgiven.

Classroom teaching became easier for me as time went on and I got well ahead of the curriculum in preparing lesson plans. I was beginning really to enjoy teaching as I realized how much new knowledge I was acquiring by the process of preparing to teach others. And, perhaps, the greatest reward was the evidence that the young sophomores of my classes were beginning to show signs of maturing.

Flying activities for the sophomores were expanded to include more field trips to distant bases in the C-47s than local orientation rides in the U-3As. By exposing the cadets in the basic Air Force

ROTC classes (freshmen and sophomores) to other air force bases, it was expected that many would be encouraged to apply for the advanced ROTC classes that would lead to a commission as a second lieutenant in the U.S. Air Force upon graduation. Also, such flights provided opportunities to enhance their interest in becoming pilots by demonstrating in flight some of the things taught them in the classroom. For example, FAA regulations prescribe the NE-ODD and SW-EVEN rules for the proper altitudes for flight in VFR (visual flight rules) conditions. That means that when flying on headings that are generally toward the north or east you must fly at an altitude of odd thousands of feet; when flying toward the south or west you must fly at an altitude of even thousands of feet. So, after seeing this done in actual flight, the cadets had a better idea of what was meant by the terms NE-ODD and SW-EVEN in the jargon of pilots.

The Air Force ROTC cadet corps was organized along similar lines to active-duty fighter groups with a group headquarters and three squadrons. Rank-wise, the cadet group commander was a cadet colonel and each squadron commander was a cadet major with staff officers of the ranks of cadet captains and first and second lieutenants. All of the cadet officers were in their junior or senior year.

Because I was teaching sophomores I did not have day-to-day contact with the cadet officers. However, I was much impressed with Cadet Colonel Willis Brown, group commander of the class of 1960. His attitude, bearing and leadership made him a standout, impressed everyone, and are worthy of mention. He also completed the Flight Indoctrination Program (FIP) that was open only to seniors. FIP included ground school classes in theory of flight, aircraft engines, meteorology, aerial navigation, and FAA regulations, as well as several hours of actual flying instruction—enough to earn a private pilot license. Upon graduation Cadet Colonel Willis Brown was commissioned Second Lieutenant Willis Brown, United States Air Force, and was awarded a baccalaureate degree for his four years of study at Howard University. Although I had not had close contact with him and his classmates, I nevertheless was proud

Lt. Col. Charles W. Dryden,
United States Air Force.

of him as a product of our AFROTC Detachment and joined everyone in wishing him well as he began active duty with the air force.

In the fall semester of 1960 my teaching assignment was changed from sophomores to seniors. The main subject, geopolitics, was right down my alley as my formal education in political science and knowledge gained in assignments as an intelligence officer helped me to prepare lesson plans and teach the subject matter. Working with seniors on a day-to-day basis was also a pleasure, especially as their leadership abilities developed with each passing week of the school year.

"My protégés" included the cadet group commander, Cadet Colonel O. B. Young, plus a staff of cadet officers of various ranks including: Klein Price, Milton White, and Ricardo Youngblood. There were others whose names have faded from memory with the years, but all were good role models for the corps of cadets. And all had "cut the mustard" at summer camp where, between the end of their junior and the start of their senior years, every advanced AFROTC cadet endured the rigors of a "boot camp" type of training at some military post. At least three of "my protégés" are commercial airline captains as this is being written: Woody Fountain, O. B. Young, and Ricardo Youngblood. And one, Rodney Coleman, was appointed assistant secretary of the air force by President Bill Clinton in 1994!

At the convocation ceremony beginning the fall 1960 semester a new president of the university made his appearance: Dr. Mordecai Johnson had retired after thirty-four years as Howard's illustrious leader and was succeeded by Dr. James H. Nabritt. Dr. Nabritt was one of the team of lawyers, led by future Supreme Court Justice Thurgood Marshall, who had scored a victory in the landmark civil rights case in the U.S. Supreme Court, *Brown v. Topeka Board of Education* in 1954.

Like Howard University the nation got a new president in the fall of 1960 by electing Massachusetts Senator John Fitzgerald Kennedy, who defeated Vice President Richard Milhous Nixon by a narrow margin of 100,000 votes. President-elect Kennedy had run a "hot," upbeat campaign that snatched victory from potential defeat to the incumbent vice president. The inauguration took place on one of the coldest days recorded in the history of the nation's capital.

Two days before inauguration day a heavy snowfall began at about 2:00 P.M., just as the Thursday afternoon ROTC drill and parade activities were beginning. The ominous weather forecast caused a cancellation of the drill activities. Government offices and private businesses throughout the city closed early to allow their employees to get home before the threatened blizzard settled in. Many motorists got caught in traffic in the city's streets and had to abandon their vehicles. There were reports of upward of 20,000 abandoned vehicles in Washington by the time of the inauguration on Saturday morning. By then the blizzard had passed, leaving Washington covered with a white blanket that gleamed in the brilliant sunshine of a crystal-clear, frigid day.

Travel to my New Jersey home was virtually impossible, what with all roads and railroads blocked by the many feet of snow and ice that the blizzard had dumped all up and down the East Coast. So I stayed in Washington that weekend. However, remembering the unpleasantness I had experienced during the Truman inauguration a dozen years before, I chose to watch the ceremony and parade from within the warmth of a friend's home. Listening to the new president's inaugural address, in which he spoke of the passing of a torch "to a new generation of Americans, born in this century" who would not permit "the slow undoing of those human rights to which this nation has always been committed," I hoped that he would fit his actions to match his words. And I thought that at least during this inauguration celebration, if I went to any restaurant in the city, I would be served and not insulted as I had been in 1949.

The spring semester brought some changes at the Air Force ROTC Detachment. First of all, Colonel Tom Money was transferred, PCS, to a new assignment at Headquarters Command located at Bolling Field, just across the Potomac from downtown Washington. I regretted his departure keenly as we had become good friends and I had really enjoyed serving in his command and the hospitality that he and his wife, Lucille, had extended at their home when they entertained the staff of the detachment and the cadet corps. Tom Money left a legacy of superb leadership in the Department of Air Science at Howard University. He also left me a "To Whom It May Concern" letter of recommendation that he had prepared at my request the year before as I had begun anticipating retirement in 1962. Dated June 10, 1960, his letter said:

> For more than nineteen years, I have known Major Charles W. Dryden as an active member of the military establishment. During approximately the past year and a half, he has worked under my direct supervision as an Assistant Professor of Air Science at Howard University, Washington, D.C.
>
> Major Dryden is one of those few persons whose personal ability is so overwhelming that it has an immediate positive impact within an organization the moment he joins it. He is unmistakably marked as a man of action, an authority in his field, and a dynamic leader. His intellect is keen and his thinking clear and sharp. He quickly integrates all relevant facts and factors of a problem and produces a logical solution long before others are fully aware of the problem. He anticipates areas where difficulties or deficiencies will obstruct the accomplishment of mission objectives and immediately identifies the type action to overcome them. He seems to be always one step ahead of everyone else because he is always thinking and planning ahead.
>
> Major Dryden approaches any problem with boundless enthusiasm and aggressiveness. His positive attitude and stimulating flow of ideas constantly inspire his associates to strive to meet his level of performance. He thinks quickly and has the ability to convey his thoughts lucidly into clear, logical and convincing language.
>
> His outstanding character and professional ability are equally matched with an effervescent personality. A sharp sense of humor, a sparkling wit and the touch of a toastmaster make him a most popular officer at gatherings.
>
> This officer is a born leader; he is an exceptionally able

staff officer; he is an officer who lives completely by the code of ethics; he is a gentleman in every sense; and he is a person of outstanding potential.
[Signed] THOMAS J. MONEY
Lt. Col., USAF
Professor of Air Science

With a recommendation like that, there can be no question why I regretted Colonel Money's transfer from Howard University.

Moreover, the second change that took place in the Department of Air Science was that Headquarters, Air University at Maxwell Field, Alabama, issued an order naming me as professor of air science to succeed Colonel Money. The order surprised me because in February I had submitted to headquarters a request for retirement from active duty effective August 31, 1961, upon completion of twenty years of continuous military service. However, following orders, I assumed command of the detachment as the school year was winding down and graduation day approached.

Graduation day brought me mixed feelings: a sense of deep pride as my protégés pinned on their gold bars as second lieutenants versus the parting-is-sweet-sorrow feeling as they were leaving.

I had another reason to be joyful, however. The guest speaker at the Air Force ROTC commissioning ceremony was Brigadier General "Rapid Robert" R. Rowland, who had been one of my flight instructors in the advanced phase of the aviation cadet program at Tuskegee Army Flying School. It was a real pleasure seeing him after twenty years and two wars had slipped into history.

Three months later a historical event shook the world when the East Germans blocked the roads linking East Berlin and West Berlin on August 13 and, the next day, began erecting a high wall of brick, concrete, and barbed wire to stem the flood of refugees fleeing the East sector. When the wall went up my plans for retirement collapsed under the weight of President Kennedy's executive order "freezing" all retirements and discharges from the armed forces until further notice. So there I was with only three weeks to go to complete my twenty years!

My replacement was already en route from overseas to join the detachment: When my request for retirement had been approved by Headquarters, Air University back in March, Major Jim Hurd, an old friend from the old days at Tuskegee, Godman, and Lockbourne, had been tapped to succeed me as the PAS. I had received notice that he was returning to the States from his assignment at Chatereaux Air Base in France. So I was going to have to move on to another assignment after overlapping with Jim Hurd for a short while to show him the ropes.

Anticipating retirement, I had enrolled in summer school courses in business administration and in marketing. My professor in both courses was Dr. H. Naylor Fitzhugh who, in later years after my retirement from the air force, was my boss at Pepsi Cola Company's world headquarters in New York City. His courses at Howard helped prepare me for the business world and for "life after military service," which was going to have to be put on hold. For how long? No one had a clue!

Early in December I received orders to report to the Washington Air Defense Sector (WAADS) at Fort Lee, Virginia, on January 4.

"Suits me fine," I thought, as I made plans to spend the holiday season at home with my family in New Jersey. Leaving the officers, NCOs, and cadets at the detachment was somewhat heartwrenching, as we had become such good friends who had shared in molding some very fine young officers. Leaving the Grays, "Mister Sonny" and "Mom" Gray, was certainly no easier for me, as they had made me feel like their own son while living in their home during the two and a half years of my sojourn in Washington.

And so, with car packed to the roof with personal gear, books, and papers, and with over twenty years of military service under my belt, I headed home for the holidays.

17 Twilight of a Lonely Eagle

» January 1962–August 1962

In the bosom of my family during the 1961 Christmas holiday season, I was happy to be with my loved ones but had a sense of foreboding and uneasiness. Blame it on the Berlin wall that had caused my retirement from active duty to be postponed indefinitely. Add to the erection of the wall in August the acceleration of nuclear testing by the USSR in September, and I, along with the rest of the world, had good reasons to be apprehensive about the future.

The fact that we had two sons, and Pete was expecting our third child in May, caused us to worry about whether the superpowers were headed toward mutual annihilation.

It was with such worrisome thoughts that I left my home in East Orange the day after celebrating Keith's second birthday on January 6. A snowstorm that had dumped a thick blanket of snow and ice all along the East Coast had made driving hazardous. But duty called, so I headed south on the New Jersey Turnpike, trying to go all the way to my new duty station at Fort Lee, Virginia, just outside of Petersburg and about a half hour drive south of Richmond.

The four-hour drive to Washington took about six hours of slipping and sliding around and past scores of cars, trucks, and buses that had stalled on the roadway or skidded off into ditches. Lightweight as it was, my German Ford Taunus kept right on going all the way to D.C., where I stayed overnight at the Bolling AFB BOQ because the highway to Richmond was impassable—snow removal equipment had not yet been able to clear the roads. By the next afternoon, however, roads into Virginia were cleared and I had no further excuse to delay reporting to Fort Lee.

Arriving at the post after retreat, I checked in at the billeting office for my room assignment in the BOQ. After unloading the car and stowing my gear in my quarters, I drove to the officers club for dinner.

Fort Lee was an old U.S. Army post, home of the Quartermaster Corps, and therefore the majority of the officers in the club were "green suiters." However, because the Air Defense Command of the U.S. Air Force had a traffic control "blockhouse" located on the fort, there was a sprinkling of air force "blue suiters" at the club.

During my tours of duty in Korea and Germany I had worked fairly closely with U.S. Army troops and thus had no problems associating professionally with troops of the other U.S. military branches. Because of interservice rivalries, however, some "blue suiters" and "green suiters" were constantly at odds with each other. Most times the rivalries were expressed in friendly banter, but sometimes rivals forgot that they were members of the same team and refused to cooperate with their other-service colleagues. In the few times that I had encountered noncooperation I wondered if the problem was the color of my skin, or my uniform, or both.

As I reported to duty at the Headquarters, WAADS orderly room the next morning, I wondered how I would fare at this new assignment. Would the "natives" turn out to be friend or foe?

I got an answer as soon as I entered the four-story, windowless "blockhouse" and reported to my new boss, Brigadier General James B. Tipton. Entering his office and saluting smartly, I said, "Major Charles Walter Dryden, reporting to duty as ordered, Sir!"

"At ease, Major," he said, amiably, returning my salute and extending his hand in greeting. "Welcome aboard, Dryden. I'm glad to have you on my battle staff at the command post. One of my operations officers will take you on a tour of this facility and brief you on what we do in here. I will depend on you to keep me and the rest of the battle staff up to date on the current intelligence about threats to our air defense sector. You may have to give us a briefing with as little as five minutes' advance notice so keep your intelligence estimates 'hot.' Is that clear?"

"Yes, Sir."

"Good. I see from your records that you served under General Davis during World War II after getting your wings at Tuskegee, so I have been looking forward to having you on my staff. You will report directly to me. Understand?"

"Yes, Sir."

"Very well, then, Major. I'll see you in the command post at the daily battle staff meeting tomorrow morning."

Rise. Snap to attention. One step backward. Salute. About face. Leave. And that was it. My introduction to Air Defense Command.

Since the reorganization of the U.S. Army Air Corps into the U.S. Air Force (USAF) as a separate branch of the armed forces in 1947, I had been assigned to units in six of the major commands of USAF, including: Tactical Air Command (TAC), when I was stationed at Lockbourne AFB; Air Training Command (ATC), at Scott AFB; Far East Air Forces (FEAF), at Yokota AB, Japan, and K-2, Korea; Continental Air Command (CONAC), at Mitchel AFB; United States Air Force, Europe (USAFE), at Ramstein AB, West Germany; and Air University Command (AUC), at AFROTC, Howard University.

And now, Air Defense Command (ADC) made it seven. "Lucky seven" it turned out to be because I was in ADC just over two months when my promotion to lieutenant colonel (L/C) came through. Per authority of Department of the Air Force Special Orders AA-290, dated March 15, 1962, my new date of rank (DOR) was January 31, 1962.

"Hallelujah!" I exulted when I got the good news.

A promotion at any time is good news. To quote my aviation cadet classmate, Clarence Jamison, who used to tease me with his "ghetto grammar," a promotion to L/C after almost ten years of wearing a major's gold leaves was "more better." And the fact that Jamie's name was also on the promotion list made it all even "much more better"! I dropped a note in the mail to Lieutenant Colonel Clarence Clifford Jamison, USAF, with one word: "Congratulations!"

The promotion compensated me for the disappointment of having had my retirement postponed indefinitely, because if I had left in August 1961 I would not have been able to wear silver leaves on my shoulders and "whipped cream" (lightening bolts and clouds) on the visor of my garrison cap—to say nothing about the higher amount of pension when I would finally be allowed to retire.

Two months later, in May, I received a letter from Headquarters, ADC informing me that retirements were being allowed again and requesting my intentions. Discussing the letter with the Headquarters, WAADS personnel people and my boss, I inferred that there was a good possibility that my name would come up on the list for promotion to full colonel in a few years—a tempting thought, but I decided to resubmit my request for retirement, and did so.

Meanwhile, while waiting for my exit date of August 31 to roll around, I plunged into my duties at the "blockhouse." Officially the facility was known as SAGE (semiautomatic ground environment) control center. Access to the windowless building required a special badge. Inside were the numerous offices occupied by officers and NCOs of various agencies involved in air traffic control, mostly military—many air force, some army, few navy and marines—and a few FAA civilians. Although routine activities involved commercial air traffic in the Atlantic Coast area for which WAADS was responsible, the critical task was to identify any and all air traffic in the sector that was "unknown," determine if it was a threat to the United States and, if so, destroy it by scrambling air defense missiles and/or aircraft.

The "eyes" of SAGE were the myriad radar installations rimming the North American continent. The "heart" was the "blue room" in each of the numerous "blockhouses" on the continent in which the subdued lighting enabled the controllers seated in front of the many TV-type screens to see and interpret what was being displayed as blips caused by the electronic impulses coming in from radar units. The "brain" of SAGE was the command post in each blockhouse where the sector commander and his battle staff took appropriate action to destroy any airborne threats to the nation coming through the sector.

In order to ensure that the system was in top working order at all times, exercises simulating "the real thing"—an actual attack by enemy aircraft or missiles—were conducted frequently, at random dates and times. All "blockhouse" personnel were on call around the clock.

I remember vividly being called by the duty officer at about 0200 hours one morning to report to the battle station at once. Rolling out of the sack and dressing swiftly, I figured the Taunus would get me there in two minutes from the BOQ. I was wrong! The Taunus could make no headway at all through the blizzard that was raging across the post, much to my shocked surprise when I went outside. There was nothing to do but hoof it through the snowdrifts piled high by the howling wind. It took me about a half hour to cover the four or five blocks to the blockhouse where I arrived chilled to the bone and covered with a crust of wet snow and ice from head to toes. But I made it.

When I reported to the boss at the command post only a skeleton crew was on hand. Many of the battle staff members lived in family quarters located in remote areas of the post and had a rough time hiking through the snowdrifts. After that experience some drastic changes were made to the SOP (standing operating procedure) for alerting members of the battle staff whenever severe weather conditions were forecast.

Experiences such as the snowstorm incident, although rare, were about the only thing that added spice and excitement to my tour of duty at Fort Lee. There were no airplanes at the fort for me to fly, and if there had been some they would not have been of any use to me anyway. I would not have been able, or more accurately, I would not have been authorized to fly them. The reason is that while I was still at Howard University and getting my flying time with the operations office at Bolling Field, I had been classified as a Flight Status Code 3 pilot.

That was a status created by the air force to include "desk jockeys," that is, those pilots, like myself, who had many hundreds of hours recorded in their Form 5s but whose primary duties did not include flying. Code 3 pilots would still receive flying pay, as long as they could pass their annual physical exam, without logging the required four hours' minimum flying time each month. This "flying pay without flying time" system was the air force's attempt to save the cost of fuel burned by non-primary-duty pilots logging their four-hour minimum each month. The presumption was that if needed in an emergency, Code 3 pilots could become proficient again swiftly.

My last flight before being placed in Code 3 status had been on September 15, 1961, when I flew a C-47 full of Air Force ROTC cadets from Bolling Field to Wright-Patterson AFB. As I touched down on the runway back at Bolling I knew that it was to be the last flight I would ever make in an air force airplane, and I tried my very best to make it the smoothest of all the thousands of landings I had made in twenty years of flying. I didn't know if I succeeded in that but I did know that that day I died a little. A bit of the light of my life went out. I had lived to fly, from my infancy, and now—it was a thing of the past.

Other activities and events had to fill the void I felt with flying no longer part of my routine. Although it didn't happen often, I was involved in court-martial trials. I had been named as a member of a special court-martial by General Tipton and, as the senior rank-ing officer on the court, I was its president. Not many cases came before the court, but one turned out to be very SPECIAL for me. It took place on May 18, 1962.

I remember the date well: not because of the offense with which the accused, a sergeant, was charged—forging the signature on a check; not because we, the court, listened to all the testimony of witnesses, reviewed all of the evidence, and then found him guilty, as charged; and not because I had announced to the court, in closed session, my intention to declare a recess until the next morning because it was already 1700 hours when we agreed on the verdict and we still had to agree on the sentence. None of the above was the reason for my certainty about the date of the case. The reason I remember the date so accurately is because even as I was announc-ing my decision to reopen the court and declare a recess until morn-ing, the court clerk handed me a note that said: "Your wife has given birth to a seven pound three ounce boy."

"Gentlemen!" I said, addressing the members of the court. "For-get what I just said about a recess. I have to go on emergency leave within an hour and I have a nine-hour drive ahead of me to get home to see my newest son. So. I want us to decide on the sergeant's sentence within the next half hour. Clear?"

"Yes, Sir, Colonel!" the five other members chorused.

"We heard you loud and clear," a major added.

Twenty minutes of discussion of the sentence options available to the court, as outlined in the *Manual for Courts-Martial,* was all we needed to reach agreement on the sentence. I don't remember what we agreed upon, but I do remember that after I reopened the court, announced the sentence, and declared the court adjourned, it took me less than a half hour to hurry out of the courtroom, with the best wishes and congratulations of the court members ringing in my ears, drive to my quarters, load the Taunus, and sign out at headquarters on the emergency leave that my boss approved to begin as of May 18, 1962—the birthday of my third son, Eric Buckley Dryden. I shall never forget that date.

Every day on the job I learned something new about the SAGE system. It was so intricate in its myriad components and subsystems that I was constantly asking questions of various persons about their particular role and how their office crew fit into the overall operation. Because many of the blockhouse people had been in Air Defense Command for years and had "grown up" with SAGE, they had an advantage over the likes of me, a newcomer to air defense. So, after a few weeks and literally hundreds of questions asked of all the blockhouse veterans, I decided that a training program was needed to facilitate the orientation and indoctrination of future newcomers.

General Tipton liked the idea of establishing such a program and gave me a green light to develop one, through consultation with all of the component agencies—communications, fighter interceptor units, missile units, radar units, the sister services of army, navy, and marines, weather forecasters, computer links, and intelligence—and draft a WAADS training directive establishing the program.

That was a tall order but I couldn't complain because I had opened my big mouth and violated one of the basic rules of getting

FAREWELL TO ARMS! In his office Brig. Gen. James B. Tipton
bids farewell to Lt. Col. Dryden, whose twenty-one years of active
duty with the U.S. Air Force ended that day, August 31, 1962.

along in the military that I had learned when I was a young lieuten-ant: Keep your eyes and ears open, your mouth and pants shut, and DON'T VOLUNTEER!

Now, as a lieutenant colonel, I was inclined to see a problem and try to do something to solve it.

So. In addition to my regular duties on the battle staff, with no-notice as well as scheduled intelligence briefings based upon con-stant reading through volumes of intelligence documents, I spent every spare moment for several weeks interviewing various persons in the blockhouse. Next came the task of drafting the training di-rective and then, finally, getting the approval of all of the agencies "to whom it may concern."

The whole process took weeks. Several weeks. Time almost ran out on me. In early August I received copies of my retirement or-ders, to be effective August 31, 1962. Working furiously to wrap it all up before leaving WAADS and the air force, I finally handed a copy of WAADS Headquarters Office Instructions Number 50–2 to General Tipton the morning of the 31st as he called me into his office to bid me farewell and Godspeed in my retirement. He had asked me weeks before if I wanted a retirement parade. "No, Gen-eral," I had replied. "I prefer to leave quietly with the good wishes of the troops rather than the curses of those who would march in a parade." And so it ended. My military career of twenty-one years. Two decades plus one year of personal experiences as well as ob-serving and sharing the experiences of many friends and comrades along the way. So many of them left their mark in the history of the world and made an impact on me, with what they did. So few of them have written about what they did.

And so I feel compelled to record some of the things that some of them did. To write one more chapter to salute some other Tus-kegee Airmen, my comrades-in-arms.

18 Contrails

>>   Landlubbers leave footprints in the sands of time,
           Aviators leave contrails in the vast reaches of space . . .
                                                    —the author

Contrails can be seen at various times of day in the skies above the earth when the conditions are right, conditions of moisture and temperature of the air through which airplanes are flying and the temperature of the gases exhausted from their engines. Contrails are seen as narrow white streaks across the blue sky, sharply defined at first, then fuzzy edged as wind currents frazzle them. Finally, they vanish. But the memory of them lingers on—how impressive they were when they were visible, somehow forcing you to look up to see them!

So it seems with many of the actions by the Tuskegee Airmen. Several "contrails" are noted in this final chapter. Several ways to identify the Tuskegee Airmen of "the Experiment." For examples, they can be identified by the numbers: 992 won their wings at Tuskegee Army Flying School (TAFS); 450 flew combat missions in North Africa, Sicily, and Italy; 66 were killed in action; 32 were taken prisoner of war; 111 enemy aircraft were shot down in the air, 25 damaged; 150 enemy aircraft were shot up on the ground, 123 damaged; 0 (zero) friendly bombers were lost to enemy air attacks (!!!); 3,000+ ground support personnel at TAFS and overseas made it possible, through their skills and efforts, for the airmen to rack up those numbers while flying combat missions in P-39s, P-40s, P-47s, and P-51s of the 332nd Fighter Group, comprising the 99th, 100th, 301st, and 302nd Fighter Squadrons.

The 477th Medium Bombardment Group, flying B-25s, comprising the 616th, 617th, 618th, and 619th Medium Bombardment Squadrons, was combat-ready, trained for combat in the Pacific, when surrender by Japan denied their approximately 200+ pilots, 100+ bombardier-navigators, and hundreds of flight engineers, radiomen, gunners, and ground support personnel a chance to demonstrate their skills in combat.

Some Tuskegee Airmen are known by their military rank, "generally" speaking: General Daniel "Chappie" James, first to wear four stars; Lieutenant General Benjamin O. Davis, Jr., first to wear three; and Major General Lucius Theus, who achieved two-star rank and was thus one of only three Tuskegee Airmen to wear stars.

Many are known by a sampling of their names and combat exploits: Charles B. Hall, first to down an enemy aircraft; James McCullen and Sherman White, first losses in combat. Benjamin O. Davis, Jr., Louis R. Purnell, and Lee Rayford flew all four aircraft in combat: P-39, P-40, P-47, and P-51. Lee Archer, Joseph D. Elsberry, and Clarence Lester each scored three aerial victories on a single mission. Roscoe Brown, Charles Brantley, and Earl Lane, flying propeller-driven P-51s, shot down German jet fighters. Gwynne Pierson sank a destroyer with machine gun fire. Howard Baugh, John Morgan, and Edward Toppins were the first replacements to join the 99th Fighter Squadron overseas in Sicily. Morgan was killed shortly thereafter in a tragic accident. However, Toppins flew 141 combat missions; Baugh flew 135. More than a normal combat tour!

Charles E. McGee flew 136 combat missions. (Later, with 100 combat missions in Korea and 172 in Viet Nam, "Chuck" McGee racked up a total of 408 combat missions in three wars, thus "painting" contrails in three war-torn skies!) Walter Palmer, a cousin of mine, assigned to the 100th Fighter Squadron, flew 158 combat missions—perhaps the highest total of all the Red Tails, as far as I have been able to determine from my griot sources.

Some others are known by a sampling of their WWII nicknames:

Fred "Stinky" Archer, Lee "Buddy" Archer, Willie "the Snake" Ashley, Harold H. "Buick" Brown, Harold H. "Oldsmobile"

TUSKEGEE AIRMEN STATUE. Sculpted by Lt. Col. Clarence L. Shivers, graduate of aviation cadet class 44-J at TAFS, this life-size statue was enshrined on May 6, 1988, at the U.S. Air Force Academy, where it occupies a central place in the academy's "Honor Court." The inscription on the base of the pedestal reads:

THE TUSKEGEE AIRMEN
OF
WORLD WAR II

They rose from adversity
Through competence, courage
Commitment, and Capacity
To serve America
On silver wings, and to set
A Standard
Few will transcend.

Brown, Sam "the Lizzard" Bruce, William "Wild Bill" Campbell, Herbert E. "Pepe" Carter, William T. "Bumps" Coleman, Hannibal "Killer" Cox, Lemuel R. "Big Buster" Custis, Charles H. "Ever So" DeBow, Clarence "Bacon" Driver, Elwood "Woody" Driver, Edward "Bulldog" Drummond, Charles W. "A-Train" Dryden, Joseph D. "Jodie" Elsberry, William "Chubby" Green, Charles B. "Seabuster" Hall, Milton R. "Baby" Hall, Richard W. "Dopey" Hall, Richard H. "Head" Harris, Fred "Little Freddie" Hutchins, Leonard "Black Jack" Jackson, Melvin T. "Red" Jackson, Daniel "Chappie" James, Clarence "Jamie Boy" Jamison, Hubert L. "Hooks" Jones, Elmore "the Whip" Kennedy, James B. "the Eel" Knighten, Herman "Ace" Lawson, Walter I. "Ghost" Lawson, Clarence "Lucky" Lester, Lewis "Highpockets" Lynch, Albert "Bootsie" Manning, William "Mattie Mae" Mattison, Chris "Hummer" Newman, Robert "Rabbit" O'Neal, Henry B. "Herky" Perry, John "Skyhawk" Porter, Wendell O. "Pretty Boy" Pruitt, Lee "Jelly" Rayford, Price de Allen "P.D." Rice, George S. "Spanky" Roberts, Marion "Tojo" Rodgers, Henry R. "Pretty Boy" Scott, Harry "Alfalfa" Shepard, Graham "Peepsight" Smith, Lowell C. "Monkey Man" Steward, William "Wild Bill" Thompson, Edward "Topper" Toppins, Andrew "Jug" Turner, James C. "Scarface" Warren, Dudley "Fearless Fosdick" Watson, Spann "the Brow" Watson, John "Mr. Death" Whitehead, James "Little Flower" Wiley, Earl "Flaps" Williams, Theodore "Brute" Wilson.

Flying together, with Lee "Buddy" Archer flying wingman for Wendell "Pretty Boy" Pruitt, two Tuskegee Airmen were nicknamed "the Gruesome Twosome," a deadly pair for any Luftwaffe pilot to tangle with!

The Tuskegee Airmen of the 332nd Fighter Group can also be identified by the medals and awards they brought home from combat overseas, including: 1 Legion of Merit, 1 Silver Star, 2 Soldiers Medals, 8 Purple Hearts, 14 Bronze Stars, 150+ Distinguished Flying Crosses, 744 Air Medals with Clusters, 1 Presidential Unit Citation, 1 Red Star of Yugoslavia (to Chubby Green for valor, fighting with the Yugoslavia underground fighters).

Meanwhile, back in the USA, 101 officers of the 477th Medium Bombardment Group, which did not get to go overseas, nevertheless earned respect for their heroism and sheer guts in insisting on their civil rights as Americans and their military rights as officers, as they tried to enter and utilize the officers club at Freeman Field, Indiana. For this "crime" they were placed under arrest in quarters. Their names were recorded on an official order, for condemnation.

Their names are listed here for acclamation because theirs are the kind of "contrails" that must never fade away.

An excerpt of the order reads as follows:

"SPECIAL ORDERS NO. 87   E-X-T-R-A-C-T   12 April 1945

19. The following named officers will proceed on or about 13 April 1945 on temporary duty to Godman Field, Ky for approximately ninety days. Subject officers are in arrest in quarters at Freeman Field, Seymour, Indiana and in arrest in transit from Freeman Field to Godman Field, Kentucky and upon arrival at Godman Field are placed in arrest in quarters at that station." The officers were: First Lieutenants Arthur L. Ward and James B. Williams; Second Lieutenants Leonard A. Altemus, Leroy A. Battle, Rudolph A. Berthoud, William W. Bowie, Jr., James W. Brown, Jr., Roy M. Chappell, Samuel Colbert, Herndon M. Cummings, Charles E. Darnell, Charles J. Dorkins, Cyril P. Dyer, Arthur O. Fisher, Leroy H. Freeman, Leroy F. Gillead, Charles S. Goldsby, Argonne F. Harden, Donald D. Harris, Glenn L. Head, Michel L. Higginbothan, Edward V. Hipps, Jr., Stephen Hostesse, Robert L. Hunter, Clifford C. Jarrett, Silas M. Jenkins, Robert B. Johnson, James E. Jones, James V. Kennedy, George H. Kydd, Robert E. Lee, George H. O. Martin, Theodore O. Mason, Melvin M. Nelson, Luther L. Oliver, Robert Payton, Jr., William C. Perkins, Roger Pines, Wardell A. Polk, George W. Prioleau, Jr., Victor L. Ranson, Walter R. Ray, Frank B. Sanders, Herbert J. Schwing, David A. Smith, Quentin B. Smith, Edward E. Tillmon, Cleophus Valentine, Calvin T. Warrick, Edward W. Watkins, James Whyte, Jr., Leonard E. Williams, Edward W. Woodward, Coleman Young; and Flight Officers Markus E. Clarkson, Marcel Clyne, Clarence C. Conway, William J. Curtis, Harry R. Dickenson, Ario Dixione, Wendell G. Freeland, Lloyd Godfrey, Donald A. Hawkins, Norman A. Holmes, Lewis C. Hubbard, Jr., Maurice J. Jackson, Jr.,

Denny C. Jefferson, McCray Jenkins, Charles E. Jones, Adolphus Lewis, Jr., Hiram E. Little, Harry S. Lum, Edward R. Lunda, Robert T. McDaniel, Alfred McKensie, Charles E. Malone, Sidney H. Marzette, Walter M. Miller, David J. Murphy, Jr., Connie Napier, Jr., John R. Perkins, Jr., Bertram W. Pitts, Frank V. Pivalo, Glenn W. Pulliam, Harris Robnett, Frederick H. Samuels, Paul W. Scott, James H. Shepherd, Calvin Smith, Alvin B. Steele, Wendell T. Stokes, Howard Storey, Edward R. Tabbanor, Charles R. Taylor, James C. Warren, Roland A. Webber, Haydel J. White, Paul L. White, Charles E. Wilson, John E. Wilson, Eugene L. Woodson.

And there were three other officers who were tried by general court-martial for resisting arrest by the provost marshal during the Freeman Field incident: Lieutenants Shirly R. Clinton, Roger C. Terry, and Marsden A. Thompson.

The Tuskegee Airmen are known by more than just the "contrails" described in this chapter. Indeed, several memorials, in the form of murals, museums, and monuments, are located at several sites across the nation that recognize and salute these American heroes of color. For instance, a fifty-foot-long mural in a main corridor of Lambert International Airport at Saint Louis, Missouri, presents a panoramic-type scene highlighting numerous individuals and events from the history of the "Tuskegee Experiment."

Exhibits based upon the persons and problems, trials and triumphs, of the Tuskegee Airmen are on display in museums in: Alabama, at Tuskegee University, in the General Daniel "Chappie" James Center for Aerospace Science and Health Education; Georgia, at the Georgia Aviation Hall of Fame on Robins Air Force Base near Warner Robins; Michigan, at the Tuskegee Airmen, Inc., museum at Fort Wayne, Detroit; and Washington, D.C., at the Aerospace Center of the Smithsonian Institution.

Monuments have been installed in: Alabama, at Tuskegee University where a "Wall of Honor" adjacent to the "Chappie" James Center holds a plaque dedicated to the Tuskegee Airmen; Ohio, at the Wright-Patterson Air Force Base Aerospace Museum, where one designed by Tuskegee Airman Lloyd Hathcock is on display; Colorado, at the Air Force Academy in the mountains near Colorado Springs, where, in a plaza next to the Cadet Chapel, there is emplaced a magnificent life-size statue of a Tuskegee Airman sculpted by Tuskegee Airman Clarence Shivers. The figure is clad in flight gear—helmet, goggles, flying suit, with maps in knee pockets, gloves, parachute slung over his shoulder—looking sky-ward. He resembles no one particular Tuskegee Airman and yet he is a symbol of all of us as the sculptor has caught, in the cocky stance of his statue, the essence of the mystique of the Tuskegee Airmen. The stance and the expression on the face seem to say, to all the world: "Yeah, I can fly. You're damn right, I can fly. And fight. And I can whip the hell out of any enemy pilot who dares to try me!"

Epilogue

"To make us love our country
 Our country ought to be lovely"

Those words, written by British statesman Edmund Burke about his country two centuries ago, are just as true today about mine—America. America, the beautiful, about which a patriotic paean proclaims: "Thine alabaster cities gleam / Undimmed by human tears. . . . "

Would that it were true—that no tears were ever shed anywhere, anytime in its history, caused by affronts to the dignity of its citizens of color, or by assaults upon their person.

How lovely would my country be if its actions did not belie its brave words that "all men are created equal" and that in this "land of the free" there are "liberty and justice for all!"

I have fought in two wars for my America because I have loved its lovely principles. From my first formal lessons in patriotism in first grade, reciting the pledge of allegiance and singing the national anthem, and throughout my three-score-and-ten years, plus five, I have loved America.

Happily, its principles have thrilled me and filled me with emotion each time I stood stiffly at attention and saluted the flag during morning reveilles and evening retreats on military posts around the world.

Sadly, however, actions by "ugly Americans" have sickened me and filled me with anger.

Despite preachments about patriotism by many Americans in high places, their policies and practices have strained and stretched my patriotism from time to time. So often my country has been unlovely that I have sometimes shed tears of sorrow, oftentimes tears of rage.

"Why so?" one might ask. "When was America not lovely to you?"

My reply:

"When the United States Army War College published its report in 1925 that purported to be an analysis of the 'physical, mental, psychological qualities and characteristics of the Negro as a subspecies of the human family' and concluded that Negroes are inferior, ignorant, and immoral, promiscuous, deceitful, and thievish. And so on, ad nauseam.

"When I was ordered to leave the officers club at Selfridge Field in Michigan.

"When 101 African American officers were placed under arrest only because they attempted to enter the officers club at Freeman Field in Indiana.

"When German prisoners of war, soldiers of America's enemy, could use all the facilities at the post exchange at Walterboro, South Carolina, and I, an American citizen who had fought the Nazis to defend America, could not. C-o-u-l-d n-o-t. COULD NOT!

"When a U.S. Army Air Corps major general told me, and hundreds of American troops under his command, that because of our color, our ethnic ancestry, we were not ready to fight and fly for our country.

"And when, most hurtfully of all, my four-year-old son was discriminated against in a kindergarten in Nutley, New Jersey, by being segregated in the classroom and denied food that his White classmates were served, on the very day that I took part in the destruction of numerous North Korean tanks and trucks—doing my patriotic duty to defend America against a foreign enemy halfway around the world! I survived my skirmishes abroad without a scratch, but I am certain that my son's psyche was wounded for his lifetime by 'enemies' right here in America."

As I recall such bitter memories I cannot help pondering some pregnant questions. For instance:

Who was my worst enemy, really?

Was it the fascist abroad or the racist at home?

Was it the Germans and North Koreans who shot at me with intent to kill, during my two wars?

Or was it the major general, and others like him, who constantly waged Jim Crow warfare against African Americans during times of peace as well as during times of war?

Or yet was it still others, like the kindergarten teacher, whose prejudice preyed on innocent children of color?

With the Germans and North Koreans I knew for sure who my enemy was. With many fellow Americans I was not at all sure!

However, I am certain about some things:

First of all, in spite of the many "ugly Americans" I have encountered who savaged my spirit by their bigotry, there have been a number of "lovely Americans" who salvaged my self-esteem by their decency. There come to mind Mary Elizabeth Sullivan, teacher in sixth grade; Agnes L. Mackin in junior high school; college professors Mario Carbone and Herbert Rosenbaum; civilian flight instructor Bill Pyhota and military flight instructors Clay Albright and Robert Rowland; senior military officers Noel F. Parrish, Arthur C. Clark, and James C. Truscott.

Second, I am certain America was changed somewhat by the achievements of the Tuskegee Airmen during World War II and thereafter as evidenced by the desegregation of the armed forces by President Truman. With that establishment of equal opportunity for all military personnel, three Tuskegee Airmen were promoted, subsequently, to the rank of general officer: General Daniel James, Lieutenant General Benjamin O. Davis, Jr., and Major General Lucius Theus. America seemed lovely then.

Third, I was certainly privileged to be a part of the "Tuskegee Experiment."

Fourth, and finally, I most certainly am enormously proud to be a Tuskegee Airman!

Glossary

AAB	Army air base
AB	Air base
AC	Aircraft commander
ADC	Air Defense Command
Aerobatic	Aerial acrobatic maneuver
AFB	Air force base
AFIT	Air Force Institute of Technology
AFR	Air force regulation
AFSC	Air force specialty code
AIC	Academic Instructor Course
Aileron	Control surface on the trailing edge of a wing, used in turns
Airacobra	Bell P-39 fighter plane
Aldis lamp	Signal lamp that has three directional beams of light (green, amber, and red) for use in directing air traffic
Altimeter setting	A number, designating the current atmospheric pressure at a given location, that a pilot sets on the altimeter on his instrument panel; 29.92 is standard sea level pressure
Ammo	Ammunition
Angels	A plane's altitude above sea level (e.g., Angels 2=2,000 feet)
AO	Airdrome officer
AOCP	Aircraft out of commission, awaiting parts
APIT	Armor-piercing, incendiary, tracer. The

	types of bullets loaded into ammunition belts for aircraft machine guns in recurring sets of 5 bullets (e.g., 2 AP, 2 I, 1 T, 2 AP, 2 I, etc.)
Armor-piercing round	A bullet that can penetrate armor plate
ATC	Air traffic control; or Air Transport Command
AUC	Air University Command
AWOL	Absent without official leave
Bail out	To jump out of an airplane
Balls out, or balls to the wall	Fly at top speed
Bandit	Enemy airplane
B-4 bag	A combination garment bag/valise with two side pockets
Big Friend	Allied bomber
Bird dog	(1) Radio compass; (2) follow-up on a project until all agencies concerned have approved it
Black Dispatch	General term referring to all newspapers and magazines publishing news about African Americans
Bogey	Unknown (i.e., whether friendly or enemy) aircraft
BOQ	Bachelor officers quarters
Bore sighting	Alignment of fixed, forward-firing aircraft machine guns to ensure that the bullets of all such guns converge at the same point ahead of the aircraft
Boring holes (through the air)	Flying without performing any specific mission, just to build up flying time
Bought the farm	Was killed in a crash or a dogfight
Break ground	Take off in an airplane
Bug out	To flee, helter skelter
Buzzing	Flying low, close to the ground
Canopy	The plastic window ("bubble") that covers the pilots' cockpit
Cartwheel, or vertical reverse	An aerial acrobatic maneuver
Caterpillar Club	An informal association of people who have had to parachute from an airplane in an emergency

CAVU	Ceiling and visibility unlimited
Chandelle	An aerial acrobatic maneuver
Checklist	An oral or written list of things to be done at a particular phase of flight (e.g., pretakeoff ———, or prelanding ———)
Check the locks	In a poker card game, saying "check" instead of betting when holding an unbeatable hand
Chug-a-lug	Drinking the entire contents of a full glass, nonstop
Chute	Parachute
CIGFTPR	Pretakeoff checklist in which the pilot checks the controls, ignition, gas, flaps, trim tabs, propellor(s), run up (of the engine at full power)
"Clear!"	Loudly spoken command by the pilot to the ground crewman outside the airplane before starting the engine, meaning "Stand clear!" (of the propellor)
Clearance	(1) Approval of a proposed flight plan; (2) permission to leave a base upon transfer by accounting for all funds and government property for which a person is responsible
CO	Commanding officer
COC	Combat Operations Center
Command pilot	The highest aeronautical rating in the U.S. Air Force, symbolized by a pair of silver wings with a star encircled by a wreath on the top of the wings
CONAC	Continental Air Command
Cone of silence	The narrow inverted cone of space, with its apex on the ground, rising above an airfield at the intersection of radio beams
Connie	Lockheed Constellation—a four-engine passenger plane
"Contact!"	See "Clear!"
Contrail	The condensation trail, visible to the naked eye, that is made by hot airplane engine exhaust gases in cold, moist air usually at high altitudes

Control stick	Stick, mounted vertically on the floor of an airplane cockpit, used by the pilot to raise or lower the nose or each wing by movement forward or aft and sideward
Cowling	A metal ring that encloses the cylinders of an airplane engine
CPTP	Civilian Pilot Training Program
CQ	Charge of quarters (an NCO on duty at a unit's orderly room after duty hours)
Cross country	Navigation training flight
Cuban 8	An aerial acrobatic maneuver
Cut the mustard	Do a job well enough to meet usual standards
DCS/O	Deputy chief of staff for operations
Dead reckoning	Aerial navigation using mainly time, distance, and speed factors to determine geographical location and track
Deck	The ground (Flying "on the deck" is flying low above it.)
Dinghy	An inflatable life raft
DNIF	Duty not involving flying (e.g., when too sick to fly)
Dodo	An aviation cadet
Dogfight	Aerial combat
DOR	Date of rank
Echelon	A type of formation of airplanes in flight
Elevator	Movable horizontal control surface in the tail of an airplane that, when moved by the pilot using the control stick, causes the airplane to go up or down
Empennage	Tail of an airplane that includes the vertical stabilizer and rudder, horizontal stabilizer and elevator
ER	Effectiveness report
ETA	Estimated time of arrival
ETE	Estimated time en route
FAA	Federal Aviation Authority
Falling leaf	An aerial acrobatic maneuver
FEAF	Far East Air Force
FIGMO	"Forget it, I've Got My Orders!"—The

	happy status of a GI possessing orders for transfer to another unit
FIP	Flight Indoctrination Program
Five by five	Perfect reception of radio transmission; e.g., perfect reception, on a scale of 1 to 5, is stated as "5 by 5" (i.e., readability 5, signal strength 5)
500 on top	A type of flight clearance, during IFR conditions, in which the airplane is flown at least 500 feet above all clouds along its flight path
Flak	Acronym for German words *flieger abwehr kanone*, meaning antiaircraft gun
Flap	Movable surface on the trailing edge of a wing for use in adjusting the angle of descent in landings
Forced landing	An actual, or simulated, emergency landing
Form 1	The daily record of the amount and type of flying activity in a USAF airplane. Each pilot who flies the plane during a given calendar day records his time and type of flight
Form 5	Flight log of each USAF aeronautically rated person
Frag order	Fragment (of a complete operations plan) that pertains to a specific unit
Fuel mixture	The ratio of fuel to air in the carburetor set by the pilot using a mixture control lever in the cockpit
Fuselage	The body of an airplane that contains the pilots' cockpit, passengers' cabin, and/or cargo compartment
Gaggle	A large formation of airplanes in flight
GCA	Ground control approach (an instrument landing method)
"Gear down," or "gear in the green," or "green gear"	Pilot's radio message to control tower operator, on final approach, that his landing gear is down and locked in place
George	Nickname for the autopilot
GI	Nickname for U.S. troops (literally, "Government Issue")

Go around	To abort an approach to landing and fly the airplane around the traffic pattern to make another approach
Goony Bird	Nickname for a C-47 transport plane
Gosport	Hollow rubber tube, between the open cockpits of early training planes, one end of which is fixed to a speaker mouthpiece in the front (instructor's) cockpit, the other end in the rear cockpit where the student attaches his end of the tube to a short metal tube in the earpiece of his helmet before each flight
Grease it	To make a smooth landing
G-2	Intelligence staff section or officer
GUMP	Prelanding checklist, meaning: Gas selector on fullest tank, fuel pumps on Undercarriage (landing gear) down and locked Mixture (fuel) control on full (or auto) rich Propellor(s) pitch control set for landing (low pitch, high RPM)
Gung ho	Eager for combat (a term originated by U.S. Marines)
Hangar queen	An airplane that is out of operation, for repairs, more often than it is flyable
Happy hour	Traditional time at officers and NCO clubs on military bases, after duty hours, when members and guests relax with or without libations
"Hawk"	Nickname for a cold, blustery wind
Head shed	Headquarters (The Pentagon is the top "head shed.")
High pitch	Propellor setting for normal cruise (with low engine RPM)
Horizontal stabilizer	Fixed horizontal surface of the empennage, to which the elevator is hinged
"Horses"	A dice game usually played at club bars
Hoss	Nickname often used by Tuskegee Airmen when greeting each other

Hot rock	A very good, sometimes flamboyant, pilot
IFR	Instrument flight rules (applicable in bad weather)
ILS	Instrument landing system (method for landing in bad weather)
Immelman	An aerial acrobatic maneuver
Incendiary round	Machine gun bullet that starts fires
In the soup	Flying in clouds, fog, or rain
In trail, or in string	Formation flying with each airplane flying in line behind the one in front of it in a follow-the-leader fashion
IP	(1) Instructor pilot; (2) initial point—point on the ground above which bombers begin their target run
IRAN	Inspection and repairs as necessary (in effect, an overhaul of a "weary" old airplane at a major maintenance depot)
Jerry	German (the enemy)
Jinking	Flying erratically, changing altitude and direction frequently to prevent antiaircraft gunners from drawing a bead on the plane (an RAF term)
JP	Junior pilot
"Jug"	Nickname for the Republic P-47 "Thunderbolt" fighter plane
KIA	Killed in action
Kittyhawk	One of the nicknames of the Curtis P-40 fighter plane
Landing stage	Several airplanes (two or more) flying around and around an airport traffic pattern and making touch and go landings
Lazy 8s	Flying-coordination training maneuvers
Lead	The distance from a moving target to the point in space ahead of it where a gunner must aim to hit the target
Lean (fuel) mixture	Low ratio of fuel to air metered to the engine cylinders by the carburetor
Liar's dice	A dice game usually played at club bars
Light lines	A series of red lights placed one at each

of twelve checkpoints, about twenty miles apart, on a route between large cities, each light flashing a different letter of the alphabet in Morse code (used as a night navigation aid in VFR conditions)

Link trainer	Flight simulator (early model)
Loop	An aerial acrobatic maneuver
Low pitch	Propellor setting for takeoffs and landings (with high engine RPM)
Macchi 202	An Italian-built fighter plane used by some Luftwaffe pilots during WWII
Mag (magneto) check	Magneto output reading during engine run-up before takeoff
MATS	Military Air Transport Service
Max cruise	Maximum cruising speed
ME-109	Messerschmidt 109, a German fighter plane
MIA	Missing in action
Mission	A task to be performed as assigned to a military unit (e.g., for bombers to destroy a target on the ground, or fighters to escort bombers to and from a target, or transport planes to move troops or cargo)
Morning report	Daily strength (i.e., present/absent) status of a military unit's assigned personnel
Morse code	Letters of the alphabet expressed in dits and dahs for radio transmission (e.g., A is . __ [dit dah]; Z is __ __ .. [dah dah dit dit])
Mustang	Nickname of the North American P-51 fighter plane
NATO	North Atlantic Treaty Organization
NCO	Noncommissioned officer
NCOIC	Noncommissioned officer-in-charge
NE-ODD	When flying on a VFR flight clearance, pilots flying north or east must maintain altitudes at *odd* thousands of feet
NLT	Not later than
NORAD	North American Air Defense
Nose wheel	Front wheel on an airplane with tricycle landing gear
Octane	Volatility rating of petroleum fuel

OD	Officer of the day, in charge of a base after duty hours
Off and on!	A favorite wake-up greeting of cadets by upperclassmen (e.g., "Alright, Dummies, off your butt and on your feet!")
Officers guide	A handbook of common practices, etiquette, and protocol for U.S. military officers
OG	Officer of the guard, assists the officer of the day
OJT	On-the-job training
Ole gal	Roommate
On the deck	(See *Deck*)
On the double	Perform a task more quickly than usual (e.g., run instead of walk)
On the gauges	Flying an airplane by reference to the instruments
Overshoot	On a landing approach, going past the safe touchdown point before contacting the ground
Over the fence	Passing above the boundary of an airfield on a takeoff or a landing
PAS	Professor of air science
PCS	Permanent change of station
Peeloff, or pitchout	Entering a traffic pattern of a base by flying above the active runway in the direction of landing then making a sharp turn to left or right and continuing the turn through 360 degrees while descending to the runway
Pinks and greens	Officers' uniforms during WWII; i.e., pink trousers and green jackets
POE	Port of embarkation
Prang	To crash
Preflight	A check of all systems and equipment of an airplane prior to takeoff to ensure proper operation
Prop	Propellor
Propshaft	In the P-39 Airacobra, a long shaft connecting the propellor to the engine through a gear box
Prop spinner	Nose cone on a propellor

Puke bag	(self-explanatory)
PX	Post exchange, a department store on a military base
Pylon 8	A flying-coordination training maneuver
Quit the trail	Give up on an assigned task or mission
Radio beacon	A signal emitted by a radio transmitter located at a particular site as an aid to navigation or landing
Radio beam	An audio highway in the air formed by the overlap of the radio signals emitted by two transmitters located at the same site, usually an airfield
Radio fix	Establish geographical position by determining the point of intersection of relative bearings of the airplane from two radio stations whose locations are shown on a map
RAF	Royal Air Force (of the United Kingdom)
R&R	Rest and recuperation
Rated	Certified as a qualified aircrew member, i.e., as a pilot, navigator, bombardier, flight surgeon, flight nurse, flight engineer, radio operator, gunner
Rat race	Several airplanes flying in trail playing "follow the leader" as the leader performs a series of acrobatic maneuvers
RBI	Reply by indorsement to a letter
Red Tails	Nickname of the 332nd Fighter Group because of the red-painted tails of their airplanes.
Reef	Make a tight turn in an airplane
Relative bearing	The angle measured clockwise from a line running due north from a radio station to a line from the airplane to the radio station
Repple depple	Replacement depot for troops arriving in a theater of operations
R-5, S-5	(See *Five by five*)
Rich (fuel) mixture	High ratio of fuel to air metered to the engine cylinders by the carburetor
RIF	Reduction in force

"Rock"	(See *Hot rock*)
Roger	Radio message acknowledging instructions or information
ROK	Republic of (South) Korea
ROKAF	Republic of (South) Korea Air Force
"Rollin' "	Pilot's report to the control tower as he begins down the runway on takeoff
RON	Remain overnight
ROTC	Reserve Officers Training Corps
Rounds	Bullets
RTU	Replacement Training Unit
Rudder	The movable vertical control surface that is hinged to the rear of the vertical stabilizer and that causes the airplane to turn when the pilot pushes the rudder pedals in the cockpit
Saint Elmo's fire	Flashes of electricity that race around the cabin window frame, tips of propellors, tips of wings when flying through clouds in some conditions of moisture and temperature
Scramble	Hurried launch of airplanes
Senior pilot	USAF aeronautical rating symbolized by a star atop silver wings
SHAPE	Supreme Headquarters Allied Powers, Europe
Shots	Inoculations
60–16	AFR 60–16, a major air force regulation that establishes rules and standards for flying operations
Slip	Side slip, or forward slip, is a flight maneuver used to lose altitude rapidly when too high above the ground in a landing approach
Slow roll	An aerial acrobatic maneuver
Smash bugs	(See *Boring holes*)
SMI	Saturday morning inspection
Snafu	Situation normal and all fouled up
Snap roll	An aerial acrobatic maneuver
SOP	Standing operating procedure

Sortie	A mission flown by one pilot; the number of sorties flown during a mission equals the number of planes on the mission
Spare(s)	The extra pilot(s) assigned to take off on a mission to replace any of the scheduled pilots who may have to abort their sortie due to engine malfunction shortly after takeoff
Spin	Airplane falling rapidly, nose down, and rotating out of control
Split-"S"	An aerial acrobatic maneuver
Spookwaffe	Nickname coined by Tuskegee Airmen to describe themselves humorously
Spot landing	Precision landing on a specific place on the ground
Spratmo, or sprat	Rumor (same as scuttlebutt)
Sputnik	Acronym for Russian phrase, "Fellow Traveler of Earth"—the first man-made satellite, launched by USSR October 4, 1957
Squared away	All ready, everything all set
Standard rate turn	A level turn through 360 degrees in two minutes
S-2	Intelligence staff officer
SW-EVEN	When on a VFR flight plan, pilots flying south or west must maintain altitudes at *even* thousands of feet
TAAF	Tuskegee Army Air Field
TAFS	Tuskegee Army Flying School
Tail dragger	Airplane with conventional landing gear: two main wheels and a tail wheel
TDY	Temporary duty
Tech order	Technical document that describes all equipment, systems, performance characteristics, and operational procedures for an airplane
TGIF	Thank God it's Friday!
TO&E	Table of organization and equipment, a document that authorizes the number and types of personnel and equipment for each type of military unit (i.e., squadron, group, wing, etc.)

Tomahawk	One of the nicknames of the Curtis P-40 fighter plane
Topkick	First sergeant (i.e., senior NCO of a military unit)
Tote board	Large (usually floor-to-ceiling) vertical, clear plastic panel on which an outline map of a theater of operations is permanently drawn and upon which clerks record with grease pencils the movements of both friendly and enemy airplanes
Touch and go	Making a landing and immediately taking off again while still rolling on the runway
Touchdown	Landing
Tracers	Machine gun bullets that show a red ember as they travel through the air, making their trajectory visible
Tricycle gear	Landing gear with two main wheels and a nose wheel
Trim tab	A small auxiliary control surface on the ailerons, elevators, and rudder that is adjustable by the pilot and helps him move those three main control surfaces in flight
TTY	Teletype
Tuskegee Airmen	The original "Tuskegee Airmen" are all of the persons who were involved in the so-called Tuskegee Experiment by the U.S. War Department to train Negroes to fly and to maintain airplanes in flying condition, from 1941 to 1946, including persons stationed or employed at Tuskegee Army Air Field and/or Moton Field, in various roles and statuses: flying officers, nonflying officers, nurses, aviation cadets, noncommissioned officers, enlisted men and women, and civilians
Tweaking	Scared, nervous
201 file	Personnel file maintained on every officer
TWX	Telegram or teletype message
UHF	Ultra high radio frequency

U.K.	United Kingdom
Undershoot	Land short of the runway
Under the hood	Practice flying of an airplane solely by reference to instruments, with a hood preventing the pilot from looking outside the cockpit, and with another pilot, not under the hood, to observe other airplanes in the area and avoid collisions
USAF	United States Air Force
USAFE	United States Air Force, Europe
USO	United Service Organization
Vertical reverse, or cartwheel	An aerial acrobatic maneuver
Vertical stabilizer	Fixed vertical surface of the empennage, to which the rudder is hinged
VFR	Visual flight rules (applicable in good weather)
VIP	Very important person
Vultee vibrator	Aviation cadets' nickname for the BT-13, basic trainer
Walk-around	Preflight visual inspection of an airplane as the pilot walks around it to examine the condition of control surfaces, wheels, tires, propellor(s), engine(s), radio antennae
Warhawk	A nickname of the Curtis P-40 fighter plane
Water Jug	P-47 "Jug" fighter plane with a water injection engine
Wheel well	The recess in the fuselage or underside of the wings of an airplane into which the wheels retract
"Wheels in the well"	An airplane with wheels retracted after takeoff
Wilco	Will comply (pilot's acknowledgment of instructions)
Wings	Surfaces that provide lift for airplanes
Yaw	An airplane's sideways skid from forward flight
Zebra	Nickname for NCOs with several stripes
Z.I.	Zone of the interior (i.e., the continental United States)

Bibliography

Davis, Benjamin O., Jr. *B. O. Davis, Jr.: American*. Washington, D.C.: Smithsonian Institution Press, 1991.

Francis, Charles E. *The Tuskegee Airmen*. Boston: Brandon Publishing Co., 1988.

Hardesty, Von, and Dominick Pisano. *Black Wings: The American Black in Aviation*. Washington, D.C.: Smithsonian Institution Press, 1984.

Jakeman, Robert J. *The Divided Skies*. Tuscaloosa: University of Alabama Press, 1992.

Osur, Alan M. *Blacks in the Army Air Forces During World War II*. Washington, D.C.: U.S. Government Printing Office, 1977.

Phelps, J. Alfred. *Chappie*. Novato, Calif.: Presidio Press, 1991.

Rose, Robert A. *Lonely Eagles*. Los Angeles: Tuskegee Airmen, Los Angeles Chapter, 1976.

Sandler, Stanley. *Segregated Skies*. Washington, D.C.: Smithsonian Institution Press, 1992.

Watson, George, Sr. *Memorable Memoirs*. New York: Carlton Press, 1987.

Index